DATE			
NOV 0 7 1988			
MAR 11 '90			

THE OECUMENICAL DOCUMENTS
OF THE FAITH

ΥΠΟΤΥΠΩΣΙΝ ΕΧΕ ΥΓΙΑΙΝΟΝΤΩΝ ΛΟΓΩΝ

THE
OECUMENICAL DOCUMENTS
OF THE FAITH

THE CREED OF NICAEA · THREE EPISTLES OF CYRIL
THE TOME OF LEO · THE CHALCEDONIAN DEFINITION

Edited with Introduction and Notes by
T. HERBERT BINDLEY

*D.D., Oxford and Durham. Sometime Principal of
Codrington College, Barbadoes ; late Rector of Denton
and Hon. Canon of Norwich Cathedral.*

FOURTH EDITION
Revised with Introduction and Notes by
F. W. GREEN

*B.D., Canon of Norwich Cathedral. Sometime
Fellow and Tutor of Merton College, Oxford.*

GREENWOOD PRESS, PUBLISHERS
WESTPORT, CONNECTICUT

Library of Congress Cataloging in Publication Data

Bindley, Thomas Herbert, 1861-1931, ed.
  The oecumenical documents of the faith.

    Reprint of the 4th ed., rev. with introd. and notes
by F. W. Green, published in 1950 by Methuen, London.
    Includes bibliographical references and indexes.
    CONTENTS: The Creed of Nicaea.--Three epistles of
Cyril.--The tome of Leo.--The Chalcedonian definition.
    1. Nicene Creed. 2. Constantinopolitan Creed.
3. Chalcedon, Council of, 451. I. Green, Frederick
Wastie, 1884-   II. Title.
[BT999.B52 1980]   238'.142   79-8708
ISBN 0-313-22197-9

The original edition of this book was first published in
November 1899.
This edition, completely revised by F. W. Green, 1950.

Reprinted with the permission of Associated Book
Publishers Ltd.

Reprinted from an original copy in the collection of the
University of Michigan Library.

Reprinted in 1980 by Greenwood Press,
a division of Congressional Information Service, Inc.
51 Riverside Avenue, Westport, Connecticut 06880

Printed in the United States of America

10 9 8 7 6 5 4 3 2 1

PREFACE TO THE FOURTH EDITION

DR. BINDLEY died on the 11th March, 1931, before he was able to take in hand a new edition of his much-used work. He had, however, left behind him an interleaved copy in which he had indicated the changes and additions he wished to make in any new edition of the work. In particular, he hoped to incorporate into the text the two sets of additional notes which he had so carefully compiled, and which did much to keep the work more abreast with recent scholarship and research. It was a misfortune that both this copy and the revised edition of the work which had been entrusted to a fellow-member of his own college were destroyed by enemy action in 1943 in the place where they had been put for security. It has been a laborious and lengthy task to rewrite the whole of that edition from the surviving notes. Nevertheless, there are compensations even to the worst of misfortunes; and the loss and delay thereby incurred have enabled the present editor to take advantage of much that has been written since, to consult scholars not available before, and, it is to be hoped, to produce a better edition than was perhaps possible in the earlier attempt. It is always difficult to enlarge or revise the work of another, and in the case of so learned a scholar as the late Dr. Bindley even presumptuous.

The present Editor therefore can only hope that the changes and additions, which, as the result of many years' continuous use both as student and teacher, he has ventured to introduce into this almost classical work, may have been not wholly unworthy of its distinguished author, and carried out in the same spirit, if not with the same learning, as it was originally conceived. At the same time he gratefully acknowledges the generous help he has received from scholars of a younger generation, without which the work of revision could never have been completed; in particular from the Warden of Keble, the Rev. H. J. Carpenter, from the Rev. Dr. R. V. Sellers, formerly Warden of St. Augustine's House, Reading, and now Professor of Systematic Theology in the University of London, and from the Rev. H. E. W. Turner, Fellow and Tutor of Lincoln College, Oxford, whose advice and assistance have been invaluable, though none of them must be held responsible for the defects and inadequacies of the work. Also he would wish specially to thank the Rev. F. E. Vokes, late Scholar of St. John's College, Cambridge, now Rector of Forncett, Norfolk, for invaluable help in revising the proofs and verifying references throughout the work, and for preparing the index; his son H. C. Green for much assistance at this as well as at other stages of preparation for the Press; and not least the Publishers for their patience over long delays.   F. W. G.

Easter, 1950

v

TABLE OF CONTENTS

vii

GENERAL INTRODUCTION

THERE are two avenues by which we may approach the documents which enshrine the Faith of the Catholic Church—the one purely dogmatic, the other historical. In the one case we deal simply with finished results, technical statements of Catholic truth; in the other we investigate the causes which led to the truth being expressed in the particular language of the formularies before us. But it is, indeed, really necessary to combine the historical with the dogmatic study of the great symbols of the Faith if we wish properly to appreciate their significance; for the exact terminology of the Creeds and their allied documents cannot be fully understood unless the history embedded in the phrases be known. In some instances this involves a knowledge of the heresies whose false or imperfect presentation of doctrine caused certain truths to be formulated by the Church in terms which at the same time excluded certain errors. This is only to say that, while the truths were undoubtedly held from the beginning, they were often latent in the Christian consciousness rather than verbally expressed, until the denial of them obliged the Church to ponder upon her Faith, and to put it into reasoned words. The finished dogmatic results, as we now have them, were not attained without much controversy, and careful sifting of language.

For example, it was not until Monarchianism in its various forms obscured the distinction of the Persons in the Godhead that the Church found it necessary to co-ordinate her belief in the Deity of the Son and of the Spirit with her intellectual hold upon monotheism. Nor was it until Arius rationalistically denied the Eternal Divinity of the Word that she had to discover terms in which to express her faith in the Essential Unity of the Father and the Son, which embraced without destroying the distinction of Person. Similarly, it was due to the attacks of Apollinarius, Nestorius, and Eutyches upon the completeness of either the Humanity or the Divinity of her Lord that the Church was led to work out the right expression of her belief in the Two Perfect Natures united in His One Divine Person.

The Trinitarian Formula—whatever its origin, whether an actual word of the Lord or adopted by the primitive Church and based on His teaching—was, as a matter of history, recognised by the Church as the " Hypotype " (ὑποτύπωσις), the outline of essential credenda, which was to be filled out and enriched as necessity arose.[1] It may be questioned whether this formula as it appears in Matt. xxviii. 19 was originally intended by the writer to be a

---

[1] Cf. Vincent Ler., Common. 23.

I

baptismal formula ; it is more likely to have been a summary of the Christian teaching concerning the nature of God as revealed in Jesus Christ. The evidence goes to show that in the first century Baptism was administered in the name of Jesus as Lord ; [1] and that the basis of all creeds is to be sought in the apostolic proclamation (κήρυγμα), the Tradition which could be summed up in the confession that Jesus is Lord (Κύριος 'Ιησοῦς) (Phil. ii. 11, Acts xvi. 31, 1 Cor. xii. 3). This is the ῥῆμα of which St. Paul writes in Eph. v. 26 and Romans x. 8. The confession required of the candidate early took an interrogative form, as is suggested by the D. text of Acts viii. 37 and 1 Pet. iii. 21 ; the latter appears to contain phrases about our Lord which correspond with the second division of the Apostles' Creed. Early in the second century, probably under the influence of the recently canonised Gospel of St. Matthew, this primitive confession was expanded into the Trinitarian formula which is first found as the form in Baptism in the Apology of Justin Martyr. [2]

It is also found in the Didache (circ. 150), which, while its date is uncertain, witnesses to an established practice. [3] Thus the doctrine of the Holy Trinity became the backbone of the various forms of creed which were later developed from the primitive formula. The Synodical letter of the Council of Constantinople (A.D. 382) recognises the Nicene Creed as an expansion of the baptismal profession. [4] Similarly the second creed of Sirmium declares : Τὸ δὲ κεφάλαιον πάσης τῆς πίστεως καὶ ἡ βεβαιότης ἐστὶν ἵνα Τριὰς ἀεὶ φυλάττηται, καθὼς ἀνέγνωμεν ἐν τῷ εὐαγγελίῳ (Matt. xxviii. 19). [5]

---

[1] See Armitage Robinson on Eph. v. 26 for references to baptism in the Name of Jesus Christ, where he remarks that the origin of the Creed is to be traced in the first instance not to the Triple Formula but to the statement of the main facts about the Lord Jesus as a prelude to baptism in His Name. For the meaning of ἐπερώτημα see Selwyn on 1 Pet. iii. 21 and Badcock, *History of the Creeds*, pp. 15 ff., where ἐπερώτημα is explained as a promise elicited by a formula or question. See Burn, *Introduction to the Creeds*, Chapter 2, and *Journal of Theological Studies*, xxxii., p. 77.

[2] Apol. i. 61 Ἐπ' ὀνόματος γὰρ τοῦ Πατρὸς τῶν ὅλων καὶ Δεσπότου Θεοῦ καὶ τοῦ Σωτῆρος ἡμῶν Ἰησοῦ Χριστοῦ καὶ Πνεύματος Ἁγίου τὸ ἐν τῷ ὕδατι τότε λουτρὸν ποιοῦνται.

[3] Ch. 7 Περὶ δὲ τοῦ βαπτίσματος οὕτω βαπτίσατε· ταῦτα πάντα προειπόντες βαπτίσατε εἰς τὸ ὄνομα τοῦ Πατρός καὶ τοῦ Υἱοῦ καὶ τοῦ Ἁγίου Πνεύματος ἐν ὕδατι ζῶντι.

[4] Theodoret HE. v. 9.

[5] Socrates 2. 30. Cf. also a well-known passage from St. Basil (Epistle 125). Δεῖ γὰρ ἡμᾶς βαπτίζεσθαι μὲν ὡς παρελάβομεν· πιστεύειν δὲ ὡς βαπτιζόμεθα, and a beautiful apostrophe in Augustine (De. Trin. xv. 51) : "Domine Deus noster, credimus in Te Patrem et Filium et Spiritum Sanctum. Neque enim diceret Veritas 'Ite baptizate omnes gentes in Nomine Patris et Filii et Spiritus Sancti,' nisi Trinitas esse. Nec baptizari nos iuberes, Domine Deus, in Eius Nomine qui non est Dominus Deus." For the question as to the subsequent validity of baptism in the Name of Jesus, see Ambrose, De Spirit. Sanct. 1, 3 ; Cyprian, Ep. lxxiii. 18 ; Pseudo-Cyprian, De Rebaptismate (I, 6, 7).

Thus the baptismal profession mentioned by Cyril [1] as in use at Jerusalem was simply

πιστεύω εἰς τὸν Πατέρα
καὶ εἰς τὸν Υἱόν
καὶ εἰς τὸ Ἅγιον Πνεῦμα

to which he adds in another place

καὶ εἰς ἓν βάπτισμα μετανοίας.

But besides this reference to Baptism there was often added a mention of the Forgiveness of Sins, Eternal Life, and the Church. Tertullian, for instance, describing the Carthaginian ritual, remarks that at the threefold immersion the candidate responded to " a good deal more " than the bare formula appointed by the Lord. His words [2] are : " Dehinc ter mergitamur amplius aliquid respondentes quam Dominus in evangelio determinavit " : and elsewhere [3] we incidentally learn that amongst the additions to the confession of the Trinity was a clause upon the Church—" Cum autem sub tribus et testatio fidei et sponsio salutis pignerentur, necessario adicitur ecclesiae mentio, quoniam ubi tres, id est Pater et Filius et Spiritus Sanctus, ibi Ecclesia quae trium corpus est."

Again, from Cyprian's Epistles on the Novatian controversy, [4] we may deduce the following baptismal interrogations :—

Credis in Deum Patrem
et in Filium Christum
et in Spiritum Sanctum ?
Credis in remissionem peccatorum
et vitam aeternam per sanctam ecclesiam ?

But we may question, especially in view of Tertullian's words, whether the interrogatory creed in Cyprian's time was as brief as this. He was only concerned in these letters to quote such clauses as assisted his argument against the position that the Novatian schismatics did not need " rebaptism " because their creed was identical with that of the Church.

Thus, besides these early examples, traces have recently been discovered of a further expansion of the earliest formulas into a rudimentary creed. Of these the best known is the ancient form embodied in the *Apostolic Tradition of Hippolytus* (A.D. 220) which indicates the use in the Church of Rome of his time, and which runs thus :—

(I believe)
In the One true God, the Father Almighty,
And in His Only Son our Lord and Saviour, Jesus Christ,
And in the Catholic Holy Church and Life Eternal. [5]

[1] Catech. xx. 4 ; xix. 9.   [2] De Corona 3.   [3] De Baptismo 6.
[4] Epist. 69 ad Magn. ; 70 ad Epist. Num.
[5] G. Dix, *Apostolic Tradition of Hippolytus*, p. 36.

We may also cite the ancient creed contained in the Dair Balaizah Papyrus discovered by Professor Flinders Petrie in 1907 and now in the Bodleian Library, possibly representing the Creed of Alexandria in the second century.[1]

> (I believe)
> In God the Father Almighty,
> And in His Only begotten Son our Lord Jesus Christ,
> And in the Spirit, the Holy,
> And in the Resurrection of the Flesh,
> And Holy Catholic Church.

The earliest known creed is probably one which has been introduced into the so-called Epistola Apostolorum, which is there said to be the creed of " the great Christianity," i.e., the Catholic Church as opposed to the heretical sects.[2]

> (I believe)
> In God the Father Almighty,
> In Jesus Christ our Saviour,
> And in the Spirit, the Holy, the Paraclete,
> In Holy Church,
> Forgiveness of Sins.

It was from these short baptismal responses that the first creeds were by expansion formed. This enlargement took place gradually, usually in view of heresies arising from time to time in various places.[3]   And although none of the creeds before the Council of Nicaea may strictly be called Oecumenical, there is a strong family likeness between them, whether in the East or the West.   Moreover, it was these local creeds differing in form but one in substance which as St. Cyril of Jerusalem tells us, the Candidates for Baptism learned by heart, but were not suffered to write down or recite except in the presence of the baptised.[4]   This baptismal creed was early called the Symbol (σύμβολον) because it was regarded either as a *token* of recognition between Christians, or, in the sense of σύμβολή, as a *Collect* summing up the main heads of belief, the things which a Christian ought to know and believe to his soul's health.[5]   But the baptismal confessions, whether brief or lengthy, which formed the Symbolum proper, did not exhaust the subject-matter of the Faith which was taught to the catechumens during their preparation for baptism or subsequently to it.   Besides the words of the Creed, St. Cyril tells us [6] they were also given a large body of Christian doctrine on such subjects as the Being and Unity of God (περὶ μοναρχίας), Creation, the Incarnation, Christ the Second

---

[1] Badcock, *History of the Creeds*, pp. 24, 26.   [2] Ibid. pp. 24, 25.
[3] But see C. H. Turner, *History and Use of Creeds*, p. 3.
[4] Catech. lect. v. 12.
[5] Rufinus of Aquileia, In Symb. Apost. 2; cf. H. J. Carpenter, *Journal of Theological Studies*, xliii., p. 1, and Badcock, *History of the Creeds*, pp. 106, 107.
[6] Catech. lect. iv.

Adam, His Birth, the Cross, the Resurrection, and the Ascension, the Future Judgment, the Holy Spirit, the Church, the Christian Doctrine of Man, his Soul and Body, his Freewill, his Resurrection, the Canon of the Scriptures, the Sacraments, together with simple rules for Christian living in a heathen world. This teaching formed the Apostolical Tradition or Rule of Faith (κάνων τῆς ἀληθείας or τῆς ἐκκλησίας, μέγιστα τῆς πιστέως κεφάλαια, cf. Origen in Ioan. 32. 16), in its Latin form, Regula Fidei.[1]

The meaning of this phrase which in its various forms is found continually recurring in the writings of this period is not free from ambiguity. Some modern scholars identify it with the Creed itself,[2] others with the Canon of Scripture.[3] There is evidence for its use in both these senses ;[4] but as neither Creed nor Canon had received their final form in the third century, it is probable that the Rule of Faith and the Creed or Scripture were not convertible terms.[5] Tertullian, indeed, appears to contrast it with the local creeds then in process of formation as " one, unalterable, and irreformable ", and " the same everywhere."[6] Moreover, he deprecates the appeal to Scripture in controversy with heretics, on the ground that it leads only to argument and uncertain conclusions, " in qua victoria aut nulla aut incerta est." For the real question is, to whom does the Faith belong, whose are the Scriptures, by whom and through whom and to whom was that Rule delivered whereby men become Christians ?[7]

Similarly St. Irenaeus, in whose writings the phrase first appears,[8] remarks in a famous passage that " if neither Christ nor the Apostles left us Scriptures, would it not have behoved us to follow the order of the *Tradition* which they handed down to those to whom they committed the Churches, to which every nation of the Barbarians assents, who believe in Christ without it being written with paper and ink, having salvation in their heart and diligently guarding the ancient tradition ? "[9] In the same way Origen's great work the

---

[1] Cf. " mensura Fidei," a phrase used by Victorinus of Petavium (Hahn, *Symbole*,[3] p. 17) ; and St. Athanasius' phrase, σκόπος ἐκκλησιαστικός c. Ar. iii. 35.

[2] Harnack, D.G. II, 26. See also Zahn, Apost. Symb., trans. Burn, p. 40.

[3] Kattenbusch, Apostolicum Symbolum II, 31 ff.

[4] Loofs, *Dogmengeschichte*,[4] p. 134.

[5] A. J. Mason in Swete, *Early History of the Church and Ministry*, p. 51.

[6] Tertullian, De Virg. Veland., 1.

[7] Idem, De Praescript. Haer. 19, of which work Badcock remarks that by Praescriptio is meant not a legal objection or demurrer entered at the beginning of a lawsuit, as is often supposed, which if maintained dispensed with going any farther into the case, but a claim preferred for the purpose of limiting the scope of the inquiry. This is the precise point of the above question, by which Tertullian claims to limit the discussion to the legitimacy of heretical appeal to Scripture. (Op. cit. p. 168.)

[8] Irenaeus, Adv. Haer. 1. 1. 20.

[9] Idem, 3. 4. 1, where he contrasts the variations of Creed and Scripture with the firm, steadfast, and undeviating faith proclaimed by the Church. Cf. 1 John v. 2.

De Principiis is professedly a commentary not on the Scripture or the Creed but on the Rule of Faith, as he remarks more than once.[1] The probable view therefore is that the Rule of Faith is not to be identified with either, but was in itself the rule of Christian teaching, the test alike of Creed and Scripture. By this these Fathers did not mean that there could be anything in the Regula Fidei which was not in Scripture, or anything corresponding to the *secret* tradition which the Gnostics claimed to have received direct from the Apostles: rather it was the Faith which the Christian Bishops as teachers received, " the same everywhere," at any rate where there were Bishops in touch with the Apostolic sees.[2]

Accordingly for this tradition both Irenaeus and Tertullian appealed to the Churches known to have been founded by the Apostles and their successors. Thus Irenaeus, speaking of the progress of the instructed Christian from Judaism into the fullness which will end in the vision of God, and the knowledge of Scriptural truth conveyed to His disciples by the Risen Christ, goes on to say, " therefore we ought to obey the Presbyters in the Church who have the succession from the Apostles as we have shown ; who along with the succession of the Episcopate have received the grace of truth (*charisma veritatis*) according to the most sure will of the Father : but to hold as suspect others who depart from the original succession." These therefore (*i.e.* the true teachers) instituted as Bishops by the Apostles in the Churches, especially that of Rome, and their successors even to our times, are the guarantees of the traditions of the Apostles throughout the whole world : " for the Apostles wished to be perfect and faultless (in the Faith) when they left them as their successors, handing on to them their own *locum magisterii*." [3]

In the same way Tertullian makes his appeal to the Apostolic Churches in which he says, " the very seats of the Apostles at this very day preside over their own places in which their own authentic writings are read. And not only to those, but also to them in Asia or Greece or Italy which can claim no Apostle or Apostolic man as their founder, as being of much later date and indeed being founded daily, who since they agree in the same Faith are by reason of their congruity in doctrine accounted not less Apostolical." In this connexion Tertullian uses the famous phrase *contesseratio hospitalitatis*,[4] a phrase derived from the token coin divided between two friends of which each kept one part. He also uses a no less significant word *auctoritas*, by which is meant not jurisdiction, but the authority of the expert, as we might speak of the authority

---

[1] Origen, De Princip. 1. 1 and *passim*.

[2] Tertullian, De Praescript. Haer. 5 and 12.

[3] Irenaeus, Adv. Haer. 3. 1. 1 ; 4. 26. 2. By *magisterium* is meant the Teacher's Chair, not as Harnack and his translators seem to have thought the seat of Government (*History of Dogma*, II, 70).

[4] De Praesc. Haer. 20 and 36. Cf. Apology 29, and Aug. Epistle xliii, 7.

of science. And this authority is both by Tertullian and Irenaeus regarded as residing geographically in the great Churches which could claim Apostles as their founders, especially that of Rome itself, of which Tertullian remarks that " her *auctoritas* is at hand for us also in Africa." This authority derives ultimately from the Apostles ; for " in the Lord's Apostles we possess our *auctoritas*, for even they did not dare to introduce anything, but faithfully declared to the nations the teaching (*disciplina*) which they had received from Christ." [1]

But lest it should be supposed that the Rule of Faith implied a petrified religion or excluded liberty of investigation or even speculation on the contents of the Christian Faith, we may note that the School of Alexandria in its greatest exponents, Clement and Origen, laid the same emphasis upon the Rule of Faith as did the more rigid and dogmatic teachers of the West. For Clement, no less than the others, all Christians are to be guided by the Rule, which he frequently mentions. Neither he himself nor his great successor has any idea of a church in which every teacher and learner was free to teach or believe without control.[2] An excellent example of the Rule of Faith is to be found in Origen's treatise *De Principiis*,[3] which as its title indicates is a commentary on the Regula Fidei as received and taught in the Church of Alexandria. He carefully distinguishes between what is integral to the Apostolic *kerygma* and what lies outside it and may be regarded as a matter of legitimate speculation, *e.g.* the origin of the soul, or the world and its destiny and, even at this time, the Holy Spirit, concerning Whom he remarks " non iam manifeste discernitur utrum natus an innatus vel filius etiam ipse Dei habendus sit." Like Tertullian and Irenaeus, Origen remarks that the Church's teaching, in spite of some who think differently from those who were before them, is preserved, being transmitted by order of succession from the Apostles, and continuing to this day in the Church ; therefore all is to be believed to be the truth which is wholly in keeping with the Apostles and Bishops of the Church.

Allowing therefore for the increasing emphasis laid by the antignostic and anti-monarchian writers of this period on Apostolic order and tradition, and for some exaggeration of phrase, the existence and authority of a Rule of Faith as a fact in the history of the Church over against the Creed and the Scriptures may be said to be proved. It is only subsequently to these writers that the phrase itself became

[1] De Praesc. Haer. 6, cf. Badcock, op. cit., p. 30.
[2] Clement, Strom. vi. 16. 3 and v. 11. 15, where he speaks of γνῶσις as coming ἐκ παραδόσεως κατὰ χάριν Θεοῦ. Cf. *charisma veritatis* in Irenaeus, (adv. Haer. iv. 40. 2).
[3] Preface 2 and 4–8. See J. A. Robinson's *Philocalia*, and Bigg, *The Christian Platonists of Alexandria*[2] (pp. 192 ff.). For Origen's rule of faith *in extenso* see F. E. Brightman in Swete, op. cit., pp. 335 ff. Cf. Mason, ibid. p. 51, who quoting Batiffol (*Église Naissante*) remarks that it might have been taken straight out of Irenaeus.

gradually restricted to the completed and greatly enlarged local creeds; while the catechetical lectures of St. Cyril of Jerusalem [1] bear witness, as we have seen, to the continued existence of the Rule as a form of general teaching. It is against a background of such a Rule of Faith that the Oecumenical Documents must be studied as authoritative interpretations of the Rule agreed upon and promulgated by the Church as binding upon its members.

To this tradition the Fathers of the Church, both Greek and Latin, were and remain the authoritative witnesses. To them all the great Scholastic Theologians and the Reformers who followed them invariably appeal, and the nature of their authority has perhaps never been so clearly put as by the greatest of all the scholastic theologians, St. Thomas Aquinas, who propounds the question whether Christ ought to have committed His teaching to writing, so as to exclude error and open the way to faith. His answer is that, " in fact, no books written by Christ are found in Holy Scripture, for three reasons : (1) On account of His own dignity ; for the more excellent the teaching, the more excellent should be the manner of teaching ; and therefore Christ, the most excellent teacher of all, used the *spoken* word that he might impress His teaching on the hearts of His hearers, as did Pythagoras and Socrates. (2) On account of the excellence of the teaching itself, which simply cannot be comprehended in writing. For if Christ had committed His teaching to writing, men would not think any more of it than of that which the Scripture itself contains. This was written in order that His teaching might in due order reach to all from Himself, while He himself taught His disciples directly, who afterwards taught others by word and writing. (3) Because of the spirituality of His teaching, which unlike the old law ought not to be written with ink but with the Spirit of the living God." [2] Thus the Church, the Body of Christ, continues to teach *ex ore* and is never tied to the written word. This is perhaps one of the reasons which led to the so-called *disciplina arcani* [3] according to which the candidate for Baptism was not allowed to write down the Creed which he had to recite at his Baptism or to read it out of a book. Nor can the Church ever renounce its *magisterium* or sovereign right to teach the Faith and to interpret the written Word. In this connexion we may note that the first Oecumenical Document of

---

[1] Novatian, De Trin. 1 and 9. Novatian uses the expression *Regula credendi*, and seems to identify it with a fixed creed. He remarks " always keep the agreement which you made with the Lord, namely that which was in the Symbolum. The words indeed are few, but it contains all the Regula which out of Scripture therein has been collected " (c. Noetum iii. 6). He is followed by Cyprian, and Augustine, Encheiridion, 56, and Serm. 186. See a good article by Ammundsen, *Journal of Theological Studies*, xiii, p. 574.

[2] Summa Theol. III. Q. 42, Art. 4.

[3] The actual phrase does not appear before the seventeenth century, according to Batiffol (L'Arcane, *Études de l'Histoire et de Théologie*, 1902). The thing itself only makes its appearance in the third century.

the Church the Apostolic Decree in Acts xv was sent out with the living voice of the Church, the written word perhaps not being regarded as sufficient (Acts xv. 30).

In particular, the authors of the Oecumenical Documents of the fourth and fifth centuries were chiefly concerned to express in unmistakable language the respective truths of the Tri-personality of the One Godhead; the true Deity of the Second and Third Persons of the Trinity; the complete and permanent Humanity united to the complete and permanent Deity of the One Christ. These truths were deduced from the Church's conscious faith as it faced the false teaching of various heretical leaders. Five typical forms of doctrinal error are more particularly dealt with in these documents—the Arian, Macedonian, Apollinarian, Nestorian, and Eutychian—to our survey of which a sixth may be prefixed—the Sabellian, as in one sense preparatory to the Arian in the region of speculative theology. Of these heresies, the Sabellian, Arian, and Macedonian were mainly Trinitarian, and the last three mainly Christological.

These, like most heresies, were the result of an exaggerated insistence upon one aspect of the Creed to the neglect of another, or of a dissociation of two truths meant to be held together, which impaired the *wholeness* of the Rule of Faith. The unity in diversity in the one Being of God, and the two natures in the one Divine Person of Christ, are examples of paradoxes and tensions which arise in any living Faith or philosophy which sets out to express the whole truth, but which, when distorted, or exaggerated on one side or the other, become heresies. The origin of heresies in the Christian Church was twofold: partly, as in the case of the Christological, they were one-sided exaggerations of theological traditions prevalent in different regions of the Christian world, such as Alexandria and Antioch; or, as in the case of the Trinitarian, they were premature solutions of the problems which inevitably confronted Christian Monotheism when it came into contact with Greek philosophy and with the Oriental speculation and mysticism generally known as Gnosticism. The Christian doctrine of the Living God, derived from Hebraic theism, was not easily reconcilable with abstract Greek ideas about God which reach their final form in some doctrine of the Absolute. The Monarchian, the Sabellian, and the Arian heresies represented attempted solutions of the problems which Judaism had already encountered in the writings of the Jewish philosopher Philo, whose speculations were destined to involve Christian theology in serious commitments. At the same time it should be realised that problems such as the relation of the finite and the infinite, the one and the many, the individual and society are not peculiar to Christianity, but are common to all forms of philosophical thought about ultimate things; and problems they will remain. For absolute truth is not revealed to the finite mind, which can receive it only in the form of apparently con-

B

tradictory though really complementary truths. The Greek Fathers at any rate were aware that the difficulties involved in Christianity were fundamentally philosophical problems, and they discussed them in terms taken from the current philosophical systems of the day. Christianity, however, is not a philosophy but a life, and a Divine Revelation, the central core of which must be preserved unimpaired at all costs, even at the expense of consistency, as both Athanasius and Cyril found themselves in the long run compelled to admit.

The function of Christian dogma as expressed in the Oecumenical Documents of the Faith was to bar the way against solutions of these tensions, which either contradicted, as in the case of Arianism, the essence of the Christian Gospel, or, as in the case of the Christological heresies, impaired its fullness. Christian dogma exists to preserve the due proportion of the deposit of faith, which heresy threatens to destroy. To this unbalanced one-sidedness of heresy must be added a moral element which is involved in its very name ($a\ddot{\iota}\rho\epsilon\sigma\iota\varsigma$) ; for heresy is often, if not always, the self-willed choice of a particular mode of thought which refuses to think with the Church. This is the meaning of those anathemas which have usually accompanied the definitions of the Church. The Church condemns the *spirit* of heresy in whatever form it is found ; and not least in the form of what St. Hilary called "irreligiosa de Deo sollicitudo," [1] which refuses to receive a revelation of the Divine Nature or mode of working which is not in accordance with its own pre-determined theories. Such a spirit of intellectual pride and self-sufficiency would have resulted in the earliest days in a transformation of the Christian religion into a philosophy, or a system of Oriental mysticism. At the same time the Church has never denied the right of the human reason to search out and develop the meaning and implications of its central doctrine. Even the modern Church could do worse than echo the penetrating words of the greatest of the Scholastic Theologians, who was steeped in the Fathers as few have ever been, when speaking of faith in God's self-revelation to man through the Church. He concludes that the act of faith does not end at the *words*, the accents, in which, though necessarily inadequate, its dogmas are pronounced, but penetrates to the Object to which they relate.[2]

[1] De Trin. 4. 6.
[2] St. Thomas Aquinas, Summa Theol. II. ii, Q. 1, Art 2. Expositio fidei in symbolo continetur. Sed in symbolo non ponuntur enuntiabilia, sed res ; non enim dicitur ibi quod Deus sit omnipotens, sed "credo in Deum omnipotentem" . . . actus autem credentis non terminatur ad enuntiabile, sed ad rem. Cf. Prestige, *God in Patristic Thought*, p. 236, and Hodgson in *Essays on the Trinity and the Incarnation*, p. 400 and *passim*.

THE CREED OF NICAEA

ΕΠΑΓΩΝΙΖΕΣΘΕ ΤΗ ΑΠΑΞ ΠΑΡΑΔΟΘΕΙΣΗ
ΤΟΙΣ ΑΓΙΟΙΣ ΠΙΣΤΕΙ

THE CREED OF NICAEA

INTRODUCTION

I. HISTORICAL

OF the circumstances which led to the Nicene Council and the precise formulation of its Creed it will be necessary to give only a very brief outline.

One day in the year 318 or 319 a discourse was delivered by Alexander, Bishop of Alexandria, on the great mystery of the Trinity in Unity. Exception was taken to its teaching by one of the Alexandrian clergy named Arius, on the ground that it tended to obliterate the distinction of the Three Persons in the Godhead, and therein savoured of Sabellianism.[1] Arius proceeded to disseminate his own views, which exaggerated those elements which he conceived to be implied in the Sonship of the Second Person, until he arrived at the point where Sonship was replaced by creature-ship, and the co-eternal and co-essential Deity of the Word was surrendered.

After repeated failures to reclaim Arius to orthodoxy, Alexander was obliged to excommunicate him. His party, however, grew in numbers, and a large council was held at Alexandria in 321 which investigated the Arian teaching and condemned it. Meanwhile Arius had found partisans in Nicomedia and in Palestine, whither he had gone after leaving Egypt. Thence he wrote to Alexander and also popularised his views both in prose and in verse (" Thalia ").[2] Alexander issued an encyclical letter (Socrates i. 6), but the heresy continued to spread in the East. The Emperor Constantine, who naturally underrated the dogmatic importance of the dispute, attempted to allay the trouble by addressing a letter to Arius and Alexander, in which he described the controversy as arising out of foolish speculation on an insignificant matter. This letter was sent by the hand of Hosius of Cordova, who appears to have been a kind of chaplain to Constantine, to Alexandria late in 324. A Synod was held there which failed to appease the Arian strife : and

---

[1] So Socrates, HE. i. 5 ; but if Constantine was correctly informed (Epist. to Alexander and Arius apud Socr. i. 7 ; cf. Sozom. i. 15), it would seem that Arius had already given utterance to his views, and that Alexander submitted a test question to his clergy. But see Kidd, *History of the Church*, Vol. II, p. 14, and Bright, *Waymarks in Church History*, Appendix B.

[2] The " Thalia," or " Banquet," was a collection of songs, dealing with the most sacred mysteries, written in a metre made infamous by its association with an obscure Maronite poet. Socr. i. 9 ; Athan. Or. c. Ar. i. 2. 4. 5 ; De Synod. 15 ; Philostorg. ii. 2. Martial, Epigr. vii. 17, terms his own poems " lasciva Thalia."

13

Hosius reported to Constantine at Nicomedia the failure of his mission.[1]

Constantine now conceived the idea of summoning a general council of bishops from all parts of the Church, whose duty it should be to settle the question of faith, and two other matters which were disturbing the unity of the Church.[2] It met at Nicaea, in Bithynia, June 19, 325. Preliminary discussions were held,[3] in which the Scriptural teaching upon the Word, Wisdom, and Son of God was carefully examined, the chief passages adduced being Prov. viii. 22 ; Matt. xix. 17, xx. 23 ; Mark xiii. 32 ; Luke ii. 52 ; John v. 19, x. 30, xiv. 28 ; Acts ii. 36 ; 1 Cor. xv. 28 ; Phil. ii. 7 ; Col. i. 15 ; Heb. i. 3. Some of the debates are described by Athanasius,[4] who himself, as Alexander's archdeacon, took a prominent part in them. When it was found that scriptural terms were accepted in an unreal sense by the Arians, the necessity was clearly forced upon the orthodox of expressing the real sense of Scripture and the true faith of the Church in terms of which the meaning could not be explained away.

Accordingly it was agreed that a dogmatic standard of faith should be adopted. An Arian Creed produced by Eusebius of Nicomedia was at once rejected for its blasphemy. Then Eusebius of Caesarea produced a creed, that of his Baptism and Consecration (Socr. i. 8), which was accepted according to his own report of the Council, as orthodox, and was approved by the Emperor. But it would hardly have been used as a basis for the new Creed, because Eusebius himself appears to have stood under condemnation for Arianism at a Council held at Antioch in the previous year,[5] and in any case the Nicene Creed differs from it in too many respects. It is more probable that the Nicene Creed like the Apostles' was a conflation from many sources, particularly from the Creeds of Antioch and its dependents, amplified by the phrases specially inserted as excluding Arian evasion ; for it was the Bishops of the Antiochene School, e.g. Eustathius, with Marcellus of Ancyra, who combined with the Western Bishops to support the homoousion.[6]

---

[1] See Kidd, op. cit., Vol. II, 21 ; Eusebius-Caes., ap. Socr. i. 8.
[2] I.e. the Paschal Question and the Meletian Schism in Egypt.
[3] Sozom. i. 17.
[4] De decretis Nic., Epist. ad Afros., De Synod., etc.
[5] See the document put out by the Council in Badcock, *History of the Creeds*, pp. 182 ff. For a discussion of its genuineness see A. E. Burn, *Council of Nicaea*, pp. 12–19. Its authenticity has been questioned chiefly on account of its use of the term *Theotokos* ; but, as Badcock remarks, that word had already been used by Origen, Hippolytus, and Eusebius himself. Other phrases appear to go back to Lucian of Antioch. On the whole question see an important article by Professor F. L. Cross in *Church Quarterly Review*, 1939, pp. 49–76, where the whole situation is reviewed, and the authenticity of the document maintained.
[6] For the close connexion between the Antiochene Tradition in Theology and Christology with that of the Western writers, such as Tertullian and Irenaeus, see Loofs' *Paulus von Samosata*, *Texte und Unter.*, Vol. 44, pp. 211–

Anathemas were appended condemning various Arian tenets. These may have been drawn from the above-mentioned Council of Antioch, which condemned Eusebius of Caesarea.

Any further remarks upon the phraseology of the Creed are reserved for the notes which follow. Meanwhile it is well to observe, first, that the method of the Nicene Council was one and the same with that of the early dogmatic apologists, namely, the reinforcement of the common tradition of the Church, which had been held from the beginning. The Council added nothing new to the facts of Apostolic belief; it simply restated them in the face of novel opinions, which would have impaired their integrity.[1] Secondly, what *was* new in connexion with the Council was its adoption of an oecumenical creed, proposed for subscription as a test of orthodoxy. Hitherto the traditional Rule of Faith had been embodied in various local formularies and creeds, catechetical and baptismal, differing verbally in the different Churches. Without interfering with these, there was now for the first time brought into existence one definite standard of right belief accepted by the representatives of the whole of Christendom.

Yet the Nicene Creed was not regarded as sacrosanct, and it never superseded the local creeds in East or West. Athanasius himself seldom refers to it in his subsequent works, nor did he make any great use of the crux of the creed, the *homoousion*, in his controversial writings. In the West the old Roman Creed continued to hold its own, and when in the sixth century a creed began to be used in the Roman Liturgy it was not the Nicene but the Creed of Constantinople which was used apparently under the impression that it was Nicene.[2] In the East its acceptance was due to the immense influence of St. Basil the Great.

It should be noted that it is regularly referred to as πίστις or μάθημα, not as σύμβολον until its conversion to a baptismal profession in the next century (Gwatkin, *Studies of Arianism*, p. 40, n. 1).

II. THEOLOGICAL

THEOLOGICALLY the Nicene Confession was the Rule of Faith explained as against Arianism, the chief objection to which in the eyes of most of the bishops was its novelty; for it is unlikely that its

---

29, and cf. Sellers, *Eustathius of Antioch* (Cambridge, 1928). A selection of creeds Eastern and Western are printed below in the Appendix, and should be carefully compared with the Nicene Creed and with each other.

[1] Cf. Athan. De Synod. 5, of the Nicene Fathers, ἔγραψαν οὐκ " Ἔδοξεν " ἀλλ' " Οὕτως πιστεύει ἡ καθολικὴ ἐκκλησία," καὶ εὐθὺς ὡμολόγησαν πῶς πιστεύουσιν, ἵνα δείξωσιν ὅτι μὴ νεώτερον ἀλλ' ἀποστολικόν ἐστιν αὐτῶν τὸ φρόνημα, καὶ ἃ ἔγραψαν οὐκ ἐξ αὐτῶν εὑρέθη, ἀλλὰ ταῦτ' ἐστιν ἅπερ ἐδίδαξαν οἱ ἀπόστολοι.

[2] See Bingham, *Christian Antiquities*, x. 4. 17.

full implications were understood by the majority. In this, as in other Oecumenical Councils, the Creed or Definition put out was strictly confined to the terms of reference in the particular controversy ; and was not intended to express the full meaning of the doctrine contained in the statement concerned. Further explanation, *e.g.* of the Sonship, and of the Holy Spirit and His relation to the Godhead, was needed and made in later Creeds or Definitions. While in each case it was the Rule of Faith which was the subject of the inquiry or of the Definition, the Church did not hesitate in its explanations to make use of terminology which went beyond the primitive Rule, and even Scripture itself, though always tested by them. The Nicene Creed in particular was essentially a recall to *religion* as opposed to the unending speculations of Origenism, a recall to the first principles of the Gospel, as faith in the redemption, and in reconciliation in Christ with a God Who is not absent from the world He created, nor so transcendent as to be out of effective touch with it. For the controversies which preceded Nicaea were seen by an influential minority to be ultimately connected, not with the logical coherence of a philosophy, but with the nature and character of God, and to be determined by the practical necessities involved in Christian monotheistic worship in the midst of a still dominant paganism.

Nevertheless, the problems which came to a head with Arianism were probably inevitable when faith ($\pi\iota\sigma\tau\iota\varsigma$) began to strive for expression in theology ($\gamma\nu\hat{\omega}\sigma\iota\varsigma$) ; though it was unfortunate that problems essentially religious and concerned primarily with the worship of the Church should have been grasped at this early date on their speculative side. For while the great Alexandrian teachers, Clement and Origen, following the Greek apologists, stood firmly on the foundation of saving religious truth as expressed in the Rule of Faith, their lesser followers developed disconnected fragments of Origen's great system, and more especially his doctrine of the Subordination of the Son or Logos to the Father. The theology of the third century assimilated in a remarkable degree the *secondary* elements of his teaching, but failed to find any satisfactory solution of the real problem, namely, how is the one God, if understood in the terms of Greek thought, to be conceived of ; what is His relation to the Universe of $\gamma\acute{\epsilon}\nu\epsilon\sigma\iota\varsigma$ and $\phi\theta o\rho\grave{a}$, and again to Him who was called in the Rule of Faith the Son of God, and to the Holy Spirit ; and how are They one, if distinct, and how distinct ?

It was at this point that Arianism stepped in with what appeared to be a coherent scheme, and armed with a new method of thought based on the logic of Aristotle. Starting from the " unoriginate " God ($\dot{a}\gamma\acute{\epsilon}\nu\nu\eta\tau o\varsigma$) transcendent and unknowable, and the predicate " Son of God," it went on logically to say that even creation is too close a relation of God with the world, and therefore in order to create the world there must first of all be an intermediary, and this instrument was called the Son of God. This was the point at which Arianism began, and where it was intrinsically wrong. For in thus stating the problem, Arianism was not only false to the biblical doctrine of Creation, and that of Redemption, which flows from it, but also involved itself in a network of syllogistic reasoning which caused it to drift further and further away from its roots in the Bible, from which, nevertheless, it was very willing to quote, especially the words in Prov. viii. 22. " The Lord created me the beginning of His ways for His works." [1] It was perhaps inevitable that Origen and his followers should have thus viewed Redemption and Creation from the cosmological side of the Logos doctrine. Where Arius went wrong was to view them in purely rationalistic terms. And while it was certain that none of the ante-Nicene specula- tions would have had any chance of influencing the Church if they had not corresponded to something in the language of St. Paul and St. John and the Wisdom literature of the Old Testament, it was left to Arius to make a logical syllogism of the central object of Christian worship, in which the major premiss was " God is unoriginate," and the minor premiss " The Son is originate " (γεννητός) and the conclusion " The Son therefore is not only inferior but other in nature to God," ξένος τοῦ υἱοῦ κατ' οὐσίαν ὁ πατήρ ; and capable of change (τρεπτός) (Athan. De Synod. 15). Or as it was put by Socrates (HE. i. 5) :

> What is true of human fatherhood is true of the relation between the Father and the Son :
> But the father's priority of existence is true of human fatherhood, therefore it is true in regard to the Father and the Son :
> Therefore once there was no Son :
> Therefore He was at some very remote period created by the Father. [2]

The *petitio principii* in the major premiss is a key to the whole heresy. It was essentially rationalistic, and in spite of every possible title of glory, even to God only Begotten (μονογενὴς Θεός) which Arius admitted, Christ remains the Son by adoption and grace, First-born among many brethren, not the Eternal Logos, but only " a word," and one among many, as he himself declared in the Thalia " Many words has God spoken : which of them was mani- fested in the flesh ? " [3] The Holy Spirit was probably placed by Arius somewhere between the Son and the creatures (τὰ κτίσματα). [4]

Such was the essential core of the Arian heresy, meriting Gwatkin's judgment that the central vice of Arianism was the incurable

---

[1] For the passages to which the Arians appealed, see Bethune-Baker, *Early History of Christian Doctrine*, pp. 161 ff.
[2] Kidd, op. cit., Vol. II, 15.
[3] Athan., De decr. Nic. 16 ; Robertson, p. 160.
[4] Athan. c. Ar. i. 2, De Syn. 15. Gwatkin, op. cit., p. 26.

badness of its method.[1]   And what strikes us chiefly in it, as in Nes-torianism, is its barren consistency.   Whatever its origin, which many connect with the martyr Lucian of Antioch, whose pupil Arius and Eusebius of Caesarea certainly were, it represented a complete break with Origen's great principle of God as the God of revelation and of love.   It was, as Athanasius never ceased to maintain, essentially *irreligious* in character.   It was, in fact, a syncretism of Christianity with Paganism, the second after Docetism to attack the cardinal doctrine of Christianity.

The earliest written document, revealing the first attempt of the Church to expel the rationalistic infection, appears in a letter bearing all the marks of the influence of Athanasius himself, which was sent by Bishop Alexander to all the bishops of the Church after a Synod held in Alexandria in or about A.D. 321, which deposed Arius.   This document (Socr. HE. i. 6; see Robertson, *Athanasius*, pp. 68 ff.) states the heads of the Arian " novelties," as they are called, put forth contrary to the Scriptures as follows :—

(1) God was not always a Father, but there was a time when God was not a Father.   The Word of God was not always, but originated ($\gamma\epsilon\nu\eta\tau\delta s$) from the things that were not, for God, Who is, has made him that was not, of that which was not; therefore there was a time when he was not, for the Son is a creature and a work.

(2) Neither is he like in essence ($o\dot{v}\sigma\dot{\iota}a$) to the Father, neither is he the true and natural Word of the Father, neither is he His true Wisdom, but he is one of the things made and created by the proper Word of God, and by the Wisdom that is in God.

(3) Wherefore he is by nature subject to change and variation ($\tau\rho\epsilon\pi\tau\delta s$), as are all rational creatures.   And the Word is foreign from the essence of the Father and is alien and separated there-from.

(4) The Word does not know the Father perfectly, neither can he see Him perfectly.   Moreover, the Son does not know his own $o\dot{v}\sigma\dot{\iota}a$ as it really is, for he was made for us, that God might create us by him, as by an instrument; and would not have existed, had not God wished to create us.

These attacks on the cardinal doctrine of the Faith were countered at Nicaea by three decisive phrases :—

(1) $\gamma\epsilon\nu\nu\eta\theta\acute{\epsilon}\nu\tau a$ $\acute{\epsilon}\kappa$ $\tau\hat{\eta}s$ $o\dot{v}\sigma\dot{\iota}as$ $\tauo\hat{v}$ $\pi a\tau\rho\grave{o}s.$
(2) $\gamma\epsilon\nu\nu\eta\theta\acute{\epsilon}\nu\tau a$ $o\dot{v}$ $\pioi\eta\theta\acute{\epsilon}\nu\tau a.$
(3) $\dot{o}\mu oo\acute{v}\sigma\iotao\nu$ $\tau\hat{\omega}$ $\pi a\tau\rho\acute{\iota}.$

to which were added four Anathemas repudiating the main Arian tenets.

We may consider the meaning of these phrases in the same order.

(1) $\acute{\epsilon}\kappa$ $\tau\hat{\eta}s$ $o\dot{v}\sigma\dot{\iota}as.$ This is the first instance of the use of this word in a Christian creed which, with its equivalents or alternatives, was destined to play so great a part in the theological and Christo-

---

[1] Op. cit., p. 273.

logical controversies of the period, more especially in connexion with the word *homoousion* in the following clause. It is therefore important to understand its meaning or meanings, as it was used by the Christian theologians of the time. Translations such as " Essence " or " Substance," derived from the Latin, are misleading as having material associations for most readers. It should be understood at the outset that the Church adopted the word and its equivalents from accepted philosophical use. Aristotle had fixed a twofold technical use of the word as having both a primary and a secondary meaning. In its primary sense οὐσία means a real individual existence, a single concrete entity or unit ; a single identical object, whether person, thing, or whatever can be said to exist in its own right. Thus, when Origen speaks of the Logos as an οὐσία[1] he was using the word to express the distinct *reality* of each of the Persons in the Blessed Trinity. Similarly, St. Athanasius defending this whole clause remarks (De Syn. 35) that it means exactly the same as do the words of the revelation of God to Moses " I am that I am," in which, as he says, we understand nothing else than the very simple and blessed and incomprehensible οὐσία itself ; " for although we be unable to master what He is, yet hearing Father and God and Almighty we understand nothing else to be meant than the very *ousia* of Him that is." And so in the treatise *ad Afros* (4) he explains the word as the same as ὑπόστασις. " Now *hypostasis* is *ousia* and means nothing else but very being (ὕπαρξις)." St. Basil can still use *ousia* of each person of the Blessed Trinity (In Incarn. 4) ; although after his acceptance of the *homoousion*, the terminology was universally adopted which defines the Trinity as one οὐσία or " unit " existing in three ὑποστάσεις.

There was, however, a secondary or more general use of the word οὐσία in which it was used as almost equivalent to *natura*, the Greek φύσις, a quality or property in which more than one individual can share, just as the word *substantia* is used by Tertullian in his definition of the Trinity ; and we shall find that its double meaning lies at the root of much of the barren controversy between Cyril and Nestorius, especially when they are trying to use the terminology of their opponents. Hence the great difficulties that both historians and theologians have incurred by failing to realise that οὐσία was before Nicaea and even later, a fluid term with no agreed meaning, and could be used interchangeably with ὑπόστασις, φύσις, πρόσωπον and εἶδος. In any case its precise meaning depended upon the particular context. It would, however, be more correct with Newman to call these terms alternatives rather than synonyms. See his note in Robertson's *Athanasius*, p. 478, where he goes on to

[1] c. Cels. vi. 64, In Ioan. i. 30. The human nature of Christ is thus called by Nestorius an οὐσία, *i.e.* a distinct reality. " Quod per se existit et non in alio." S. Thom. Aq., Summa Theol. I, Q. 29, Art. 2 (on *subsistentia*).

say that in one sense Natura and Substantia and Hypostasis are synonymous, as one and all denoting *Una Res*, which is Almighty God (cf. Athan. De Orat. iii. 11 and Epiphanius, Haer. 72, 73).

At the same time it should be understood that Dr. Prestige, in further research subsequent to that of Bishop Strong, Dr. Bethune-Baker, and Dr. Brightman,[1] has drawn from Athanasius and the post-Nicene Fathers, a further refinement in the meaning of *ousia*, which he distinguishes from *hypostasis* as subject from object. *Ousia* is therefore to be understood as the reality of a thing with reference to its analysis or interior content; *hypostasis*, in reference to the same symbol as external object of perception or consciousness. οὐσία therefore might be translated " unit." Such an explanation of the terms seems to make it far more possible to understand the doctrine of the Cappadocian Fathers, in that God in His eternal relationship of Father, Son, and Spirit, is One in His *ousia*, but to Himself and to us exists and appears as Three; God is one Object in Himself and three Objects to Himself and by revelation to men.[2] What then is the relation of *ousia* to the Latin *substantia* or *essentia*? It will be remembered that the Latins from Tertullian onwards, when speaking of the Trinity, used the expression *una substantia, tres personae*. But *substantia* is strictly speaking a translation of the Greek ὑπόστασις rather than of οὐσία ; and if the Greeks thought of God as one *ousia* and three *hypostases* or objects, the Latins took a different view and thought of God as one Object and three Subjects inhering in Him. The Latins used the phrase *una substantia* to express both unity and identity. Cf. Tertullian " Tres autem non statu sed gradu, nec substantia sed forma, nec potestate sed specie, unius autem substantiae et unius status et unius potestatis " (Adv. Prax. 2). The word *essentia* was not favoured except by St. Augustine (De Trin. 7. 10) and fell out of use. On the other hand, the term ὑπόστασις does not occur in the Creed until the Third Appended Anathema, in which it is denied that the Son is ἐξ ἑτέρας ὑποστάσεως ἢ οὐσίας. Did the Nicene Fathers use it as synonymous with *ousia*? Opinion has been divided. Bishop Bull (1634) maintained a difference, as against Petavius (1644), on the ground that *ousia* was intended for the Arians, *hypostasis* for the semi-Arians. Newman is probably right in his view that these terms are alternatives rather than synonyms ; *ousia* being the expression used among the Easterns, and *hypostasis* among the Westerns, as being the equivalent of their own *substantia* (cf. Theodoret, Eranistes, Dialogue I and Loofs, *Texte u. Unter.*, Vol. 44, pp. 250 f.). This view is confirmed by Dr. Prestige who thinks that the word *hypostasis* was added to the Anathema as supplying a link between

---

[1] Strong, *Journal of Theological Studies*, ii. 224 ; iii. 22. J. F. Bethune-Baker, *Journal of Theological Studies*, iii. 291 ; *Texts and Studies*, vii. 1. Brightman in Bigg, *Christian Platonists of Alexandria*, 2nd edition, pp. 203–205.

[2] *God in Patristic Thought*, p. 249, cf. 169.

the East and the West in the Trinitarian controversies of that date. Athanasius himself writing to the Bishops of Africa (ad Afros 4) remarked at a later date that the word *hypostasis* signified exactly the same as *ousia*, with the connotation of αὐτὸ τὸ ὄν, or real being, and was supported in this view by Epiphanius [1] and Cyril at the Council of Alexandria in 361 (Socr. iii. 7) when it was declared that such expressions as οὐσία and ὑπόστασις ought not to be used in reference to God : for the former is not employed in Holy Scripture, and the Apostle misapplied the term ὑπόστασις in attempting to describe what is ineffable (Heb. i. 1). Later they decided that in refutation of Sabellianism the term ὑπόστασις was admissible in default of more appropriate language, " lest it should be supposed that one Thing was indicated by a Three-fold designation. Whereas we ought rather to believe that each one of those named in the Trinity is the whole of God in his own proper ὑπόστασις.'' Socrates goes on to say that " if any expression of our judgment on this matter be permitted, it appears to us that the ancient Greek philosophers have given a varying definition of οὐσία, but have not taken the slightest notice of ὑπόστασις, a barbarous term not to be found in any of the ancients but only used by poets in its original meaning of sediment at the bottom of wine. Yet the modern philosophers frequently use it instead of οὐσία.''

Meanwhile the Latins preferred to adhere to their own terminology and never understood the subtlety of the Greek mind. But much confusion was caused by the use of *persona*, begun by Tertullian, which later became the Latin equivalent of ὑπόστασις with the result that both terms became associated in the Latin mind with ideas of personality. St. Jerome (Ep. xv. 1) vigorously protested against the Cappadocian formula of the Holy Trinity because he was Latin and therefore made no attempt to understand what the Greeks meant by *hypostasis*. At the same time it must be recognised that the confusion that arose about the use of this term was partly the result of its varying use in Holy Scripture, to which the Fathers always most strictly adhered. In the Epistle to the Hebrews the word occurs in both a transitive and intransitive sense : transitively in Heb. xi. 1 where the R.V. margin has " Faith is the giving substance (or reality) to things hoped for '' ; while in Heb. i. 3 it is used intransitively for the being, nature, or content of God Himself of which the Eternal Son is the " Express Image.'' In view of these two shades of meaning, which Dr. Prestige so carefully distinguishes, it should not be difficult to understand how the word came to be used as at once synonymous with and at the same time distinct from *ousia*. If God be regarded in His own absolute existence He is one

---

[1] He asks the Arians (Haer. 69. 3) if they do not know that οὐσία and ὑπόστασις have exactly the same meaning. In his other book, the *Ancoratus*, he maintains that the term ὁμοούσιον implies the existence of a single *hypostasis*.

hypostasis or Object, but if we think of Him as Father, Son, and
Holy Spirit, He is Three (op. cit., p. 250, etc.). Cf. on the whole
question Bigg, op. cit., pp. 201–214.

(2) γεννηθέντα οὐ ποιηθέντα. It was the vice of Origenism to
import into Christian theology the biological ideas current in
Gnosticism. For this reason Athanasius is careful to explain exactly
what is implied in the word γεννηθέντα in this clause of the Creed.
" What is from the Being (οὐσία) of the Father and proper to Him
is *entirely* the Son ; for it is all one thing to say that God is wholly
participated, and that He begets. And what does begetting signify
but a Son ? And what is partaken from the Father is the Son . . .
and beholding the Son we see the Father. For the thought (ἔννοια)
and comprehension of the Son by us is, as the Scripture says,
knowledge concerning the Father, because He is the proper offspring
(γέννημα) from His οὐσία. And since to be partaken no one of us
would call affection or division of God's Being (for it has been
shown and acknowledged that God is participated, and to be
participated is the same thing as to beget), therefore that which is
begotten is neither affection nor division of that blessed οὐσία.
Hence it is not incredible that God should have a Son, the offspring
of His own οὐσία ; nor do we imply affection or division of God's
οὐσία ; but rather are acknowledging the genuine and true and only
begotten of God. So we believe " (c. Ar. i. 16, Robertson, p. 316,
cf. Augustine, De Trin. ii. 13. " Non enim aliud est esse de Patre,
idest nasci de Patre, quam videre Patrem ").

At the same time much difficulty was caused by the prevailing
use, in which Athanasius himself shared, of the term γέννημα[1] as
applied to the Logos or Son. Athanasius explains again very
carefully that it was a right expression ; for it is to be contrasted
with the term γενητός meaning " derived," the opposite of the
word ἀγένητος which could strictly speaking be applied only to
God the Father. If God is ἀγένητος, His express image or
effulgence (Heb. i. 2) is not γενητός, " a derived thing," but γέννημα,
that is, belonging to the Father, who would not be Father unless
there was a γέννημα to justify the name. His Fatherhood, as
Athanasius himself was never tired of telling the Arians, belongs
to His Nature eternally and unalterably. To the Arians, on the
other hand, γέννημα meant the same as κτίσμα, " a creature " ; and
with some justification, for the word is constantly found in Greek
authors as applied to an inanimate object ; while the parallel word
spelt with one " ν " hardly ever occurs. Arius therefore called

---

[1] On the uses of the word in its many cognates and derivatives, see
Prestige, *God in Patristic Thought*, pp. 151 ff., who has much to say on the con-
fusion in the MSS. between the two spellings. Differing from Lightfoot,
Apostolic Fathers (Ignatius, Vol. 1, pp. 268, 269), he shows that the terms γενητός
and ἀγέννητος and their cognates were, until after the Arian heresy, used inter-
changeably. All, however, as he rightly remarks, as applied to God or
Christ, derive from the Hellenistic side of a deep line of cleavage between
Scriptural and philosophical Christianity.

the Son κτίσμα, though not as one of the κτίσματα, and γέννημα, though not as one of the γεννήματα. But the generation of the Son is not a successive *act of the Father's Will*, but a *necessary property of His Nature*. To signify that the generation of the Son (as also the Spiration of the Holy Spirit) is at once present and enduring we may say with Origen that " the Son is always *being* begotten." It is, however, better to say with Augustine and Gregory that " the Son is always begotten " (not *semper nascitur* but *semper natus*) in order to exclude the notion that the Generation or Procession of Persons in the Trinity is a *series of successive operations* and not the eternal duration, including, in human language, past, present, and future, of the changeless energy of God (cf. St. Thom. Aq., Summa Theol. I, Q. 42, Art. 2).

(3) ὁμοούσιον τῷ πατρί. This, the third crucial anti-Arian phrase, was selected by the Council as concentrating in itself the force of various Scriptural expressions which denoted the real Godhead of the Son. It was, as Robertson remarks (*Athanasius*, Intro., p. xvii), the work of two concurrent influences in the Council, the anti-Origenists or Antiochenes of the East, such as Marcellus of Ancyra and Eustathius of Antioch, in alliance with the Roman delegates and the Western bishops headed by Hosius of Cordova " who presided both at Nicaea and Sardica " and " put forth the Nicene Confession." (Athan. De Synod. 42.) Athanasius himself, great as was his influence as the young supporter of his Bishop Alexander, was not himself its author nor, indeed, were any of the Alexandrian theologians, who in the previous century had rejected the expression at the Council of Antioch in 269. This was the Council which condemned Paul of Samosata, who according to one account had used the word himself to safeguard, as he thought, the unity of God. Of Athanasius, it has been said that he was moulded by the *homoousion* but did not mould it himself.[1] Indeed, it is highly probable that Athanasius only learned the full implications of the term from the West, where the emphasis had always been laid on the *unius substantiae*, rather than on the *tres personae* = τρεῖς ὑποστάσεις as in the School of Alexandria. On the other hand, the phrase had been disowned by Eusebius of Nicomedia on the ground that it implied the true Sonship (Ambros. De Fid. iii. 15, § 125); and by Arius himself in the Thalia (Athan. De Synod. 15). The main body of the bishops present probably used the phrase, in spite of its doubtful antecedents, in the sense of " of the same kind or nature ", the sense in which the word had been used in philosophical and scientific writing, by Clement and Origen, and by Dionysius of Alexandria (247–265), who had to deny the charge brought against him by his Western namesake that he denied Christ to be ὁμοούσιος with God, because, as he states, a Son is clearly of the same nature with a Father (ὁμοφυής). From which it may be inferred that at

[1] Athanasius' account of the reasons for its adoption are given in De decr. Nic. 18 and 21 ff., ad Afros. 6.

the actual Council the only purpose of its use was to place beyond possibility of doubt that the Son is God in exactly the same sense as the Father, without reference to the later problem of the relation between the Persons. (See Dr. Prestige, *God in Patristic Thought*, p. 213.) So St. Basil seems to have thought (Epistle 52). The opposition to the *homoousion* seems to have been threefold. In the first place it was not Scriptural. But, as Athanasius afterwards remarked, if not actually in Scripture, it nevertheless conveyed better than any other term the full sense of Scripture (de Decr. Nic. 21). The second objection which the conservatives as a whole felt, certainly those who were under the influence of the School of Alexandria, was that it tended to obscure the reality and distinctness of the Three Persons, even if it was not actually Sabellian. And, thirdly, it was regarded as having a material connotation. Thus Eusebius of Caesarea, who accepted the word reluctantly and with qualifications, wrote to his Diocese that the word was not intended in the sense attaching to physical objects, but was intended to mean that the Son was not in any way as one of the " originate " things ($\gamma\epsilon\nu\eta\tau\acute{a}$) ; but that He is in every way *like* the Father alone who begat Him, and that He is not of any other *hypostasis*, but out of the Father (Letter to his diocese on the Nicene Creed, § 4). To the use of $\dot{o}\mu oo\acute{u}\sigma\iota os$ in this sense the conservatives such as Eusebius of Caesarea and his supporters agreed. And it was only ten years after the Council, when Marcellus of Ancyra published his work on the Trinity, that opposition to the *homoousion*, as being Sabellian, arose.

The minority party, however, under Hosius undoubtedly thought that the term implied a great deal more than this, and intended it to do so. This is proved by the description which Athanasius in his later treatises gave of the proceedings of the Council. These further implications were not at first clearly perceived even by Athanasius himself. For to the Westerns the word implied *identity* ($\tau a \upsilon\tau\acute{o}\tau\eta s$) as well as equality or unity in the Godhead ; while the Easterns naturally preferred the *homoiousion* because the plurality meant more to them than the identity. Athanasius in the treatise *De Decretis* maintained that the Arians were prepared to accept this well-known substitute as well as the phrase which occurs in several Eastern Creeds, $\dot{a}\pi a\rho\acute{a}\lambda\lambda a\kappa\tau os$ $\epsilon\dot{\iota}\kappa\acute{\omega}\nu$, of the Logos, but that not even with the addition $\kappa a\tau'$ $o\dot{\upsilon}\sigma\acute{\iota}a\nu$ was it regarded as sufficient in itself ; and that by saying this the Arians showed clearly that $\dot{\epsilon}\kappa$ $\tau\hat{\eta}s$ $o\dot{\upsilon}\sigma\acute{\iota}as$ or $\dot{o}\mu oo\acute{u}\sigma\iota os$ was destructive of their " catch-words of impiety " such as " created " and " work " and " originated " and " alterable " and " that He was not before His generation." He concludes by repeating again and again the illustration of the relation of radiance ($\dot{a}\pi a\acute{\upsilon}\gamma a\sigma\mu a$) to the light. In the treatise *De Synodis* (42) he adds the warning, however, not to press the metaphor too far, when you argue from material analogies to God ; just as in giving the title " offspring " or " Son " we entertain no material ideas about Him, nor do we admit that there is in the *homoousion* any failure to transcend physical notions. It is in this treatise that we see Athanasius developing the *homoousion* from its original Nicene connotation—namely, "one in nature" into the important conception of *identity* (ταυτότης) of substance or being, as its true meaning. This is the last of the great and important group of writings of his third exile, written in 359 after the Arianising Councils of Ariminium and Seleucia, in which he turns from abuse of the Arians to a careful statement in vindication of the Nicene Faith. In other words, Athanasius had now penetrated into the deeper meaning of the *homoousion*, in which it has come to mean that *all* the Father is in the Son and in the Holy Ghost ; and it was in this sense that it was finally accepted by Basil and the Cappodocian Fathers in the formulation of the Faith of Nicaea as one οὐσία existing in three ὑποστάσεις or presentations of God. The importance of this is seen in the fact that it marked the end after a long struggle of what was known as "subordinationism," the idea, however expressed, that the Father is God, and the Son and the Spirit God in the second and third place from Him, and with some sense of subordination to Him.[1] For the extension of the *homoousion* to the Holy Spirit, see Prestige, op. cit., p. 221, and Athanasius, Ad Serapion. i. 2.

The *homoousion*, however, was not only an uncompromising refutation of Arianism, it was also, when taken with the words which next follow, "By whom all things were made" a positive assertion of the Christian doctrine of Creation. The central doctrine of the Redemption has at times in the history of the Church been allowed to obscure the no less vital doctrine of Creation, with fatal results to the wholeness of Catholic teaching about the doctrine of man, the Fall, and the Atonement. At the Council of Nicaea the Arian doctrine was condemned which denied that God could act *directly* in Creation, and therefore in Redemption also, and it was maintained in the strongest terms that He "by whom all things were made" was identical in Being with God ; and that the God Who created us is the same also as redeemed us. As Professor Hodgson remarks "perhaps the most difficult task for Christian philosophy is the thinking out of its doctrine of Creation in which it is essential that man be conceived both as owing his existence to God and made of nothing other than God, and yet also in a real sense distinct from and other than God" (*Bazaar of Heracleides*, p. xxxiv).

[1] Prestige, op. cit., pp. xxix and xxx, also p. 235 ; Robertson, *Athanasius*, pp. xxvii and xxviii. For the Latin view see Prestige, op. cit., pp. 220 and 221. Cf. also Athanasius, De Decretis 23, Theodoret, HE. i. 12.

C

THE CREED OF NICAEA

1 Πιστεύομεν
 εἰς ἕνα Θεὸν Πατέρα παντοκράτορα
  πάντων ὁρατῶν τε καὶ ἀοράτων ποιητήν·
 καὶ εἰς ἕνα Κύριον Ἰησοῦν Χριστόν
5   τὸν Υἱὸν τοῦ Θεοῦ,
   γεννηθέντα ἐκ τοῦ Πατρὸς μονογενῆ
   τουτέστιν ἐκ τῆς οὐσίας τοῦ Πατρός
   Θεὸν ἐκ Θεοῦ,
   Φῶς ἐκ Φωτός,
10   Θεὸν ἀληθινὸν ἐκ Θεοῦ ἀληθινοῦ,
   γεννηθέντα, οὐ ποιηθέντα,
   ὁμοούσιον τῷ Πατρί,
  δι' οὗ τὰ πάντα ἐγένετο
   τά τε ἐν τῷ οὐρανῷ καὶ τὰ ἐν τῇ γῇ,
15   τὸν δι' ἡμᾶς τοὺς ἀνθρώπους, καὶ
   διὰ τὴν ἡμετέραν σωτηρίαν, κατελθόντα,
   καὶ σαρκωθέντα,
   καὶ ἐνανθρωπήσαντα,
   παθόντα
20   καὶ ἀναστάντα τῇ τρίτῃ ἡμέρᾳ,
   ἀνελθόντα εἰς τοὺς οὐρανούς,
   ἐρχόμενον κρῖναι ζῶντας καὶ νεκρούς.
 καὶ εἰς τὸ Ἅγιον Πνεῦμα.
 Τοὺς δὲ λέγοντας Ἦν ποτε ὅτε οὐκ ἦν,
25   καὶ Πρὶν γεννηθῆναι οὐκ ἦν,
  καὶ ὅτι Ἐξ οὐκ ὄντων ἐγένετο,
   ἢ Ἐξ ἑτέρας ὑποστάσεως ἢ οὐσίας φάσκοντας
    εἶναι
   ἢ κτιστόν
30   ἢ τρεπτόν
   ἢ ἀλλοιωτὸν τὸν Υἱὸν τοῦ Θεοῦ,
 τούτους ἀναθεματίζει ἡ ἁγία καθολικὴ καὶ ἀποστολικὴ ἐκκλησία.

NOTES ON THE CREED OF NICAEA

TEXT. In the lack of any authentic Acts of the Council, the primary authorities for the Text of the Creed are Eusebius of Caesarea, and Athanasius. The former embodied the Creed in a letter written to his diocese at the time of the Council, which is extant in four recensions :—

(1) Appendix to Athan. De decr. syn. Nic : (2) Socrates, HE. i. 8 : (3) Theodoret, HE. i. 12 ; Mansi II, p. 916 : (4) Gelasius, Hist. Conc. Nic. ii. 35 ; this last possessing no independent value. The first three are referred to below as E^A, E^S, E^T.

Athanasius himself gave the Text of the Creed in his letter to Jovian, 3 (Robertson, p. 568), which is also inserted by Theodoret in his history, iv. 3. Other authorities are Basil, Epist. 125, Cyril of Alex. Epist. 3 ad Nest., and a document presented by Eustathius of Sebaste and others to Pope Liberius in 365 (apud Socr. iv. 12). These are referred to respectively as *A*, *S*, *B*, *C*, *Eust.*

None of the variations are important, but it may be well to note them at once.

Line 2   εἰς τὸν ἕνα Κύριον   *A.*
4   εἰς ἕνα μονογενῆ Θεὸν Κ. ᾽Ι. Χ.   *Eust.*
6   *omit* μονογενῆ   *Eust.*
9   καὶ φῶς ἐκ φ.   *S.* E^T.
14   ἐπὶ τῆς γῆς   *A, Eust.*
15   *omit* τὸν   *S.*
18   *omit* καὶ E^S, *A, B.*
21   *omit* τοὺς   *C, Eust.*
22   καὶ πάλιν ἐρχ.   *C.*
23   τὸ Π. τὸ ῞Αγ. E^S.
29   *omit* ἢ κτιστόν   *C,* E^T, *Eust.*
32   *omit* τούτους   *S,* E^T.
       omit ἁγία   *C,* E^{SA}, *Eust.*
       omit καὶ ἀποστολική E^A.

On the variations in the Text read in the Council of Chalcedon, see below, p. 194 f.

The earliest known translation of the Nicene Creed into Latin is that of Hilary of Poitiers, De Synodis et De Fid. Orientalium, 84 (Watson's translation, *Nicene and post-Nicene Fathers*, p. 26), which adds "Nostrum" in the Second Article and omits δι᾽ ἡμᾶς τοὺς ἀνθρώπους in the same (cf. also Rufinus, in Eus. HE. ii. 6, and Leo, Epistle 134).

Πιστεύομεν. Conciliar creeds were naturally couched in the plural number, and baptismal creeds, as naturally, in the singular : cf. Cyr. Jer. Catech. xix. 9 ; xx. 4. The latter was the general cast of Western creeds. Some of the Liturgical Eastern creeds are likewise in the singular number ; e.g. Apost. Const. vii. 41 ; " Liturgy of St. James " (πιστεύω), Brightman, Liturgies E. and W., p. 42 ; " Liturgy of Syr. Jacobites " (Priest, " We believe " ; congregation, " I believe "), ibid. p. 82 ; " Liturgy of St. Mark " (πιστεύω), ibid. p. 124 ; " Ninth Century Byzantine Liturgy " (πιστεύω) ibid. p. 321 ; and this use has asserted itself in the modern Greek Orthodox Church. In Augustine the form varies. The creed commented on in De Fid. et Symb. was seemingly in the plural ; but in Ser. ad Catech. the creed which begins with the singular number continues in the second article with " Jesus Christ our Lord."

The distinction between πιστεύειν εἰς and πιστεύειν with the dative is strongly emphasised by Augustine Tract. xxix in Ioan. 6 : " Hoc est opus Dei ut credatis in Eum quem Ille misit. Ut credatis in Eum, non ut credatis Ei. Sed si creditis in Eum, creditis Ei : non autem continuo qui credit Ei, credit in Eum. Nam et daemones credebant Ei, non credebant in Eum. . . . Quid est ergo credere in Eum ? Credendo amare, credendo diligere, credendo in Eum ire et Eius membris incorporari " (cf. Tract. liv. 3, and the Commentary on John ii. 11). The distinction, however, is peculiar to the Latin Fathers and reappears in the English Homily on Faith. That it is not recognised by any of the Greek Fathers makes it doubtful whether it can be pressed in the Creed, which as Bishop Pearson remarks " being nothing else but a brief comprehension of the most necessary matters of Faith, whatever else is contained in it beside the first word ' I believe ' can be nothing else but part of those verities to be believed ; and the act of belief nothing but an assent to them as divinely credible and infallible truths." The use of πιστεύειν εἰς in the Gospels is with one exception (Matt. xviii. 6 = Mark ix. 42) peculiar to St. John, who also has the alternative construction ; the explanation probably being that Aramaic, with which the Fourth Gospel has so many affinities, uses both indifferently ; while, in the most crucial instance of all, Abraham's act of justifying faith, is translated in the LXX (Gen. xv. 6) ἐπίστευσεν Ἀβραμ τῷ Θεῷ. St. Paul also uses both constructions. See Pearson on the Creed ad loc. with the important note (K). Cf. John iii. 18, iv. 21, x. 38, xiv. 11, vi. 29, 30, ix. 35, xi. 26, xiv. 1 ; Acts. x. 43, xxvi, 27, xxvii. 25 ; Gal. ii. 16 ; Phil. i. 29 ; 1 Pet. i. 8. Compare also Rufinus in the note following.

2. ἕνα Θεόν. Emphasis is laid on the Unity of God in all creeds which were in use where philosophical speculation or Gnostic heresy denied the unity of the First Principle : Gaul (Irenaeus iii. 4. 1), Carthage (Tertullian, de Virg. Vel. 1, adv. Prax. 2, de praescr.

haer. 13 [not Cyprian]), the East (Origen, De Princ. i. praef., Socr. HE. ii. 10, Euseb.-Caes. ibid. i. 8, Cyr.-Jer. Catech. vi. vii. 1). By far the most frequently quoted passage is that in The Shepherd of Hermas, which is quoted by St. Irenaeus as Scripture : καλῶς οὖν εἶπεν ἡ γραφὴ ἡ λέγουσα Πρῶτον πάντων πιστευσον ὅτι εἷς ἐστὶν ὁ Θεός, ὁ τὰ πάντα κτίσας καὶ καταρτίσας καὶ ποιήσας ἐκ τοῦ μὴ ὄντος εἰς τὸ εἶναι τὰ πάντα (Irenaeus iv. 34. 2 ; Hermas, Mand. I).

Rufinus is no doubt right in tracing the phrases ἕνα Θεόν . . . ἕνα Κύριον I. X. to St. Paul's words, 1 Cor. viii. 6. " Orientales ecclesiae omnes paene ita tradunt, Credo in Uno Deo Patre et rursus in sequenti sermone ubi nos dicimus Et in Christo Jesu unico Filio Eius Domino nostro, illi tradunt Et in Uno Domino nostro . . . Unum scilicet Deum et Unum Dominum, secundum auctoritatem Pauli Apostoli profitentes " (Rufin. in symb. 4). But the recurrence of the numeral again before " Holy Spirit " in the third division of some earlier creeds, e.g. those of Caesarea, Jerusalem, Alexandria, seems rather to show that the purport of its insertion in each case was to mark the distinctness of the Three Persons in the Godhead. Indeed Eusebius' own words imply this :

πιστεύομεν οὖν καὶ ὁμολογοῦμεν ἕνα μόνον καὶ ἀληθινὸν καὶ ἀγαθὸν Θεὸν καὶ ἕνα τὸν μονογενῆ αὐτοῦ Υἱὸν καὶ ἓν μόνον Πνεῦμα ἅγιον ; with which we may compare the anti-Sabellian appendix to his Creed τούτων ἕκαστον εἶναι καὶ ὑπάρχειν πιστεύοντες Πατέρα ἀληθῶς Πατέρα καὶ Θεὸν ἀληθῶς Υἱὸν καὶ Πνεῦμα Ἅγιον ἀληθῶς Ἅγιον Πνεῦμα (cf. Athan. De Decretis vi. 8, ad Afros. v., De Incarn. 3, and Clement Epist. i. 1).

2. Πάτερα. Cf. Eph. iv. 6, εἷς Θεὸς καὶ πατὴρ πάντων and 1 Cor. viii. 6 ἐξ οὗ τὰ πάντα. With the exception of the creeds of Marcellus (apud Epiphan. Haer. 72) and Tertullian (in all three forms),[1] this word is found in this position in all creeds. Yet the idea of Fatherhood is implied even in those creeds which omit the word, by the use of such phrases as Filius eius, Dei Filius, in the following section. The use of the term Father in the sense of Creator is frequent in the early Fathers, e.g. Clement, Epist. 19, " the Father and Creator of the whole World " ; also Novatian (De Trin. 2), who writes " Ipse qui virtutum omnium et Deus et parens est " ; and Irenaeus (iv. 34. 1) " Non ergo angeli fecerunt nos, nec nos plasmaverunt, nec angeli potuerunt imaginem facere Dei, nec alius quis praeter Verbum Domini, nec virtus longe absistens a Patre universorum."

2. παντοκράτορα. " All sovereign." The word asserts the universal dominion of God, and is inadequately represented by " omnipotens," " almighty," in the Latin and English creeds.

---

[1] Tertullian cites the Creed of North Africa in De Praesc. Haer. 13 ; De Virg. Veland. 1. (the most complete) and Adv. Prax. 1. 16. He is evidently quoting the Regula Fidei, but there is no mention of the Father in any of these passages.

παντοκράτωρ belongs to Biblical Greek, and is used in the versions to translate both צבאות "(Lord of) Hosts," and שׁדי, "Almighty," 2 Sam. v. 10, vii. 8, 26, etc.; Job. v. 17, viii. 5. In the N.T. it is used (nine times in the Apocalypse), but appears (2 Cor. vi. 18) in a quotation from the LXX. which is difficult to trace (perhaps 2 Sam. vii. 8). It invests the idea of God with a spiritual and moral not a philosophical significance. Cf. Cyril. Catech. viii. 3, παντο-κράτωρ γὰρ ἐστὶν ὁ πάντων κρατῶν, ὁ πάντων ἐξουσιάζων. Cf. Theoph. ad Autol. i. 4; Greg. Nyss. contr. Eunom. ii.; Rufin. in symb. 5; Novatian De Trin. 2.

Some later creeds of North Africa known to St. Augustine expanded the term *omnipotentem* by the addition of " Universorum Creatorem, regem saeculorum (1 Tim. i. 17), immutatum et invisibilem," [1] which is explained thus " Ipse est quippe Deus Omnipotens, qui in primo radio mundi cunctum ex nihil fecit, qui est ante saecula, qui fecit et regit saecula. Non enim tempore augetur aut loco dividitur aut aliqua natura continetur aut terminatur, sed manens apud se et in se ipso plane et perpetua aeternitas, qui nec comprehenditur nec cogitari potest ut longe manens."

3. πάντων ὁρατῶν τε καὶ ἀοράτων ποιητήν. Some creeds have ἁπάντων, *e.g.* Caesarea and the Apostolic Constitutions. The Creed known as Constantinopolitan inserts the clause " Maker of Heaven and Earth " which also appears in latest form of the Roman Creed, adopted probably from the Creed of Niceta of Remesiana (see Badcock, p. 72).

This clause is characteristically Eastern. It was the tendency of Oriental mysticism to lay exaggerated stress on the position and functions of unseen spiritual powers, and it was therefore necessary to assert their dependence upon the First Principle. Especially did the dualistic theories, which constantly troubled the East, and penetrated the West, in the form of Gnostic heresies which separated the Supreme God from the Creator of the world, necessitate the insertion of some words in the Creeds to identify the Creator or Demiurge with the One God. See the forms given by Irenaeus i. 2. 1, τὸν πεποιηκότα τὸν οὐρανὸν καὶ τὴν γῆν καὶ τὰς θαλάσσας καὶ πάντα τὰ ἐν αὐτοῖς : iii. 4. 1, fabricatorem caeli et terrae et omnium quae in eis sunt; and Tertullian, De Praescr. Haer. 13, De Virg. Veland. 1, mundi creatorem. Similarly the Jerusalem Creed, ποιητὴν οὐρανοῦ καὶ γῆς ; whence it passed into the Epiphanian and later forms, but did not establish itself in the Western creeds until the seventh century. Cf. Origen, c. Cels. i. 25, ἢ γὰρ ἀορίστως ὁμολογοῦσιν τὸ κοινὸν ὄνομα, τό, ὁ Θεός, ἢ καὶ μετὰ προσθήκης τῆς, ὁ δημιουργὸς τῶν ὅλων, ὁ ποιητὴς οὐρανοῦ καὶ γῆς—words which seem to point to such a clause in the Creed of Alexandria.

The true doctrine of creation was expressed by Athanasius De

---

[1] See Hahn, pp. 58, 61. Cf. pseudo-Augustine, Serm. in redd. symb. ccxv.

Inc. 3, where he cites Herm. Mand. 1, Heb. xi. 3 and adds that
" God is good, or rather is essentially the source of goodness;
nor would one that is good be grudging of anything; whence
grudging existence to none He has made all things out of nothing
by his own Word which was Christ our Lord " (see below on
δι᾽ οὗ τὰ πάντα ἐγένετο).

4. καί. It will be noted that in the Second Clause belief is
asserted not explicitly in the Second Person of the Trinity but in
the *Incarnate Lord*, in what was called the *economy* (οἰκονομία).
Who that Person is constitutes the substance of the next clauses.
Cf. John xiv. 1. 4.

4. ἕνα Κύριον Ἰησοῦν Χριστόν. Εἷς Κύριος comes from Eph. iv.
5 : the whole phrase from 1 Cor. viii. 6. This is the historic title
borne by the Second Person of the Trinity Incarnate. It contains three titles (i) Κύριος, the title given, from the very beginning,
to the risen and ascended Christ, the foundation of the baptismal
formula subsequently enlarged into the threefold Name. As we
have seen, the confession of Jesus as Lord was the primary qualification for Christian baptism. Actually, however, the correspondence is not between Κύριος and δοῦλος (though St. Paul was
referring to that contrast when describing himself as servant or
slave of Jesus Christ), but between the Κύριος and His ἐκκλησία.
It must be remembered that the name of Κύριος first appeared
under the Aramaic form of *Maran*, which means *our* Lord. Jesus
is our Lord because we belong to Him as members of His *ecclesia*.
Κύριος and ἐκκλησία are correlatives; they belong to each other as
the Head to the Body, and we cannot think of the Lord without
thinking of the Church and the community. The presence of
Christ constitutes the Church; and the reference therefore in
the title of Κύριος is probably to Matt. xviii. 20, an early oracle
of Palestinian Christianity, rather than to St. Paul's declaration in
Phil. ii. 2. See *Mysterium Christi*, p. 112, and cf. Hort on 1 Pet.
ii. 3 ; Selwyn, *The First Epistle of St. Peter*, pp. 157 and 193.

(ii). Ἰησοῦς = יְשׁוּעַ. The human name meaning Saviour. Luke
i. 31, ii. 21 ; Matt. i. 21.

(iii). Χριστός = מָשִׁיחַ, the Messiah, or the Anointed One. John i.
41, iv. 25 ; Luke ii. 32 ; Acts ii. 31 ; Rom. xv. 8, 12. It means
the fulfiller of Jewish national expectations and prophecy and,
through these, of Gentile longings and aspirations, the " Desire
of all the nations." (Haggai ii. 7.)

5. τὸν Υἱὸν τοῦ Θεοῦ. The fact of the Divine Sonship stands
prominently forward, τὸν Υἱὸν replacing τὸν Λόγον of the earlier
Eastern creeds. This is the case in nearly all subsequent creeds,
and in view of the Arian tenet, it would naturally be insisted on by
the orthodox at Nicaea.

The Son of God is the name attributed in the Old Testament
to Israel itself (Exod. iv. 22, 23 ; Hos. xi. 1) ; and in the New

Testament to the *Incarnate* Revealer of the Father, and is so used of Himself by Christ in the Fourth Gospel (John v. 19 and *passim*). The earlier Christian writers still retained this use, as can be seen in such expressions of Irenaeus as " Ipse Filius mensura Dei . . . visibile est invisibilis Dei, quoniam et capit eum " (iv. 6). Loofs remarks that the transference of the expression " Son," from the sense of Jesus as Messiah to that of the Second Person was the most momentous point in the pluralistic development of Christian Theology and of Monophysite Christology [1] (see note on Marcellus of Ancyra, p. 42).

The order of the names Jesus Christ in this place is to be noted, universal in the Eastern Creeds, though not in all Western. St. Leo, however, has the same order, which is decisive for the early Roman Creed. But Hippolytus, Novatian, and Tertullian reverse the order.

6. γεννηθέντα ἐκ τοῦ Πατρός. This clause is taken from the Alexandrian, Antiochene, and Jerusalem Creeds, all of which add, with the Caesarean (which reads γεγεννημένον), πρὸ πάντων τῶν αἰώνων. These last words were probably omitted here for the sake of grammatical clearness. They retained their natural place in the Constantinopolitan Creed, which followed a different construction from the Nicene. They witness to the Eternal Generation of the Son, but the expression is not scriptural. Our Lord's own phrase (John xvii. 5) is πρὸ τοῦ τὸν κόσμον εἶναι or (ibid. 24) πρὸ καταβολῆς κόσμου.

The Arians admitted the Son's Generation from the Father, but rejected the logical consequence of this admission in the case of a Generation which was divine and unique. True Generation from a Divine Being must imply in the One Generated the possession of the same Divine Nature, and the Generation itself must therefore be of an eternal character. Ἐκ τοῦ Πατρός was thus explained and defined as ἐκ τῆς οὐσίας and ὁμοούσιος. See further, on the anathemas. Hilary of Poitiers (De Trin. viii. 13) argued the unity of Nature, as opposed to a mere concord of will between the Father and the Son, from the unity of all who partake of the Eucharist. This union results (he says) from the Father being in Christ and Christ in us. (Cf. Hooker, E.P., v. 67. 11.)

6. μονογενῆ. *Unique*, rather than Only Begotten as in the Latin translations *unicus* or *unigenitus*.[2] What gives this word its importance is its association with the title Θεός in the Prologue of the

---

[1] *Paulus von Samosata, Texte und Unter.*, Vol. 44, p. 313 and refs.

[2] μονογενής was represented in the Latin Creeds by *unicus*, and so St. Leo in his Tome translates it ; but elsewhere in his writings he employs *unigenitus*. The old Latin versions give *unicus*, but the Vulgate has *unigenitus* and this form prevailed eventually in the Latin creeds from the fourth century onwards.

Fourth Gospel (John i. 18), where the best attested reading is μονογενὴς θεός, ὁ ὢν εἰς τὸν κόλπον τοῦ Πατρός, ἐκεῖνος ἐξηγήσατο.[1]

As Hort remarks, the force of this important word in its original context is to contrast the unique relation of the Incarnate Logos to the Deity with the adopted sonship given to those who believe on His name (John i. 12). He goes on to remark that the word, which is found in all creeds Eastern and Western, connects the two great Christological thoughts of the Prologue, the Perfect Godhead of the Logos, and the Godhead of the Logos made Flesh (John i. 14), Jesus Christ, named in the rest of the Gospel the Son. Thus Hort finds in this word the Scriptural foundation of the pre-temporal Sonship within the Godhead, as distinguished from the manifested Sonship of the Incarnation : for to the attribute Θεός already given to the Logos as Revealer, is now (in verse 14) added the attribute μονογενής, already suggested in verse 12. Then in the last and crowning verse 18 of the Prologue the two elements are brought together, associating Deity with the Logos as Son, as expressly as it has been associated with Him as the revealing Word. We may compare the words of Cyril of Alexandria, ἐπειδὴ γὰρ ἔφη μονογενῆ καὶ Θεόν, τίθησιν εὐθύς, ὁ ὢν ἐν τοῖς κόλποις τοῦ Πατρός, ἵνα νοήται καὶ υἱὸς ἐξ αὐτοῦ καὶ ἐν αὐτῷ φυσικῶς. (Comm. in Ioan. i. 10 on John i. 18.) In this way, as Cyril saw, St. John leads his readers from the idea of revelation implied in the Logos doctrine, under which he condenses so much of the scattered teaching of our Lord and the earlier Apostles, to the deeper mystery of the Unique Sonship, which after the Prologue he employs generally. Similarly we may compare the Definition of the Council of Chalcedon (l. 123, p. 193) ἀλλ' ἕνα καὶ τὸν αὐτὸν υἱὸν καὶ μονογενῆ Θεόν, Λόγον, Κύριον Ἰ. Χ. and Athanasius' favourite phrase ἴδιον τῆς τοῦ Πατρὸς οὐσίας γέννημα, which is the best commentary on the word.

In the Arian controversy it was not of great dogmatic importance, inasmuch as it was accepted by the Arians and its force evaded by making " generation " synonymous with " creation " : nor for them did the uniqueness of the Son's generation exempt Him from creatureship. See the letter of Arius to Eusebius of Nicomedia in Theodoret HE. i. 5. In the dated Creed of Sirmium (A.D. 359) μονογενῆ is explained by μόνον ἐκ μόνου, words which were substituted for the Nicene τουτέστιν ἐκ τῆς οὐσίας τοῦ Πατρός.

Instances of the Arian use of μονογενής occur in Arius' own letter

[1] The phrase μονογενὴς θεός disappears utterly after this date from MSS. and Creeds alike, probably as the result of the rise to supremacy of the Constantinople Creed. At the same time it may be noted that all Creeds and statements of doctrine were built up out of disjointed sentences ; and with a similar accumulation of appositional phrases as in the Nicene Creed may usefully be compared those in the Synodical Letter of the previous Council of Antioch (A.D. 269) which condemned Paul of Samosata. τοῦτον δὲ τὸν υἱὸν γεννητόν, μονογενῆ υἱόν, εἰκόνα τοῦ ἀοράτου θεοῦ τυγχάνοντα, πρωτότοκον πάσης κτίσεως, σοφίαν καὶ λόγον καὶ δύναμιν θεοῦ πρὸ αἰώνων ὄντα, οὐ προγνώσει, ἀλλ' οὐσίᾳ καὶ ὑποστάσει θεόν, θεοῦ υἱόν. (Hahn, p. 178.)

to Eusebius of Nicomedia, θελήματι καὶ βουλῇ ὑπέστη πρὸ χρόνων
καὶ πρὸ αἰώνων πλήρης Θεὸς μονογενὴς ἀναλλοίωτος, and in his
"Blasphemies" (apud Athan. De Synod. 15), Λοιπὸν ὁ Ὑιὸς οὐκ ὢν
(ὑπῆρξε δὲ θελήσει πατρῴᾳ), μονογενὴς Θεός ἐστιν. It is similarly
joined with Θεός in the Lucianic (Second Antiochene, "Dedication")
Creed; in a creed of Marcellus (apud Euseb. contr. Marc. i. 4),
εἰς τὸν Ὑιὸν αὐτοῦ τοῦ μονογενῆ Θεόν: and in precisely identical
words in the Creed of Theophronius (Third Antiochene) (Athan.
De Synod. 24). In the Homoion Creed of Acacius at Seleucia
the phrase is practically Nicene, Θεὸν ἐκ Θεοῦ μονογενῆ (Athan. De
Synod. 29), and so in the profession of Eustathius and other
Homoiousians (Socr. iv. 12), εἰς ἕνα μονογενῆ Θεόν, K. 'I. X.

7. τουτέστιν ἐκ τῆς οὐσίας τοῦ Πατρός. It remains to consider
the place of these words in the Nicene Creed in connexion with
the construction of the whole clause γεννηθέντα ἐκ τοῦ Πατρός,
μονογενῆ, τουτέστιν ἐκ τῆς οὐσίας τοῦ Πατρός, Θεὸν ἐκ Θεοῦ. Hort
believed that it was necessary to read the whole sentence together
as one, μονογενῆ doing "double duty," combined alike with ἐκ τοῦ
Πατρός and with Θεὸν ἐκ Θεοῦ; the clause, τουτέστιν ἐκ τῆς
οὐσίας τοῦ Πατρός being parenthetic; and thus connecting μονογενῆ
directly with Θεὸν ἐκ Θεοῦ, as in John i. 18. In favour of this view,
which of course makes an awkward overloaded sentence, it may be
urged that both Athanasius (De Decretis 19; ad Afros. 5) and
Eusebius (ad Caes. 5) regard τουτέστιν ἐκ τῆς οὐσίας τοῦ Πατρός
as interpreting the former phrase γεννηθέντα ἐκ τοῦ Πατρός. It was a
kind of commentary, and is incidentally defended by Athanasius
with reference to former theologians only, but not as belonging
to any known creed (De Decretis 19, 35: ad Afros. 5), all the
rest of the clause in question being taken from other creeds.
Moreover, in the Creed of Jerusalem [1] we find that the corresponding clause runs thus: τὸν υἱὸν τοῦ Θεοῦ τὸν μονογενῆ
γεννηθέντα ἐκ τοῦ Πατρὸς Θεὸν ἀληθινὸν πρὸ πάντων τῶν αἰώνων,
with which may be compared the Lucianic Creed of Antioch, which
has τὸν υἱὸν αὐτοῦ τὸν μονογενῆ Θεὸν δι' οὗ τὰ πάντα, τὸν γεννηθέντα
πρὸ τῶν αἰώνων ἐκ τοῦ Πατρὸς, Θεὸν ἐκ Θεοῦ, ὅλον ἐξ ὅλου, μόνον ἐκ
μόνου. On the other hand, in the Creed of Caesarea the clause "God
of God" appears as an independent one. As Hort remarks, it is
improbable that the Bishops at Nicaea should have so weakened
what they found in the Jerusalem and Antiochene Creeds by substituting for the phrase which indicates the *Divinity* of Christ
the word "Son," in which it is not necessarily implied, and which
would make the clause γεννηθέντα ἐκ τοῦ Πατρός redundant. The
whole clause, overloaded as it is, illustrates the construction of
the Nicene Creed as a conflation of existing authentic creeds of the
centres of the Catholic Church East and West. The clause, as

---

[1] Cyril of Jerusalem, Catech. Lect. iv. 7. Cf. Eusebius, Demonstratio Ev.
12. 7; Cyril Alex. Epist. 3 ad Nest. (2nd Oecumenical Document).

Hort maintains, thus understood declares the full divinity of the Saviour in words of unusual clearness. The parenthesis had to come in somewhere, and what better place could be found for it, even at the cost of losing the full force of the Scriptural expression μονογενῆ Θεόν? At the same time it is, of course, simpler to understand both the word μονογενῆ and the clause which follows it as explanatory of γεννηθέντα ἐκ τοῦ Πατρός, and to take " God of God " independently as a fresh clause in apposition to the preceding phrase, and as adopted from the Caesarean Creed.

ἐκ τῆς οὐσίας τοῦ Πατρός was, as we have already remarked, the first of the three crucial phrases which were found by the Council to be imperatively needed to secure the reality of the Sonship. The incidental accounts which we possess of the course of the debates show that the force of other phrases, whether taken from Scripture or from existing creeds, was evaded by the Arians. None of the phrases was absolutely new, as Athanasius pointed out ; [1] ἐκ τῆς οὐσίας, e.g., had been used by Theognostus of Alexandria in his Hypotyposes towards the end of the third century ; Eusebius of Nicomedia had distinctly rejected it in his letter to Paulinus of Tyre ; [2] and the Arians generally thought that it subjected God to necessity, but Athanasius showed that *necessity* was not a correct term to use in describing that which was inherent in the *Nature* of God.[3]

8. Θεὸν ἐκ Θεοῦ. These words, as we have seen, were taken from the Creed of Caesarea. The preposition (ἐκ) denotes origin and derivation from the Father as Fons Deitatis. The absolute possession of life from another is the essential character of Sonship ; John v. 26 ; cf. viii. 42 ; xvi. 28, and Augustine, Tract. xlvii. in Ioan. 8, " Ab Illo processit ut Deus, ut aequalis, ut Filius Unicus, ut Verbum Patris." Compare the Valentinian Ptolemaeus on John i. 1 quoted by Irenaeus i. 1. 18 (ed. Harvey), τὸ ἐκ Θεοῦ γεννηθὲν Θεός ἐστιν.

9. Φῶς ἐκ Φωτός. Heb. i. 3 naturally suggested the comparison of the simultaneous birth of light and its source with the Eternal Generation of the Son from the Father ; and it became a favourite simile with Christian writers. Cf. Justin Martyr, Dial. 128 ; Tatian, Orat. 5 ; Origen, De Princip. iv. 28 ; Tertullian, Apol. 21 (" lumen de lumine ") ; adv. Prax 8, 13 ; Dionysius-Alex., apud Athan. De Sent. Dion. 18 ; Athan. De Synod. 41. 8, De Decr. Nic. 23 and 25 (citing Theognostus) ; Augustine, Serm. ad Catech. 8.

10. Θεὸν ἀληθινὸν ἐκ Θεοῦ ἀληθινοῦ. The words probably occurred in the Jerusalem Creed. Athanasius, however, used this phrase,

---

[1] Athan. De Decr. 25 ; cf. ibid. 19, ad Afros. 5, De Synod. 33 foll., Epist. Euseb. Caes.

[2] Theodor. HE. i. 6, οὐκ ἐκ τῆς οὐσίας αὐτοῦ γεγονός.

[3] Athan. Orat. iii. 62–66.

citing I John v. 20, Exposit. Fid. I. Cf. Orat. c. Arian. iii. 9, ἔδωκεν ἡμῖν ὅτι τοῦ ἀληθινοῦ Πατρός ἀληθινόν ἐστι γέννημα : and again, αὐτὸς δὲ ὁ Υἱὸς ἐκ τοῦ Πατρός ἐστί φύσει καὶ ἀληθινὸν γέννημα.

11. γεννηθέντα οὐ ποιηθέντα. This is the second crucial phrase of the Council ; and in defence of it Athanasius (De Decr. Nic. 25 foll.) quotes Dionysius of Alexandria and his namesake of Rome as witnesses to the blasphemy of terming the Son a " creature " or a " work." That the Logos was ποιηθέντα was the great Arian contention. They ranked Him amongst the creatures of God (Encycl. of Alexander, Socr. i. 6). Arius' own words in his letter to Alexander (ap. Athan. De Synod. 16) were ὑποστή-σαντα ἰδίῳ θελήματι ἄτρεπτον καὶ ἀναλλοίωτον, κτίσμα τοῦ Θεοῦ τέλειον ἀλλ' οὐχ ὡς ἓν τῶν κτισμάτων. But the words ἰδίῳ θελήματι rob the concession of ἄτρεπτον of its value (see below on τρεπτόν), while οὐχ ὡς ἓν τῶν κτισμάτων is a refinement which yet does not remove the Logos from the category of beings separate from the Father's nature.

13. δι' οὗ τὰ πάντα ἐγένετο. This clause was taken from the Caesarean Creed and is based on I Cor. viii. 6, John i. 3 and 10, Col. i. 16. These passages of Scripture reflect the theological thought familiar to the Hellenistic-Jewish world of the first century represented pre-èminently by Philo and the Alexandrian schools, and summed up in the three titles applied to our Lord by St. Paul, εἰκὼν τοῦ θεοῦ τοῦ ἀοράτου, πρωτότοκος πάσης κτίσεως, ἡ ἀρχὴ (Col. i. 15–18 ; cf. Rev. iii. 14, ἀρχὴ τῆς κτίσεως τοῦ θεοῦ) ; He is, as Trench says, not only " principium principatus," but " principium princi-pans." The Apostolic teaching as enlarged by this conception main-tains that the Logos is no longer a philosophical abstraction but a Divine Person. As Lightfoot writes in his important note on Col. i. 16 : " All the laws and purposes which guide the creation and government of the Universe reside in Him, the Eternal Word, as their meeting-point. The Apostolic doctrine of the Logos teaches us to regard the Eternal Word as holding the same relation to the Universe which the Incarnate Christ holds to the Church. He is the source of its life, the centre of all its developments, the mainspring of all its motions." The fundamental conception of the Logos further involves the idea of mediation between God and Creation. A perverted view of the nature of that mediation lay at the root of Arianism as it had before of Gnosticism, which drew from it the wrong inference that the Son is therefore Himself a created being. For a valuable discussion of the idea of the Logos as the Archetype of Creation, the expression of the mind and purpose of God, see Burney, " Christ as the ἀρχὴ of Creation," *Journal of Theological Studies*, xxvii., pp. 160 ff. ; and for the use of the idea of the Mediator to elucidate the philosophical problem of creation *ex nihilo*, see Webb, *God and Personality*, pp. 163 ff.

It is interesting to note that Athanasius makes use of this clause in defence of the *homoousion* in the important writing *De Synodis* (52): " why deny him the title of one with the Father if this illuminating and creative power specially proper to the Father is indeed, as the Creed says, His, without Whom the Father neither frames nor is known, for all things consist through Him and in Him ? For what is it to be ὁμοφυής with the Father but to be one in οὐσία with Him ?" It will, however, be noted that the expression " By whom all things were made " is applied by Marcellus of Ancyra, Theodore of Mopsuestia, and some of the Antiochene Fathers to the Son Incarnate : perhaps in the attempt to cut the ground from under the feet of the Arians, and in order to take out of their hands the titles mentioned above, and to refer them only to the spiritual creation and to the Logos as Head of the Church. Actually, however, all creation, material and spiritual, is included in this clause.

15. τὸν δι' ἡμᾶς τοὺς ἀνθρώπους καὶ διὰ τὴν ἡμετέραν σωτηρίαν. These words appear to be peculiar to the Nicene Creed, the Caesarean having only διὰ τὴν ἡμετέραν σωτηρίαν σαρκωθέντα ; the double phrase was probably intended to emphasise as against the Arians the fact that the humiliation implied in the following word κατελθόντα was not, as they said, a mark of the inherent imperfection of the Logos, but alien to Him, though assumed by Him for our sakes. Westcott (" Gospel of Creation," Essay in *Epistles of St. John*, p. 315) quotes Osiander, who finds support in the distinction of these two clauses for the Scotist view of the necessity of the Incarnation apart from human sin. More probably the words were inserted in view of the Arian blasphemy that the Son's existence was in some sense relative to ours and were intended to say that He was not made for our sakes but He did become incarnate for us. The Arian view is given by Alexander (Encycl. apud Socr. i. 6), δι' ἡμᾶς γὰρ πεποίηται, ἵνα ἡμᾶς δι' αὐτοῦ ὡς δι' ὀργάνου κτίσῃ ὁ Θεός· καὶ οὐκ ἂν ὑπέστη εἰ μὴ ἡμᾶς ὁ Θεὸς ἤθελεν ποιῆσαι. And again by Athan., Encycl. ad Episcop. Aegypt. 12, τότε γὰρ γέγονεν ὅτε βεβούληται αὐτὸν ὁ Θεὸς δημιουργῆσαι· ἐν γὰρ τῶν πάντων ἔργων ἐστὶ καὶ αὐτός ; and again, quoting the Thalia, Or. c. Ar. i. 5, εἶτα θελήσας ἡμᾶς δημιουργῆσαι, τότε δὴ πεποίηκεν ἕνα τινά, καὶ ὠνόμασεν αὐτὸν Λόγον καὶ Σοφίαν καὶ Υἱόν, ἵνα ἡμᾶς δι' αὐτὸν δημιουργήσῃ.

16. κατελθόντα. This verb did not appear in the Caesarean or Jerusalem Creeds and was probably taken from the Antiochene. But the whole phrase κατελθόντα ἐκ τῶν οὐρανῶν as it stands in the Constantinopolitan Creed is found in effect in Cyril's Catechetical Lectures iv. 9, διὰ τὰς ἁμαρτίας ἡμῶν ἐξ οὐρανῶν κατῆλθεν ἐπὶ τῆς γῆς.

17. σαρκωθέντα. The word implies the assumption of a passible humanity and a human life, although of a perfect man, lived under the conditions, including ignorance, of fallen man. Our Lord came " in likeness of flesh of sin " (Rom. viii. 3). For the bearing

of this phrase on the doctrine of the Kenosis see notes on Cyril's Epistles and Leo's Tome, pp. 122, 175. The word itself is not found in the New Testament, but occurs in late medical writers in the sense of to " make or grow fleshy." The first occurrence of the word in Patristic Greek is in the Rule of Faith in Irenaeus i. 2, where Irenaeus has σαρκωθέντα ὑπὲρ τῆς ἡμετέρας σωτηρίας. Arius and Euzoius also wrote σαρκωθέντα, according to Socrates, i. 26, though Sozomen, ii. 27, gives σάρκα ἀναλαβόντα, and this is the more usual expression : e.g. in the Creed of the Apost. Constit. ; the First Antiochene or Eusebian encyclical of 341 (Socr. ii. 10, Athan. De Synod. 22) ; the Homoion Creed of Seleucia (359, Socr. ii. 40, Athan. De Synod. 29). σαρκωθέντα stood alone in the Caesarean Creed, but the Council rightly felt that by itself it was not an effective safeguard of the Incarnation from Arian evasion. It did not, for instance, exclude the Lucianic tenet that the Word took flesh only, without a human soul (Epiphan. Ancor. 33, Λουκιανὸς γὰρ καὶ πάντες Λουκιανισταὶ ἀρνοῦνται τὸν Υἱὸν τοῦ Θεοῦ ψυχὴν εἰληφέναι· σάρκα μὲν μόνον φασὶν ἐσχηκέναι. Cf. Lucian's Confession of Faith, apud Ruf. on Euseb. HE. ix. 6, in Routh, Rel. Sacr. iv. p. 6, " Deus . . . Sapientiam suam misit in hunc mundum carne vestitam "). Nor does it lift the Incarnation above the level of a mere Theophany. The Council therefore added from the Jerusalem Creed ἐνανθρωπήσαντα, " dwelt amongst men as man " ; and the two verbs together correspond to St. John's ὁ Λόγος σὰρξ ἐγένετο καὶ ἐσκήνωσεν ἐν ἡμῖν (John i. 14).

The Arian view was unequivocally expressed in the Creed of Eudoxius of Constantinople—σαρκωθέντα οὐκ ἐνανθρωπήσαντα· οὔτε γὰρ ψυχὴν ἀνθρωπίνην ἀνείληφεν, ἀλλὰ σὰρξ γέγονεν, ἵνα διὰ σαρκὸς τοῖς ἀνθρώποις ὡς διὰ παραπετάσματος Θεὸς ἡμῖν χρηματίσῃ· οὐ δύο φύσεις, ἐπεὶ μὴ τέλειος ἦν ἄνθρωπος, ἀλλ' ἀντὶ ψυχῆς Θεὸς ἐν σαρκί (Hahn, p. 261. Cf. Ps.-Athan. c. Apollin. i. 15, ii. 3). In order expressly to reject this heresy and Apollinarian developments of it, the Armenian Church expanded this clause of their creed as follows—ἐνανθρώπησεν, ἐγεννήθη τελείως ἐκ Μαρίας τῆς ἁγίας παρθένου διὰ Π. Ἁγ. ὥστε λαβεῖν σῶμα καὶ ψυχὴν καὶ νοῦν καὶ πάντα ὅσα ἐστὶν ἐν ἀνθρώπῳ ἀληθινῶς καὶ οὐ δοκήσει (Hahn, p. 152). Justin Martyr employed the rarer expression ἀνδρούμενον, Apol. i. 31.

18. ἐνανθρωπήσαντα. The verb is rare except in ecclesiastical Greek, and is not used in the N.T. Here it replaces ἐν ἀνθρώποις πολιτευσάμενον of Caesarea. It is intended to express the permanent union of God with Human Nature ; but, as was afterwards proved, it was not sufficiently technical to exclude heretical theories as to the mode of the union, whether by the conversion of the Godhead into flesh (as in Apollinarianism), or by union with a human person (Nestorianism ; see Cyril, Epist. 2 ad Nest.).

No clause dealing with the mode of the Incarnation finds place in the Nicene Creed. Eastern Creeds generally contained one,

e.g. that of Niceta of Remesiana. The two operations, Luke i.
35, Matt. i. 20, are variously expressed in Creeds, generally in
Greek by ἐκ followed by the simple copula (καί), but more usually
in Latin by "*de* Sp. S. *ex* Maria V.*"* Augustine (De Fid. et
Symb. 8) has "*per* Sp. S. *ex* V.M. "; and so Leo in his Tome and
generally in the West. For an interesting view on the mode of
the Incarnation, see Hilary, De Trin. i. 19, iv. 15 (Watson, *Library
of Nicene and Post-Nicene Fathers*, pp. 45, 75) and cf. H. J. Carpenter,
Journal of Theological Studies, xl., p. 137.

Such a clause was useful in excluding the Apollinarian and
Valentinian notions that the Body of Christ was not derived from
the substance of His mother (see note below on the Tome, 2).
It naturally found a place in the Constantinopolitan Creed, and
had often been dwelt upon by Cyril in his lectures : *e.g.* iv. 9, γεννηθεὶς ἐξ ἁγίας παρθένου καὶ ʿΑγίου Πνεύματος, xii. 3, ἐκ παρθένου καὶ
Πν. ʿΑγ. κατὰ τὸ εὐαγγέλιον ἐνανθρωπήσαντα.

19. παθόντα. So the Caesarean Creed, simply ; no description
of the mode of the Passion being added. The Jerusalem Creed
read instead σταυρωθέντα καὶ ταφέντα ; and some of the earlier
Western Creeds seem to have inserted the historic detail of the name
of the Roman procurator : *e.g.* Iren. iii. 4. 1, " passus sub Pontio
Pilato " ; Tertull. De Virg. Veland. 1, "crucifixum sub P. Pilato " ;
so the Constantinopolitan, σταυρωθέντα τε ὑπὲρ ἡμῶν ἐπὶ Π. Πιλάτου
καὶ παθόντα. This express mention of Pilate by name is of constant
recurrence in early Christian writings ; Acts iii. 13, iv. 27 ; 1 Tim.
vi. 13 ; Ignat. Magn. 11 ; Trall. 9 ; Smyrn. 1 ; Just. Mart. Apol.
i. 13 ; Dial. 30 ; and it was doubtless from Christian sources that
Tacitus gained his knowledge (Ann. xv. 44) " Auctor nominis
ejus Chrestus Tiberio imperitante per procuratorem P. Pilatum
supplicio adfectus erat." Its appearance in early statements of
Christian belief or in those quoted above shows that it may well
date from a time when in preaching to the heathen it was necessary
to insist on the historic reality of the Passion. Augustine says
that it was intended to fix the date of the Crucifixion (De Fid. et
Symb. 11, " Addendum enim erat iudicis nomen propter temporum
cognitionem "). If this is true, it shows that the original tradition
which formed the basis of the Creed was drawn up in Syria, where
the name of the Procurator would be used more naturally than that
of a distant and wholly unknown Emperor to date an event in the
Provinces. But neither this phrase nor the previous Latin phrase
" born by the Holy Ghost of the Virgin Mary " occur in any fixed
creed earlier than the fourth century, except possibly that of Hippolytus which, however, shows signs of later additions. (See
G. Dix, *Apostolic Tradition*, p. 36.)

ταφέντα. The Burial, as an article of the faith, was indeed ranked
by St. Paul amongst the " first principles " of Christian instruction,
because of its importance in leading to the Resurrection (1 Cor. xv,

3). Cyril himself in his Lectures also dwells upon Christ's Descent into Hades, though the clause itself does not appear in the collected text of his creed as usually given. Catech. iv. 11, κατῆλθεν εἰς τὰ καταχθόνια ; xiv. 18. 19, κατελθόντα εἰς ᾅδην. The phrase is found also in the Sirmian " Dated " Creed of May 22, 359, drawn up by Valens and Ursacius, and read five days later at Ariminum—καὶ εἰς τὰ καταχθόνια κατελθόντα, and this is its first actual appearance in a creed. This Arian formulary, after a revision at Nice on October 10, which left this phrase unaltered, was finally adopted at Constantinople on December 31, with the reading καὶ εἰς τὰ καταχθόνια κατεληλυθότα (Socr. ii. 37. 41 ; Theodoret. HE. ii. 16). The clause is next found in the orthodox Creed of Aquileia as given by Rufinus, A.D. 390—" Descendit in inferna "—neither the Roman nor Eastern Creeds possessing it (Ruf. in Symb. Ap. 18). There can be little doubt that the fact of our Lord's descent into Hades did form part of the regular instruction delivered to catechumens, although it might not be formulated in the Creed. As Rufinus says (loc. cit.), it was implied in the clause "was buried." There was severance of soul and body. The body was laid in the tomb, the spirit went to the place of the departed. Our Lord's death was a real death ; and so the clause has its importance as excluding Docetic notions, and as emphasising the existence of the human soul in Christ, which the Arians and Apollinarians denied.

In the Western Latin Creeds the inseparable Hypostatic Union of God the Son with both the soul and the body is expressed by the subject of each verb being the same—" Mortuus, sepultus, descendit " (cf. Ps.-Athan. c. Apollin. i. 18, ii. 15). Cyril of Alexandria, in his Second Letter to Nestorius, argues for a real Incarnation on the same ground of the identity of *Hypostasis* of the Only begotten with Him who suffered.

20. ἀναστάντα τῇ τρίτῃ ἡμέρᾳ. All complete creeds contain clauses couched in nearly identical terms on the Resurrection, Ascension, and Second Advent ; the Constantinopolitan Creed adding to this clause from 1 Cor. xv. 4, κατὰ τὰς γραφάς, where the allusion is no doubt to Ps. xvi. 10, Hos. vi. 2, and to Christ's words, Luke xxiv. 46, Mk. viii. 31, 34, cf. John ii. 19. Athan., De Inc. 26, gives three reasons for this particular period of three days : (a) Not on the same day, lest the real death should be denied ; (b) not on the second day, lest His incorruption should not be clearly manifested ; (c) not later than the third day, lest the identification of His body should be questioned and the events forgotten.

21. ἀνελθόντα εἰς τοὺς οὐρανούς. The phrase is not to be limited to the sense of a literal local ascent. The visible departure which the disciples witnessed (Luke xxiv. 51 ; Acts i. 9) was symbolical of the definite withdrawal of the Risen Lord into the higher plane of spiritual being upon which He had entered *as Man* concurrently with His Resurrection (cf. Eph. iv. 10 ; Heb. vii. 26).

Note the omission here, as in the Caesarean Creed, of any clause relating to the Session at the right hand of God. Place is given it in the Creeds of Jerusalem, Constantinople, and Antioch, as well as in the three " forms " given by Tertullian. The metaphor denotes the position of honour and felicity (1 Kings ii. 19; Ps. xvi. 11, cx. 1), power and sovereignty (Matt. xxvi. 64; Heb. viii. 1). It is based upon Eph. i. 20; 1 Pet. iii. 22; Col. iii. 1; Heb. i. 3, x. 12, xii. 2; cf. Rom. viii. 34; Acts vii. 56; 1 Cor. xv. 25. Cf. Primasius (cited by Westcott on Heb. viii. 1). " Plenitudinem majestatis summamque gloriam beatitudinis et prosperitatis debemus per dexteram intelligere in qua Filius sedet."

Cyril, in his Lectures, xi. 17, xiv. 27–30, arguing against Arianism, emphatically urges that the Session at the right hand, with the possession of the Divine Glory which it implied, belonged to the Son from all eternity, and did not begin after His Ascension. Hence perhaps the change from καθίσαντα of the early Jerusalem Creed to the present tense, καθεζόμενον, in C. But the point intended by the clause is that the Incarnate Son, Jesus Christ, in His twofold Nature, Human as well as Divine, assumed by His Ascension that Divine position and glory which had ever been His in His Divine Nature. The throne of God is *now* shared (Rev. iii. 21) by One who is clad in our nature, the perfect Sympathiser (Heb. v. 1–10), the unceasing Intercessor (Heb. vii. 25), the Advocate turned towards the Father (1 John ii. 1). Cf. Iren. i. 2. 1, καὶ τὴν ἔνσαρκον εἰς τοὺς οὐρανοὺς ἀνάληψιν (" et *in carne* in caelos ascensionem "); Athan. Expos. Fid. 1, ἡμῖν ἔδειξεν ἄνοδόν τε εἰς οὐρανοὺς ὅπου πρόδρομος εἰσῆλθεν ὑπὲρ ἡμῶν ὁ κυριακὸς ἄνθρωπος (= the Lord's Humanity) ἐν ᾧ μέλλει κρίνειν ζῶντας καὶ νεκρούς. Ruf. in Symb. Ap. 31, " Ascendit ergo ad caelos, non ubi Verbum Deus ante non fuerat, quippe qui semper erat in caelis et manebat in Patre, sed ubi Verbum caro factum ante non sedebat." This doctrine has been the inspiration of such hymns as Michael Bruce's " Where high the heavenly temple stands"; and Dr. Bright's stanza—

" His Manhood pleads where now It lives
On heaven's eternal throne."

22. ἐρχόμενον κρῖναι ζῶντας καὶ νεκρούς. The phrase comes originally from 1 Pet. iv. 5. The present participle should be given its own force. The " coming " in present judgments is not less true than that doctrine of the Lord's Second Advent, which was prominent in the minds of the early Christians, who naturally regarded the " coming " rather as an event than a process (Acts xvii. 31; Rom. ii. 16; 1 Thess. ii. 19, v. 4; 2 Tim. iv. 1; Rev. xx. 12). The future participle ἥξοντα is found only in the Caesarean of the Greek creeds; but the familiar influence of the Latin " venturus " has penetrated even into the English translation of ἐρχόμενον in the " Nicene " Creed.

The Caesarean Creed also added πάλιν ἐν δόξῃ after ἥξοντα.

D

This idea of the "glorious majesty" is strictly Scriptural (Matt. xvi. 27, xxiv. 30, xxv. 31 ; Mark viii. 38, xiii. 26 ; Luke ix. 26, xxi. 27), and found a place in the majority of creeds, Western and Eastern. Irenaeus, i. 1. 2, καὶ τὴν ἐκ τῶν οὐρανῶν ἐν τῇ δόξῃ τοῦ Πατρὸς παρουσίαν αὐτοῦ : ibid. iii. 4. 1, " in gloria venturus"; Tertullian, De Praescr. Haer. 13, "venturus cum claritate"; Lucian of Antioch, πάλιν ἐρχόμενον μετὰ δόξης καὶ δυνάμεως : Jerusalem, ἐρχόμενον ἐν δόξῃ : Constantinopolitan, πάλιν ἐρχόμενον μετὰ δόξης.

A further clause stood in the Jerusalem Creed (as in the Apost. Const. vii. 41, and in the Constantinopolitan) expressive of the eternity of Christ's regal office, in words taken directly from Luke i. 33—οὗ τῆς βασιλείας οὐκ ἔσται τέλος. The phrase was valuable against a minor deduction from an erroneous conception of the Logos which was associated with the name of Marcellus. " The theory ascribed to him was that the Logos was an impersonal Divine power, immanent from eternity in God, but issuing from Him in the act of creation, and entering at last into relation with the human person of Jesus, who thus became God's ' Son.' But this ' expansion ' of the original Divine unity would be followed by a ' contraction ' (συστολή), when the Logos would retire from Jesus, and God would again be all in all " (Bright, *Notes on the Canons*, p. 86). 1 Cor. xv. 24 was therefore naturally but wrongly interpreted as the surrender by Christ of such kingship as must for ever belong to Him.

This is, of course, only a rough-and-ready description of Marcellus' teaching. Marcellus was one of the most interesting theologians of the Nicene period, though only fragments [1] of his writings have survived, the rest having suffered the fate of so many "heretical" writings, a fate which Nestorius' Apologia [2] only escaped by a pseudonym. Hence the need of caution in accepting the statements of his many Arian and semi-Arian enemies, such as Eusebius of Caesarea, who wrote a book against him. Marcellus was one of a group of strong supporters of the *homoousion* at Nicaea, and as such was suspected of Sabellianism in the reaction which followed. Epiphanius, who classes him with Paul of Samosata,[3] was correct, in so far as Marcellus inherited much of the teaching characteristic of the theology of Antioch, with its distrust of the pluralism of Origen and Alexandria, which he regarded as too much influenced by pagan philosophy. He represented an attack upon Arianism not otherwise developed, which exercised much influence upon Apollinarianism. (See Raven, *Apollinarianism*, p. 162.) While accepting the terminology of Sonship in the Nicene Creed, he thought that the emphasis upon the title Son

---

[1] Edited by Klostermann (Berlinen Corpus, Eusebius Bd. IV).

[2] Known as the *Bazaar of Heracleides*, see p. 88.

[3] In whom the two theologies had already clashed, when Paul was condemned in 269 by a panel of Alexandrian judges, headed by the Presbyter Malchion.

rather than Logos favoured the tritheistic and subordinationist doctrines popular at Alexandria, and gave a handle to the Arians. Accordingly he reverted to a doctrine of the Logos, which differed widely from that which Origen had derived from the teaching of Philo and the Greek Apologists. Starting, like the rest of his school, from a profound sense of the unity (μοναρχία) of God, which he shared with Athanasius and the Westerns, he continued the Antiochene attempt to safeguard it by representing the Trinity as an " unfolding " or " increase " of God for His purposes of creation and redemption (cf. Col. ii. 19). Reviving the Stoic ideas, if not the terms, of Theophilus of Antioch,[1] who was the first to employ the actual word τριάς, he regarded the Logos as at first " immanent " (ἐνδιάθετος) in the Deity, the indivisible Monad (Μονὰς ἀδιαίρετος θεότητος) ; and as coming forth (προφορικός) as an active power (δραστικὴ ἐνέργεια) for those purposes.[2] At the Incarnation the Logos united to a human nature became also " Son of God " for the redemption of man. And similarly the Spirit contained within the Logos issued forth from God and became operative in the Church after the Incarnation of the Logos.[3] And thus, he continues, the Monad appears as extended into Trinity (ἡ Μονὰς φαίνεται πλατυνομένη εἰς Τριάδα Fr. 67). This he called διαστολή (expansion), which when the purposes of God in creation and redemption are fulfilled, will be as it were reversed (συστολή, contraction) in order that the Logos may be once more in God qua Logos, as He was formerly before the world was (Fr. 50). Speculation of this kind was common in the pre-Nicene Church and can be paralleled in Irenaeus, Tertullian, and Novatian. Such modes of thought were, however, no longer pursued after the Cappadocian Fathers, Basil and the two Gregories, following Athanasius, formulated a doctrine of the Trinity which, while effectively safeguarding the " Monarchia," finally eliminated all traces of the pluralism and subordinationism of Alexandria.[4]

When the Eusebians condemned Marcellus at the second council

---

[1] Ad Autolycum (Otto) 2. 10 ; cf. Epiphanius De Trin. 32.

[2] ἐνεργείας ἡ τοῦ Κόσμου γένεσις ἐδεῖτο δραστικῆς. Marcellus, Klostermann Fragments 60 and 53 ; cf. also Fr. 73, where the Logos is called a δύναμις remaining within the Deity ; by which is meant more than a mere quality ; cf. Justin Martyr Dial. 61 and Tertullian, who exhibits many of the same ideas as Marcellus, e.g. Adv. Prax. 7 ; Sermo in Patre semper et apud Deum semper ; cf. 23 ; Filium semet habens etsi porrectum in terram.

[3] Fr. 71 ; ἐνεργείᾳ ἡ Θεότης μόνη πλατύνεσθαι δοκεῖ ὥστε εἰκότως μονὰς ὄντως ἐστιν ἀδιαίρετος, cf. Epiphanius' statement (Haer. 72. 1) which, if correct, will make him suspect of Sabellianism, but it is doubtful, and in any case very little is known about Sabellianism.

[4] As examples of similar tendencies the following passages may be quoted : Irenaeus, v. 36. 2 ; Tertullian, Adv. Prax. 23 ; Eo Spiritui qui Sermone inerat ; ibid. 7 ; ibid. 26 ; portio totius quae cessura sit in Filii nomen. Cf. Novatian, De Trin. 31 ; a quo solo [sc. Patre] haec vis emissa, etiam in Filium tradita et directa, rursum substantiae per communionem ad Patrem revolvitur.

of Sirmium (351) it was not for Sabellianism, but because he contended that the Son of God had taken His beginning from Mary, his principal work being regarded as merely unfortunate (Raven, op. cit., p. 95). Athanasius [1] refused to condemn him by name, and the West did not do so, and even then reluctantly, till 380.

As in the case of Paul of Samosata, it was in his doctrine of the Incarnation that Marcellus was most vulnerable. It cannot be denied that he, like the rest of the Antiochene school, failed to achieve unity in his doctrine of the Person of Christ. The Logos was one and the " Son " another, and he never succeeded in bringing them together, as did Irenaeus and Tertullian. Yet it is clear that in his treatment of the " economy " Marcellus was developing, if erroneously, the ancient scriptural tradition, ultimately derived from St. Paul, of Christ as the Second Adam (1 Cor. xv. 21 and 45), the Man from Heaven, and the Beginner of a new creation; the doctrine known to St. Ignatius of Antioch as the οἰκονομία εἰς καινὸν ἄνθρωπον (Eph. xx.). According to Marcellus it was the function of the Incarnate Logos to accomplish as " Son " the purpose of God in creation, and to " restore all things in Christ " and in particular the lordship over creation which man by his sin had lost. The Logos therefore according to Marcellus " adopted " the man (*i.e.* human nature, as so often in the Fathers) " that he might perform the first fruits of man's primaeval authority." The " Man " thus united to the Logos has by his unity with Him become Son of God, ἄφθαρτος, ἀθάνατος, σύνθρονος Θεῷ.[2] It was, of course, this " Kingdom " or authority and Lordship over creation, thus restored by and in man united to the Logos which was to be ultimately surrendered that God might be all in all.[3] This interpretation of 1 Cor. xv. 28 was not accepted by the Church, as the Creeds of Constantinople, Apostolic Constitutions and Jerusalem indicate. In all other respects Marcellus' substantial orthodoxy was proved by the creed which he exhibited to Pope Julius when at Rome in 340; when he even pleaded for the full recognition of the phraseology of Sonship as adopted at Nicaea.[4]

---

[1] It should be noted that the 4th Oration against the Arians which discusses the Marcellan doctrines is no longer regarded as a genuine work of Athanasius. For the view of Athanasius himself see Contra Ar. 1. 50, Hist. Ar. 20, De Synod. 27, De Decretis 26, De Sent. Dion. 13, and Feltoe, *Dionysius of Alexandria*, pp. 169 f. (Cambridge Texts.)

[2] Fr. 110, cf. Irenaeus, iii. 19. 6, ὁ Λόγος ἥνωσεν τὸν ἄνθρωπον τῷ Θεῷ· εἰ γὰρ μὴ ἄνθρωπος ἐνίκησεν τὸν ἀντίπαλον τοῦ ἀνθρώπου οὐκ ἂν δικαίως ἐνικήθη ὁ ἐχθρός.

[3] Cf. Irenaeus, v. 36. 2.

[4] For further discussion see Raven, *Apollinarianism*, pp. 161 ff., who maintains that Marcellus regarded the Incarnation as a temporary theophany; and the Logos Incarnate or Son as " passible " like the Arian Son. What is certain is that Marcellus, like many other early theologians, had not thought out the implications of his speculations; he admits that what became of the flesh (or human nature) of the Logos has not been revealed (Fr. 117–121), Kidd, op. cit., vol. ii, pp. 65–7. Cf. also Prestige, op. cit., p. 207, and Rawlinson, *Essays on the Trinity and the Incarnation*, pp. 260–70.

Cyril of Jerusalem (Catech. Lect. iv. 15 and xv. 27) also explicitly denies Marcellus' interpretation. The importance of Marcellus lies in his grasp of the Christian doctrine of Creation, and of the dangers in Arianism to that fundamental belief; thus he saw further than many of his contemporaries into the implications of the *homoousion*, which as the friend of Athanasius he so strongly upheld.

23. Καί. The copula must again be given its full significance. The doctrine of the Holy Trinity, which is thus implicitly asserted, formed, as has been already said, the framework of these more elaborate expressions of the Faith. Athanasius has an interesting passage on this point (ad Afros. 11) in the concluding paragraph of the Encyclical Letter written in 369, when Arianism was nearing its end in the West, against the Creed of the Council of Ariminum, the last attempt to supersede the Nicene Creed: Αὕτη γὰρ ἡ ἐν Νικαίᾳ σύνοδος ἀληθῶς στηλογραφία κατὰ πάσης αἱρέσεώς ἐστιν, αὕτη καὶ τοὺς βλασφημοῦντας εἰς τὸ Π κτίσμα ἀνατρέπει. εἰρηκότες γ νεῦμα τὸ Ἅγιον καὶ λέγοντας αὖ το πίστεως, ἐπήγαγον εὐθὺς Πιστε ἀρ οἱ πατέρες περὶ τῆς εἰς τὸν Υἱὸν τελείαν καὶ πλήρη τὴν εἰς τὴν υομεν καὶ εἰς τὸ Πνεῦμα τὸ Ἅγιον, ἵνα τὸν χαρακτῆρα τῆς ἐν Χριστ Ἁγίαν Τριάδα πίστιν ὁμολογήσαντες, καθολικῆς ἐκκλ ἐν τούτῳ πίστεως, καὶ τὴν διδασκαλίαν τῆς καὶ παρὰ πᾶσι ησίας τηκε, κ γνωρίσωσι. Δῆλον γὰρ καὶ παρ' ὑμῖν τοῦτο σχοίῃ τῇ καθέσαν, ᾧ αἱ οὐδεὶς ἂν Χριστιανῶν ἀμφίβολον εἰς ἀλλ' εἰς ἕνα ν διάνοι ατέρς οὐκ ἔστιν ἡμῶν ἡ πίστις εἰς τὴν κτίσιν, ἀοράτων ποιητ Θεὸν Π ἷς ἕ α παντοκράτορα, πάντων ὁρατῶν τε καὶ τον μονογενῆ· ἥν· καὶ ε να Κύριον Ἰησοῦν Χριστὸν, τὸν Υἱὸν αὐτοῦ ι ι καὶ εἰς ἕν Πνεῦμα Ἅγιον· ἕνα Θεὸν τὸν ἐν τῇ ἁγίᾳ καὶ τελε ᾳ Τριάδ γινωσκόμενον (cf. ad Jovian. 4).

23. εἰς τὸ Ἅγιον Πνεῦμα. The Caesarean, Alexandrian, and Jerusalem Creeds in uniformity with the first two articles—εἰς ἕνα Θεόν . . . εἰς ἕνα Κύριον Ἰ. Χ.—read here εἰς ἕν Πν. Ἅγιον, and it seems strange that ἕν should have dropped out, particularly as it has direct Scriptural authority (Eph. iv. 4; 1 Cor. xii. 13). Athanasius himself naturally uses this form when referring to the Nicene Creed as really a confession of faith in the Holy Trinity, ad Afros. 11 (quoted in last note), and so also Alexander of Alexandria, apud Theodoret HE. i. 4. Cf. John Damasc. De fide orth. 8, ὁμοίως πιστεύομεν εἰς ἕν Πν. Ἅγιον, κ.τ.λ. This brief mention of the Third Person of the Holy Trinity indicates the undeveloped character of the doctrine of the Holy Spirit in the ante-Nicene period. St. Basil's treatise De Spiritu Sancto is the first attempt at a formal treatment of the doctrine in Christian theology. On the " Spirit Christology " of the period see Loofs' *Theophilus of Antioch*, *Texte und Unter.*, Vol. 46, pp. 101–205.

24. Τοὺς δὲ λέγοντας, κ.τ.λ. The anathematisms which follow are an integral part of the document, although they do not add anything

to the substance of the Creed, but only condemn a number of Arian statements respecting the Second Person of the Trinity, which were contrary to the Church's teaching and untenable in her communion. Their presence shows that the Council did not intend its creed to be a baptismal symbol or a popular declarative creed superseding the existing formularies of the different local churches, but simply a dogmatic standard constructed for a particular emergency, and proposed for signature as a test of orthodoxy.

Had the Council intended to draw up a complete creed, there were clauses at hand in the Creed of Jerusalem, on the Paraclete, Baptism, Forgiveness of Sins, the Church, the Resurrection, and Eternal Life ; but evidently neither Eusebius of Caesarea, who had only quoted the creed of his Church as far as the clause πιστεύομεν καὶ εἰς ἓν Πνεῦμα Ἅγιον, nor the Council generally thought it necessary to cite or insert clauses on subjects as to which no heterodoxy had been expressed—" confessi sunt quod negabatur ; tacuerunt de quo nemo quaerebat " (Jerome, Epist. 84 ad Pam. et Ocean.). Compare on this point of omission the Eusebian encyclical of Antioch in 341, which, while fairly adequate on the Second Person, ends πιστεύομεν καὶ εἰς τὸ Ἅγιον Πνεῦμα. Εἰ δὲ δεῖ προσθεῖναι πιστεύομεν καὶ περὶ σαρκὸς ἀναστάσεως καὶ ζωῆς αἰωνίου (Athan. De Synod. 22 ; Socr. ii. 10). Cf. J. Th. St. i 14 ff.

It was not until the Ephesian Council in 431 that N was converted into a baptismal profession (canon 7), and not until Chalcedon in 451 that it was termed a σύμβολον. The Council of Laodicaea (canon 7) in 363 spoke generally of τὰ τῆς πίστεως σύμβολα, but without distinct reference to the Nicene Creed. The anathematisms were naturally not taken over into local creeds, which were otherwise expanded from the Nicene. They are, however, still retained, and expanded to include similar denials respecting the Holy Spirit, in the enlarged creed recited in the Armenian liturgy (Hahn, p. 153 ; Brightman, op. cit., p. 426).

The object of the anathematisms was to afford no loophole for the evasion of the strict meaning of the terms used in the Creed. Some of the anathemas appended to various Arianising creeds did offer such loopholes : e.g. the insertion of χρόνος and ὡς ἓν τῶν κτισμάτων in the anathemas of the Dedication Creed of 341.

24. Ἦν ποτε ὅτε οὐκ ἦν. " Once He was not." This phrase was intended by Arius to deny the eternal co-existence of the Son with the Father (Alexander ap. Theodoret HE. i. 4 ; id. encycl. ap. Socr. i. 6 ; Athan. Or. c. Arian. i. 5, etc.). Arius' rationalistic temper of mind led him to import into Divine relations some of those limitations which are necessarily inherent in human relations. As a human son is posterior in time to his father, so Arius concluded that the Divine Son must be of later existence than the Divine Father. " There was," therefore, " when He did not exist." He overlooked the fact that " Father " and " Son " are correlative

terms, not necessarily involving any notions of before and after; and that even in the human sphere fatherhood and sonship spring into co-existence simultaneously (cf. Athan., Or. c. Arian, i. 26 foll., iii. 6). The Catholic doctrine of this Eternal relation had been expressed by Origen, De Princ. iv. 1. 28, οὐκ ἔστιν ὅτε οὐκ ἦν, a direct negative to the Arian teaching; Hom. in Ierem. ix. 4, ἀεὶ γεννᾷ ὁ Πατὴρ τὸν Υἱόν: cf. De Princ. i. 2. 4, 10, and apud Apol. Pamphil. pro Orig., ὁ Σωτὴρ ἀεὶ γεννᾶται (Routh, Rel. Sacr. iv. 304); and by Dionysius of Rome contr. Sabell. apud Athan. De Decr. Nic. 26, εἰ γὰρ γέγονεν Υἱός, ἦν ὅτε οὐκ ἦν· ἀεὶ δὲ ἦν, εἴ γε ἐν τῷ Πατρί ἐστι, ὡς αὐτός φησι, καὶ εἰ Λόγος καὶ Σοφία καὶ Δύναμις ὁ Χριστός—passages which show that the Arian position had been already met and refuted in the third century, and that the Catholic theology was fixed long before the date usually assigned to it. Cf. Alexander writing to Alexander of Byzantium in 324, (Theodoret HE. i. 4), ἀνάγκη τὸν Πατέρα ἀεὶ εἶναι Πατέρα. Ἔστι δὲ Πατὴρ ἀεὶ παρόντος τοῦ Υἱοῦ δι' ὃν χρηματίζει Πατήρ. And again, apud Epist. Ar. ad Euseb. Nicom., ib. i. 5, ἀεὶ ὁ Θεός, ἀεὶ ὁ Υἱός· οὔτε ἐπινοίᾳ οὔτε ἀτόμῳ τινὶ προάγει ὁ Θεὸς τοῦ Υἱοῦ· ἀεὶ Θεός, ἀεὶ Υἱός. Neither in thought nor at any point of time is God prior to the Son.

25. Πρὶν γεννηθῆναι οὐκ ἦν. This formula, which Arius used in his letter to Alexander, οὐκ ἦν πρὸ τοῦ γεννηθῆναι (Athan. De Synod. 16); and again to Eusebius of Nicomedia—πρὶν γεννηθῇ οὐκ ἦν— (Theodoret HE. i. 5) his words are "we say and believe, have taught and teach that the Son is not ἀγέννητος, οὐδὲ μέρος ἀγεννήτου κατ' οὐδένα τρόπον, οὐδὲ ἐξ ὑποκειμένου τινός, ἀλλὰ τῷ θελήματι καὶ βουλῇ ὑπέστη πρὸ χρόνων καὶ πρὸ αἰώνων. πλήρης Θεὸς μονογενὴς ἀναλλοίωτος καὶ πρὶν γεννηθῇ ἤτοι κτισθῇ ἢ ὁρισθῇ ἢ θεμελιωθῇ οὐκ ἦν· ἀγέννητος γὰρ οὐκ ἦν· It is obvious from this that the whole error of Arianism was contained in its major premiss, i.e. that there is only one Agennetos, namely God; the Son being ex hypothesi γεννητός (begotten) cannot therefore be in the same sense God; and if not God, then in some measure created (κτιστός) and not eternal. It will be noted that the Arians argued from agennetos (unbegotten), not from agenetos, which means underived, not unbegotten; which was contrasted with genetos (derived). As Dr. Prestige remarks, it was common ground with all parties that the Father alone was agenetos; and Origen attempted to indicate the derived character of the Son's Being by calling him genetos. The Arians adopted this terminology and made it imply that the Father alone was uncreated and the Son virtually a creature. For to the Arian mind gennema (γέννημα) was equivalent to ποίημα (something made), and gennetos to "created." In other words, the Arians to be consistent denied any essential difference between the two senses and spellings of agenetos (agennetos): and in order to be still more logical they had to abolish the distinction between

the positive terms *genetos* and *gennetos*. Aetius and Eunomius throughout the argument with Athanasius proceeded on the assumption that *agennetos* implied everything that was involved in the *agenetos* of the philosophical schools. If God is wholly *agennetos*, He cannot have begotten a Son *substantially* (ἐκ τῆς οὐσίας); for that would imply division of His substance. But *gennema* the Son may be, the act being one of creation and not of generation. In other words, generation became among the Arians equivalent to creation.

Does this anathema mean the same as the foregoing ? Doubtless all these anathemas refer to the Arian stock phrases, all of which had their root in the Arian syllogism, " if Son, then later in time and inferior in being to the Father." But there was more to it than that, as Bishop Bull [1] long ago saw. This term *gennesis* had been used in another school, that of Asia Minor, to express other things than the eternity of the Son as explained by Origen. It had been used to express the *economy* (οἰκονομία) in Creation and in Redemption, according to the texts " Thou art My Son ; this day have I begotten Thee," Ps. ii. 7. " The Lord begat me the beginning of His works," Prov. viii. 22. This was good Scriptural language. And the question therefore is : is this yet another illustration of the comprehensive character of the Nicene formula, in that this anathema was intended not to exclude those, who while maintaining the eternity of the Logos, regarded Him as " Son " only in creation and redemption ; and therefore said that in any case, even before His generation in the Scriptural sense, the Son eternally existed as Logos in the Father, as we have seen Marcellus of Ancyra understood it. Newman, however, assumes that all Catholics thought alike in this matter.

26. ἐξ οὐκ ὄντων ἐγένετο. This also was Arius' own phrase : Athan. De Synod. 14 ; Alexand. encycl. Socr. i. 8 ; Arius' letter to Euseb. Nicom., Theodoret HE. i. 4. It became the watchword of the thorough-going Arians, the Anomoeans, who were termed in consequence " Exoukontians," Socr. ii. 45 ; Athan. De Synod. 31. Theodoret HE. iv. 3. It is directly opposed by the ἐκ τῆς οὐσίας of the Creed.

27. ἐξ ἑτέρας ὑποστάσεως ἢ οὐσίας. That the Son was foreign in essence to the Father was taught by Arius in his Thalia (apud Athan. De Synod. 15, Ξένος τοῦ Υἱοῦ κατ' οὐσίαν ὁ Πατήρ) and by Eusebius of Nicomedia (Epist. ad Paulin. Tyr. apud Theodoret HE. i. 6, οὐκ ἐκ τῆς οὐσίας αὐτοῦ γεγονός . . . ἀλλ' ἕτερον τῇ φύσει). He

---

[1] *Nicene Creed.* For this idea of the Sonship see Loofs' *Paulus von Samosata, Texte und Unter.*, Vol. 44, p. 243. Cf. Ps. Athan. Or. 4, c. Arian, 15 : οἱ μὲν γὰρ τὸν ἄνθρωπον, ὃν ἔλαβεν ὁ σωτήρ, αὐτὸν εἶναι τὸν υἱὸν λέγουσιν· οἱ δὲ τὸ συναμφότερον, τόν τε ἄνθρωπον καὶ τὸν λόγον, υἱὸν τότε γεγενῆσθαι ὅτε συνήφθησαν· ἄλλοι δὲ εἰσιν οἱ λέγοντες αὐτὸν τὸν λόγον τότε υἱὸν γεγενῆσθαι, ὅτε ἐνηνθρώπησεν, "ἀπὸ γὰρ λόγου," φασί, "γέγονεν υἱὸς οὐκ ὢν πρότερον υἱὸς ἀλλὰ λόγος μόνον."

bases this solely on unintelligent and literal understanding of the stock text, Prov. viii. 22, "The Lord begat me the beginning of His works."

29. κτιστόν. This word is read here by Socr. i. 8, and in Eusebius' transcript of the Creed in his letter, according to Socrates and Athanasius. Theodoret alone omits it from the Eusebian transcript, and it was omitted in the version of the Creed read in the second Session at Chalcedon (Mansi, vi. 956).

The "creatureship" was a corollary of the denial of a *true* Sonship. Here was shown the illogical position of Arianism. It began by emphasising the Sonship, and ended by robbing it of its verity. For Sonship implies community of nature with the Father, whereas Arianism, by denying the ὁμοούσιον, placed the Son amongst created beings, and made Him in consequence alien to the nature of the Father. "If Son, then not creature ; if creature, then not Son," said Athanasius, tersely summing up the dilemma (De decr. Nic. 13). The Arian view developed as its premisses were pushed home. Arius did not at first see what his original denial involved. By insistence on the ἀγεννησία of true Deity, the Son fell into the order of κτιστά, and therefore was ἀλλότριος καὶ ἀνόμοιος κατὰ πάντα τῆς τοῦ Πατρὸς οὐσίας καὶ ἰδιότητος (Athan. Or. c. Ar. i. 6). The attribution to such a being of Divine titles was simple paganism : indeed, Arian thought was largely coloured with polytheistic conceptions of Deity (Or. c. Ar. i. 10, 18 ; ad Episc. Aeg. 4, 13).

30. τρεπτὸν ἢ ἀλλοιωτόν. By τρεπτόν, "capable of moral change," the Arians meant in effect "peccable". Φᾶσιν αὐτὸν τρεπτῆς εἶναι φύσεως, ἀρετῆς τε καὶ κακίας ἐπιδεκτικόν, wrote Alexander to his namesake of Byzantium (Theodor. HE. i. 4), describing Arius' teaching. Οὐκ ἔστιν ἄτρεπτος, ὡς ὁ Πατήρ, ἀλλὰ τρεπτός ἐστι φύσει, ὡς τὰ κτίσματα, sang Arius in his Thalia (Athan. Or. c. Ar. i. 9). In another place Arius made the immutability dependent upon the Son's own volition : ὑποστήσαντα ἰδίῳ θελήματι ἄτρεπτον καὶ ἀναλλοίωτον (Epist. to Alex. ap. Athan. De Synod. 16) ; cf. the Thalia (Athan. ibid. 5), καὶ τῇ μὲν φύσει, ὥσπερ πάντες, οὕτω καὶ αὐτὸς ὁ Λόγος ἐστὶ τρεπτός, τῷ δὲ ἰδίῳ αὐτεξουσίῳ, ἕως βούλεται, μενεῖ καλός· ὅτε μέντοι θέλει, δύναται τρέπεσθαι καὶ αὐτὸς ὥσπερ καὶ ἡμεῖς, τρεπτῆς ὢν φύσεως : and Arian blasphemies quoted by Athan. ad Episc. Aeg. 12, καὶ τῇ μὲν φύσει τρεπτός ἐστι, τῷ δὲ ἰδίῳ αὐτεξουσίῳ, ὡς βούλεται, μένει καλός, ὅτε μέντοι θέλει, δύναται τρέπεσθαι καὶ αὐτὸς ὥσπερ καὶ τὰ πάντα.

Alexander's encyclical (Socr. i. 6) relates how the question had been pushed home—" Could the Word of God be changed (τραπῆναι) as the Devil changed ? " And the answer was, " Yes, he could ; for he was τρεπτῆς φύσεως, γενητὸς καὶ τρεπτὸς ὑπάρχων." Athanasius of Anazarbus boldly said that the Son of God was one of the hundred sheep (Athan. De Synod. 17).

APPENDICES
TO
THE CREED OF NICAEA

I. CREED OF CAESAREA

Of this Creed which Eusebius submitted at the Council of Nicaea in proof of his orthodoxy he remarks " as in our first catechetical instruction and at the time of our baptism we received from the Bishop who was before us, and as we have learned from the Holy Scriptures, and alike as Presbyter and as Bishop were wont to believe and teach ; so now we believe and thus declare our faith."

This takes the Creed back at least to the end of the third century. But in view of Eusebius' condemnation for heresy in 321 it is possible that he may have strengthened it somewhat in the interval, *e.g.* by such phrases as Θεὸν ἐκ Θεοῦ, Φῶς ἐκ Φωτός, Ζωὴν ἐκ Ζωῆς.

Epist. Euseb. apud Socr. i. 8.

Theod. i. 12.

Athan. App. to De Decr. Nic.

Πιστεύομεν εἰς ἕνα Θεὸν Πατέρα παντοκράτορα,
τὸν τῶν ἁπάντων ὁρατῶν τε καὶ ἀοράτων ποιητήν·
καὶ εἰς ἕνα Κύριον Ἰησοῦν Χριστόν,
τὸν τοῦ Θεοῦ Λόγον,
Θεὸν ἐκ Θεοῦ,
Φῶς ἐκ Φωτός,
Ζωὴν ἐκ Ζωῆς,
Υἱὸν μονογενῆ,
πρωτότοκον πάσης κτίσεως,
πρὸ πάντων τῶν αἰώνων ἐκ τοῦ Πατρὸς γεγεννημένον,
δι' οὗ καὶ ἐγένετο τὰ πάντα·
τὸν διὰ τὴν ἡμετέραν σωτηρίαν σαρκωθέντα,
καὶ ἐν ἀνθρώποις πολιτευσάμενον,
καὶ παθόντα,
καὶ ἀναστάντα τῇ τρίτῃ ἡμέρᾳ,
καὶ ἀνελθόντα πρὸς τὸν Πατέρα,
καὶ ἥξοντα πάλιν ἐν δόξῃ κρῖναι ζῶντας καὶ νεκρούς·
πιστεύομεν καὶ εἰς ἓν Πνεῦμα Ἅγιον.

*   *   *   *

II. CREED OF JERUSALEM

Collected from the Catechetical Lectures of Cyril

THE catechetical lectures of Cyril were delivered in the year 348 when he was still a Presbyter. The Creed is, of course, conjectural, but all its phrases can be traced in the Lectures except σαρκωθέντα καὶ ἐνανθρωπήσαντα, σταυρωθέντα καὶ ταφέντα, which have been restored in the text-books. Possibly concerning the Incarnation the phrasing should be γεννηθέντα ἐκ τῆς παρθένου καὶ τοῦ Ἁγίου Πνεύματος. Both these Creeds show signs of Antiochene influence (see below, p. 58).

Πιστεύομεν εἰς ἕνα Θεὸν Πατέρα παντοκράτορα,
  ποιητὴν οὐρανοῦ καὶ γῆς, ὁρατῶν τε πάντων καὶ ἀοράτων·
καὶ εἰς ἕνα Κύριον Ἰησοῦν Χριστόν,
  τὸν Υἱὸν τοῦ Θεοῦ τὸν μονογενῆ,
  τὸν ἐκ τοῦ Πατρὸς γεννηθέντα πρὸ πάντων τῶν αἰώνων
  δι' οὗ τὰ πάντα ἐγένετο,
  σαρκωθέντα καὶ ἐνανθρωπήσαντα,
  σταυρωθέντα καὶ ταφέντα,
  ἀναστάντα τῇ τρίτῃ ἡμέρᾳ,
  καὶ ἀνελθόντα εἰς τοὺς οὐρανούς,
  καὶ καθίσαντα ἐκ δεξιῶν τοῦ Πατρός,
  καὶ ἐρχόμενον ἐν δόξῃ κρῖναι ζῶντας καὶ νεκρούς,
  οὗ τῆς βασιλείας οὐκ ἔσται τέλος·
καὶ εἰς ἕν Ἅγιον Πνεῦμα,
  τὸν παράκλητον
  τὸ λαλῆσαν ἐν τοῖς προφήταις·
καὶ εἰς ἓν βάπτισμα μετανοίας εἰς ἄφεσιν ἁμαρτιῶν·
καὶ εἰς μίαν ἁγίαν καθολικὴν ἐκκλησίαν·
καὶ εἰς σαρκὸς ἀνάστασιν·
καὶ εἰς ζωὴν αἰώνιον.

III. CREED OF ALEXANDRIA

This is best found in the Creed of Arius and Euzoius (Hahn, *Symbole*, pp. 256 f.).

Πιστεύομεν εἰς ἕνα Θεὸν Πατέρα παντοκράτορα·
Καὶ εἰς Κύριον Ἰησοῦν Χριστόν,
τὸν Υἱὸν Αὐτοῦ,
τὸν ἐξ Αὐτοῦ (πρὸ πάντων τῶν αἰώνων)
γεγεννημένον (Θεὸν) Λόγον,
δι' οὗ τὰ πάντα ἐγένετο
(τά τε ἐν τοῖς οὐρανοῖς καὶ τὰ ἐπὶ τῆς γῆς),
τὸν κατελθόντα,
καὶ σαρκωθέντα,
καὶ παθόντα,
καὶ ἀναστάντα,
ἀνελθόντα εἰς τοὺς οὐρανούς,
καὶ πάλιν ἐρχόμενον
κρῖναι ζῶντας καὶ νεκρούς·
Καὶ εἰς τὸ Ἅγιον Πνεῦμα·
Καὶ εἰς σαρκὸς ἀνάστασιν·
Καὶ εἰς ζωὴν τοῦ μέλλοντος αἰῶνος·
(καὶ εἰς βασιλείαν οὐρανῶν)
Καὶ εἰς μίαν καθολικὴν ἐκκλησίαν
(τοῦ Θεοῦ, τὴν ἀπὸ περάτων ἕως περάτων)

IV. CREED OF THE APOSTOLIC CONSTITUTIONS

vii. 41

This document is an Arian production of the late fourth century, and is one of a series of documents all claiming to be Apostolic— the Didascalia of the Apostles, the Apostolic Constitutions, and the Apostolic Church Order—all of which assert or imply a meeting of the Apostles at Jerusalem ; and in the Didascalia they are said to have drawn up some form of faith. That in the Apostolic Constitutions, which is printed below, while showing traces of Antiochene influence, is based in general outline on the Apostolic Tradition of Hippolytus already alluded to (Dix, op. cit. p. 36). It will be noted that it contains the clause " Whose Kingdom shall have no end " added by the Council of Constantinople to N, which also appears in the letter of Marcellus of Ancyra to Pope Julius and in the Creed of Epiphanius (see p. 60).

Πιστεύω καὶ βαπτίζομαι εἰς ἕνα ἀγέννητον μόνον ἀληθινὸν Θεὸν
    παντοκράτορα, τὸν Πατέρα τοῦ Χριστοῦ,
    κτίστην καὶ δημιουργὸν τῶν ἁπάντων.
    ἐξ οὗ τὰ πάντα·
καὶ εἰς τὸν Κύριον Ἰησοῦν τὸν Χριστόν
    τὸν μονογενῆ αὐτοῦ Υἱόν
    τὸν πρωτότοκον πάσης κτίσεως
    τὸν πρὸ αἰώνων εὐδοκίᾳ τοῦ Πατρὸς γεννηθέντα
    δι' οὗ τὰ πάντα ἐγένετο τὰ ἐν οὐρανοῖς καὶ ἐπὶ γῆς ὁρατά τε
      καὶ ἀόρατα,
    τὸν ἐπ' ἐσχάτων τῶν ἡμερῶν κατελθόντα ἐξ οὐρανῶν καὶ
      σάρκα ἀναλαβόντα,
    ἐκ τῆς ἁγίας παρθένου Μαρίας γεννηθέντα,
    καὶ πολιτευσάμενον ὁσίως κατὰ τοὺς νόμους τοῦ Θεοῦ καὶ
      Πατρὸς αὐτοῦ,
    καὶ σταυρωθέντα ἐπὶ Ποντίου Πιλάτου,
    καὶ ἀποθανόντα ὑπὲρ ἡμῶν,
    καὶ ἀναστάντα ἐκ τῶν νεκρῶν μετὰ τὸ παθεῖν τῇ τρίτῃ ἡμέρᾳ,
    καὶ ἀνελθόντα εἰς τοὺς οὐρανούς,
    καὶ καθεσθέντα ἐν δεξιᾷ τοῦ Πατρός,
    καὶ πάλιν ἐρχόμενον ἐπὶ συντελείᾳ τοῦ αἰῶνος μετὰ δόξης
      κρῖναι ζῶντας καὶ νεκρούς,
    οὗ τῆς βασιλείας οὐκ ἔσται τέλος·
βαπτίζομαι καὶ εἰς τὸ Πνεῦμα τὸ Ἅγιον,
    τοῦτ' ἐστὶν τὸν παράκλητον,
    τὸ ἐνεργῆσαν ἐν πᾶσιν τοῖς ἀπ' αἰῶνος ἁγίοις,

ὕστερον δὲ ἀποσταλὲν παρὰ τοῦ Πατρὸς κατὰ τὴν εὐαγγελίαν
τοῦ Σωτῆρος ἡμῶν καὶ Κυρίου Ἰησοῦ Χριστοῦ,
καὶ μετὰ τοὺς ἀποστόλους δὲ πᾶσιν τοῖς πιστεύουσιν ἐν τῇ
ἁγίᾳ καθολικῇ καὶ ἀποστολικῇ ἐκκλησίᾳ·
εἰς σαρκὸς ἀνάστασιν,
καὶ εἰς ἄφεσιν ἁμαρτιῶν,
καὶ εἰς βασιλείαν οὐρανῶν,
καὶ εἰς ζωὴν τοῦ μέλλοντος αἰῶνος.

E

V. CREEDS OF ANTIOCH

The Creed of Antioch is important as being that of the third city of the Roman Empire.[1] Until the rise of Constantinople there were only two cities of first-class importance in the Christian East, Antioch and Alexandria; and their influence on their neighbourhood and beyond it was necessarily great. They had their own respective theological traditions, which, as we have seen, met at Nicaea. Soon after Nicaea, Antioch began to be overshadowed by the growing influence of Constantinople or new Rome. Antiochene Christianity, as we can see from the New Testament, had a strong missionary interest (Acts xv), and Theodoret's statement that it was at Antioch that the ancient antiphonal singing was first introduced,[2] witnesses to a widespread liturgical and therefore credal influence on the part of this great centre of Christianity. The various Councils of Bishops, held both before and after Nicaea at Antioch, were doubtless a means of propagating such influence, as they are the evidence of its central position in the East. This influence was paramount in Asia Minor, where Ephesus had ceased to count as of ecclesiastical importance. In fact, as Duchesne[3] remarks, up to the reign of Theodosius (379–95) Antioch remained Queen of the East, the centre to which the Greek Empire looked as its chief ecclesiastical metropolis, the ancient churches of Asia and the Christian communities of the Diocese of Thrace being drawn into its circle of influence. At the same time it would be wrong to ignore the intrusion of active Alexandrian influence in Asia Minor and Antioch in the time of Paul of Samosata and Lucian the Martyr.

We have no extant Creed of Antioch in full before the " Ecthesis " adopted by the Dedication Council of Antioch in 341. This was said by the Council to have been written by Lucian the Martyr of Antioch and head of a local school of theology. His teaching approximated to the Logos doctrine of Alexandria, stressed the separate and subordinate hypostasis of the Logos-Son, and as some writers think led directly to the system of Arius, who had certainly sat at the feet of Lucian.[4] This creed, amplified by

[1] Josephus, B.J. iii. 2, 4.
[2] In the time of Bishop Leontius (344–57). Duchesne, *Christian Worship*, p. 114. Theodoret HE. ii. 19.
[3] Duchesne, *Ancient History of the Church*, Vol. 1, p. 323 ; Socrates HE. vi. 8 ; Theodoret HE. iii. 19 ; cf. Lightfoot, *Apostolic Fathers*, Part II, i, p. 31.
[4] Considerable uncertainty surrounds the name of Lucian. Most Church historians—*e.g.* Harnack and Bethune-Baker—regard him as the parent of Arianism and as closely connected with Paul of Samosata. Others,

58

references to Scripture, characteristic of the school of Antioch, is given by Athanasius, De Synod. 23 and in a Latin version by Hilary, De Synod. 29 (cf. Socrates, HE. ii. 10). It is printed in full below so as to stand as an example of the reaction against Nicaea begun at the Council of the Dedication, which was important as coming between that of Rome (340), which vindicated Athanasius and Marcellus, and that of Sardica, which confirmed Nicaea and the *homoousion*. Especially noteworthy are the various phrases substituted for the *homoousion* of the Son. Quite apart from these obvious additions, it is nowhere claimed that this was the Creed of Antioch itself, however much it may express the substantial orthodoxy of Lucian. We must therefore look elsewhere for the Creed of this great Church; and it is probably to be found in the following formulas: (1) The version given in Latin by Cassian (De Incarn. vi. 3) in opposition to Nestorius, whose baptismal profession it was supposed to be.

Cass. de incarn. vi. 3

Credo in unum et solum verum Deum, Patrem omnipotentem,
creatorem omnium visibilium et invisibilium creaturarum:
Et in Dominum nostrum Iesum Christum,
Filium eius unigenitum,
et Primogenitum totius creaturae,
ex eo natum ante omnia saecula
et non factum,
Deum verum ex Deo vero,
homoousion Patri,
per quem et saecula campaginata sunt et omnia facta:
Qui propter nos venit,
et natus est ex Maria virgine,
et crucifixus sub Pontio Pilato
et sepultus,
et tertia die resurrexit secundum scripturas,
et in caelos ascendit,
et iterum veniet iudicare vivos et mortuos.

This is only a fragment, as is also (2) that given in Greek in a treatise by Eusebius of Dorylaeum (Mansi, iv. 1109) preserved in the Acts of the Council of Ephesus (431) as follows:—

such as Gwatkin, maintain that there is nothing really against him but the leaning of his disciples towards Arianism (*Studies of Arianism*, p. 17 (n.)). On the other hand, Loofs had come to the conclusion that there were two Lucians, one the martyr in the persecution of Diocletian, and another Paul's successor at Antioch. For the evidence see Loofs, *Paulus von Samosata, Texte und Unter.*, vol. 44, pp. 180–6; and for a good English version and discussion see R. V. Sellers, *Eustathius of Antioch* (Cambridge, 1928), p. 10. See also Harnack, *History of Dogma*, Vol. 2, p. 582; Bethune-Baker, *History of Christian Doctrine*, p. 110; Raven, *Apollinarianism*, pp. 72 f.

. . . .

. . . .

Θεὸν ἀληθινὸν ἐκ Θεοῦ ἀληθινοῦ,
ὁμοούσιον τῷ Πατρί,
δι' οὗ καὶ οἱ αἰῶνες κατηρτίσθησαν καὶ τὰ πάντα ἐγένετο·
τὸν δι' ἡμᾶς κατελθόντα
καὶ γεννηθέντα ἐκ Μαρίας τῆς ἁγίας τῆς ἀειπαρθένου,
καὶ σταυρωθέντα ἐπὶ Ποντίου Πιλάτου

. . . .

. . . .

Chrys.	καὶ εἰς ἁμαρτιῶν ἄφεσιν,
Chrys.	καὶ εἰς νεκρῶν ἀνάστασιν,
Chrys.	καὶ εἰς ζωὴν αἰώνιον.

If it could be proved that the Creed of Marcellus of Ancyra, which he submitted in 340 to Pope Julius as evidence of his orthodoxy was, as he himself is said to have claimed, his own Creed, that is, the Creed of his Church and Baptism (Epiphanius, Adv. Haer. lxxii) it could, with its obvious resemblances to the old Roman Creed, be regarded as an important link between Eastern and Western Creeds. The majority of scholars, however, do not accept Badcock's view (op. cit., pp. 58, 69) that it was, in fact, the Creed of Ancyra, but believe that it was the Roman Creed to which Marcellus subscribed to save his orthodoxy. Such a link, however, might be said to exist in the Creed of Niceta of Remesiana, whose Eastern character is proved by its close correspondence with Eastern Creeds of the fourth century. Marks of the East may be noted in the epithet *catholicam* after *ecclesiam*, and the characteristically Eastern clause *caeli et terrae Creatorem*. These Creeds are printed below for comparison.

The Creed of Niceta of Remesiana (Burn, *Niceta*, p. lxxxiv)	The Creed of Marcellus
Credo in Deum Patrem omnipotentem,	Πιστεύω εἰς Θεὸν παντοκράτορα
caeli et terrae Creatorem ;	
Et in Filium ejus Iesum Christum	Καὶ εἰς Χριστὸν Ἰησοῦν,
(Dominum nostrum ?)	τὸν Υἱὸν Αὐτοῦ τὸν μονογενῆ,
	τὸν Κύριον ἡμῶν,
natum ex Spiritu Sancto et ex virgine Maria,	τὸν γεννηθέντα ἐκ Πνεύματος Ἁγίου
	καὶ Μαρίας τῆς παρθένου,
passum sub Pontio Pilato,	τὸν ἐπὶ Ποντίου Πιλάτου σταυρωθέντα

The Creed of Niceta of Remesiana (Burn, *Niceta*, p. lxxxiv)	The Creed of Marcellus
crucifixum, mortuum,	καὶ ταφέντα,
tertia die resurrexit vivus a mortuis,	καὶ τῇ τρίτῃ ἡμέρᾳ
ascendit in caelos,	ἀναστάντα ἐκ τῶν νεκρῶν,
sedet ad dexteram Patris	ἀναβάντα εἰς τοὺς οὐρανούς
inde venturus iudicare vivos et mortuos ;	καὶ καθήμενον ἐν δεξιᾷ τοῦ Πατρός,
Et in Spiritum Sanctum ;	ὅθεν ἔρχεται κρίνειν ζῶντας καὶ νεκρούς·
Sanctam ecclesiam catholicam ;	Καὶ εἰς τὸ Ἅγιον Πνεῦμα·
Communionem sanctorum ;	Ἁγίαν ἐκκλησίαν·
Remissionem peccatorum ;	Ἄφεσιν ἁμαρτιῶν·
Carnis resurrectionem ;	Σαρκὸς ἀνάστασιν·
Et vitam aeternam.	Ζωὴν αἰώνιον.

Such is the Creed of Niceta, a mid-way form looking evidently to Rome but deriving, like his Liturgy, from Asia Minor. The Creed was translated into Latin because Niceta, though a Greek, preached to a congregation composed largely of the Roman Legionaries. Similar resemblances to this Creed are to be found in the Psalter of Athelstan (Badcock, op. cit., p. 63) given in a Liturgy which betrays close affinity to Syrian liturgies. Do either of these represent the original Creed of Antioch ?

Further light is thrown on the Creed of Antioch by reference to documents of undoubted Antiochene origin, such as those mentioned above, those of the successive Councils of Antioch in 341, the Macrostich of 345, and lastly the Creeds of Cappadocia and Auxentius,[1] which may have been that of Apollinarius of Laodicea. The probable conclusion is that the original Creed of Antioch was a short and simple one like the Roman and Western Creeds which underwent enlargement at the hands of various bishops and Councils, and survives in some liturgies such as that of the Apostolic Constitutions.

(3) The Lucianic Creed is probably the result of two revisions of the original baptismal creed of Antioch, which was amplified, first, by Lucian, with the insertion of Scriptural phrases and an anti-Sabellian appendix, and then enlarged at Antioch in 341 by a few other phrases and the addition of the two anathemas, which seem specially adapted to admit of Arian subscription, by their inclusion of χρόνον in the first, and ὡς ἓν τῶν κτισμάτων (and its parallels) in the second.[2]

---

[1] Badcock, op. cit., p. 49.
[2] Cf. Arius' letter to Alexander, apud. Athan. De Synod. 16, ἄτρεπτον καὶ ἀναλλοίωτον κτίσμα τοῦ Θεοῦ τέλειον, ἀλλ' οὐχ ὡς ἓν τῶν κτισμάτων· γέννημα, ἀλλ' οὐχ ὡς ἓν τῶν γεγεννημένων.

Πιστεύομεν (ἀκολούθως τῇ εὐαγγελικῇ καὶ ἀποστολικῇ παραδόσει)
εἰς ἕνα Θεὸν Πατέρα παντοκράτορα,
    τὸν τῶν ὅλων δημιουργόν τε καὶ ποιητὴν
    καὶ προνοητήν,
    ἐξ οὗ τὰ πάντα·
καὶ εἰς ἕνα Κύριον Ἰησοῦν Χριστόν,
    τὸν Υἱὸν αὐτοῦ τὸν μονογενῆ Θεόν,
    δι' οὗ τὰ πάντα,
    τὸν γεννηθέντα πρὸ τῶν αἰώνων ἐκ τοῦ Πατρός,
    Θεὸν ἐκ Θεοῦ
    ὅλον ἐξ ὅλου, μόνον ἐκ μόνου,
    τέλειον ἐκ τελείου, βασιλέα ἐκ βασιλέως,
    Κύριον ἀπὸ Κυρίου,
    Λόγον ζῶντα, Σοφίαν ζῶσαν,
    Φῶς ἀληθινὸν, ὁδὸν, ἀλήθειαν, ἀνάστασιν, ποιμένα,
    θύραν,
    ἄτρεπτον τε καὶ ἀναλλοίωτον,
    τῆς θεότητος οὐσίας τε καὶ βουλῆς καὶ δυνάμεως καὶ
    δόξης τοῦ Πατρὸς ἀπαράλλακτον εἰκόνα,
    τὸν πρωτότοκον πάσης κτίσεως
    τὸν ὄντα ἐν ἀρχῇ πρὸς τὸν Θεόν, Λόγον Θεοῦ, κατὰ τὸ
    εἰρημένον ἐν τῷ εὐαγγελίῳ Καὶ Θεὸς ἦν ὁ Λόγος,
    δι' οὗ τὰ πάντα ἐγένετο, καὶ ἐν ᾧ τὰ πάντα συνέστη-
    κεν·
    τὸν ἐπ' ἐσχάτων τῶν ἡμερῶν κατελθόντα ἄνωθεν,
    καὶ γεννηθέντα ἐκ παρθένου κατὰ τὰς γραφάς,
    καὶ ἄνθρωπον γενόμενον,
    μεσίτην Θεοῦ καὶ ἀνθρώπων, ἀπόστολόν τε τῆς
    πίστεως ἡμῶν, καὶ ἀρχηγὸν τῆς ζωῆς, ὥς φησιν ὅτι
    Καταβέβηκα ἐκ τοῦ οὐρανοῦ οὐχ ἵνα ποιῶ τὸ θέλημα
    τὸ ἐμὸν ἀλλὰ τὸ θέλημα τοῦ πέμψαντός με·
    τὸν παθόντα ὑπὲρ ἡμῶν,
    καὶ ἀναστάντα ὑπὲρ ἡμῶν τῇ τρίτῃ ἡμέρᾳ,
    καὶ ἀνελθόντα εἰς οὐρανούς,
    καὶ καθεσθέντα ἐν δεξιᾷ τοῦ Πατρός,
    καὶ πάλιν ἐρχόμενον μετὰ δόξης καὶ δυναμέως κρῖναι
    ζῶντας καὶ νεκρούς·
καὶ εἰς τὸ Πνεῦμα τὸ Ἅγιον
    τὸ εἰς παράκλησιν καὶ ἁγιασμὸν καὶ
    τελείωσιν τοῖς πιστεύουσι διδόμενον
καθὼς καὶ ὁ Κύριος ἡμῶν Ἰησοῦς Χριστὸς διετάξατο τοῖς μαθηταῖς
λέγων Πορευθέντες μαθητεύσατε πάντα τὰ ἔθνη βαπτίζοντες αὐτοὺς
εἰς τὸ ὄνομα τοῦ Πατρὸς καὶ τοῦ Υἱοῦ καὶ τοῦ Ἁγίου Πνεύματος·
δηλονότι Πατρὸς ἀληθῶς Πατρὸς ὄντος, Υἱοῦ δὲ ἀληθῶς Υἱοῦ ὄντος,
τοῦ δὲ Ἁγίου Πνεύματος ἀληθῶς Ἁγίου Πνεύματος ὄντος, τῶν
ὀνομάτων οὐχ ἁπλῶς οὐδὲ ἀργῶς κειμένων, ἀλλὰ σημαινόντων ἀκριβῶς
τὴν οἰκείαν ἑκάστου τῶν ὀνομαζομένων ὑπόστασίν τε καὶ τάξιν καὶ
δόξαν· ὡς εἶναι τῇ μὲν ὑποστάσει τρία, τῇ δὲ συμφωνίᾳ ἕν.

Ταύτην οὖν ἔχοντες τὴν πίστιν καὶ ἐξ ἀρχῆς καὶ μέχρι τέλους ἔχοντες ἐνώπιον τοῦ Θεοῦ καὶ τοῦ Χριστοῦ, πᾶσαν αἱρετικὴν κακοδοξίαν ἀναθεματίζομεν.

καὶ εἴ τις παρὰ τὴν ὑγιῆ τῶν γραφῶν ὀρθὴν πίστιν διδάσκει, λέγων ἢ χρόνον ἢ καιρὸν ἢ αἰῶνα ἢ εἶναι ἢ γεγονέναι πρὸ τοῦ γεννηθῆναι τὸν Ὑιόν, ἀνάθεμα ἔστω.

καὶ εἴ τις λέγει τὸν Ὑιὸν κτίσμα ὡς ἓν τῶν κτισμάτων ἢ γέννημα ὡς ἓν τῶν γεννημάτων, ἢ ποίημα ὡς ἓν τῶν ποιημάτων, καὶ μὴ ὡς αἱ θεῖαι γραφαὶ παραδέδωκεν, τῶν προειρημένων ἕκαστον ἀφ᾽ ἑκάστου· ἢ εἴ τι ἄλλο διδάσκει, ἢ εὐαγγελίζεται, παρ᾽ ὃ παρελάβομεν, ἀνάθεμα ἔστω.

Ἡμεῖς γὰρ πᾶσι τοῖς ἐκ τῶν θείων γραφῶν παραδεδομένοις ὑπό τε προφητῶν καὶ ἀποστόλων ἀληθινῶς τε καὶ ἐμφόβως καὶ πιστεύομεν καὶ ἀκολουθοῦμεν.

VI. CREED OF CONSTANTINOPLE

Πιστεύομεν εἰς ἕνα Θεὸν Πατέρα παντοκράτορα
    ποιητὴν οὐρανοῦ καὶ γῆς, ὁρατῶν τε πάντων καὶ ἀοράτων·
καὶ εἰς ἕνα Κύριον Ἰησοῦν Χριστόν
    τὸν Υἱὸν τοῦ Θεοῦ τὸν Μονογενῆ,
    τὸν ἐκ τοῦ Πατρὸς γεννηθέντα πρὸ πάντων τῶν αἰώνων,
    Φῶς ἐκ Φωτός,
    Θεὸν ἀληθινὸν ἐκ Θεοῦ ἀληθινοῦ,
    γεννηθέντα οὐ ποιηθέντα,
    ὁμοούσιον τῷ Πατρί,
    δι' οὗ τὰ πάντα ἐγένετο·
    τὸν δι' ἡμᾶς τοὺς ἀνθρώπους καὶ διὰ τὴν ἡμετέραν σωτη-
        ρίαν κατελθόντα ἐκ τῶν οὐρανῶν,
    καὶ σαρκωθέντα ἐκ Πνεύματος Ἁγίου καὶ Μαρίας τῆς
        παρθένου,
    καὶ ἐνανθρωπήσαντα,
    σταυρωθέντα τε ὑπὲρ ἡμῶν ἐπὶ Ποντίου Πιλάτου,
    καὶ παθόντα, καὶ ταφέντα,
    καὶ ἀναστάντα τῇ τρίτῃ ἡμέρᾳ κατὰ τὰς γραφάς,
    καὶ ἀνελθόντα εἰς τοὺς οὐρανούς,
    καὶ καθεζόμενον ἐκ δεξιῶν τοῦ Πατρός,
    καὶ πάλιν ἐρχόμενον μετὰ δόξης κρῖναι ζῶντας καὶ νεκρούς,
    οὗ τῆς βασιλείας οὐκ ἔσται τέλος·
καὶ εἰς τὸ Πνεῦμα τὸ Ἅγιον τὸ Κύριον τὸ Ζωοποιόν,
    τὸ ἐκ τοῦ Πατρὸς ἐκπορευόμενον,
    τὸ σὺν Πατρί καὶ Υἱῷ συνπροσκυνούμενον καὶ συνδοξαζόμε-
        νον,
    τὸ λαλῆσαν διὰ τῶν προφητῶν·
    εἰς μίαν ἁγίαν καθολικὴν καὶ ἀποστολικὴν ἐκκλησίαν·
    ὁμολογοῦμεν ἓν βάπτισμα εἰς ἄφεσιν ἁμαρτιῶν.
    προσδοκῶμεν ἀνάστασιν νεκρῶν,
    καὶ ζωὴν τοῦ μέλλοντος αἰῶνος.

                                                    Ἀμήν.

The history of this formulary, which is known as " C," is of special interest because it is the Creed which is the almost universal use of Christendom, supplanting the original Nicene symbol (N) and usurping its name. It is, in fact, a document of very different character from N ; and the one assured result of the minute examination to which it has been subjected in recent years is that, whatever its origin, it is not a mere enlargement of that Creed. Its origin must be sought in other and probably more local sources. Its authorship is a matter of conjecture and needs further investigation. Dr. Hort's theory expounded in *Two Dissertations* (1876) was long held to be the most reasonable. He suggested that a revision and enrichment of the old Baptismal Creed of Jerusalem may have been carried out by Cyril about the years 363–4, after his return to his diocese on the accession of Julian, at the time when he and his friend Meletius had finally severed themselves from the Acacian (Homoian and Homoiousian) party, and decisively adopted the Nicene standard in its integrity. Dr. Hort supposed that Cyril himself presented his Creed thus revised to the Council of Constantinople (381) in support of his orthodoxy. One long Nicene extract, which included the all-important ὁμοούσιον, vindicated the loyalty of the document to the Nicene faith; and for the rest it proceeded on Jerusalem lines, incorporating words and phrases from Cyril's own lectures, from the creeds of sister churches, and from Scriptural sources. The Nicene anathemas were naturally not appended, as the Creed was intended for general eccelesiastical purposes.

Subsequent investigation, however, has challenged the obvious plausibility of this theory.

(1) Two Nicene clauses, which might have been expected, were not employed: (a) ἐκ τοῦ Πατρὸς τουτέστιν ἐκ τῆς οὐσίας τοῦ Πατρὸς; and (b) the defining phrase, τά τε ἐν τῷ οὐρανῷ καὶ τὰ ἐν τῇ γῇ after δι' οὗ τὰ πάντα ἐγένετο.

(2) The " Creed " of Jerusalem is itself only a *conjectural* composition from sentences in Cyril's " Catechetical Lectures." [1]

(3) The enlarged Creed has all the marks of close association not with Jerusalem but with Constantinople, *e.g.* its strongly anti-Macedonian character as shown in the additions to the brief Nicene clause on the Holy Spirit. Macedonianism was a heresy not of Jerusalem but of Constantinople.

(4) While it is true that the first six clauses may be verbally identical with the conjectural Creed of Jerusalem, the other more important additions are difficult to explain on the assumption that they were made by Cyril. Even if it is admitted that the " Nicene " insertions were made by him to mark his transition to full orthodoxy, and the clause " of the Holy Ghost and the Virgin Mary " inserted to guard against Apollinarianism, that is not sufficient to account for the additions of " For us men ", " Under Pontius Pilate," and " according to the Scriptures." Still more difficult is it to explain the almost complete rewriting of the third section. It is hardly likely that any Bishop would have introduced such arbitrary changes on his own authority into his diocesan creed.

(5) Most of the additional clauses in the Creed of Constantinople (C) can be traced equally well to other local creeds, *e.g.* that of the Apostolic Constitutions and other creeds dependent on Antioch. The new clause " Whose Kingdom shall have no end " seems to be the only one which can with any probability be traced to Jerusalem.

[1] See *Journal of Theological Studies*, iv, 285, and Bethune-Baker, *Christian Doctrine*, pp. 188 f.

A more probable explanation, therefore, is that suggested by Dr. Kunze,[1] namely, that " C " was the Creed professed at his Baptism and Consecration by Nectarius, the Praetor of the City, who was elected to succeed St. Gregory of Nazianzus in the See of Constantinople. ‖ As such, it would naturally be entered upon the Acts of the Council, just as the Caesarean Creed recited by Eusebius was entered in the Acts at Nicaea, and later, the Creed of Charisius of Philadelphia came into the Acts of the Council of Ephesus. Moreover, this suggestion receives some support from the words in which Callinicus of Apamea recorded his vote in favour of the Chalcedonian Definition in 451, which incorporated the original Creed of Nicaea, together with the Creed of the 150 Fathers at Constantinople. He evidently connected this latter Creed with the Ordination of Nectarius, for he said : ʽΗ σύνοδος ἡ ἐν τῇ τῶν Νικαέων συγκροτηθεῖσα παρὰ τῶν τιή ἁγίων πατέρων καὶ τῶν ρύ τῶν ἐν τῇ μεγαλωνύμῳ Κωνσταντινουπόλει ἐπὶ τῇ χειροτονίᾳ εὐλαβεστάτου Νεκταρίου τοῦ ἐπισκόπου.[2]

If this hypothesis be accepted, most of the difficulties surrounding the origin of C have disappeared. For it is on the face of it only natural that the Creed proposed by the candidate for Baptism and Consecration should be that of the Church of his baptism, which he was to rule, rather than that of another Church such as Jerusalem or even the Nicene Creed which was not at that time a baptismal one. The conclusion therefore reached on a full review of the evidence by Dr. Badcock is that all those clauses in which the Creed of Constantinople differs from that of Nicaea can be explained without bringing in Cyril at all. He thinks that the work of the Council would normally have stopped with the recital of the Creed of Nicaea, had it not been for the Baptism of Nectarius, who would naturally have been consecrated on the basis of the Creed of that Church as recently " enlarged " by the Council of 381, and accepted as agreeable to N. The evidence of such an enlargement as made or approved by the Council of Constantinople may be summarised as follows :

(1) The Council's Letter in 381 to the Emperor described its work as falling into three divisions : (a) it had renewed concord, (b) it had promulgated short rules or definitions (συντόμους ὅρους) confirming the faith of the Fathers at Nicaea, and anathematising the heresies that had grown up contrary to the same, (c) in addition to these things it had decreed certain previous Canons for the good ordering of the Church. (Mansi, Concilia iii. 557; cf. iv. 102 and 104.)

(2) This letter must be read in connexion with the Epistle of the Council in 382 to Pope Damasus and others, which stated that, for the proof of their orthodoxy, it was sufficient for them to refer to

---

[1] *Das nicänische-konstantinopolitanische Symbol* (Leipzig 1898) ; cf. Gibson, *The Three Creeds*, pp. 171–3.
[2] Mansi, vii. 36.

the " Tome from Antioch " ; [1] and to a similar Formulary " recently put out by the Imperial Synod in Constantinople in which the Faith was confessed in an enlarged form (πλατύτερον τὴν πίστιν) and an anathematisation was made in writing of the heresies newly arisen ".[2]

(3) St. Leo in the Tome refers to one clause in the enlarged Creed in the words " qui est de Spiritu Sancto et Maria Virgine " as the common and universal profession of the faithful. Nestorius also used this clause as well as others as being in the Nicene Creed, and was reproached by Cyril for so doing. (Adv. Nest. 1. 6. 8.) [3]

(4) Flavian, Bishop of Constantinople, writing to the Emperor Theodosius I in 449 says : " Always following the Holy Scriptures and the Expositions of the Holy Fathers gathered together at Nicaea and at Constantinople " (Mansi, vi. 541). To which may be added the words in a dialogue falsely attributed to Athanasius in which it is admitted by the orthodox disputant that (at the Council) things were added to the Nicene Creed, though nothing contrary to it (De Sanc. Trin. Dial. iii ; Migne, P.G. xxviii. 1204).

(5) The Council of Chalcedon and its successors refer, as did Flavian, to both N and C. In its fifth session, after the recital of both, the Definition continues : " The present holy, great and ecumenical Synod decrees that the Faith of the 318 Fathers shall remain inviolate, and on account of the Pneumatomachi it confirms the doctrine subsequently delivered concerning the substance of the Spirit by the 150 Fathers who assembled in the imperial city, which they made known to all, not as adducing anything left lacking by their predecessors, but making distinct by written (or scriptural) testimonies their conception concerning the Holy Spirit against those who were trying to set aside His sovereignty." (See *Definition of Chalcedon*, p. 192 ; Mansi, vi. 956–958.)

From this evidence it can rightly be concluded that the Council of Constantinople officially added or approved these additions to the local Creed in opposition to the new heresies, naming Apollinarianism, Macedonianism, and the doctrine of Marcellus of Ancyra.[4]

There remains the problem of the long silence about C. It

---

[1] The Tome from Antioch was the Synodical Letter of the 153 Bishops presided over by Meletius in 379 and condemning all errors from Arianism to date. See Bright, *Canons*, xxii, pp. 113 f.

[2] Theodoret HE. v. 9, οἰκουμενικῆς here = *imperial*, not *ecumenical* in the ecclesiastical sense of the word. The mediaeval historian Nicephorus Callistus (HE. xi. 13) is the only authority for the information that the Council entrusted the selection of the additional language to St. Gregory of Nyssa, who frequently uses the expression " Giver of Life " as applied to the Holy Ghost.

[3] Cf. Loofs, *Nestoriana*, p. 337–8, and Nestorius' own words to Pope Caelestine (Mansi, iv. 1022).

[4] For a full statement of the evidence and on the whole question see Badcock, 2nd Edn. Chapter 13, and A. E. Burn, *Nicene Creed*.

was at one time supposed that it was known to Epiphanius, Bishop of Salamis, who died in 403, a writer always in close touch with Jerusalem, and like Cyril and Meletius of Antioch present at the Council of Constantinople in 381. In 374 he wrote an Exposition of the doctrine of the Trinity called "Ancoratus" (the Anchored one), in the last chapter but one of which he inserts a Creed which differs from C only by the addition of the two Nicene clauses omitted in that Creed. It is, however, now regarded as highly probable that the text of the Ancoratus has been altered, and that the creed which Epiphanius inserted at this point was the Creed of Nicaea, and that the existing text is a compilation of both. In this case it must be admitted that nothing is heard of C until seventy-seven years later, when the Imperial Commission at Chalcedon referred, as we have seen, to the Exposition of the " 150 Fathers who met at a later date." We must therefore fall back on the explanation that the Council of 381 was not at once regarded as oecumenical ; [1] a fact which would illustrate the accepted belief that the authority of a General Council depends not on itself but on its subsequent recognition by the consent of the Church. Constantinople naturally did not at this period regard itself as the equal either of Rome or Alexandria. In the latter the tradition was at all times hostile to additions to the Nicene Creed, as can be seen in the concluding words of the Definition of Chalcedon repeated in the later Oecumenical Councils forbidding the putting out of any other Creed.

The causes of its ultimate displacement of N are not far to seek. We need not dwell upon the fact that the latter was constructed to meet a special want, while its anathemas rendered it unsuitable for baptismal use ; and that C, both in stateliness of rhythm and in fullness of doctrinal statement, was superior to the Nicene and eminently suited for liturgical recitation. In any case it would be sufficient that it was popularly believed to have been commended by the Council of Constantinople and that it was known to be the Creed of the Church of the Imperial City. Moreover, as Hort suggests, when C is set side by side with contemporary creeds of similar composition its true intention becomes yet clearer. The traditions which invested it with associations borrowed from Nicaea have been negatived by historical evidence ; but comparison with the revised Creeds of other Churches clothes it with new and better associations, belonging to the peaceful life and growth of the Church renewed after the disastrous interruption of Arianism. The opening years of this happier period have, as Dr. Hort remarks, left no more characteristic monument than the one Creed which united East and West in the confession of a true Faith, as illuminated by the light of the highest Greek theology. [2]

[1] In the West, indeed, it was not formally recognised till the sixth century. See Kidd, op. cit., Vol. II, p. 288.
[2] Hort, *Two Dissertations*, p. 137.

We now proceed to comment on such clauses in this Creed as have not been remarked upon in the previous notes upon the Nicene.

τὸ Πνεῦμα τὸ Ἅγιον τὸ Κύριον τὸ Ζωοποιόν. A triad of epithets is here employed to emphasise the real Deity of the Spirit in view of the Macedonian heresy which denied it, and the uncertainty which in the first four centuries surrounded the Doctrine of the Third Person. He is declared to be different from all other spirits as one who is Holy, Divine, and Life-giving.[1]

τὸ Ἅγιον. Cf. John xiv. 26. This epithet expresses the essential characteristic of the Divine Spirit and sums up the teaching of both Old and New Testaments. The idea of a Divine Spirit is common to all religions. Primitive man was aware of strange experiences which seem to him to come from without in the form of dreams or of some kind of possession. To experiences of this kind the Greeks gave the name of πνεῦμα, and the Hebrews that of *Ruach*, which always means a third thing in addition to the body and soul of man, and belonging to another world. At its highest level this conception included inspiration and genius of every kind.[2] In religion it has been defined as " the numinous "[3] which is universal in the experience of human beings. The Prophets of the Old Testament, however, followed by St. Paul and St. John in the New, drew a distinction between spiritual phenomena of any such kind and what they call " Holy " Spirit. St. Paul (1 Cor. xii. 3) especially warned the Corinthians that those who speak in the spirit do not necessarily speak with the Holy Ghost; while to St. John (1 John iv. 1) the discernment of spirits is a vital element in their equipment as Christians. The prophets of the Old Testament drew a similar distinction between their own vocational experiences and the ecstatic outbursts of the " sons of the prophets " and other possessed men. It was thus the function of a prophet by whom the *Holy* Spirit spoke to make clear the distinction between God and the world, the Spirit of God and the human spirit at its highest (Isa. vi. 6) as well as that between the world of God and the world of demons, or between true and false religion. In other words, in the Old Testament the Spirit is the power and nearness of a God transcendent in His ethical holiness and separation from men, which is the root meaning of the word Holy.

But in the New Testament the Spirit is always regarded after Pentecost as the Spirit of Jesus;[4] the Power and Presence of God working through the glorified humanity of the Incarnate.[5] In the Johannine writings the Holy Spirit is a " Paraclete " Who has been given to the Church and is operative in her for ever. Henceforth

---

[1] Cf. Cyril, Catech. Lect. xvi. 6.   [2] Cf. Ex. xxxi. 3, 1 Sam. x. 6, etc.
[3] See Otto, *The Idea of the Holy*, p. 7.   [4] Cf. Acts xvi. 7; 1 Pet. i. 10.
[5] Cf. Milligan, *The Resurrection of Christ*, pp. 195 and 265.

the Office of the Prophet becomes subordinate to that of the Apostle; and rules are laid down by the Apostle to test the authenticity of the prophetic word. " Hereby shall ye know the Spirit of God (the Spirit of Truth, *i.e.* the real Spirit); every spirit which confesseth that Jesus Christ is come in the flesh is of God : and every (prophetic) spirit which does not confess that Jesus Christ is come in the flesh is not of God." (1 John iv. 2 f.) In other words, prophecy is now confined within the limits assigned to it by the Incarnation and the apostolic witness to the same in the Church, lest it should threaten the *finality* of the revelation in Christ; as indeed happened later in the heresy of Montanism.

On the other hand, the Creed does not actually use the word *Theos* in connexion with the Holy Spirit as it did with the Son or Logos. But compare the statement of Gregory Nazianzen, who was a member of the Council of 381 and actually Archbishop of Constantinople until his resignation and the election of Nectarius : " Of the ordained men among ourselves some have conceived the Spirit as an activity, some as a creature, some as God, and some have not known which, out of reverence for the Scriptures, as they say; because those Scriptures did not make the matter clear either way." (Ep. vi.) Again, " Is the Spirit God? Most certainly. Well then is He consubstantial? Yes, if He is God." (Ep. x.) Cf. the letter to Cledonius, where, speaking of the Nicene Faith, he continues " completing in doctrine that which was incompletely said by them (*i.e.* N) concerning the Holy Spirit; for that question had not then been mooted, namely that we are to believe that the Father, Son and Holy Spirit are of one Godhead, thus confessing the Spirit to be God." Tertullian was the first to call the Holy Spirit " Deus " in his Montanist treatise " Adversus Praxean." Basil himself in his great treatise on the Holy Spirit does not expressly use the word *Theos* of the Holy Ghost, nor, according to Origen, did the original Apostles. Cf. Origen, In. Ioan ii. 6 ; De Prin. ii. 2. See Bigg, *Christian Platonists of Alexandria* (2nd Edn.), p. 213.

τὸ Κύριον. Cf. 2 Cor. iii. 17, 18. This word is decisive against the Macedonian heresy that the Spirit was not only a creature but also one of the ministering spirits differing from the Angels only in degree. (Athanasius, Ep. ad Serap. i. 1.) Cyril of Jerusalem evidently had this in mind when he wrote (Catech. iv. 16): " Those who teach blasphemous things of Him, who with the Father and the Son is exalted with the glory of the Godhead . . . who halloweth and deifieth all " ; and again xvi. 23, where he speaks of the Spirit as the Governor and Teacher and Sanctifier of all the spiritual hosts. τὰ μέν εἰς λειτουργίαν ἀποστελλόμενα, τὸ δὲ ἐρευνᾷ καὶ τὰ βάθη τοῦ Θεοῦ.

τὸ Ζωοποιόν. Life-giving, not merely Life-transmitting. The Spirit is life-giving because He is himself Life (Rom. viii. 2.

τὸ Πνεῦμα τῆς Ζωῆς). This epithet, like the others, is Scriptural (John vi. 63 ; 2 Cor. iii. 6) and is thus explained by Athanasius (ad Serap. i. 23), τὰ δὲ κτίσματα . . . . ζωοποιούμενά ἐστι δι᾿ αὐτοῦ, τὸ δὲ μὴ μέτεχον ζωῆς ἀλλ᾿ αὐτὸ μετεχόμενον καὶ ζωοποιοῦν τὰ κτίσματα, ποίαν ἔχει συγγένειαν πρὸς τὰ γενητά, ἢ πῶς ὅλως ἂν εἴη τῶν κτισμάτων, ἅπερ ἐν ἐκείνῳ παρὰ τοῦ Λόγου ζωοποιεῖται ; This epithet is also Cyrilline, Catech. vii. 16, xvi. 12.

The Holy Spirit is Life-giving in creation, giving and sustaining life and order and beauty ; in human history, moulding the character and shaping the destiny of individuals, nations and races ; in grace, first imparting spiritual life and then renewing and strengthening it ; above all and specially He is creative of the Church, being the Spirit of Christ, whose presence He accomplishes in those incorporated by baptism into the Body of Christ on earth. Hence He is termed " Creator Spiritus." See Mason, *Faith of the Gospel*, pp. 225 f.

The Spirit, however, is ὁμοούσιον with the Father and the Son. Cf. Ps.-Athanasius, c. Apoll. i. 9, ὁμοούσιος γὰρ ἡ Τριάς : ad Serap. i.27. Probably the Nicene keyword was felt, when the Macedonian controversy arose, to be too closely attached to the doctrine of the Second Person to be used again with wisdom. Yet Damasus (apud Theodoret HE. v. 11) used the phrase " of one and the same essence (μιᾶς καὶ τῆς αὐτῆς οὐσίας) with the Father and the Son " : and later it became the usual term : *e.g.* Epiph. Haer. 74 ; Invocation in Liturgy of St. Mark (Brightman, op. cit., p. 134) ; Creed of Charisius (Hahn, p. 319). The doctrine of the co-essential Trinity had been clearly stated by Tertullian, Adv. Prax. 2, " Tres autem non statu sed gradu, nec substantia sed forma, nec potestate sed specie ; unius autem substantiae," etc.

ἐκ τοῦ Πατρὸς ἐκπορευόμενον. As, in the language of Scripture which is followed in the technical confessions of the Church, the relation of the Son to the Father is described by the term " generation," so that of the Spirit is termed " procession," both being ineffable eternal relations. The phrase combines 1 Cor. ii. 12 with John xv. 26 ; it is frequent in Athanasius, ad Serap. i. 15, 20, 22, 25 ; iii. 2. Procession is according to Gregory of Nyssa the peculiar character (ἰδίωμα) of the Spirit, His mode of being (τρόπος ὑπάρξεως), as γεννησία is that of the Son, and ἀγεννησία that of the Father (Non tres Dei, Migne, XLV, 133).

ἐκ τοῦ Πατρός has the same force here as when used of the Son ; that is, it denotes co-essentiality. The Son is ἐκ τοῦ Πατρὸς γεννηθέντα : the Spirit ἐκ τοῦ Πατρὸς ἐκπορευόμενον. There was a difficulty felt on the subject of this nomenclature, and Ps.-Athan himself unconsciously stated it in arguing for the Sonship of the Logos, Orat. c. Ar. iv. 15, εἰ δὲ ἐκ τοῦ Θεοῦ ἐστιν, διὰ τί μὴ συνορῶσιν ὅτι τὸ ἔκ τινος ὑπάρχον υἱός ἐστιν ἐκείνου ἐξ οὗ καὶ ἔστιν ; this would involve the Spirit being also " Son " because of ἐκ τοῦ

Πατρός. The Arians seized upon the point and were rebuked (ad Serap. i. 15–17) on the ground that speculation was irreverent.

The temporal mission of the Spirit is not referred to in this Creed, though it finds a place in Tertullian, De Praescr. Haer. 13, " misisse vicariam vim Spiritus Sancti qui credentes agat"; Adv. Prax. 2, " Qui exinde miserit secundum promissionem suam a Patre Spiritum Sanctum Paracletum," and many other pre-Nicene writings.

On the " Filioque" addition in the West, see detached note, p. 78.

τὸ σὺν Π. καὶ Υ. συμπροσκυνούμενον καὶ συνδοξαζόμενον. This clause cannot be traced to any earlier Creed that has been preserved; but the diction resembles that of Athanasius, ad Serap. i. 31, τὸ συνδοξαζόμενον Πατρὶ καὶ Υἱῷ καὶ θεολογούμενον μετὰ τοῦ Λόγου: ad Iov. ad fin. συνεδόξασαν αὐτὸ τῷ Πατρὶ καὶ τῷ Υἱῷ. The resemblance to the language of the Creed found in the common text of Cyril, Catech. iv. 16, disappears in the critical text of Reischl.

The idea underlying this clause is that the association of the Spirit with the Father and Son in equal worship and doxology exhibited the constant Christian belief in His co-essential Deity. The lex adorandi expressed the lex credendi. On the " Gloria Patri" see Basil, De Sp. Sancto, 4, 73. Somewhat similarly an anonymous writer, probably Hippolytus or Gaius, apud Eus. HE. v. 28, had appealed to the devotional hymnody of the Church as testifying to the Deity of Christ. On the value of liturgical formularies as preservative of the truth see Bull, Serm. 13, " The ancient Liturgies were so framed that they were a kind of system of orthodox divinity and antidotes against heresy," etc.

τὸ λαλῆσαν διὰ τῶν προφητῶν. This clause expresses the Scriptural teaching on the inspiration of " holy men of God " (2 Pet. i. 21). It thus unites the old Dispensation with the new, showing that there was no such antagonism between them as Marcion held, but that it was the same Spirit of God who spake in times past through the prophets (Heb. i. 1), who now, speaks through the Church to the hearts and consciences of Christians; cf., too, Mark xiii. 11. Still there is no reason for excluding a reference also to the prophets of the early Church: Acts xi. 27; xiii. 1; xv. 32; 1 Cor. xi.–xiv.; Rom. xii. 6; Eph. iii. 5; iv. 11; cf. Mark xiii. 11. See Selwyn's important note on 1 Pet. i. 10–11.

εἰς μίαν . . . ἐκκλησίαν. Following a group of clauses introduced by καί (implying πιστεύομεν), another καί would have been natural here, especially as the clauses are not grouped under ὁμολογοῦμεν (Hort). A clause referring to the Church was customary in early creeds: e.g. Cyprian (Ep. lxx. lxxvi.); Arius and Euzoius (Socr. i. 26); Marcellus (Epiphan. Haer. 72); early Creed of Jerusalem (but after εἰς ἓν βάπτισμα κ.τ.λ.); and Tertullian alludes to some recognition of the Church in the creed (De Bapt. 6, 11), although he does not give it a place in the Rule of Faith which he sets out at length.

It is remarkable that some Latin versions (followed by our English) have ignored εἰς, and read " et unam sanctam," etc., without any Greek authority.

The preposition here, as in the first opening of the creed, is important : it implies belief in the Church as an article of faith no less essential than those which precede it. On the Church as the Body of Christ and its implications, see an interesting study by A. E. J. Rawlinson in *Mysterium Christi*, pp. 225 ff.

The word ἐκκλησία was employed by the Greek translators to represent the Hebrew word which connoted the gathering together of the representative heads of the people of Israel, and the calling together of the congregation. The use of the word in St. Stephen's apology (Acts vii. 38) of the ancient congregation of Israel gives the key to its transferred use, general in the New Testament, of the Christian congregation, the Body of Christ assembled for the Eucharist, the true Israel of God. (Cf. Hort, *Christian Ecclesia*, pp. 3 ff.)

This clause εἰς μίαν . . . ἐκκλησίαν and the following ones are placed in the third division of the Creed under the Article dealing with the Holy Spirit, because the Church is now living under His Dispensation, and from Him draws all her life and powers of grace.

The four " notes " or inward characteristics of the Church here given are Unity, Holiness, Catholicity, and Apostolicity. The first and fourth are originally peculiar to Eastern Creeds. The second alone finds place in the Cyprianic Creed and that of Marcellus. The third first occurs in a creed (after appearing in the Nicene anathemas) in that of Arius and Euzoius (328) then in the Jerusalem Creed (along with the first and second), the Apost. Const. (along with the second and fourth), but not in a Western Creed until about the year 400 (see the Creed of Niceta of Remesiana in Burn, op. cit., p. 48).[1]

We may now examine them separately.

μίαν. Strictly speaking the unity of the Church is necessarily an invisible unity, since the greater number of its members have already passed beyond the veil. The unity is that of the one Body of Christ quickened by the One Spirit (Eph. iv. 6). On earth the unity is imperfectly realised. For a fuller discussion of the implications of this word, see F. W. Puller, *Primitive Saints and the See of Rome*, Lecture VI. See also St. Cyprian's great work *De Unitate Ecclesiae* 15, in which he interprets the Petrine passage (Matt. xvi.

---

[1] With these " notes " may be compared the three characteristics of " the Visible Church of Christ " given in Article XIX ; and the points enumerated in Acts ii. 41, 42 Baptism, Apostles' doctrine (opposed to heresy), the κοινωνία (opposed to schism), the Breaking of the Bread (Holy Communion), the Prayers (Liturgical Services).

F

18–19) in the sense of unity of foundation rather than of government or organisation.

ἁγίαν. The holiness of the Church is a necessary consequence of its constitution, though again imperfectly realised in its members, for it is the Body of Christ and the Temple of His Spirit. Thus, notwithstanding grave defects in the individual members, St. Paul addresses his letters to the "Holy ones" (ἁγίοις) in the various Churches. Cf. Acts ix. 32, Jude 3. The omission of this epithet in the Prayer Book version of this Creed may have been deliberate, possibly the action of Cranmer, as was certainly the case in his omission of the word εἰς before "the Church" and all that follows. But it should be noted that Latin versions dated from the 3rd Council of Toledo (589) usually omit the word "holy," as do all the late manuscripts of the definition of Chalcedon (see *Church Quarterly Review*, viii, 372).

καθολικήν. This epithet occurs in the Creed of Niceta of Remesiana, and like "Sanctorum communio" is typically Eastern. The word also occurs in the very early Creed of the Dair Balaizah Papyrus (see p. 4).

This epithet is thus explained by Cyril : Καθολικὴ μὲν οὖν καλεῖται διὰ τὸ κατὰ πάσης εἶναι τῆς οἰκουμένης ἀπὸ περάτων γῆς ἕως περάτων· καὶ διὰ τὸ διδάσκειν καθολικῶς καὶ ἀνελλιπῶς ἅπαντα τὰ εἰς γνῶσιν ἀνθρώπων ἐλθεῖν ὀφείλοντα δόγματα περί τε ὁρατῶν καὶ ἀοράτων πραγμάτων, ἐπιουρανίων τε καὶ ἐπιγείων, καὶ διὰ τὸ πᾶν γένος ἀνθρώπων εἰς εὐσέβειαν ὑποτάσσειν, ἀρχόντων τε καὶ ἀρχομένων, λογίων τε καὶ ἰδιωτῶν· καὶ διὰ τὸ καθολικῶς ἰατρεύειν μὲν καὶ θεραπεύειν ἅπαν τὸ τῶν ἁμαρτιῶν εἶδος τῶν διὰ ψυχῆς καὶ σώματος ἐπιτελουμένων, κεκτῆσθαι δὲ ἐν αὐτῇ πᾶσαν ἰδέαν ὀνομαζομένης ἀρετῆς ἐν ἔργοις τε καὶ λόγοις καὶ πνευματικοῖς παντοίοις χαρίσμασιν (Catech. xviii. 23). The original ecclesiastical use of the word is to denote "universal," "general," as opposed to "particular." So Ignatius, Smyrn. 8 (church); Justin Martyr, Dial. 82 and Theophilus, ad Autol. i. 13 (resurrection); Mart. Poly. (church). Thus it became easy for it to be used as a definite epithet for the orthodox body distinct from local schisms, and so to denote that organism which preserved the truth distinct from heresy. Examples of this sense will be found in Clement, Alex. Strom. vii. 106, 107; and in Latin in the "Muratorian Fragment." (Lightfoot, *Ignatius*, ii. 310.) Cf. Pacian, ad Symp. *passim*; Augustine, De Civ. Dei, xiii. 12, "Universa ecclesia ex multis constat ecclesiis."

ἀποστολικήν. The Church is built upon the foundation of the Apostles (Eph. ii. 20; 1 Cor. xii. 25; cf. Acts ii. 42). It dates from their days, preserves their doctrine, and continues their authority and ministry, which is that of Christ Himself (John xx. 21–23); and we may compare Clement Alex., Strom. vii. 108; and Tertullian's words already quoted, De Praescr. Haer. 20: "The

Apostles founded Churches, others received the Faith from these, and therefore though there are so many and so great Churches there is only one, the original one from the Apostles from which come all. So all are original and all Apostolic." This " note " also confirms what we have already noticed, the primacy of the Apostolic over the prophetic office ; and for this reason the ministry of the Church must always be Apostolic rather than prophetic, without in any way excluding the latter. For the spirit of prophecy in the Christian dispensation is the Spirit of Jesus (Acts xvi. 7), witnessing always to the historical life of God in the Flesh and confined to that final revelation (Rev. xix. 20). For a useful discussion of this note see *Mysterium Christi*, pp. 93 ff.

ἐν βάπτισμα. The Jerusalem Creed, no doubt under the influence of Mark i. 4 and parallels, added μετανοίας, which also stood in the shorter baptismal confessions. John's was the baptism of repentance only (Acts xix. 4) ; Christ's is also a baptism of regeneration (Matt. iii. 11) ; cf. Basil, De Sp. Sancto, 36. Ambrose, in Luc. iii. 3, " Aliud fuit baptisma paenitentiae, aliud gratiae est " (quoted by Swete on Mark i. 4). The phrase comes from Eph. iv. 5, and denotes one and the same baptism into the Name of the Blessed Trinity, whereby all are admitted into the One Body. The repetition of the spiritual birth is, of course, as impossible as that of the physical birth (John iii. 4). For the baptismal controversy between Cyprian and others who held that heretical and schismatical baptism was invalid, as against the Roman view later held against the Donatists by St. Augustine who admitted it, and the doctrine of the Sacraments involved in this controversy, see C. H. Turner in Swete, *Early History of the Church and Ministry*, pp. 152–69 ; Kidd, *Church History*, Vol. 2, pp. 411 ff. ; Bethune-Baker, op. cit., pp. 24, 386 ff., Bright, *Notes on the Canons*, p. 67 ; Armitage Robinson, *Epistle to the Ephesians*, pp. 206 ff.

εἰς ἄφεσιν ἁμαρτιῶν. The remission of sins necessarily follows from the nature of the sacrament of baptism (Acts ii. 38). The spiritual sphere of existence upon which the believer enters is a sphere of forgiveness, and though acts of sin may be committed they may be daily remitted. " Semel abluimus baptismate, cotidie abluimus oratione " (Augustine, Serm. ad Catech. xv). It must be remembered that there is a further analogy between the spiritual birth and the physical birth besides that of the impossibility of repetition ; neither is a guarantee of freedom from the possibility of disease and death in its own sphere.

There is nothing corresponding to the clause in the later Roman Creed known to St. Augustine, namely " the Communion of Saints," unless it is intended to be covered by the reference to one baptism. This could be the case only if that expression is taken in the sense of " communio in sacris " *i.e.* the sacraments, which perhaps was the original meaning of the clause. See Badcock, op. cit., pp. 242 ff. ;

Zahn, *Apostles' Creed*, Eng. trans., pp. 188 ff. ; Swete, *Apostles' Creed*, pp. 82 ff. ; cf. *Journal of Theological Studies*, vol. xxi., pp. 106 ff. On other interpretations of " Sanctorum Communio " cf. Zahn, *Apostles' Creed*, pp. 188 ff. ; Burn, *Niceta*, p. lxxvi.

ἀνάστασιν νεκρῶν. The phrase is Pauline, 1 Cor. xv. 21, " a resurrection of dead persons " ; that is, the general resurrection, and the form of expression excludes any false notions which might attach to the word σαρκός (*carnis*). Indeed, the phrase σαρκὸς ἀνάστασις (*resurrectio carnis*), though common in early creeds, occurs nowhere in Scripture, and its unguarded use amongst Christians gave rise to heathen scoffs and misinterpretations. Cyril avoided it in his Lectures, though it stood in his Creed (xviii. 1, 22, 28). The Aquileian *huius carnis* [1] was still more open to misconstruction, although it was really only meant to guard the " identity " of the future resurrection body with the present earthly one. According to St. Paul's illustration this " identity " is analogous to that of the seed and the plant (1 Cor. xv. 36), where the principle of life is continuous, though the outer organism wherein that life manifested itself is *changed*. The essential identity of the body therefore, which even in this life is dependent upon constant change, will be preserved through the changes involved in death and dissolution ; *alter et idem*. Cf. Luke xxiv. 39.

Christianity knows nothing of the " immortality of the soul " apart from the body. That was a conception of pagan philosophy which is really destructive of the belief in the continuance of our distinct and complete personal existence. The Christian doctrine teaches the restoration of the full personality of the individual which exists, as we know it, only in the vital union of body and soul (cf. Matt. x. 28). *Personal* identity may be held to consist in a fundamental, individualised energy which is gifted with the power of clothing itself with a suitable organism adapted to its environment. " By the Resurrection of the dead is meant the summoning of the whole man, soul and body, from death to Life in the Spirit. Just as man was once called into existence in the flesh in this transient world, so the resurrection is a new creation. Just as man's creation is indissolubly bound up with the existence of the world, and his existence is inseparably connected with the existence of the world, so man's new creation cannot be conceived apart from a new creation of the world of which it may be said that ' there shall be no more death.' " (Sasse in *Mysterium Christi*, p. 103 ; cf. the following article.)

Ζωὴν τοῦ μέλλοντος αἰῶνος. This expression replaces the ζωὴν αἰώνιον of earlier creeds, which was also the general Western form

[1] *Huius carnis* appears also in the Creed of Niceta of Remesiana (Hahn, p. 47), and in the creed delivered at the *traditio symboli* on Palm Sunday in the Mozarabic ritual (Hahn, p. 69). Zahn quotes also Pseudo-Aug. Serm. 242, and Missale Florentinum in Caspari, iv. 302.

of the article, *vitam aeternam*; but the Apost. Const. and Arius and Euzoius (Socr. i. 26) read, εἰς Ζωὴν τοῦ μέλλοντος αἰῶνος. Following on the above, this future life means " the beginning of a new World epoch; the end of the old and the beginning of a new aeon; the dawn of the new world of eternity and the Spirit." This dawn has as it were been anticipated in the resurrection of Christ, which is an eschatological event, the future become present; the end turned into beginning; so Christ is named " the beginning of the (new) creation of God." (Rev. iii. 14.)

Ζωή. Life is independent of time. Eternal life consists in the knowledge of God (John xvii. 3; 1 John v. 20) advanced, illuminated, and intensified by the Beatific Vision (1 John iii. 2).

NOTE ON THE CLAUSE "FILIOQUE"

To those who have studied the obscure history of the Creed of Constantinople, the vexed question of the Filioque clause will no longer present the same difficulty as was felt when it was thought to be an addition to the original Nicene Creed. Moreover, recent investigation into the history of the Great Schism which divided the East from the West forbids us to attach the same crucial importance to the controversy on this clause as was at one time the case.[1]

The history of the addition is obscure, but the date of its first appearance in a creed can (if the received texts are to be trusted) be fixed exactly. The third Council of Toledo, A.D. 589, was summoned by King Reccared in order that the Visigoths in Spain, who had hitherto professed the Arian faith, might publicly proclaim their renunciation of Arianism and adherence to Catholicism. The Council accordingly recited first the original Creed of Nicaea; and then the "Symbol of the 150" as in the Chalcedonian Definition, but with two additions : (a) *Deum de Deo* (= Θεὸν ἐκ Θεοῦ *of Nicaea*); (b) *et Filio* ("a Patre *et Filio* procedentem "). No reason can be assigned for these insertions save that they were believed to belong to the true text of the Creed, and were therefore, if not in the exemplar already, either written mechanically by the scribe or inserted because he thought that they ought to be there. Once inserted, the liturgical use of the Creed made the additions familiar.

The East has never admitted the second insertion, which was not apparently detected until the beginning of the ninth century; nor would Pope Leo the Third, while upholding the doctrine, admit the insertion into the Creed at Rome, although pressed by Charlemagne and Legates from the Council of Aachen, A.D. 809, to do so.[2] Thus at Rome, alone of Western churches, the Constantinopolitan Creed was without the addition, and Leo's Silver Shields [3] witnessed to

---

[1] See G. Every, *The Byzantine Patriarchate*, p. 186 and other references.

[2] The fact that it appears twice in some texts of the Creed of the Council of Toledo in 400—"The Father is unbegotten, the Son begotten, the Paraclete not begotten, but proceeding from the Father and the Son " (the phrase " a Patre Filioque procedens " occurs twice) (Hahn, p. 210) makes it probable that the insertion belongs to a stage of the local Arian controversy. Dr. Neale suggested that her acute controversy with Arianism led the Spanish Church to dislike the idea that the Father should have an attribute, namely of producing the Holy Ghost, which the Son had not, and therefore to make the addition to the Constantinopolitan Creed (Neale, *History of the Holy Eastern Church*, Introduction, ii. 1153 ; and cf. Swete, *History of the Doctrine of the Procession of the Holy Spirit*, p. 164). But see Burn, *Nicene Creed*, who does not accept the word "Filioque" in the Creed of the Council of Toledo.

[3] For Leo's Silver Shields in the Latin version see *Journal of Theological Studies*, October 1900, p. 110.

the original text of the symbol. When the insertion of the Filioque was first recognised at Rome is unknown.[1] Probably it came into popular use there when Benedict VIII (A.D. 1014) adopted the custom of chanting the Creed in the Liturgy. The Lateran Council of 1214 made *de fide* the definition "Spiritus Sanctus a Patre Filioque aequaliter procedit." The Decree of the Council of Florence 1439 went farther, explaining that the Greek δι' υἱοῦ must be understood by Catholics as if "ad hanc intelligentiam tendit, Filium quoque esse secundum Graecos quidem causam (αἰτίαν), secundum Latinos vero principium subsistentiae Spiritus Sancti sicut et Patrem." [2]

The doctrine of the Double Procession was probably brought to the English from Rome by Augustine, and was naturally held by them from the first. Gregory the Great had taught it explicitly,[3] and it found expression in the Synodal Letter of the Council of Heathfield (680).[4] Still more emphatic was the action of the Reformers, who imported it into the Litany of 1544, and into the Articles of 1563, Article V being taken from the Conference of Wurtemburg (1522).[5]

The substance of the doctrine, however, was from an early date widely if not universally held by Christian writers, though not necessarily in the same form. Those who inherited the pluralistic and subordinationist theology of Origen, who called the Holy Spirit a "γενητόν," "made by the Son," [6] came to teach that the Holy Spirit "proceeded" from the Father "through the Son." This phrase, however, is rarely found except in eirenic writings after the controversy had begun; an early example of which is a letter of Tarasius, Patriarch of Constantinople, to the Pope in 787 at the Second Council of Nicaea in which he proclaims his faith, εἰς τὸ Πνεῦμα τὸ Ἅγιον τὸ Κύριον καὶ Ζωοποιοῦν τὸ ἐκ τοῦ Πατρὸς δι' υἱοῦ ἐκπορευόμενον.[7] In earlier writers influenced by Origen and the school of Alexandria, the usual expression is that the Spirit "receives from the Son"; and later that "He shines forth or is revealed through the Son." Even Epiphanius, the inveterate opponent of Origen, taught that the Spirit "proceeds from the Father and receives from the Son"; "is out of the same sub-

[1] But see Pearson on the Creed, Article Eight; and Neale, op. cit., ii. 1167. It is certain that it received formal recognition and sanction in the Second Council of Lyon, A.D. 1274.

[2] Hefele, *Concilia*, vii, p. 748.

[3] Gregory, Moral. i. 22; Hom. in Evang. 11. 26.

[4] Bede, HE. iv. 17. See also *Church Quarterly Review*, iii, p. 445.

[5] Gibson, *Articles*, p. 198. It is, however, archaeologically interesting that in the Stowe Missal the Filioque is the work of a later handwriting between the lines of the Nicene Creed, which is without it. This shows that the addition spread rather slowly in this country between 589 and 1014. I owe this information to the Rev. E. Every of Merton College.

[6] Origen, In Ioan. xi. 6. See Swete, *Apostles' Creed*, pp. 30 ff.

[7] Mansi, xii. 122.

stance of the Father and the Son." Gregory of Nyssa [1] uses the
expression that the Holy Spirit is attached to (ἔχεται) the Only-
Begotten; Cyril of Alexandria's belief in the Double Procession
is equally clear; though the chief thing he insisted upon was His
mission from the Son.[2] On the other hand, the Antiochene school
represented by Theodore of Mopsuestia and Theodoret explicitly
denied the Double Procession. " If Cyril means that the Spirit
has His existence from the Son, or through the Son," says Theodoret
in answer to Cyril's Ninth Anathema, " we reject this teaching as
blasphemous and impious." It is, however, doubtful if either
Cyril [3] or any other Greek Father ever maintained that the Spirit
proceeded from the Son in the same way that he proceeds from
the Father; though as we have seen something very like this became
de fide at Rome. Dr. Prestige maintains that the Cappadocian
Fathers in adopting the *homoousion* found the solution of the
problem of the Divine Monarchia which the Antiochenes had failed
to discover.[4] Thus, Gregory of Nyssa explains the procession
(ἐκπόρευσις) of the Spirit as the completion of that attribute of
generation which was as much an attribute of the Godhead in the
idea of the Fathers as unity and omnipotence.[5] According to
them the Godhead is the whole Trinity and not one Person of It.
But in the West the doctrine of the Double Procession was not
derived from the teaching of Origen and Alexandria but from the
" economic " tradition which found its fullest expression in Irenaeus
and Tertullian. Thus Tertullian wrote " Spiritum non aliunde
puto quam a Patre per Filium " ; " Tertius est Spiritus a Deo et
Filio ; sicut tertius a radice fructus ex frutice, et tertius a fonte
rivus ex flumine, et tertius a sole apex ex radio. . . . Ita Trinitas
per consertos et connectos gradus a Patre decurrens monarchiae
nihil obstrepit." [6] Even more clearly St. Augustine following
St. Ambrose states " Filius de Patre natus est, et Spiritus Sanctus
de Patre principaliter et sine ullo temporis intervallo dante com-
muniter et de utroque procedit." Again " His aliquis forsitan
quaerat utrum et a Filio procedat Spiritus Sanctus. Filius enim

[1] Greg. Nyss., Adv. Maced. ii. 10 ; c. Eun., Migne 45. 464 B, C ; Non
tres Dei, Migne 45. 133 B, C, quoted by Prestige, op. cit., p. 252. Basil, Ep.
xxviii. 4 ; De Sp. Sanct. 64.
[2] Cyril of Alexandria, Adv. Nest. 9e ; Dial de Trin. 618e ; In Ioan.
858b–859e ; and for Cyril's doctrine as a whole see passages cited by Swete,
pp. 143 ff., and Pusey, " *A Letter on the Clause ' And the Son' in the Nicene
Creed.*"
[3] Cyril, Epist. 3 ad Nest., 9th Anath. For the Creed ascribed to Theodore
see Hahn, *Symbole,*[3] p. 302. For Theodore of Mopsuestia see Prestige, op.
cit., p. 250.
[4] Op. cit., pp. 256 f.
[5] Greg. Nyss., Non tres Dei, Migne 45. 125, 133.
[6] Tertullian, Adv. Prax. 4 and 8. Cf. Hilary of Poitiers, De Trin. xii.
55, 57, who, probably under Eastern influence, has " ex Patre per Filium,"
and cf. for the " economic " tradition Rawlinson, *Essays on the Trinity and
Incarnation*, p. 258, and Loofs, *Paulus von Samosata*, p. 212.

solius Patris est Filius et Pater solius Filii est pater : Spiritus autem sanctus non est unius eorum Spiritus sed amborum." Again, commenting on John xxi. 22, he asks, " Quid enim alius significavit illa insufflatio nisi quod procedat Spiritus Sanctus et de Ipso ? " And again, " Insufflando significavit Spiritum Sanctum non Patris solius esse Spiritum, sed et suum." [1] The clause itself was probably inserted against some heresy, possibly a revival of Adoptionism becoming prevalent in the West. Thus, the doctrine hardens into the teaching of the Schoolmen as represented by St. Thomas Aquinas, who remarks that there was no other way of distinguishing between the Second and the Third Persons of the Blessed Trinity. " Si Spiritus Sanctus non esset a Filio, nullo modo posset ab Eo personaliter distingui." (Summa Theol. I., Q. 36, Art. 2.)

In conclusion, the Scriptural proofs usually cited in support of the doctrine—namely, John xiv. 16, 17 ; xv. 26 ; xvi. 14 ; xx. 22 ; Rom. viii. 9, 10, etc.—are inconclusive because they can equally well refer only to the temporal mission of the Holy Ghost, as the Power of God working through the glorified humanity of the Incarnate Son, which the Greeks, of course, have never questioned. What they have consistently questioned is the legitimacy of transferring Scriptural expressions of this kind to the eternal relationships of the Holy Trinity, about which the oecumenical Faith has defined nothing beyond the consubstantiality of the Three Persons. But they are undoubtedly right in maintaining the protest of the Orthodox Church that the *Filioque* was the forerunner of other definitions of the faith which the Western Church has made obligatory, without consulting the Eastern, and thereby begun a process which has culminated in the Vatican decrees of 1870. " Change the Creed," it is said, " on your own authority and you finally claim an authority over the Creed."

On the whole subject see Prestige, op. cit., pp. 249–55 and 292 ; Burn, *Introduction to the Creeds*, pp. 114 ff. ; Swete, *History of the Doctrine of the Procession of the Holy Spirit*, pp. 143 ff. ; Gibson, *Articles*, and *The Three Creeds*, pp. 212 ff. ; Mansi, ix. 977 ; Badcock, op. cit., pp. 215 ff. Cf. *Church Quarterly Review*, Vol. 3, pp. 42 ff.

[1] Augustine, De Trin. xv. 47, xc. 9 ; In Ioan. xvi. 13 ; cxxii. 4 ; Ambrose, De Spirit. Sanct. i. 11 ; Theodoret, v. 47b (Berlin Corpus). Cf. Chrysostom, Hom. lxxii, quoted by Gibson, op. cit., p. 214.

VII. CREEDS OF EPIPHANIUS

A. THE SHORTER FORM

At the end of Chapter 118 of the Ancoratus (the chapter in which this Creed occurs) Epiphanius remarks that " it was handed down from the Holy Apostles and in the Church, the Holy City, from all the Bishops at that time about 310 in number." By the Holy City may be meant either Nicaea itself or, as Kattenbusch thought, Jerusalem, or as Holl thinks, the Church itself. In any case the 310 must mean Nicaea. Compare the words of Theodoret, HE. ii. 27. " The Faith which was founded at Nicaea according to the authority of the Apostles." Hence the conclusion that the Creed which precedes this sentence was intended to be N and not C and was originally so written. See p. 68.

Ancoratus 118.

Πιστεύομεν εἰς ἕνα Θεὸν Πατέρα παντοκράτορα
  ποιητὴν οὐρανοῦ τε καὶ γῆς, ὁρατῶν τε πάντων καὶ ἀοράτων·
καὶ εἰς ἕνα Κύριον Ἰησοῦν Χριστόν,
  τὸν Υἱὸν τοῦ Θεοῦ τὸν μονογενῆ
  τὸν ἐκ τοῦ Πατρὸς γεννηθέντα πρὸ πάντων τῶν αἰώνων,
  τουτέστιν ἐκ τῆς οὐσίας τοῦ Πατρός,
  Φῶς ἐκ Φωτός,
  Θεὸν ἀληθινὸν ἐκ Θεοῦ ἀληθινοῦ,
  γεννηθέντα οὐ ποιηθέντα,
  ὁμοούσιον τῷ Πατρί,
  δι' οὗ τὰ πάντα ἐγένετο, τά τε ἐν τοῖς οὐρανοῖς καὶ τὰ ἐν τῇ γῇ·
  τὸν δι' ἡμᾶς τοὺς ἀνθρώπους καὶ διὰ τὴν ἡμετέραν σωτηρίαν
    κατελθόντα ἐκ τῶν οὐρανῶν,
  καὶ σαρκωθέντα ἐκ Πνεύματος Ἁγίου καὶ Μαρίας τῆς παρθένου,
  καὶ ἐνανθρωπήσαντα,
  σταυρωθέντα τε ὑπὲρ ἡμῶν ἐπὶ Ποντίου Πιλάτου,
  καὶ παθόντα καὶ ταφέντα,
  καὶ ἀναστάντα τῇ τρίτῃ ἡμέρᾳ κατὰ τὰς γραφάς,
  καὶ ἀνελθόντα εἰς τοὺς οὐρανούς,
  καὶ καθεζόμενον ἐκ δεξιῶν τοῦ Πατρός,
  καὶ πάλιν ἐρχόμενον μετὰ δόξης κρῖναι ζῶντας καὶ νεκρούς,
  οὗ τῆς βασιλείας οὐκ ἔσται τέλος·
καὶ εἰς τὸ Πνεῦμα τὸ ἅγιον τὸ κύριον καὶ τὸ ζωοποιόν,
  τὸ ἐκ τοῦ Πατρὸς ἐκπορευόμενον,
  τὸ σὺν Πατρὶ καὶ Υἱῷ συμπροσκυνούμενον καὶ συνδοξαζό-
    μενον,
  τὸ λαλῆσαν διὰ τῶν προφητῶν·
εἰς μίαν ἁγίαν καθολικὴν καὶ ἀποστολικὴν ἐκκλησίαν.
ὁμολογοῦμεν ἓν βάπτισμα εἰς ἄφεσιν ἁμαρτιῶν·

προσδοκῶμεν ἀνάστασιν νεκρῶν
καὶ ζωὴν τοῦ μέλλοντος αἰῶνος.
Ἀμήν.

Τοὺς δὲ λέγοντας Ἦν ποτε ὅτε οὐκ ἦν, καὶ πρὶν γεννηθῆναι οὐκ
ἦν, ἢ ὅτι ἐξ οὐκ ὄντων ἐγένετο, ἢ ἐξ ἑτέρας ὑποστάσεως ἢ
οὐσίας φάσκοντας εἶναι ῥευστὸν ἢ ἀλλοιωτὸν τὸν τοῦ Θεοῦ
Υἱόν, τούτους ἀναθεματίζει ἡ καθολικὴ καὶ ἀποστολικὴ
ἐκκλησία.

B. THE LONGER FORM

THIS Creed is in reality an annotated edition of N with catechetical
explanations not suitable for repetition, but a sort of syllabus of
instruction; with the addition of certain clauses which can be
paralleled in the Creeds of Antioch, and may be assumed to be
derived from the local baptismal creed of Salamis in Cyprus, of
which Epiphanius was Bishop. In this respect it strongly resembles
the Creed of Jerome, the Armenian Creed, and a document known
as " Interpretatio in symbolum." (See Badcock, p. 51.)

Ancoratus 119.

Πιστεύομεν εἰς ἕνα Θεόν, Πατέρα παντοκράτορα, πάντων ἀοράτων τε
    καὶ ὁρατῶν ποιητήν·
καὶ εἰς ἕνα Κύριον Ἰησοῦν Χριστόν, τὸν Υἱὸν τοῦ Θεοῦ,
    γεννηθέντα ἐκ Θεοῦ Πατρὸς μονογενῆ
    τουτέστιν ἐκ τῆς οὐσίας τοῦ Πατρός
    Θεὸν ἐκ Θεοῦ, Φῶς ἐκ Φωτός, Θεὸν ἀληθινὸν ἐκ Θεοῦ ἀληθινοῦ,
    γεννηθέντα οὐ ποιηθέντα,
    ὁμοούσιον τῷ Πατρί,
    δι' οὗ τὰ πάντα ἐγένετο, τά τε ἐν τοῖς οὐρανοῖς καὶ τὰ ἐν τῇ γῇ,
        ὁρατά τε καὶ ἀόρατα.
    τὸν δι' ἡμᾶς τοὺς ἀνθρώπους καὶ διὰ τὴν ἡμετέραν σωτηρίαν
        κατελθόντα καὶ σαρκωθέντα, τουτέστι γεννηθέντα τελείως
        ἐκ τῆς ἁγίας Μαρίας τῆς ἀειπαρθένου διὰ Πνεύματος
        Ἁγίου,
    ἐνανθρωπήσαντα, τουτέστι τέλειον ἄνθρωπον λαβόντα, ψυχὴν
        καὶ σῶμα καὶ νοῦν καὶ πάντα, εἴ τι ἐστὶν ἄνθρωπος, χωρὶς
        ἁμαρτίας, οὐκ ἀπὸ σπέρματος ἀνδρός, οὐδὲ ἐν ἀνθρώπῳ,
        ἀλλ' εἰς ἑαυτὸν σάρκα ἀναπλάσαντα εἰς μίαν ἁγίαν ἑνότητα·
        οὐ καθάπερ ἐν προφήταις ἐνέπνευσέ τε καὶ ἐλάλησε καὶ
        ἐνήργησεν, ἀλλὰ τελείως ἐνανθρωπήσαντα (ὁ γὰρ Λόγος
        σὰρξ ἐγένετο, οὐ τροπὴν ὑποστὰς οὐδὲ μεταβαλὼν τὴν
        ἑαυτοῦ θεότητα εἰς ἀνθρωπότητα), εἰς μίαν συνενώσαντα
        ἑαυτοῦ ἁγίαν τελειότητά τε καὶ θεότητα (εἷς γάρ ἐστι
        Κύριος Ἰησοῦς Χριστὸς καὶ οὐ δύο, ὁ αὐτὸς Θεός, ὁ αὐτὸς
        Κύριος, ὁ αὐτὸς βασιλεύς).
    παθόντα δὲ τὸν αὐτὸν ἐν σαρκί,
    καὶ ἀναστάντα καὶ ἀνελθόντα εἰς τοὺς οὐρανοὺς ἐν αὐτῷ τῷ
        σώματι

ἐνδόξως καθίσαντα ἐν δεξιᾷ τοῦ Πατρός,
ἐρχόμενον ἐν αὐτῷ τῷ σώματι ἐν δόξῃ κρῖναι ζῶντας καὶ νεκρούς,
οὗ τῆς βασιλείας οὐκ ἔσται τέλος·
καὶ εἰς τὸ Ἅγιον Πνεῦμα πιστεύομεν,
τὸ λαλῆσαν ἐν νόμῳ καὶ κηρῦξαν ἐν τοῖς προφήταις καὶ κατα-
βὰν ἐπὶ τὸν Ἰορδάνην, λαλοῦν ἐν ἀποστόλοις, οἰκοῦν ἐν
ἁγίοις·
οὕτως δὲ πιστεύομεν ἐν αὐτῷ ὅτι ἐστὶν Πνεῦμα Ἅγιον,
Πνεῦμα Θεοῦ, Πνεῦμα τέλειον, Πνεῦμα παράκλητον, ἄκτισ-
τον,
ἐκ τοῦ Πατρὸς ἐκπορευόμενον καὶ ἐκ τοῦ Υἱοῦ λαμβανόμενον
καὶ πιστευόμενον.
πιστεύομεν εἰς μίαν καθολικὴν καὶ ἀποστολικὴν ἐκκλησίαν
καὶ εἰς ἓν βάπτισμα μετανοίας,
καὶ εἰς ἀνάστασιν νεκρῶν καὶ κρίσιν δικαίαν ψυχῶν καὶ
σωμάτων,
καὶ εἰς βασιλείαν οὐρανῶν καὶ εἰς ζωὴν αἰώνιον.
Τοὺς δὲ λέγοντας ὅτι ἦν ποτε ὅτε οὐκ ἦν ὁ Υἱὸς ἢ τὸ Πνεῦμα τὸ
Ἅγιον, ἢ ὅτι ἐξ οὐκ ὄντων ἐγένετο ἢ ἐξ ἑτέρας ὑποστάσεως ἢ οὐσίας,
φάσκοντας εἶναι τρεπτὸν ἢ ἀλλοιωτὸν τὸν Υἱὸν τοῦ Θεοῦ ἢ τὸ Ἅγιον
Πνεῦμα, τούτους ἀναθεματίζει ἡ καθολικὴ καὶ ἀποστολικὴ ἐκκλησία,
ἡ μήτηρ ὑμῶν τε καὶ ἡμῶν· καὶ πάλιν ἀναθεματίζομεν τοὺς μὴ ὁμολο-
γοῦντας ἀνάστασιν νεκρῶν καὶ πάσας τὰς αἱρέσεις τὰς μὴ ἐκ ταύτης
τῆς ὀρθῆς πίστεως οὔσας.

THE EPISTLES OF CYRIL

II. AND III. TO NESTORIUS AND TO JOHN OF ANTIOCH

TU REX GLORIAE, CHRISTE,
TU PATRIS SEMPITERNUS ES FILIUS.

TU AD LIBERANDUM MUNDUM SUSCEPISTI HOMINEM
NON HORRUISTI VIRGINIS UTERUM.

THE EPISTLES OF CYRIL

INTRODUCTION

I. HISTORICAL

THE circumstances which led to the intervention of Cyril in the Nestorian controversy must be briefly told.

After the death of Archbishop Sisinnius, at the close of the year 427, Nestorius, a priest of Antioch and pupil of Theodore of Mopsuestia (392–428), was consecrated in April 428 to the see of Constantinople. He took with him from Antioch a domestic chaplain (*syncellus*) named Anastasius, who was an ardent disciple of Theodore's teaching and methods of thought.[1] In one of his Advent sermons upon the Incarnation Anastasius decried the Catholic practice of calling the Virgin Mary *Theotokos*—Θεοτόκον τὴν Μαρίαν καλείτω μηδείς· Μαρία γὰρ ἄνθρωπος ἦν· ὑπὸ ἀνθρώπου δὲ Θεὸν τεχθῆναι ἀδύνατον. (Socr. vii. 32.)

This teaching Nestorius publicly approved, and he himself preached a course of sermons in which he drew a distinction between " Emmanuel," born of Mary, and the Logos who dwelt in him.[2] Eusebius, a lawyer, afterwards Bishop of Dorylaeum, led the Catholic opposition to this erroneous doctrine, and denounced Nestorius as a heretic, confronting him with his own creed (see above, p. 59). Marius Mercator at the same time published a tract against Nestorius ; but neither he nor Eusebius accurately grasped the vital point of the heresy. They treated it as if it was Trinitarian instead of Christological. Nestorius never denied the *hypostasis* of the Word : he did deny that the Word really became Flesh.

Nestorius' sermons soon began to circulate at Rome and in Egypt, particularly amongst the monks. Cyril, in his Paschal homily for Easter, 429, written early in January, took occasion to dwell upon the unity of Christ's Person, and the doctrinal value of the Virgin's title of *Theotokos* ; and when his attention was especially drawn to the mischief which Nestorius' sermons were doing he issued an encyclical letter to the Monks of Egypt in which he stated the Catholic doctrine of the Incarnation.

This encyclical reached Nestorius in Constantinople and kindled his keen resentment against Cyril, whom he proceeded to calumniate. Meanwhile Pope Caelestine, into whose hands Nestorius' sermons

---

[1] On the widespread influence of Theodore and his responsibility for Nestorianism and Pelagianism see the *Church Quarterly Review*, i. 115 ff.

[2] These sermons are extant in a Latin version made by Marius Mercator, the opponent of Pelagius, also a native of Africa (418–60) and are most easily available in Loofs' *Nestoriana*.

had come, wrote to Cyril asking if they really were productions of Nestorius. Upon this Cyril wrote to Nestorius, urging him to restore peace by employing the term *Theotokos* (Epist. ad Nestor. 1). Nestorius' reply was conciliatory but evasive. And he now took the opportunity of writing to Caelestine respecting four Pelagian bishops at Constantinople, and ending his letter with an attack upon the Catholics, who called the Virgin *Theotokos*. The Pope did not know Greek, and therefore knew Cyril and Nestorius only in translation. On the receipt of this letter, therefore, and the tracts which accompanied it, Caelestine employed Cassian, who knew both, to refute Nestorius. This he did in seven books on the Incarnation. This Cassian was to be the opponent of Pelagius, revealing the subtle connexion between Nestorianism and Pelagianism, to which attention has so often been called. Meanwhile Cyril had received from his agents at Constantinople copies of further Nestorian writings, and also learnt the names of his calumniators, who turned out to be certain Alexandrians who had been convicted for various crimes. Hereupon, in February 430 he wrote his Second Letter to Nestorius, which now follows (Epist. 2 ad Nest., *Obloquuntur*).

It must, however, at the outset be made clear that the controversy reveals both Cyril and Nestorius in no happy light. Nestorius himself was a rigorous persecutor, and Cyril betrays throughout antagonism not only to Nestorius himself but also to his See, which he regarded as upstart, challenging the hitherto undisputed authority of Alexandria. Much, therefore, must be discounted in the assertions on either side against the other. Similarly, in the Christological aspect of the controversy, it is now regarded as questionable whether Nestorius himself was a Nestorian in the strict sense of that term. The older Church histories were written before the discovery early in the twentieth century of Nestorius' Apologia concealed under the cryptic name of the *Bazaar of Heracleides*, in which he vindicates his orthodoxy in terms which show that he would have accepted the definition of the Council of Chalcedon. But this vindication of Nestorius need not in any way detract from the claim of Cyril to be regarded as a sincere, able, and devoted defender of the traditional Christian faith in its catholicity and antiquity. Throughout the following notes it should also be borne in mind that the controversy is in essence not one between two eminent teachers or between two rival sees, but between two ancient Christologies, which had persisted in their separation and continued to persist on parallel lines despite the attempt made at Chalcedon to reconcile them by a compromising formula. For full discussion of the disputants and their views and the historical position in general, see Kidd, *Church History*, vol. 3, pp. 192–216; Duchesne, *Ancient History of the Church*, vol. 3, pp. 219 ff.; Dorner, *Doctrine of the Person of Christ*, II. 1. 51 ff. On the doctrinal position of Nestorius see Bethune-

Baker, *Nestorius and His Teaching* (Cambridge, 1908); Loofs, *Nestorius and His Place in Christian Doctrine* (Cambridge, 1914); *Journal of Theological Studies*, April 1911, January and April 1915, October 1917; Mason, *Chalcedonian Doctrine*, pp. 26 ff.; Driver and Hodgson, *Bazaar of Heracleides*, Introduction and Notes; Sellers, *Two Ancient Christologies*, pp. 143 ff.; Prestige, *Fathers and Heretics*, pp. 247 ff.

II. THEOLOGICAL

THE Christological controversies of the fourth and fifth centuries followed all too quickly upon the Council of Nicaea, before the Church had time to give precision to the still fluid terminology, in which both the theological and Christological doctrines had been or were to be expressed. This partly explains their bewildering character and difficulty. It would be wrong to suppose that they were the direct result of Arianism itself; their roots can already be discerned in the Christology of Lucian of Antioch,[1] the teacher of Arius, as well as in the controversy between Paul of Samosata and his Alexandrian judges in 269. It is commonly supposed that Arius taught a Christology according to which, by a sort of inverted *kenosis*, the Logos took the place of the human soul (ψυχή) in Christ; a theory adopted, though with important differences, by Apollinarius, Bishop of Laodicea (*c.* 390). The reason for the addition of ἐνανθρωπήσαντα to σαρκωθέντα in the Nicene Creed was probably to guard against theories of this kind, which denied a real Incarnation of the Son of God. The Creed of Arius and Euzoius (see p. 55) has only σαρκωθέντα which, combined with παθόντα, was a doubtfully orthodox statement. But it was orthodox in comparison with the Anomoean Creed of Eudoxius, Bishop of Constantinople (370), which asserted καὶ εἰς Κύριον . . . (πιστεύομεν) σαρκωθέντα οὐκ ἐνανθρωπήσαντα, οὔτε γὰρ ψυχὴν ἀνθρωπίνην ἀνείληφεν ἀλλὰ σάρξ γέγονεν . . . οὐ δύο φύσεις, ἐπεὶ μὴ τέλειος ἦν ἄνθρωπος ἀλλ' ἀντὶ ψυχῆς Θεὸς ἔνσαρκος, μία τὸ ὅλον κατὰ σύνθεσιν φύσις. (Doctrina Incarnationis, 9.) The Letter of St. Athanasius to Epictetus, Bishop of Corinth (370), which was later regarded as a standard of orthodoxy by Alexandrians and Antiochenes alike, together with the two letters of the same date to Adelphicus and Maximus [2] reveal the extremes of two positions in Christology existing side by side in the Greek world, and recognisable as exaggerations of the two schools of thought connected with Alexandria and Antioch. These crude Christological representations on the one side and the other began

---

[1] See Bethune-Baker, *Early History of Christian Doctrine*, p. 111; Gwatkin, *Arianism*, p. 17. It must, however, be remembered that the evidence for the Christological doctrines attributed to Lucian and Arius is uncertain and fragmentary. See also Epiphanius (Ancoratus, 23), a writer not to be implicitly trusted in his statements about heretics.

[2] All these are translated in Robertson, *Athanasius*, pp. 570 ff.

G

to receive definite expression in the teaching of Apollinarius, which was directed not so much against Arianism as against the great Antiochene doctors, Eustathius of Antioch and Diodore of Tarsus. Against their doctrine of ἄλλος καὶ ἄλλος (a twofold Sonship), in the Person of Christ, a parallelism elaborated by their successors Theodore of Mopsuestia and Nestorius, Apollinarius revived the Lucianic idea of the Λόγος σαρκωθείς, according to which, as the result of a mixture (σύγχυσις, κρᾶσις, or μίξις) of the two elements, there is but one *composite* nature of Christ, a doctrine which lies at the root of the movement in Christology afterwards known as Monophysitism.

To speculations, attempting on the one side or the other to explain or define the mode of the Incarnation, Athanasius, followed by Cyril of Alexandria and afterwards by Leo, opposed the Christian Rule of Faith as it had been received through such teachers as Cyril of Jerusalem, Methodius, Ambrose, Cyprian, Irenaeus, Ignatius, and finally St. Paul himself (Rom. i. 3). The doctrine of Athanasius [1] based on that Rule, as developed by such teachers, maintained (1) that the Logos incarnate is one Person (εἷς) but existing in two " conditions," Godhead and Manhood, which are not in Him two " persons," ἄλλος καὶ ἄλλος, but rather ἄλλο καὶ ἄλλο, two elements (πράγματα) indivisible (ἀδιάκριτα) but never confused or mixed (ἀσύγχυτα). The two Elements, however, are not parallel, as the Antiochenes since Paul of Samosata, but not Ignatius, had taught. Nor are they interchangeable ; though attempts were made by the use of what was called ἀντίδοσις or in Latin *communicatio idiomatum*, whereby the sayings and doings of our Lord in the Gospels are attributed to Him in either Nature, each being in absolute possession of the other. (2) An important addition to this is the idea found already in the De Incarnatione (cc. 8 and 30) that the Logos " makes His own " (ἰδιοποιεῖται) the human nature with the mind and sufferings of the

---

[1] The majority of scholars hold that the works *Contra Arianos*, Book IV, and the two books against Apollinarius, cannot be attributed to Athanasius himself, though they are evidently by one of the same school. But some writers, such as Weigl, still hold them to be genuine, and from them are able to attribute to Athanasius a far more elaborate Christology than would appear from the rest of his works. There are resemblances in c. Apoll. to the Letter Ad Epictetum, but the fact that Apollinarius is nowhere mentioned by name suggests that the author was a contemporary and acquainted with Athanasius. Very much of Book I is occupied with criticisms of ideas which cannot by any stretch of imagination be supposed to concern Apollinarius. The second book appears to be a compendium of the first, and the emphasis laid on the charge of being a follower both of Arius and Paul of Samosata is evidence that it was not the work of Athanasius. It also shows knowledge of the Nestorian and Monophysite controversies, and probably belongs to the middle of the fifth or to the early sixth century. The first mention of this book was by Proclus at the Council of 553. See Raven, *Apollinarianism*, pp. 242–9 ; and for the Christology of Athanasius apart from these works see Sellers, *Two Ancient Christologies*, pp. 33 ff., and Prestige, *Fathers and Heretics*, pp. 137 ff.

"Man" (ἄνθρωπος), which in Athanasius meant real humanity in all its fullness (c. Ar. iii. 22. 53–56; ad Epict. 6; De Incarn. 18). (3) This union was and remains a mystery not to be comprehended by the understanding: but that the higher is the dominant element (τὸ ἡγεμονικόν), a phrase used by Plato in his trichotomy of the soul, is taken for granted by Athanasius as implicit in the Rule of Faith. Nevertheless, the whole position of Athanasius, as of Cyril, rests on a real *religious* interest and the need of a genuine, complete, and personal Saviour, who is God and Man, Body, Soul and Spirit, as alone able to accomplish the redemption of sinful man. Such a unity he could not see either in the rending of the mystery "into a Dyad of Sons" (Def. Chalced. 1. 101) or in the elimination or diminution of one of the two elements. His soteriology sought for a doctrine of Christ already to be found in Irenaeus, wherein Creator and created need not be forever divided, or lost in the confusion of natures (ad Adelph. 3; ad Max. 2). Athanasius safeguards what was called by later authors μία θεανδρικὴ ἐνέργεια,[1] and always looked to the *fact* of Christ as one composite Whole, though it must be admitted that he failed to approach the philosophical side of the question, which is what the Antiochenes and Apollinarius were trying to do.

The same must be said of Cyril, who accepted the Rule of Faith as understood by Athanasius, even to the extent of adopting phrases which were erroneously attributed to Athanasius, but really belong to Apollinarius. Cyril's position is not free from ambiguity, nor is he a wholly consistent theologian. He has been described as an " eclectic " thinker, whose view is sometimes distorted or exaggerated by animus against his great opponent, by political considerations, and by ecclesiastical ambition, which made him ready at times to approach nearer to the position of such men as John of Antioch and Theodoret, the representatives of Antiochene Christology in his period. To Athanasius' Rule of Faith Cyril may be said to have added the following developments:

(1) While, like Athanasius, making Christ's Person, the One Lord, the foundation of his whole teaching, he added without qualification the two " natures " (δύο φύσεις), a phrase which he took over from the Cappadocian Fathers, Basil and the two Gregories, who had adopted a mediating position between the two schools, thus giving precision to Athanasius' ἄλλο καὶ ἄλλο and guarding against errors on both sides.

(2) He adopted the Apollinarian phrase, thinking it to be Athanasian, μία φύσις τοῦ Λόγου σεσαρκωμένη or σεσαρκωμένου, but left it ambiguous as to the sense in which φύσις is used, whether as " nature " in the ordinary sense of the word, or as equivalent or alternative to ὑπόστασις and perhaps to the Latin *persona*, and as some would say, to πρόσωπον (cf. Def. Chalced. ll. 121–2); though it cannot always be clear when Cyril is accommodating himself to the

[1] I.e. Dionysius the Areopagite and Severus.

position of his critics. If, however, he was using the word φύσις in its ordinary meaning of "nature," Cyril must be declared a Monophysite as Dr. Raven believes him to be (op. cit., p. 231). If the latter, he is merely reproducing in another form the ἄλλο καὶ ἄλλο of the Athanasian Christology. Certainly Apollinarius meant by that phrase that the Logos is His own φύσις, which is now incarnate (σεσαρκωμένη), and the Person who from eternity was simple and single is now composite; in other words, Jesus Christ, is μία φύσις, one and the same Person or *Hypostasis*.[1]

(3) Cyril, again following Athanasius but with greater precision, adopted a position akin to that in the preceding paragraph, viz., that a distinction must be drawn between the Λόγος ἄσαρκος and the Λόγος ἔνσαρκος—the Logos before the Incarnation, and the Logos Incarnate regarded as θεικῶς and σωματικῶς ἐνεργῶν (De Recta Fide ad Reg.). That is to say, that which cannot be attributed to the Logos Discarnate, *e.g.* Suffering or Exaltation, can be attributed to Him as Christ Incarnate.

(4) Cyril constantly repeats the phrase ἐκ δυοῖν φυσέων of the One Christ and Son, but after the union there can be no such division. Not that he thought of the two Natures in abstraction; both are real, but after the Incarnation they are *recognised* as two θεωρίᾳ μόνῃ—that is, to contemplation only (Adv. Nest. 2). It follows that the Incarnate Christ was more properly described as One from both (εἷς ἐξ ἀμφοῖν), a formula not adopted at Chalcedon in deference to Leo's protest as being too close to the teaching of Eutyches. The word "recognized" (γνωριζόμενον), however, with all that it implies was adopted at Chalcedon (Def. 1. 119), as was also the word *prosopon* as alternative to *hypostasis*, to satisfy the Antiochenes.

(5) Cyril while making the fullest use of the *communicatio idiomatum* carries further than Athanasius did the idea of the *kenosis*—a speculation in which Hilary of Poitiers, the friend and pupil of the Cappadocian Fathers, who allowed the idea of progress (προκοπή : *e.g.* Basil, Ep. clxxvi. 1 ; cf. Athanasius, De Synod. 26, 45) in the human life of the Logos, had led the way. Cyril said that the Logos *voluntarily* allowed the *measures* (τὰ μέτρα), that is to say, the experiences of humanity, to "prevail" in the case of Christ,[2] though he does not solve the problem of our Lord's human knowledge.

In studying the Oecumenical Documents we are not concerned with the more subtle developments of Cyril's Christology. They should be read in such works as *Quod Unus Sit Christus* (Pusey's

---

[1] Whether this implies what we should in modern terms call personality or subject remains doubtful. See a Letter of the late Canon Lacey published in Rawlinson, *Essays on the Trinity and Incarnation*, p. 392 ; but it must not be assumed that either Athanasius or Cyril would have called the Logos the *Subject* of an inspired Humanity or even of a human experience.

[2] See note on κένωσιν, Ep. 3 ad Nest, l. 204 (p. 121).

Edition, vol. vii, part i, pp. 230 ff.) and in his most recent expositor Weigl, *Christologie vom Tode des Athanasius bis zum Ausbruch des nestorianischen Streites*, pp. 373–429 ; also Sellers, op. cit., pp. 85 ff., and Prestige, *Fathers and Heretics*, pp. 338, 341 ff. ; the last two especially for his doctrine of *kenosis*.

Cyril's Letter has the added weight of being conciliar, being dated in the official manner of councils, and in particular of that which met usually at Alexandria before Lent (Kidd, op. cit., vol. 3, p. 214).

ANALYSIS OF CYRIL'S SECOND LETTER TO NESTORIUS

A. *Introduction.*

Injurious reports about me are being circulated by unworthy persons, whom God will judge.

Let me remind you to hold fast and teach the true faith, lest you cause any to stumble.

B. *Doctrinal.*

The meaning of the Nicene Faith in the Incarnation: not conversion of the Godhead into flesh, or into a whole man; but by a hypostatic Union with soul and flesh the WORD became MAN, the two different Natures, Godhead and Manhood, retaining their diversity, yet uniting to make One Lord and Christ and Son.

Hence the Word has two generations—

> Begotten before the ages of the Father,
> Begotten also, after the flesh, of the Virgin;

not a mere man upon whom the Word descended, but the Word Himself born in His Human Nature.

Thus God suffered and died and rose again, not in His Godhead, but in His Manhood.

So we worship One Christ, not a man along with (σύν) the Word.

To reject this Hypostatic Union is to make Two Sons.

It was not a union of the Word to a human person, but the Word became flesh; *i.e.* He partook of our flesh and blood, yet still remained God. This is the teaching of catholicity and antiquity.

Thus the Virgin is Theotokos, not the bearer of the Godhead, but of the Word as regards His complete Humanity.

C. *Conclusion.*

Do you so think and teach, and preserve peace to all.

ΕΠΙΣΤΟΛΗ ΔΕΥΤΕΡΑ ΑΓΙΟΥ

ΚΥΡΙΛΛΟΥ

ΠΡΟΣ ΝΕΣΤΟΡΙΟΝ

Τῷ εὐλαβεστάτῳ καὶ θεοφιλεστάτῳ συλλειτουργῷ Νεστορίῳ Κύριλλος ἐν
Κυρίῳ χαίρειν   5

ΚΑΤΑΦΛΥΑΡΟΥΣΙ μὲν, ὡς μανθάνω, τινὲς τῆς ἐμῆς ὑπολήψεως
ἐπὶ τῆς σῆς θεοσεβείας· καὶ τοῦτο συχνῶς, τὰς τῶν ἐν τέλει συνόδους
καιροφυλακοῦντες μάλιστα, καὶ τάχα που καὶ τέρπειν οἰόμενοι τὴν σὴν
ἀκοήν· καὶ ἀβουλήτους πέμπουσι φωνάς, ἠδικημένοι μὲν οὐδέν, ἐλεγχ-
θέντες δὲ καὶ τοῦτο χρηστῶς· ὁ μέν, ὅτι τυφλοὺς ἠδίκει καὶ πένητας· ὁ 10
δέ, ὡς μητρὶ ξίφος ἐπανατείνας· ὁ δέ, θεραπαίνῃ συγκεκλοφὼς χρυσίον
ἀλλότριον, καὶ τοιαύτην ἐσχηκὼς ἀεὶ τὴν ὑπόληψιν, ἣν οὐκ ἂν εὔξαιτό
τις συμβῆναί τισι καὶ τῶν λίαν ἐχθρῶν. πλὴν οὐ πολὺς τῶν τοιούτων
ὁ λόγος ἐμοί, ἵνα μήτε ὑπὲρ τὸν δεσπότην καὶ διδάσκαλον, μήτε μὴν
ὑπὲρ τοὺς πατέρας τὸ τῆς ἐνούσης ἐμοὶ βραχύτητος ἐκτείνοιμι μέτρον. 15
οὐ γὰρ ἐνδέχεται τὰς τῶν φαύλων διαδρᾶναι σκαιότητας, ὡς ἂν
ἕλοιτό τις διαβιοῦν. ἀλλ᾽ ἐκεῖνοι μὲν ἀρᾶς καὶ πικρίας   Rom. iii. 14.
μεστὸν ἔχοντες τὸ στόμα, τῷ πάντων ἀπολογήσονται Κριτῇ· τετρά-
ψομαι δὲ πάλιν ἐγὼ πρὸς τὸ ὅτι μάλιστα πρέπον ἐμαυτῷ, καὶ
ὑπομνήσω καὶ νῦν, ὡς ἀδελφὸν ἐν Χριστῷ, τῆς διδασκαλίας τὸν λόγον 20
καὶ τὸ ἐπὶ τῇ πίστει φρόνημα μετὰ πάσης ἀσφαλείας ποιεῖσθαι πρὸς
τοὺς λαούς· ἐννοεῖν τε ὅτι τὸ σκανδαλίσαι καὶ μόνον ἕνα   Matt. xviii. 6.
τῶν μικρῶν τῶν πιστευόντων εἰς Χριστόν, ἀφόρητον ἔχει τὴν ἀγανάκτη-
σιν· εἰ δὲ δὴ πληθὺς εἴη τοσαύτη τῶν λελυπημένων, πῶς οὐχ ἁπάσης
εὐτεχνίας ἐν χρείᾳ καθεστήκαμεν, πρός γε τὸ δεῖν ἐμφρόνως περιελεῖν 25
τὰ σκάνδαλα, καὶ τὸν ὑγιῆ τῆς πίστεως κατευρῦναι λόγον τοῖς ζητοῦσι
τὸ ἀληθές ; ἔσται δὲ τοῦτο καὶ μάλα ὀρθῶς, εἰ τοῖς τῶν ἁγίων πατέρων
περιτυγχάνοντες λόγοις, περὶ πολλοῦ τε αὐτοὺς ποιεῖσθαι σπουδάζοιμεν,
καὶ δοκιμάζοντες ἑαυτούς, εἰ ἐσμὲν ἐν τῇ πίστει, κατὰ τὸ   2 Cor. xiii. 5.
γεγραμμένον, ταῖς ἐκείνων ὀρθαῖς καὶ ἀνεπιλήπτοις δόξαις τὰς ἐν ἡμῖν 30
ἐννοίας εὖ μάλα συμπλάττοιμεν.
   Ἔφη τοίνυν ἡ ἁγία καὶ μεγάλη σύνοδος, αὐτὸν τὸν ἐκ Θεοῦ καὶ
Πατρὸς κατὰ φύσιν γεννηθέντα Υἱὸν μονογενῆ, τὸν ἐκ Θεοῦ ἀληθινοῦ
Θεὸν ἀληθινόν, τὸ φῶς τὸ ἐκ τοῦ φωτός, τὸν δι᾽ οὗ τὰ πάντα
πεποίηκεν ὁ Πατήρ, κατελθεῖν, σαρκωθῆναι, ἐνανθρωπῆσαι, παθεῖν, 35
ἀναστῆναι τῇ τρίτῃ ἡμέρᾳ, καὶ ἀνελθεῖν εἰς οὐρανούς. τούτοις καὶ
ἡμᾶς ἕπεσθαι δεῖ καὶ τοῖς λόγοις καὶ τοῖς δόγμασιν, ἐννοοῦντας τί
τὸ σαρκωθῆναι καὶ ἐνανθρωπῆσαι δηλοῖ τὸν ἐκ Θεοῦ Λόγον· οὐ γάρ
φαμεν, ὅτι ἡ τοῦ Λόγου φύσις μεταποιηθεῖσα γέγονε σάρξ, ἀλλ᾽ οὐδὲ
ὅτι εἰς ὅλον ἄνθρωπον μετεβλήθη, τὸν ἐκ ψυχῆς καὶ σώματος· ἐκεῖνο δὲ 40
μᾶλλον, ὅτι σάρκα ἐψυχωμένην ψυχῇ λογικῇ ἑνώσας ὁ Λόγος ἑαυτῷ
καθ᾽ ὑπόστασιν ἀφράστως τε καὶ ἀπερινοήτως, γέγονεν ἄνθρωπος καὶ

95

κεχρημάτικεν υἱὸς ἀνθρώπου, οὐ κατὰ θέλησιν μόνην ἢ εὐδοκίαν, ἀλλ'
οὐδὲ ὡς ἐν προσλήψει προσώπου μόνου· καὶ ὅτι διάφοροι μὲν αἱ πρὸς
45 ἑνότητα τὴν ἀληθινὴν συνενεχθεῖσαι φύσεις, εἷς δὲ ἐξ ἀμφοῖν Χριστὸς
καὶ Υἱός· οὐχ ὡς τῆς τῶν φύσεων διαφορᾶς ἀνῃρημένης διὰ τὴν ἕνωσιν,
ἀποτελεσασῶν δὲ μᾶλλον ἡμῖν τὸν ἕνα Κύριον καὶ Χριστὸν καὶ Υἱὸν
θεότητός τε καὶ ἀνθρωπότητος, διὰ τῆς ἀφράστου καὶ ἀπορρήτου πρὸς
ἑνότητα συνδρομῆς. οὕτω τε λέγεται, καίτοι πρὸ αἰώνων ἔχων τὴν
50 ὕπαρξιν καὶ γεννηθεὶς ἐκ Πατρός, γεννηθῆναι καὶ κατὰ σάρκα ἐκ
γυναικός, οὐχ ὡς τῆς θείας αὐτοῦ φύσεως ἀρχὴν τοῦ εἶναι λαβούσης ἐν
τῇ ἁγίᾳ παρθένῳ, οὔτε μὴν δεηθείσης ἀναγκαίως δι' ἑαυτὴν δευτέρας
γεννήσεως μετὰ τὴν ἐκ Πατρός· ἔστι γὰρ εἰκαῖόν τε ὁμοῦ καὶ ἀμαθὲς
τὸν ὑπάρχοντα πρὸ παντὸς αἰῶνος καὶ συναΐδιον τῷ Πατρὶ, δεῖσθαι
55 Nic. Symb.　λέγειν ἀρχῆς τῆς εἰς τὸ εἶναι δευτέρας· ἐπειδὴ δὲ " δι'
ἡμᾶς καὶ διὰ τὴν ἡμετέραν σωτηρίαν " ἑνώσας ἑαυτῷ ὁ Λόγος καθ'
ὑπόστασιν τὸ ἀνθρώπινον, προῆλθεν ἐκ γυναικός, ταύτῃτοι λέγεται
γεννηθῆναι σαρκικῶς. οὐ γὰρ πρῶτον ἄνθρωπος ἐγεννήθη κοινὸς ἐκ
τῆς ἁγίας παρθένου, εἶθ' οὕτω καταπεφοίτηκεν ἐπ' αὐτὸν ὁ Λόγος·
60 ἀλλ' ἐξ αὐτῆς μήτρας ἑνωθεὶς, ὑπομεῖναι λέγεται γέννησιν σαρκικὴν,
ὡς τῆς ἰδίας σαρκὸς τὴν γέννησιν οἰκειούμενος. οὕτω φαμὲν αὐτὸν
καὶ παθεῖν καὶ ἀναστῆναι· οὐχ ὡς τοῦ Θεοῦ Λόγου παθόντος εἰς ἰδίαν
φύσιν ἢ πληγὰς ἢ διατρήσεις ἥλων ἤγουν τὰ ἕτερα τῶν τραυμάτων·
ἀπαθὲς γὰρ τὸ θεῖον ὅτι καὶ ἀσώματον· ἐπειδὴ δὲ τὸ γεγονὸς αὐτοῦ
65 ἴδιον σῶμα πέπονθε, ταῦτα πάλιν αὐτὸς λέγεται παθεῖν ὑπὲρ ἡμῶν· ἦν
γὰρ ὁ ἀπαθὴς ἐν τῷ πάσχοντι σώματι. κατὰ τὸν ἴσον δὲ τρόπον καὶ
ἐπὶ τοῦ τεθνάναι νοοῦμεν. ἀθάνατος μὲν γὰρ κατὰ φύσιν καὶ ἄφθαρτος
καὶ ζωὴ καὶ ζωοποιός ἐστιν ὁ τοῦ Θεοῦ Λόγος· ἐπειδὴ δὲ τὸ ἴδιον
Heb. ii. 9.　αὐτοῦ πάλιν σῶμα χάριτι Θεοῦ, καθά φησιν ὁ Παῦλος,
70 ὑπὲρ παντὸς ἐγεύσατο θανάτου, λέγεται παθεῖν αὐτὸς τὸν ὑπὲρ ἡμῶν
θάνατον· οὐχ ὡς εἰς πεῖραν ἐλθὼν τοῦ θανάτου, τό γε ἧκον εἰς τὴν
αὐτοῦ φύσιν· ἀποπληξία γὰρ τοῦτο λέγειν ἢ φρονεῖν· ἀλλ' ὅτι
καθάπερ ἔφην ἀρτίως, ἡ σὰρξ αὐτοῦ ἐγεύσατο θανάτου. οὕτω καὶ,
ἐγηγερμένης αὐτοῦ τῆς σαρκός, πάλιν ἡ ἀνάστασις αὐτοῦ λέγεται, οὐχ
75 ὡς πεσόντος εἰς φθοράν· μὴ γένοιτο· ἀλλ' ὅτι τὸ αὐτοῦ πάλιν ἐγήγερται
σῶμα. οὕτω Χριστὸν ἕνα καὶ Κύριον ὁμολογήσομεν, οὐχ ὡς ἄνθρωπον
συμπροσκυνοῦντες τῷ Λόγῳ, ἵνα μὴ τομῆς φαντασία παρεισκρίνηται,
διὰ τοῦ λέγειν τό Σύν· ἀλλ' ὡς ἕνα καὶ τὸν αὐτὸν προσκυνοῦντες, ὅτι μὴ
ἀλλότριον τοῦ Λόγου τὸ σῶμα αὐτοῦ, μεθ' οὗ καὶ αὐτὸς συνεδρεύει τῷ
80 Πατρί· οὐχ ὡς δύο πάλιν συνεδρευόντων υἱῶν, ἀλλ' ὡς ἑνὸς καθ'
ἕνωσιν μετὰ τῆς σαρκός. ἐὰν δὲ τὴν καθ' ὑπόστασιν ἕνωσιν ἢ ὡς
ἀνέφικτον ἢ ὡς ἀκαλλῆ παραιτώμεθα, ἐμπίπτομεν εἰς τὸ δύο λέγειν
υἱούς· ἀνάγκη γὰρ πᾶσα διορίσαι, καὶ εἰπεῖν τὸν μὲν, ἄνθρωπον ἰδικῶς,
τῇ τοῦ Υἱοῦ κλήσει τετιμημένον· ἰδικῶς δὲ πάλιν, τὸν ἐκ Θεοῦ Λόγον,
85 υἱότητος ὄνομά τε καὶ χρῆμα ἔχοντα φυσικῶς.
　　Οὐ διαιρετέον τοιγαροῦν εἰς υἱοὺς δύο τὸν ἕνα Κύριον Ἰησοῦν
Χριστόν. ὀνήσει δὲ κατ' οὐδένα τρόπον τὸν ὀρθὸν τῆς πίστεως λόγον
εἰς τὸ οὕτως ἔχειν, κἂν εἰ προσώπων ἕνωσιν ἐπιφημίζωσί τινες· οὐ γὰρ
John i. 14.　εἴρηκεν ἡ γραφή, ὅτι ὁ Λόγος ἀνθρώπου πρόσωπον ἥνωσεν
90 ἑαυτῷ, ἀλλ' ὅτι γέγονε σάρξ. τὸ δὲ σάρκα γενέσθαι τὸν Λόγον, οὐδὲν

ἔτερόν ἐστιν, εἰ μὴ ὅτι παραπλησίως ἡμῖν μετέσχεν Heb. ii. 14.
αἵματος καὶ σαρκός, ἴδιόν τε σῶμα τὸ ἡμῶν ἐποιήσατο, καὶ προῆλθεν
ἄνθρωπος ἐκ γυναικός· οὐκ ἀποβεβληκὼς τὸ εἶναι Θεὸς καὶ τὸ ἐκ
Θεοῦ γεννηθῆναι Πατρός, ἀλλὰ καὶ ἐν προσλήψει σαρκὸς μεμενηκὼς
ὅπερ ἦν. τοῦτο πρεσβεύει πανταχοῦ τῆς ἀκριβοῦς πίστεως ὁ λόγος· 95
οὕτως εὑρήσομεν τοὺς ἁγίους πεφρονηκότας πατέρας· οὕτω τεθαρρήκασι
θεοτόκον εἰπεῖν τὴν ἁγίαν παρθένον· οὐχ ὡς τῆς τοῦ Λόγου φύσεως
ἤτοι τῆς θεότητος αὐτοῦ τὴν ἀρχὴν τοῦ εἶναι λαβούσης ἐκ τῆς ἁγίας
παρθένου· ἀλλ' ὡς γεννηθέντος ἐξ αὐτῆς τοῦ ἁγίου σώματος, ψυχωθέντος
λογικῶς, ᾧ καὶ καθ' ὑπόστασιν ἐνωθεὶς ὁ Λόγος, γεννηθῆναι λέγεται 100
κατὰ σάρκα.

Ταῦτα καὶ νῦν ἐξ ἀγάπης τῆς ἐν Χριστῷ γράφων παρακαλῶ ὡς
ἀδελφὸν καὶ διαμαρτύρομαι ἐνώπιον τοῦ Χριστοῦ καὶ τῶν 1 Tim. v. 21.
ἐκλεκτῶν ἀγγέλων, ταῦτα μεθ' ἡμῶν καὶ φρονεῖν καὶ διδάσκειν· ἵνα
σώζηται τῶν ἐκκλησιῶν ἡ εἰρήνη, καὶ τῆς ὁμονοίας καὶ ἀγάπης ὁ 105
σύνδεσμος ἀρραγὴς διαμένῃ τοῖς ἱερεῦσι τοῦ Θεοῦ.

NOTES ON CYRIL'S SECOND LETTER TO NESTORIUS

8. Τέρπειν οἰόμενοι τὴν σὴν ἀκοήν. Alluding to the long-established jealousy between the sees of Constantinople and Alexandria, which had no doubt led these excommunicated persons to seek refuge at Constantinople.

39. ἡ τοῦ Λόγου φύσις μεταποιηθεῖσα, κ.τ.λ. This was a tenet of the extreme exponents of Apollinarianism. Curiously enough, Apollinarianism, though due to a recoil from Arianism, was yet in its first position—the denial of the human mind in Christ—in agreement with it (pseudo-Athanasius, c. Apoll. ii. 3). The heresy passed through three stages of development. First, the human, νοῦς, as being the seat of sinful thoughts and inclinations, was considered to imply the Arian τρεπτόν, and was surrendered for its place to be supplied by the Divine Logos. Next, the human body which Christ took from the Virgin was deemed to be, by His assumption of it, made co-essential with the Deity. Lastly, it was held that Christ's Body was not of human but of heavenly origin— ἐξ οὐρανοῦ—a portion of the Deity materialised, as it were; " the Godhead converted into flesh." See again Epist. 3, and Leo's Tome, § 2, where Eutyches is charged with a revival of this notion. Athanasius had argued against the Arians (Orat. iii. 30) that the σάρξ of John i. 14 was equivalent to ἄνθρωπος, and the two coarser forms of Apollinarianism were combated very fully in his Epistle to Epictetus of Corinth in 372, the acceptance of which became a test of orthodoxy in the Nestorian controversy (see Epist. ad Ioan. ad fin.). Apollinarius himself distinguished between the *anima rationalis* and the *anima animans*. The latter he allowed that Christ possessed (Theodoret, Dial. 2), but a few of his followers seem to have even denied this. See Leo, Serm. 24 in Nat. Dom. 4.[1]

39. οὐδὲ ὅτι εἰς ὅλον ἄνθρωπον μετεβλήθη. Cf. Athanasius, Or. c. Ar. ii. 47, καὶ γὰρ ὥσπερ 'Ιωάννου ἀκούσαντες ὁ Λόγος σάρξ ἐγένετο, οὐκ αὐτὸν ὅλον σάρκα νοοῦμεν τὸν Λόγον, ἀλλὰ σάρκα ἐνδυσάμενον καὶ γενόμενον; Gregory Naz. Epist. ci, cii, ad Cled. contr. Apoll. Cf., too, the twelfth anathema of the first Sirmian Creed, Socr. ii. 30, Εἴ τις τὸ 'Ο Λόγος σάρξ ἐγένετο ἀκούων, τὸν Λόγον εἰς

---

[1] This heresy was first condemned at the Council of Alexandria 362 (Socr. iii. 7; Athanasius, Tom. ad Ant.). Apollinarius himself, it must be remembered, was represented at the Council and accepted its decisions. See Raven, op. cit., pp. 103–12. On the whole subject of Apollinarius and Apollinarianism see Kidd, Vol. II, p. 213 ff.

σάρκα μεταβεβλῆσθαι νομίζοι, ἢ τροπὴν ὑπομεμενηκότα ἀνειληφέναι τὴν σάρκα λέγοι, ἀνάθεμα ἔστω : and see the comments of Hilary of Poitiers upon it, De Synod. 48.

41. ἑνώσας ὁ Λ. ἑαυτῷ καθ' ὑπόστασιν. The use of the term ἕνωσις, like συνάφεια, for the " mode " of the Incarnation, was common to both sides and to all early Christology. The question was, what kind of union ? Cyril maintained that it was " hypostatic " (καθ' ὑπόστασιν) (see note on ousia and hypostasis, p. 19). It is probable that Cyril did not intend by the use of this term to imply any metaphysical theory of the union, for he was always careful to say that the union is wholly mysterious, ineffable, and incapable of any philosophical explanation ; nor does he anywhere offer one. What he implies by the phrase is that the union was not merely a *moral* one (σχετική), a union of will or an association between two beings, but so close and organic that it would be impossible after the Incarnation to speak of the two natures as two " objects," but only of one ὑπόστασις, i.e. Christ in His two Natures acts in both, in the same way as God exists in the Trinity in Threefold fashion. Even so, Christ after the Incarnation exists, acts, and speaks, both humanly and divinely, as one Person. Nestorius, on the other hand, while, of course, not denying the obvious orthodoxy of this, the Catholic and traditional view, was consciously attempting a philosophical explanation of the mode of the Incarnation, which, as he thought, safeguarded better the no less important truth of the two complete and active natures in Christ. Hence he insisted that the union was to be found in what he called the *prosopon* (πρόσωπον), that is to say, in the sharing of a common sphere of activity by two centres of life. The result of this was, as maintained by Cyril, " to rend the mystery of the Incarnation into a Dyad of Sons " (Def. Chalced. l. 101). While the whole question is doubtful and the terminology fluid, the simplest explanation is that the two antagonists were all the time at cross purposes. For Cyril appears to use the term *hypostasis* in the Trinitarian sense of *persona* according to the prevailing use since the Cappadocian Fathers formulated the doctrine of the Trinity ; and a difference between *hypostasis* and *ousia* was thenceforth accepted. Whereas Nestorius probably was adhering to the old Nicene use of the terms as synonymous,[1] with the result that he insisted as strongly on the *two ousiai* in the Person of Christ as did St. Athanasius and the Nicene Fathers on the *one ousia* of Father and Son. Prestige remarks : " The mind which can bear to talk about two *ousiai* in Christ is in danger of losing its grip on the doctrine of God " (*God in Patristic Thought*, p. 274).

43. κατὰ θέλησιν μόνην ἢ εὐδοκίαν. This was the position of Theodore, whom Nestorius followed ; by κατ' εὐδοκίαν was meant

[1] Cf. Def. Chalced. l. 121.

a union of grace or divine favour or preference.[1] The Antiochene
Fathers preferred to use the terminology of grace and indwelling;
the two terms are identical when applied to the Incarnation and
belief in Christ.[2] Nestorius did not, in fact, teach what Cyril
called a " moral " union (κατὰ θέλησιν), a union resulting from the
fact that the two Natures in Christ both willed alike, true as that
of course is : for he makes the unity of will the *consequence* of the
union, not its ground, just as in the orthodox position.   Nor did he
teach that the " Man " Jesus Christ was granted by the grace of God
complete Unity with the Logos or Son.   Both these positions were
expressly repudiated by Nestorius in the *Bazaar*.[3] What he did
say was that the union must be *voluntary*, *i.e.* as far as the Logos
is concerned all through the Incarnate Life.   The word θέλησις
(willing) in their terminology must be understood to refer to
the will of *God*.   The Antiochenes opposed to Cyril's " hypostatic
union " a " voluntary union," because the Logos Himself has been
willing to take the body and soul of a rational and intelligent person.
Hence the union of God the Word, it is maintained, is neither κατ'
οὐσίαν nor κατὰ φύσιν but a union κατ' εὐδοκίαν.   The reason why
Nestorius steadily refused the hypostatic union, was because he
thought that Cyril meant by it a " physical " union such as exists
between the body and soul, which seemed to him to subject the
Divine principle to the necessities of a natural constitution :   cf.
the Quicunque Vult :   " For as the reasonable soul and flesh is one
man, so God and Man is one Christ."

Employing this terminology, Theodore of Mopsuestia distinguished
three kinds of Divine Indwelling ; God is present everywhere κατ'
οὐσίαν, or κατ' ἐνέργειαν, *i.e.* by His very Nature or activity.   This
is sound orthodox teaching.   Secondly, He is present in His saints
in a different way which He calls κατ' εὐδοκίαν, *i.e.* by grace or God's
good will and favour.   Thirdly, in Jesus He dwelt indeed by grace,
but also, more than that, as " in a Son," inasmuch as the Son by
nature took to Himself " man " to dwell in him.   Nestorius in
his earliest sermon used such language, as did also Flavian of
Constantinople, and spoke of Christ's indwelling as " in a temple "
and of His wearing of the flesh as a vesture or employing it as an
instrument. (See Swete, *Theodore of Mopsuestia*, vol. 2, p. 294, and
Dr. L. Patterson, *Theodore of Mopsuestia*, pp. 30 ff. Loofs, op. cit.,
pp. 290–2, and *Nestoriana*, p. 220.)

44. On the history and meaning of πρόσωπον see Prestige,
Fathers and Heretics, pp. 287 ff. ; Hodgson and Driver, *Bazaar*,
Appendix III, pp. 402 ff. Loofs has given to this term as used in
this controversy the now accepted meaning of the " external undivided appearance " of any object or person (op. cit., p. 76).

[1] ἡ καλλίστη καὶ ἀρίστη θέλησις τοῦ θεοῦ, Theodore of Mopsuestia, De Incarn·
vii. (Swete, ii, p. 294).
[2] Cf. J. H. Newman, *Lectures on Justification*, pp. 148 ff.
[3] *Bazaar*, p. 70 ; cf. also pp. 163 and notes, 179, 181 ff.

45. εἷς δὲ ἐξ ἀμφοῖν Χριστὸς καὶ Ὑιός. This was a phrase rejected at Chalcedon in favour of ἐν δυοῖν φύσεσιν ; and the result was the Monophysite heresy. Eutyches fastened on it, but it will be noted that Cyril disclaims any idea of a mixture, maintaining the traditional statement about the two natures current since the time of Tertullian ; cf. Adv. Prax. 27, where occurs the famous phrase " salva est utriusque proprietas substantiae." Cf. Vincent Lerin., Common. 13.

46. οὐχ ὡς τῆς τῶν φύσεων διαφορᾶς ἀνῃρημένης διὰ τὴν ἔνωσιν. This truth was constantly emphasised in the Christological controversies, and these very words of Cyril were adopted in the letter of the Council of Ephesus to the deposed Nestorius (apud Leo, Epist. xxvi, Flav. ad Leon.), and were also incorporated in the Chalcedonian Definitio Fidei.[1]

It may be useful to add at this point a summary of Nestorius' position as stated again and again in the Bazaar. To Cyril's phrase ἔνωσις καθ' ὑπόστασιν Nestorius never ceased to oppose one or other of the phrases based on the term πρόσωπον, to express the mode of the union of the Godhead and Manhood in Christ. It is clear that Nestorius meant by this expression something much more important and real than mere " appearance," for which he always uses the word σχῆμα. In the judgment of Loofs, followed by Dr. Hodgson, Nestorius may have had behind him a philosophical doctrine which was not to be despised, though it does not appear it could ever be a satisfactory basis for a doctrine of the Person of Christ. In his philosophy everything had its πρόσωπον, its kind of being seen and judged. That more was meant than mere " appearance " is indicated by such passages in the Bazaar as the following : " Although the prosopon exists not without ousia, the ousia and the prosopon are not the same " (p. 170). Again " in order that we may not, like Sabellius, make the prosopon without hypostasis and without ousia " (p. 228). It looks then as if in the metaphysic of Nestorius everything has its ousia, its phusis, and its prosopon, which is something in its make up which differs from its ousia or hypostasis and its phusis and means the undivided external appearance of a thing. A unity therefore of the Person of Christ must be a unity in one or more of these elements ; and thus there are three possible kinds of unity ; the union of the Persons in the Trinity is a unity of ousia or hypostasis, as the Nicene Creed had said. But as, in the view of Nestorius, Godhead and Manhood are mutually exclusive terms,[2] they must remain distinct in Christ if He is to be perfect God and perfect Man. For if they are fused, as Nestorius supposed to be the case in Cyril's hypostatic union, Christ will be neither God nor Man but some new kind of composite Being (Bazaar, pp. 22, 26, and 27, and cf. p. 320). Similarly if the union

---

[1] § 4. Cf. Vincent Ler., Common. 13.
[2] So the Antiochene philosopher Nemesius of Emesa (fourth to fifth centuries) (De Natura hominis, P.G. xl).

were one of *phusis*—that is to say, the same sort of union that exists between body and soul in man (as the Athanasian Creed posits)—the Godhead and the Manhood cannot be so united in Christ; for such a union would seem to subject the divine element in Him to some sort of physical compulsion as in the case with soul and body in man.[1]   There remains the union in a *prosopon*, considered as an objectively real element in the *being* of a thing; that indivisible *ousia* in which the various elements of the *phusis* are united, so as to form an external undivided appearance of the whole.   Thus, while we cannot find the union of two different kinds of existence either in their *ousia* or in their *phusis*, we can think of them as being identical in their appearances (πρόσωπα), which in the Incarnation may be said to overlap and so the two Elements will have one *prosopon*.   This is a tenable position so long as it is realised that for Nestorius the *prosopon* is no *mere* appearance but an objectively real element in the being of a thing without which the thing would not be what it is; for the *prosopon* which was not the *prosopon* of an *ousia* would be a mere illusion, and neither the Manhood nor the Godhead of Christ was that.   On the other hand, an *ousia* without a *prosopon* would be equally unthinkable.   A "prosopic" union, therefore, in his view was, indeed, the only kind of real union possible in this particular case. Passages which suggest the above interpretation of *prosopon* will be found in pp. 22–31, 146–7 of the *Bazaar*, and especially pp. 189 and 190, where the famous statement occurs that "the prosopon of the Manhood is the Godhead and the prosopon of the Godhead is the Manhood"; an expression which seems to imply a sort of interchange or overlapping of the *prosopa*; an attempt to put into philosophical form what Leo states in the Tome, where the several actions and deeds of the one Christ are said to exhibit at one time humanity, at another divinity, in a life which presented one undivided appearance (Tome of Leo 4).   It will, of course, be understood that by *prosopon* is meant not merely the face or appearance of Jesus Christ but everything that He said or did, thereby manifesting both natures in a common exterior.

47.   τὸν ἕνα Κύριον καὶ Χριστὸν καὶ Υἱόν.   Cyril's most characteristic statement and his most valuable contribution to Christology.

48.   ἀφράστου καὶ ἀπορρήτου.   Cyril echoes Athanasius in insisting on the mysteriousness of the Incarnation; see *e.g.* Athan., c. Arian. i, 41.   Cf. Augustin. Serm. 215, "Deo gratias, quia id quod competenter non potest dici, potest fideliter credi!" ibid., 244 "Expone quomodo natus si semper fuit.   Non expono; non possum."

48.   πρὸς ἑνότητα συνδρομῆς.   Here Cyril uses another favourite phrase which at the same time appears to allow some concession to his opponent's position.

---

[1] *Bazaar*, pp. 38, 179, 304; cf. Loofs, *Nestorius*, p. 68.

61. οὕτω φαμὲν αὐτὸν καὶ παθεῖν. Since the Logos Incarnate is the subject, as we have seen, of all that is said of Jesus Christ in the Bible, it is right also to speak of the words or actions in either nature as the words or actions of God. This Ignatius of Antioch had already done (Ephesians vii. 2 with Lightfoot's note). Accordingly, St. Paul spoke of the crucifixion of the Lord of Glory. (1 Cor. ii. 8) and of Second Man being " from heaven " (1 Cor. xv. 47), and St. John of the Son of Man being " in heaven " (John iii. 13). The technical term for this method of speaking is *antidosis* (ἀντίδοσις) or *communicatio idiomatum*, whereby all that can be predicated of the Divine or Human Nature may with equal propriety be predicated of the One Divine Person of Christ. It is the Person who acts or suffers ; it is His Nature, Divine and Human, which makes Him capable of either (Hooker, *Ecclesiastical Polity*, bk. v, 52). Leo also drew this out at length in the Tome. (§ 5) Nestorius would not allow that this method of speech could be used without inconsistency, as indeed Cyril was already aware when he resorted to such paraphrases as ἀπαθῶς ἔπαθεν, or, as in line 64, ἀπαθὲς γὰρ τὸ θεῖον ὅτι καὶ ἀσώματον and at the same time ἦν ὁ ἀπαθὴς ἐν τῷ πάσχοντι σώματι. But a *body* does not suffer. See, however, *Bazaar*, p. 241, where Nestorius does seem to allow a qualified validity to this method.

76. οὐχ ὡς ἄνθρωπον συμπροσκυνοῦντες τῷ Λόγῳ. See below on Anath. 8.

92. προῆλθεν ἄνθρωπος ἐκ γυναικός. So again in Epist. iii, but the phrase is Athanasian, ad Epict. 12, ἐκ δὲ Μαρίας αὐτὸς ὁ Λόγος σάρκα λαβὼν προῆλθεν ἄνθρωπος. Cf. c. Apoll., i. 9, Θεὸς Λόγος ἐκ παρθένου τῆς ἁγίας Μαρίας προελθὼν ἄνθρωπος.

94. μεμενηκὼς ὅπερ ἦν. " Mansit quod erat." The phrase was the sheet anchor of Catholic Christology, Alexandrian, Antiochene and Western. Cf. St. Augustine, In Ioan. 8. " Natus de matre, non recedens a Patre."

97. θεοτόκον. " She who bare (as to His Human Nature) Him who is God."
This epithet was of very ancient use in the language of the Church ; Theodoret (HE. iv. 12) refers to " the Apostolical Tradition," and indeed its equivalent is found in Scripture : Luke i. 43, ἡ μήτηρ τοῦ Κυρίου μου. Cf. Ignatius, Ephes. 18, ὁ γὰρ Θεὸς ἡμῶν Ἰησοῦς ὁ Χριστὸς ἐκυοφορήθη ὑπὸ Μαρίας κατ' οἰκονομίαν. The usual Latin equivalent was " Deipara," but Tertullian practically used the phrase " Mater Dei" (De Pat. 3, " Nasci se Deus in utero patitur matris "), and Leo (Serm. xxi, Epist. clxv) used " Dei genetrix." Origen (according to Socr. vii. 32), in his commentary on Rom. i. 5, gave an ample exposition of the use of the word : ἑρμηνεύων πῶς " Θεοτόκος " λέγεται πλάτεως ἐξήτασε. Eusebius

himself used it (Vit. Const. iii. 43), and placed in the mouth of Constantine in his Oration (ad Sanct. Coet. 11) the expression Θεοῦ μήτηρ κόρη. Alexander (Theodoret, HE. i. 4) spoke of Christ taking a body, ἐκ τῆς θεοτόκου Μαρίας, and so Athanasius, Or. c. Ar. iii. 14, 29, 33 ; iv. 32 ; Cyril Jer., Catech. x. 19 ; Ambrose, Hexem. v. 20 (Mater Dei).

In the confession of faith called *De Fide et Incarnatione* attributed to Apollinarius, the title *Theotokos* occurs three times. It is also found in his Epistle to Jovian in which occurs the famous phrase wrongly attributed to Athanasius μία φύσις τοῦ θεοῦ Λόγου σεσαρκωμένη. In this letter Apollinarius and his Synod protest that neither they nor any sane person speaks of the flesh of Christ as consubstantial with God, but only as individually united with the Logos to form one *prosopon*, one *hypostasis*, wholly one and wholly God (cf. Def. Chalced. l. 121), and that in consequence of this inseparable union, and not of any divinity of the body apart from such union, the Virgin is *Theotokos*, and if this belief in the reality and result of the union be rejected, she will no longer be believed to be *Theotokos*. Apollinarius appealed to the title " Mother of God," applied to the Virgin in current theological language, in confirmation of his Christology. It had already been the subject of an attack upon him by Theodore of Mopsuestia.[1] From his words it is probable that the term *Theotokos* was at that time popular but not universally accepted. Evidently it had already become the subject of party strife. But the title is carefully restricted in the Definition of Chalcedon by the addition of the words κατὰ τὴν ἀνθρωπότητα (Raven, op. cit., p. 211 ; Def. Chalced. l. 117).

Nestorius objected to the term as implying the ascription of a human mode of existence to the divine *ousia*, though he was willing to accept it if properly safeguarded ; but he preferred *Christotokos* (see Ep. ad Caelest.), or *Theodochos*, as in Sermon vii. Duchesne pertinently adds that this term had not been prescribed by any council (op. cit., III, 236). At Nicaea those who accepted the *homoousion* had been allowed to specify that they did not use that term in a Sabellian sense. Even so did Nestorius in the case of the term *Theotokos*.

[1] C. Apoll. iii, Fr. 1, Swete, *Theodore of Mopsuestia, etc.*, ii, pp. 313 ff.

THE THIRD EPISTLE (SYNODICAL) OF CYRIL TO NESTORIUS

INTRODUCTION

NESTORIUS in his reply to Cyril's second letter put his finger on the weak point in Cyril's argument: praising him for disclaiming the notion that the Word in His own nature was capable of suffering; but denying Cyril's consistency in making the disclaimer, which, however, was in effect concealed by language which had the appearance of predicating suffering and death of the divine Word Himself. He proceeds to the use of the texts about the Lord's humanity in the old style, showing that to it belong the nativity and other human experiences; but so closely was He connected with the Godhead that the Godhead might be said to appropriate the acts of the humanity; and the communion between them, he argued, issued in one *prosopon* which is called Christ or Emmanuel. Mary, therefore, had better be called *Christotokos*, for *Theotokos* he regarded as pagan because it involved a notion that the Godhead was born of her.[1] In April 430 Cyril answered Pope Caelestine's letter of the previous year (Easter, 429), and a council at Rome in August condemned Nestorius, giving him ten days to recant. The matter was placed in the hands of Cyril, who held a council at Alexandria in November, which drew up this Third Letter, to which twelve anathematisms were appended (Epist. ad Nest. 3, " Cum Salvator "). It was sent at once to Constantinople, along with Caelestine's letter, by the hands of four bishops.

Meanwhile Theodosius the Second, whose two sisters, Arcadia and Marina, Cyril unwisely endeavoured to influence against Nestorius, the Empress Pulcheria being strongly Orthodox,[2] on November 17 had issued the summons for a General Council to meet next Pentecost.

[1] Mansi, iv. 891.
[2] See *Bazaar*, pp. 96, 97, for Nestorius' bitter complaint against Cyril about this matter.

ANALYSIS OF CYRIL'S THIRD LETTER

WITH TWELVE ANATHEMAS

A. *Introduction.*

Our reasons for writing: Duty to Christ, to the Faith, and to the scandalised Church.

B. *Hortatory.*

Uniting our counsel with that of the Roman Synod, we exhort you to refrain from perversion of the Truth under pain of excommunication.

Your excommunication of others is disannulled. You must accept the right sense of the Nicene formulary as well as its terms, and abjure your profane doctrines in the anathematisms appended hereunto.

C. *Doctrinal.*

The Nicene Creed.

The doctrine of the Incarnation: the Word was made Flesh, yet remained God. There was no change of Flesh into the Nature of God, nor of the Nature of God into Flesh. While a Child in the Virgin's lap He yet filled Creation as God.

The Hypostatic Union: we worship One Christ, GOD and MAN united in one Hypostasis,

 not merely connected by dignity or authority,

 not admitting of a double application of the title Christ,

 not a God-carrying man,

 but a true Union of Natures, like that of soul and body.

Thus there is One Christ, Son, and Lord,

 not a conjunction of man and Word in a union of honour,

 or of juxtaposition,

 or of " accidental " participation.

Indeed, " conjunction " is an inadequate term ;

 " union " is the right expression.

He did indeed speak of His Father as His God,

 but this was in virtue of the " emptying."

We refuse to say, " I worship him who is worn on account of Him that wore him,"

or, " The assumed is called God along with the Assumer."

Christ is ONE, not two, who suffered, died, and rose again.

We partake of the Holy Eucharist because it is the Flesh of One who is GOD, and therefore Life-giving.

The words of Christ in the Gospels are referable to One Person in Two Natures; some pertain to His Godhead, and some to His Manhood.

He is High Priest, not for Himself, but for us only. His Holy Spirit manifests His Glory to man.

By virtue of the Hypostatic Union the Virgin Mary is Theotokos—not that the Word had His beginning from her, nor that He needed a birth in time, but He blessed our birth, and removed the curse, and sanctified marriage.

D. *Conclusion.*

This is the true ancient Faith, to which you must unequivocally assent.

E. *Appendix.*

It is necessary for you to subscribe the following anathematisms :
Anathema to him who

(1) denies that the Virgin is Theotokos,

(2) denies that the Word is Personally united to Flesh, ONE CHRIST,

(3) severs Christ into two persons joined in dignity,

(4) refers Scriptural sayings respecting Christ to two different Hypostases, one human and one Divine,

(5) asserts that Christ is a God-carrying man,

(6) denies that the Word is alike God and Man,

(7) asserts that the man Jesus was energized by God the Word,

(8) asserts that co-worship is due to a man assumed by God the Word,

(9) denies that the Spirit was Christ's Own,

(10) denies that our High Priest was the very Word of God, who offered for us only,

(11) denies that Christ's Flesh is that of the Life-giving Word,

(12) denies that the Word Himself suffered and died in the Flesh.

ΕΠΙΣΤΟΛΗ ΤΡΙΤΗ ΤΟΥ ΑΓΙΟΥ

ΚΥΡΙΛΛΟΥ

ΠΡΟΣ ΝΕΣΤΟΡΙΟΝ

Τῷ εὐλαβεστάτῳ καὶ θεοσεβεστάτῳ συλλειτουργῷ Νεστορίῳ Κύριλλος καὶ ἡ συνελθοῦσα
5 σύνοδος ἐν Ἀλεξανδρείᾳ ἐκ τῆς Αἰγυπτιακῆς διοικήσεως ἐν κυρίῳ χαίρειν.

ΤΟΥ Σωτῆρος ἡμῶν λέγοντος ἐναργῶς Ὁ φιλῶν πατέρα ἢ μητέρα
Matt. x. 37.   ὑπὲρ ἐμὲ οὐκ ἔστι μου ἄξιος, καὶ ὁ φιλῶν υἱὸν ἢ θυγατέρα
ὑπὲρ ἐμὲ οὐκ ἔστι μου ἄξιος, τί πάθωμεν ἡμεῖς, οἱ παρὰ τῆς σῆς
εὐλαβείας ἀπαιτούμενοι τὸ ὑπεραγαπᾶσθαι τοῦ πάντων ἡμῶν Σωτῆρος
10 Χριστοῦ ; τίς ἡμᾶς ἐν ἡμέρᾳ κρίσεως ὀνῆσαι δυνήσεται ; ἢ ποίαν
εὑρήσομεν τὴν ἀπολογίαν, σιωπὴν οὕτω τιμήσαντες τὴν μακρὰν ἐπὶ
ταῖς παρὰ σοῦ γενομέναις κατ᾽ αὐτοῦ δυσφημίαις ; καὶ εἰ μὲν σαυτὸν
ἠδίκεις μόνον, τὰ τοιαῦτα φρονῶν καὶ διδάσκων, ἥττων ἂν ἦν ἡ
φροντίς· ἐπειδὴ δὲ πᾶσαν ἐσκανδάλισας ἐκκλησίαν, καὶ ζύμην αἱρέσεως
15 ἀήθους τε καὶ ξένης ἐμβέβληκας τοῖς λαοῖς· καὶ οὐχὶ τοῖς ἐκεῖσε
μόνοις, ἀλλὰ γὰρ καὶ τοῖς ἁπανταχοῦ, περιηνέχθη γὰρ τῶν σῶν
ἐξηγήσεων τὰ βιβλία· ποῖος ἔτι ταῖς παρ᾽ ἡμῶν σιωπαῖς ἀρκέσει
λόγος ; ἢ πῶς οὐκ ἀνάγκη μνησθῆναι λέγοντος τοῦ Χριστοῦ Μὴ
νομίσητε ὅτι ἦλθον βαλεῖν εἰρήνην ἐπὶ τὴν γῆν· οὐκ ἦλθον βαλεῖν
20 εἰρήνην, ἀλλὰ μάχαιραν· ἦλθον γὰρ διχάσαι ἄνθρωπον κατὰ τοῦ
πατρὸς αὐτοῦ, καὶ θυγατέρα κατὰ τῆς μητρὸς αὐτῆς. πίστεως γὰρ
ἀδικουμένης, ἐρρέτω μὲν ὡς ἕωλος καὶ ἐπισφαλὴς ἡ πρὸς γονέας
αἰδώς· ἠρεμείτω δὲ καὶ ὁ τῆς εἰς τέκνα καὶ ἀδελφοὺς φιλοστοργίας
νόμος, καὶ τοῦ ζῆν ἀμείνων ἔστω λοιπὸν τοῖς εὐσεβέσιν ὁ θάνατος,
25 Heb. xi. 35.   ἵνα κρείττονος ἀναστάσεως τύχωσι, κατὰ τὸ γεγραμμένον.
Ἰδοὺ τοίνυν ὁμοῦ τῇ ἁγίᾳ συνόδῳ, τῇ κατὰ τὴν μεγάλην Ῥώμην
συνειλεγμένῃ, προεδρεύοντος τοῦ ὁσιωτάτου καὶ θεοσεβεστάτου
ἀδελφοῦ καὶ συλλειτουργοῦ ἡμῶν Κελεστίνου τοῦ ἐπισκόπου καὶ τρίτῳ
σοι τούτῳ διαμαρτυρόμεθα γράμματι, συμβουλεύοντες ἀποσχέσθαι τῶν
30 οὕτω σκαιῶν καὶ ἐξεστραμμένων δογμάτων, ἃ καὶ φρονεῖς καὶ
διδάσκεις, ἀνθελέσθαι δὲ τὴν ὀρθὴν πίστιν, τὴν ταῖς ἐκκλησίαις παραδοθεῖσαν ἐξ ἀρχῆς διὰ τῶν ἁγίων ἀποστόλων καὶ εὐαγγελιστῶν, οἳ καὶ
Luke i. 2.   αὐτόπται καὶ ὑπηρέται τοῦ λόγου γεγόνασιν· ἢ εἰ μὴ τοῦτο
δράσειεν ἡ σὴ εὐλάβεια, κατὰ τὴν ὁρισθεῖσαν προθεσμίαν ἐν τοῖς
35 γράμμασι τοῦ μνημονευθέντος ὁσιωτάτου καὶ θεοσεβεστάτου ἐπισκόπου
καὶ συλλειτουργοῦ ἡμῶν τῆς Ῥωμαίων Κελεστίνου, γίνωσκε σαυτὸν
οὐδένα κλῆρον ἔχοντα μεθ᾽ ἡμῶν, οὐδὲ τόπον ἢ λόγον ἐν τοῖς ἱερεῦσι
τοῦ Θεοῦ καὶ ἐπισκόποις. οὐδὲ γὰρ ἐνδέχεται περιιδεῖν ἡμᾶς ἐκκλησίας
οὕτω τεθορυβημένας καὶ σκανδαλισθέντας λαοὺς καὶ πίστιν ὀρθὴν
40 ἀθετουμένην καὶ διασπώμενα παρὰ σοῦ τὰ ποίμνια, τοῦ σώζειν ὀφείλ-
οντος, εἴπερ ἦσθα καθ᾽ ἡμᾶς ὀρθῆς δόξης ἐραστής, τὴν τῶν ἁγίων

108

πατέρων ἰχνηλατῶν εὐσέβειαν. ἅπασι δὲ τοῖς παρὰ τῆς σῆς εὐλαβείας
κεχωρισμένοις διὰ τὴν πίστιν, ἢ καθαιρεθεῖσι λαϊκοῖς τε καὶ κλη-
ρικοῖς, κοινωνικοὶ πάντες ἐσμέν. οὐ γάρ ἐστι δίκαιον τοὺς ὀρθὰ
φρονεῖν ἐγνωκότας σαῖς ἀδικεῖσθαι ψήφοις, ὅτι σοὶ καλῶς ποι- 45
οῦντες ἀντειρήκασι. τοῦτο γὰρ αὐτὸ καταμεμήνυκας ἐν τῇ ἐπιστολῇ
τῇ γραφείσῃ παρὰ σοῦ πρὸς τὸν τῆς μεγάλης Ῥώμης ἁγιώτατον
συνεπίσκοπον ἡμῶν Κελεστῖνον. οὐκ ἀρκέσει δὲ τῇ σῇ εὐλαβείᾳ τὸ
συνομολογῆσαι μόνον τὸ τῆς πίστεως σύμβολον, τὸ ἐκτεθὲν κατὰ
καιροὺς ἐν Ἁγίῳ Πνεύματι παρὰ τῆς ἁγίας καὶ μεγάλης συνόδου, τῆς 50
κατὰ καιροὺς συναχθείσης ἐν τῇ Νικαέων· νενόηκας γὰρ καὶ ἡρμήνευσας
οὐκ ὀρθῶς αὐτό, διεστραμμένως δὲ μᾶλλον κἂν ὁμολογῇς τῇ φωνῇ τὴν
λέξιν· ἀλλὰ γὰρ ἀκόλουθον ἐγγράφως καὶ ἐνωμότως ὁμολογῆσαι, ὅτι
καὶ ἀναθεματίζεις μὲν τὰ σαυτοῦ μιαρὰ καὶ βέβηλα δόγματα, φρονήσεις
δὲ καὶ διδάξεις, ἃ καὶ ἡμεῖς ἅπαντες, οἵ τε κατὰ τὴν ἑσπέραν καὶ τὴν 55
ἑῴαν ἐπίσκοποι καὶ διδάσκαλοι καὶ λαῶν ἡγούμενοι. συνέθετο δὲ καὶ
ἡ κατὰ τὴν Ῥώμην ἁγία σύνοδος, καὶ ἡμεῖς ἅπαντες, ὡς ὀρθῶς ἐχούσαις
καὶ ἀνεπιλήπτως, ταῖς γραφείσαις ἐπιστολαῖς πρὸς τὴν σὴν εὐλάβειαν
παρὰ τῆς Ἀλεξανδρέων ἐκκλησίας. ὑπετάξαμεν δὲ τούτοις ἡμῶν τοῖς
γράμμασιν, ἅ τε δεῖ φρονεῖν καὶ διδάσκειν, καὶ ὧν ἀπέχεσθαι προσήκει. 60
Αὕτη γὰρ τῆς καθολικῆς καὶ ἀποστολικῆς ἐκκλησίας ἡ πίστις, ᾗ
συναινοῦσιν ἅπαντες, οἵ τε κατὰ τὴν ἑσπέραν καὶ τὴν ἑῴαν ὀρθόδοξοι
ἐπίσκοποι·

ΠΙΣΤΕΥΟΜΕΝ εἰς ἕνα Θεὸν Πατέρα παντοκράτορα, πάντων ὁρατῶν τε καὶ ἀοράτων
ποιητήν· καὶ εἰς ἕνα Κύριον Ἰησοῦν Χριστόν, τὸν Υἱὸν τοῦ Θεοῦ, γεννηθέντα ἐκ τοῦ Πατρός, 65
μονογενῆ, τουτέστιν ἐκ τῆς οὐσίας τοῦ Πατρός· Θεὸν ἐκ Θεοῦ, Φῶς ἐκ Φωτός, Θεὸν
ἀληθινὸν ἐκ Θεοῦ ἀληθινοῦ· γεννηθέντα, οὐ ποιηθέντα, ὁμοούσιον τῷ Πατρί· δι᾿ οὗ τὰ
πάντα ἐγένετο, τά τε ἐν τῷ οὐρανῷ καὶ τὰ ἐν τῇ γῇ· τὸν δι᾿ ἡμᾶς τοὺς ἀνθρώπους καὶ
διὰ τὴν ἡμετέραν σωτηρίαν κατελθόντα καὶ σαρκωθέντα καὶ ἐνανθρωπήσαντα· παθόντα
καὶ ἀναστάντα τῇ τρίτῃ ἡμέρᾳ· ἀνελθόντα εἰς οὐρανούς, ἐρχόμενον κρῖναι ζῶντας καὶ 70
νεκρούς· καὶ εἰς τὸ Ἅγιον Πνεῦμα. τοὺς δὲ λέγοντας *Ην ποτε ὅτε οὐκ ἦν, καί Πρὶν
γεννηθῆναι οὐκ ἦν, καὶ ὅτι ἐξ οὐκ ὄντων ἐγένετο, ἢ ἐξ ἑτέρας ὑποστάσεως ἢ οὐσίας
φάσκοντας εἶναι ἢ τρεπτὸν ἢ ἀλλοιωτὸν τὸν Υἱὸν τοῦ Θεοῦ, τούτους ἀναθεματίζει
ἡ καθολικὴ καὶ ἀποστολικὴ ἐκκλησία.

Ἑπόμενοι δὲ πανταχῇ ταῖς τῶν ἁγίων πατέρων ὁμολογίαις, αἷς 75
πεποίηνται, λαλοῦντος ἐν αὐτοῖς τοῦ Ἁγίου Πνεύματος, καὶ τῶν ἐν
αὐτοῖς ἐννοιῶν ἰχνηλατοῦντες τὸν σκοπόν, καὶ βασιλικὴν ὥσπερ
ἐρχόμενοι τρίβον, φαμὲν ὅτι αὐτὸς ὁ Μονογενὴς τοῦ Θεοῦ Λόγος, ὁ ἐξ
αὐτῆς γεννηθεὶς τῆς οὐσίας τοῦ Πατρός, ὁ ἐκ Θεοῦ ἀληθινοῦ Θεὸς
ἀληθινός, τὸ Φῶς τὸ ἐκ τοῦ Φωτός, ὁ δι᾿ οὗ τὰ πάντα ἐγένετο, τά τε 80
ἐν τῷ οὐρανῷ καὶ τὰ ἐν τῇ γῇ, τῆς ἡμετέρας ἕνεκα σωτηρίας κατελθών,
καὶ καθεὶς ἑαυτὸν εἰς κένωσιν, ἐσαρκώθη τε καὶ ἐνηνθρώπησε, τουτέστι,
σάρκα λαβὼν ἐκ τῆς ἁγίας παρθένου, καὶ ἰδίαν αὐτὴν ποιησάμενος ἐκ
μήτρας, τὴν καθ᾿ ἡμᾶς ὑπέμεινε γέννησιν, καὶ προῆλθεν ἄνθρωπος ἐκ
γυναικός, οὐχ ὅπερ ἦν ἀποβεβληκώς, ἀλλ᾿ εἰ καὶ γέγονεν ἐν προσλήψει 85
σαρκὸς καὶ αἵματος καὶ οὕτω μεμενηκὼς ὅπερ ἦν, Θεὸς δηλονότι
φύσει τε καὶ ἀληθείᾳ· οὔτε δὲ τὴν σάρκα φαμὲν εἰς θεότητος τραπῆναι

φύσιν, οὔτε μὴν εἰς φύσιν σαρκὸς τὴν ἀπόρρητον τοῦ Θεοῦ Λόγου
παρενεχθῆναι φύσιν, ἄτρεπτος γὰρ ἐστι καὶ ἀναλλοίωτος παντελῶς ὁ

90 Cf. John viii. 35.   αὐτὸς ἀεὶ μένων κατὰ τὰς γραφάς· ὁρώμενος δὲ καὶ
ibid. x. 30.   βρέφος καὶ ἐσπαργανωμένος, ὢν ἔτι καὶ ἐν κόλπῳ τῆς
Mal. iii. 6.   τεκούσης παρθένου, πᾶσαν ἐπλήρου τὴν κτίσιν ὡς Θεὸς,
καὶ σύνεδρος ἦν τῷ γεγεννηκότι. τὸ γὰρ θεῖον ἄποσόν τε ἐστὶ καὶ
ἀμέγεθες καὶ περιορισμὸν οὐκ ἀνέχεται.

95   Ἡνῶσθαί γε μὴν σαρκὶ καθ' ὑπόστασιν ὁμολογοῦντες τὸν Λόγον,
ἕνα προσκυνοῦμεν Υἱὸν καὶ Κύριον Ἰησοῦν Χριστόν, οὔτε ἀνὰ μέρος
τιθέντες καὶ διορίζοντες ἄνθρωπον καὶ Θεόν, ὡς συνημμένους ἀλλήλοις
τῇ τῆς ἀξίας καὶ αὐθεντίας ἑνότητι· κενοφωνία γὰρ τοῦτο καὶ ἔτερον
οὐδέν· οὔτε μὴν Χριστὸν ἰδικῶς ὀνομάζοντες τὸν ἐκ Θεοῦ Λόγον, καὶ
100 ὁμοίως ἰδικῶς ὡς χριστὸν ἕτερον τὸν ἐκ γυναικός· ἀλλ' ἕνα μόνον
εἰδότες Χριστὸν τὸν ἐκ Θεοῦ καὶ Πατρὸς Λόγον μετὰ τῆς ἰδίας
σαρκός. τότε γὰρ ἀνθρωπίνως κέχρισται μεθ' ἡμῶν, καίτοι τοῖς
ἀξίοις τοῦ λαβεῖν τὸ Πνεῦμα διδοὺς αὐτός, καὶ οὐκ ἐκ μέτρου, καθά
John iii. 34.   φησιν ὁ μακάριος εὐαγγελιστὴς Ἰωάννης. ἀλλ' οὐδ'
105 ἐκεῖνό φαμεν, ὅτι κατῴκησεν ὁ ἐκ Θεοῦ Λόγος, ὡς ἐν ἀνθρώπῳ κοινῷ
τῷ ἐκ τῆς ἁγίας παρθένου γεγεννημένῳ, ἵνα μὴ θεοφόρος ἄνθρωπος
John i. 14.   νοοῖτο Χριστός. εἰ γὰρ καὶ ἐσκήνωσεν ἐν ἡμῖν ὁ Λόγος,
Col. ii. 9.   εἴρηται δὲ καὶ ἐν Χριστῷ κατοικῆσαι πᾶν τὸ πλήρωμα τῆς
θεότητος σωματικῶς· ἀλλ' οὖν ἐννοῶμεν, ὅτι γενόμενος σάρξ, οὐχ
110 ὥσπερ ἐν τοῖς ἁγίοις κατοικῆσαι λέγεται, κατὰ τὸν ἴσον καὶ ἐν αὐτῷ
τρόπον γενέσθαι διοριζόμεθα τὴν κατοίκησιν· ἀλλ' ἑνωθεὶς κατὰ
φύσιν καὶ οὐκ εἰς σάρκα τραπείς, τοιαύτην ἐποιήσατο τὴν κατοίκησιν,
ἣν ἂν ἔχειν λέγοιτο καὶ ἡ τοῦ ἀνθρώπου ψυχὴ πρὸς τὸ ἴδιον ἑαυτῆς
σῶμα.

115   Εἷς οὖν ἄρα Χριστὸς καὶ Υἱὸς καὶ Κύριος, οὐχ ὡς συνάφειαν ἁπλῶς
τὴν ὡς ἑνότητι τῆς ἀξίας ἤγουν αὐθεντίας ἔχοντος ἀνθρώπου πρὸς
Θεόν· οὐ γὰρ ἑνοῖ τὰς φύσεις ἡ ἰσοτιμία, καὶ γοῦν Πέτρος τε καὶ
Ἰωάννης, ἰσότιμοι μὲν ἀλλήλοις, καθὸ καὶ ἀπόστολοι καὶ ἅγιοι
μαθηταί, πλὴν οὐχ εἷς οἱ δύο· οὔτε μὴν κατὰ παράθεσιν τὸν τῆς
120 συναφείας νοοῦμεν τρόπον, οὐκ ἀπόχρη γὰρ τοῦτο πρὸς ἕνωσιν φυσι-
κήν· οὔτε μὴν ὡς κατὰ μέθεξιν σχετικήν, ὡς καὶ ἡμεῖς κολλώμενοι
1 Cor. vi. 17.   τῷ Κυρίῳ, κατὰ τὸ γεγραμμένον, ἐν πνεῦμά ἐσμεν πρὸς
αὐτόν· μᾶλλον δὲ τὸ τῆς συναφείας ὄνομα παραιτούμεθα, ὡς οὐκ ἔχον
ἱκανῶς σημῆναι τὴν ἕνωσιν. ἀλλ' οὐδὲ Θεὸν ἢ Δεσπότην τοῦ Χριστοῦ
125 τὸν ἐκ Θεοῦ Πατρὸς Λόγον ὀνομάζομεν· ἵνα μὴ πάλιν ἀναφανδὸν
τέμνωμεν εἰς δύο τὸν ἕνα Χριστὸν καὶ Υἱὸν καὶ Κύριον, καὶ δυσφημίας
ἐγκλήματι περιπέσωμεν, Θεὸν ἑαυτοῦ καὶ Δεσπότην ποιοῦντες αὐτόν.
ἑνωθεὶς γὰρ, ὡς ἤδη προείπομεν, ὁ τοῦ Θεοῦ Λόγος σαρκὶ καθ'
ὑπόστασιν, Θεὸς μέν ἐστι τῶν ὅλων, δεσπόζει δὲ τοῦ παντός· οὔτε δὲ
130 αὐτὸς ἑαυτοῦ δοῦλός ἐστιν, οὔτε Δεσπότης· εὔηθες γὰρ, μᾶλλον δὲ
ἤδη καὶ δυσσεβές, τὸ οὕτω φρονεῖν ἢ λέγειν. ἔφη μὲν γὰρ Θεὸν
John xx. 17.   ἑαυτοῦ τὸν Πατέρα καίτοι Θεὸς ὢν φύσει καὶ ἐκ τῆς
οὐσίας αὐτοῦ, ἀλλ' οὐκ ἠγνοήκαμεν, ὅτι μετὰ τοῦ εἶναι Θεὸς, καὶ
ἄνθρωπος γέγονεν ὁ ὑπὸ Θεῷ, κατά γε τὸν πρέποντα νόμον τῇ τῆς
135 ἀνθρωπότητος φύσει. αὐτὸς δὲ ἑαυτοῦ πῶς ἂν γένοιτο Θεὸς ἢ

Δεσπότης; οὐκοῦν, ὡς ἄνθρωπος, καὶ ὅσον ἧκεν εἴς γε τὸ πρέπον τοῖς τῆς κενώσεως μέτροις, ὑπὸ Θεῷ μεθ᾽ ἡμῶν ἑαυτὸν εἶναί φησιν. οὕτω γέγονε καὶ ὑπὸ νόμον, καίτοι λαλήσας αὐτὸς τὸν νόμον καὶ Gal. iv. 5. νομοθέτης ὑπάρχων, ὡς Θεός.

Παραιτούμεθα δὲ λέγειν ἐπὶ Χριστοῦ Διὰ τὸν φοροῦντα τὸν φορούμε- 140 νον σέβω, διὰ τὸν ἀόρατον προσκυνῶ τὸν ὁρώμενον, φρικτὸν δὲ πρὸς τούτῳ κἀκεῖνο εἰπεῖν Ὁ ληφθεὶς τῷ λαβόντι συγχρηματίζει Θεός. ὁ γὰρ ταῦτα λέγων διατέμνει πάλιν εἰς δύο χριστούς, καὶ ἄνθρωπον ἵστησιν ἀνὰ μέρος ἰδικῶς καὶ Θεὸν ὁμοίως· ἀρνεῖται γὰρ ὁμολογουμένως τὴν ἕνωσιν, καθ᾽ ἣν οὐχ ὡς ἕτερος ἑτέρῳ συμπροσκυνεῖταί τις, οὔτε 145 μὴν συγχρηματίζει Θεός· ἀλλ᾽ εἰς νοεῖται Χριστὸς Ἰησοῦς, Υἱὸς Μονογενής, μιᾷ προσκυνήσει τιμώμενος μετὰ τῆς ἰδίας σαρκός. ὁμολογοῦμεν δέ, ὅτι αὐτὸς ὁ ἐκ Θεοῦ Πατρὸς γεννηθεὶς Υἱὸς καὶ Θεὸς Μονογενὴς καίτοι κατὰ φύσιν ἰδίαν ὑπάρχων ἀπαθής, σαρκὶ I Peter iv. I. πέπονθεν ὑπὲρ ἡμῶν, κατὰ τὰς γραφάς· καὶ ἦν ἐν τῷ σταυρωθέντι 150 σώματι τὰ τῆς ἰδίας σαρκὸς ἀπαθῶς οἰκειούμενος πάθη, χάριτι δὲ Θεοῦ καὶ ὑπὲρ παντὸς ἐγεύσατο θανάτου, διδοὺς αὐτῷ τὸ Heb. ii. 9. ἴδιον σῶμα, καίτοι κατὰ φύσιν ὑπάρχων ζωή, καὶ αὐτὸς ὢν ἡ ἀνάστασις. ἵνα γὰρ ἀρρήτῳ δυνάμει πατήσας τὸν θάνατον, ὡς ἔν γε δὴ πρώτῃ τῇ ἰδίᾳ σαρκί, γένηται πρωτότοκος ἐκ John xi. 25.
Col. i. 18. 155
I Cor. xv. 20. νεκρῶν καὶ ἀπαρχὴ τῶν κεκοιμημένων, ὁδοποιήσῃ τε τῇ ἀνθρώπου φύσει τὴν εἰς ἀφθαρσίαν ἀναδρομήν, χάριτι Θεοῦ, καθάπερ ἔφημεν ἀρτίως, ὑπὲρ παντὸς ἐγεύσατο θανάτου· τριήμερος Heb. ii. 9. δὲ ἀνεβίω σκυλεύσας τὸν ᾅδην. ὥστε κἂν λέγηται δι᾽ ἀνθρώπου γενέσθαι ἡ ἀνάστασις τῶν νεκρῶν, ἀλλὰ νοοῦμεν ἄνθρωπον I Cor. xv. 21. 160 τὸν ἐκ Θεοῦ γεγονότα Λόγον· καὶ λελύσθαι δι᾽ αὐτοῦ τοῦ θανάτου τὸ κράτος· ἥξει δὲ κατὰ καιροὺς ὡς εἷς Υἱὸς καὶ Κύριος ἐν τῇ δόξῃ τοῦ Πατρός, ἵνα κρίνῃ τὴν οἰκουμένην ἐν δικαιοσύνῃ, καθὰ Acts xvii. 31. γέγραπται.

Ἀναγκαίως δὲ κἀκεῖνο προσθήσομεν· καταγγέλλοντες γὰρ τὸν κατὰ 165 σάρκα θάνατον τοῦ Μονογενοῦς Υἱοῦ τοῦ Θεοῦ, τουτέστιν, I Cor. xi. 26. Ἰησοῦ Χριστοῦ, τήν τε ἐκ νεκρῶν ἀναβίωσιν, καὶ τὴν εἰς οὐρανοὺς ἀνάληψιν ὁμολογοῦντες, τὴν ἀναίμακτον ἐν ταῖς ἐκκλησίαις τελοῦμεν λατρείαν· πρόσιμέν τε οὕτω ταῖς μυστικαῖς εὐλογίαις καὶ ἁγιαζόμεθα, μέτοχοι γινόμενοι τῆς τε ἁγίας σαρκὸς καὶ τοῦ τιμίου αἵματος τοῦ 170 πάντων ἡμῶν Σωτῆρος Χριστοῦ. καὶ οὐχ ὡς σάρκα κοινὴν δεχόμενοι, μὴ γένοιτο· οὔτε μὴν ὡς ἀνδρὸς ἡγιασμένου καὶ συναφθέντος τῷ Λόγῳ κατὰ τὴν ἑνότητα τῆς ἀξίας, ἤγουν ὡς θείαν ἐνοίκησιν ἐσχηκότος· ἀλλ᾽ ὡς ζωοποιὸν ἀληθῶς καὶ ἰδίαν αὐτοῦ τοῦ Λόγου. ζωὴ γὰρ ὢν κατὰ φύσιν ὡς Θεός, ἐπειδὴ γέγονεν ἓν πρὸς τὴν ἑαυτοῦ σάρκα, ζωοποιὸν 175 ἀπέφηνεν αὐτήν. ὥστε κἂν λέγῃ πρὸς ἡμᾶς Ἀμὴν ἀμὴν John vi. 53. λέγω ὑμῖν, ἐὰν μὴ φάγητε τὴν σάρκα τοῦ υἱοῦ τοῦ ἀνθρώπου καὶ πίητε αὐτοῦ τὸ αἷμα· οὐχ ὡς ἀνθρώπου τῶν καθ᾽ ἡμᾶς ἑνὸς καὶ αὐτὴν εἶναι λογιούμεθα, πῶς γὰρ ἡ ἀνθρώπου σὰρξ ζωοποιὸς ἔσται, κατὰ φύσιν τὴν ἑαυτῆς; ἀλλ᾽ ὡς ἰδίαν ἀληθῶς γενομένην τοῦ δι᾽ ἡμᾶς καὶ 180 υἱοῦ ἀνθρώπου γεγονότος τε καὶ χρηματίσαντος.

Τὰς δέ γε ἐν τοῖς εὐαγγελίοις τοῦ Σωτῆρος ἡμῶν φωνάς, οὔτε ὑποστάσεσι δυσὶν οὔτε μὴν προσώποις καταμερίζομεν· οὐ γάρ ἐστι

διπλοῦς ὁ εἷς καὶ μόνος Χριστός, κἂν ἐκ δύο νοῆται καὶ διαφόρων
185 πραγμάτων εἰς ἑνότητα τὴν ἀμέριστον συνενηνεγμένος, καθάπερ
ἀμέλει καὶ ἄνθρωπος ἐκ ψυχῆς νοεῖται καὶ σώματος, καὶ οὐ διπλοῦς
μᾶλλον, ἀλλ᾽ εἷς ἐξ ἀμφοῖν· ἀλλὰ τάς τε ἀνθρωπίνας. καὶ πρός γε
τούτῳ τὰς θεϊκὰς, παρ᾽ ἑνὸς εἰρῆσθαι διακεισόμεθα φρονοῦντες ὀρθῶς.
ὅταν μὲν γὰρ θεοπρεπῶς λέγῃ περὶ ἑαυτοῦ Ὁ ἑωρακὼς ἐμὲ ἑώρακε
190 John xiv. 9.   τὸν Πατέρα, καὶ Ἐγὼ καὶ ὁ Πατὴρ ἕν ἐσμεν, τὴν θείαν
ibid. x. 30.   αὐτοῦ καὶ ἀπόρρητον ἐννοοῦμεν φύσιν, καθ᾽ ἣν καὶ ἕν
ἐστι πρὸς τὸν ἑαυτοῦ Πατέρα διὰ τὴν ταυτότητα τῆς οὐσίας, εἰκών
τε καὶ χαρακτὴρ καὶ ἀπαύγασμα τῆς δόξης αὐτοῦ·
2 Cor. iv. 4, Col.
i. 15, Heb. i. 3.   ὅταν δὲ τὸ τῆς ἀνθρωπότητος μέτρον οὐκ ἀτιμάζων,
195 τοῖς Ἰουδαίοις προσλαλῇ Νῦν δέ με ζητεῖτε ἀποκτεῖναι,
ἄνθρωπον ὃς τὴν ἀλήθειαν ὑμῖν λελάληκα, πάλιν οὐδὲν ἧττον αὐτὸν
τὸν ἐν ἰσότητί τε καὶ ὁμοιότητι τοῦ Πατρὸς Θεὸν Λόγον καὶ ἐκ τῶν
τῆς ἀνθρωπότητος αὐτοῦ μέτρων ἐπιγινώσκομεν. εἰ γάρ ἐστιν ἀναγκαῖον τὸ πιστεύειν, ὅτι Θεὸς ὢν φύσει γέγονε σὰρξ, ἤγουν ἄνθρωπος
200 ἐμψυχωμένος ψυχῇ λογικῇ· ποῖον ἂν ἔχοι λόγον τὸ ἐπαισχύνεσθαί
τινας ταῖς παρ᾽ αὐτοῦ φωναῖς, εἰ γεγόνασιν ἀνθρωποπρεπῶς; εἰ γὰρ
παραιτοῖτο τοὺς ἀνθρώπῳ πρέποντας λόγους, τίς ὁ ἀναγκάσας γενέσθαι
καθ᾽ ἡμᾶς ἄνθρωπον; ὁ δὲ καθεὶς ἑαυτὸν δι᾽ ἡμᾶς εἰς ἑκούσιον
κένωσιν, διὰ ποίαν αἰτίαν παραιτοῖτο ἂν τοὺς τῇ κενώσει πρέποντας
205 λόγους; ἑνὶ τοιγαροῦν προσώπῳ τὰς ἐν τοῖς εὐαγγελίοις πάσας
1 Cor. viii. 6.   ἀναθετέον φωνὰς, ὑποστάσει μιᾷ τῇ τοῦ Λόγου σεσαρκωμένῃ.
Κύριος γὰρ εἷς Ἰησοῦς Χριστός, κατὰ τὰς γραφάς.
Heb. iii. 1.   Εἰ δὲ δὴ καλοῖτο καὶ ἀπόστολος καὶ ἀρχιερεύς τῆς
ὁμολογίας ἡμῶν, ὡς ἱερουργῶν τῷ Θεῷ καὶ Πατρὶ τὴν πρὸς ἡμῶν
210 αὐτῷ τε καὶ δι᾽ αὐτοῦ τῷ Θεῷ καὶ Πατρὶ προσκομιζομένην τῆς
πίστεως ὁμολογίαν· καὶ μὴν καὶ εἰς τὸ Ἅγιον Πνεῦμα· πάλιν αὐτὸν
εἶναί φαμεν τὸν ἐκ Θεοῦ κατὰ φύσιν Υἱὸν Μονογενῆ, καὶ οὐκ ἀνθρώπῳ
προσνεμοῦμεν παρ᾽ αὐτὸν ἑτέρῳ, τό τε τῆς ἱερωσύνης ὄνομα, καὶ
1 Tim. ii. 5.   αὐτὸ δὲ τὸ χρῆμα· γέγονε γὰρ μεσίτης Θεοῦ καὶ ἀνθρώπων
215 Eph. v. 2.   καὶ διαλλακτὴς εἰς εἰρήνην· ἑαυτὸν ἀναθεὶς εἰς ὀσμὴν
Heb. x. 5–7.   εὐωδίας τῷ Θεῷ καὶ Πατρί. τοιγάρτοι καὶ ἔφασκε Θυσίαν
Ps. xl. 6–8.   καὶ προσφορὰν οὐκ ἠθέλησας, ὁλοκαυτώματα καὶ περὶ
ἁμαρτίας οὐκ ηὐδόκησας, σῶμα δὲ κατηρτίσω μοι· τότε εἶπον Ἰδοὺ
ἥκω, ἐν κεφαλίδι βιβλίου γέγραπται περὶ ἐμοῦ, τοῦ ποιῆσαι, ὁ Θεὸς, τὸ
220 θέλημά σου. προσκεκόμικε γὰρ ὑπὲρ ἡμῶν εἰς ὀσμὴν εὐωδίας τὸ
ἴδιον σῶμα, καὶ οὐχ ὑπέρ γε μᾶλλον ἑαυτοῦ. ποίας γὰρ ἂν ἐδεήθη
προσφορᾶς ἢ θυσίας ὑπὲρ ἑαυτοῦ, κρείττων ἁπάσης ἁμαρτίας ὑπάρχων
Rom. iii. 23.   ὡς Θεός; εἰ γὰρ πάντες ἥμαρτον καὶ ὑστεροῦνται τῆς δόξης
τοῦ Θεοῦ, καθὸ γεγόναμεν ἡμεῖς ἕτοιμοι πρὸς παραφορὰν, καὶ κατηρ-
225 ρώστησεν ἡ ἀνθρώπου φύσις τὴν ἁμαρτίαν (αὐτὸς δὲ οὐχ οὕτω), καὶ
ἡττώμεθα διὰ τοῦτο τῆς δόξης αὐτοῦ· πῶς ἂν εἴη λοιπὸν ἀμφίβολον,
ὅτι τέθυται δι᾽ ἡμᾶς καὶ ὑπὲρ ἡμῶν ὁ ἀμνὸς ὁ ἀληθινός; καὶ τὸ λέγειν
ὅτι προσκεκόμικεν ἑαυτὸν ὑπέρ τε ἑαυτοῦ καὶ ἡμῶν, ἀμοιρήσειεν ἂν
οὐδαμῶς τῶν εἰς δυσσέβειαν ἐγκλημάτων· πεπλημμέληκε γὰρ κατ᾽
230 οὐδένα τρόπον, οὔτε μὴν ἐποίησεν ἁμαρτίαν. ποίας οὖν ἐδεήθη
προσφορᾶς, ἁμαρτίας οὐκ οὔσης, ἐφ᾽ ᾗπερ ἂν γένοιτο καὶ μάλα εἰκότως;

THE EPISTLES OF CYRIL 113

Ὅταν δὲ λέγῃ περὶ τοῦ Πνεύματος Ἐκεῖνος ἐμὲ δοξάσει· John xvi. 14.
νοοῦντες ὀρθῶς, οὐχ ὡς δόξης ἐπιδεᾶ τῆς παρ' ἑτέρου φαμὲν, τὸν ἕνα
Χριστὸν καὶ Υἱὸν τὴν παρὰ τοῦ Ἁγίου Πνεύματος δόξαν ἑλεῖν· ὅτι
μηδὲ κρεῖττον αὐτοῦ καὶ ὑπὲρ αὐτὸν τὸ Πνεῦμα αὐτοῦ. ἐπειδὴ δὲ εἰς 235
ἔνδειξιν τῆς ἑαυτοῦ θεότητος ἐχρῆτο τῷ ἰδίῳ Πνεύματι πρὸς μεγαλουρ-
γίαν, δεδοξάσθαι παρ' αὐτοῦ φησιν, ὥσπερ ἂν εἰ καί τις λέγοι τῶν
καθ' ἡμᾶς περὶ τῆς ἐνούσης ἰσχύος αὐτῷ τυχὸν ἤγουν ἐπιστήμης τῆς
ἐφ' ὁτῳοῦν, ὅτι δοξάσουσιν ἐμέ. εἰ γὰρ καὶ ἔστιν ἐν ὑποστάσει τὸ
Πνεῦμα ἰδικῇ, καὶ δὴ καὶ νοεῖται καθ' ἑαυτό, καθὸ Πνεῦμά ἐστι καὶ 240
οὐχ Υἱός· ἀλλ' οὖν ἐστιν οὐκ ἀλλότριον αὐτοῦ· πνεῦμα γὰρ ἀληθείας
ὠνόμασται, καὶ ἔστι Χριστὸς ἡ ἀλήθεια· καὶ προχεῖται John xv. 26.
παρ' αὐτοῦ, καθάπερ ἀμέλει καὶ ἐκ τοῦ Θεοῦ καὶ Πατρός. ibid. xiv. 6.
ἐνεργήσαν τοιγαροῦν τὸ Πνεῦμα καὶ διὰ χειρὸς τῶν ἁγίων ἀποστόλων τὰ
παράδοξα μετὰ τὸ ἀνελθεῖν τὸν Κύριον ἡμῶν Ἰησοῦν τὸν Χριστὸν εἰς 245
τὸν οὐρανόν, ἐδόξασεν αὐτόν. ἐπιστεύθη γὰρ, ὅτι Θεὸς κατὰ φύσιν
ἐστὶ πάλιν αὐτὸς ἐνεργῶν διὰ τοῦ ἰδίου Πνεύματος. διὰ τοῦτο καὶ
ἔφασκεν Ὅτι ἐκ τοῦ ἐμοῦ λήψεται, καὶ ἀναγγελεῖ ὑμῖν. John xvi. 14.
καὶ οὔτι που φαμέν, ὡς ἐκ μετοχῆς τὸ Πνεῦμά ἐστι σοφόν τε καὶ
δυνατόν· παντέλειον γὰρ καὶ ἀπροσδεές ἐστι παντὸς ἀγαθοῦ. ἐπειδὴ 250
δὲ τῆς τοῦ Πατρὸς δυνάμεως καὶ σοφίας, τουτέστι τοῦ Υἱοῦ, Πνεῦμά
ἐστιν, αὐτόχρημα σοφία ἐστὶ καὶ δύναμις.
Ἐπειδὴ δὲ Θεὸν ἑνωθέντα σαρκὶ καθ' ὑπόστασιν ἡ ἁγία παρθένος
ἐκτέτοκε σαρκικῶς, ταύτῃτοι καὶ θεοτόκον εἶναί φαμεν αὐτήν, οὐχ ὡς
τῆς τοῦ Λόγου φύσεως τῆς ὑπάρξεως τὴν ἀρχὴν ἐχούσης ἀπὸ σαρκός· ἦν 255
γὰρ ἐν ἀρχῇ καὶ Θεὸς ἦν ὁ Λόγος καὶ ὁ Λόγος ἦν πρὸς τὸν John i. 1.
Θεόν, καὶ αὐτός ἐστι τῶν αἰώνων ὁ ποιητής, συναΐδιος τῷ Πατρί, καὶ τῶν
ὅλων ὁ δημιουργός· ἀλλ' ὡς ἤδη προείπομεν, ἐπειδὴ καθ' ὑπόστασιν
ἐνώσας ἑαυτῷ τὸ ἀνθρώπινον, καὶ ἐκ μήτρας αὐτῆς γέννησιν ὑπέμεινε
σαρκικήν, οὐχ ὡς δεηθεὶς ἀναγκαίως, ἤτοι διὰ τὴν ἰδίαν φύσιν, καὶ τῆς 260
ἐν χρόνῳ καὶ ἐν ἐσχάτοις τοῦ αἰῶνος καιροῖς γεννήσεως· ἀλλ' ἵνα καὶ
αὐτὴν τῆς ὑπάρξεως ἡμῶν εὐλογήσῃ τὴν ἀρχήν· καὶ τεκούσης γυναικὸς
αὐτὸν ἑνωθέντα σαρκί, παύσηται λοιπὸν ἡ κατὰ παντὸς τοῦ γένους
ἀρά, πέμπουσα πρὸς θάνατον τὰ ἐκ γῆς ἡμῶν σώματα, καὶ τό Ἐν
λύπαις τέξῃ τέκνα δι' αὐτοῦ καταργούμενον, ἀληθὲς Gen. iii. 16. 265
ἀποφήνῃ τὸ διὰ τῆς τοῦ προφήτου φωνῆς Κατέπιεν ὁ θάνατος ἰσχύσας,
καὶ πάλιν ἀφεῖλεν ὁ Θεὸς πᾶν δάκρυον ἀπὸ παντὸς Isa. xxv. 8.
προσώπου. ταύτης γὰρ ἕνεκα τῆς αἰτίας φαμὲν αὐτὸν Apoc. vii. 17.
οἰκονομικῶς καὶ αὐτὸν εὐλογῆσαι τὸν γάμον, καὶ ἀπελθεῖν κεκλημένον
ἐν Κανᾷ τῆς Γαλιλαίας ὁμοῦ τοῖς ἁγίοις ἀποστόλοις. John ii. 2. 270
Ταῦτα φρονεῖν δεδιδάγμεθα παρά τε τῶν ἁγίων ἀποστόλων καὶ
εὐαγγελιστῶν καὶ πάσης δὲ τῆς θεοπνεύστου γραφῆς, καὶ ἐκ τῆς τῶν
μακαρίων πατέρων ἀληθοῦς ὁμολογίας. τούτοις ἅπασι καὶ τὴν σὴν
εὐλάβειαν συναινέσαι χρή, καὶ συνθέσθαι δίχα δόλου παντός. ἃ δέ
ἐστιν ἀναγκαῖον ἀναθεματίσαι τὴν σὴν εὐλάβειαν, ὑποτέτακται τῇδε 275
ἡμῶν τῇ ἐπιστολῇ.
α'. Εἴ τις οὐχ ὁμολογεῖ Θεὸν εἶναι κατὰ ἀλήθειαν τὸν Ἐμμανουήλ,
καὶ διὰ τοῦτο θεοτόκον τὴν ἁγίαν παρθένον· γεγέννηκε γὰρ σαρκικῶς
σάρκα γεγονότα τὸν ἐκ Θεοῦ Λόγον· ἀνάθεμα ἔστω.

280 β'. Εἴ τις οὐχ ὁμολογεῖ σαρκὶ καθ' ὑπόστασιν ἡνῶσθαι τὸν ἐκ Θεοῦ
Πατρὸς Λόγον, ἕνα τε εἶναι Χριστὸν μετὰ τῆς ἰδίας σαρκός, τὸν αὐτὸν
δηλόνοτι Θεόν τε ὁμοῦ καὶ ἄνθρωπον, ἀνάθεμα ἔστω.

γ'. Εἴ τις ἐπὶ τοῦ ἑνὸς Χριστοῦ διαιρεῖ τὰς ὑποστάσεις μετὰ τὴν
ἕνωσιν, μόνῃ συνάπτων αὐτὰς συναφείᾳ τῇ κατὰ τὴν ἀξίαν, ἤγουν
285 αὐθεντίαν ἢ δυναστείαν, καὶ οὐχὶ δὴ μᾶλλον συνόδῳ τῇ καθ' ἕνωσιν
φυσικήν, ἀνάθεμα ἔστω.

δ'. Εἴ τις προσώποις δυσὶν ἤγουν ὑποστάσεσι τάς τε ἐν τοῖς εὐαγγελικοῖς καὶ ἀποστολικοῖς συγγράμμασι διανέμει φωνάς, ἢ ἐπὶ Χριστῷ
παρὰ τῶν ἁγίων λεγομένας, ἢ παρ' αὐτοῦ περὶ ἑαυτοῦ· καὶ τὰς μὲν ὡς
290 ἀνθρώπῳ παρὰ τὸν ἐκ Θεοῦ Λόγον ἰδικῶς νοουμένῳ προσάπτει, τὰς δὲ
ὡς θεοπρεπεῖς μόνῳ τῷ ἐκ Θεοῦ Πατρὸς Λόγῳ, ἀνάθεμα ἔστω.

ε'. Εἴ τις τολμᾷ λέγειν θεοφόρον ἄνθρωπον τὸν Χριστόν, καὶ οὐχὶ
John i. 14.   δὴ μᾶλλον Θεὸν εἶναι κατὰ ἀλήθειαν, ὡς Υἱὸν ἕνα καὶ φύσει,
Heb. ii. 14.   καθὸ γέγονε σὰρξ ὁ Λόγος καὶ κεκοινώνηκε παραπλησίως
295 ἡμῖν αἵματος καὶ σαρκός, ἀνάθεμα ἔστω.

ϛ'. Εἴ τις λέγει Θεὸν ἢ Δεσπότην εἶναι τοῦ Χριστοῦ τὸν ἐκ Θεοῦ
Πατρὸς Λόγον, καὶ οὐχὶ δὴ μᾶλλον τὸν αὐτὸν ὁμολογεῖ Θεόν τε ὁμοῦ
καὶ ἄνθρωπον, ὡς γεγονότος σαρκὸς τοῦ Λόγου κατὰ τὰς γραφάς,
ἀνάθεμα ἔστω.

300 ζ'. Εἴ τις φησίν, ὡς ἄνθρωπον ἐνηργῆσθαι παρὰ τοῦ Θεοῦ Λόγου
τὸν Ἰησοῦν καὶ τὴν τοῦ Μονογενοῦς εὐδοξίαν περιῆφθαι, ὡς ἑτέρῳ
παρ' αὐτὸν ὑπάρχοντι, ἀνάθεμα ἔστω.

η'. Εἴ τις τολμᾷ λέγειν τὸν ἀναληφθέντα ἄνθρωπον συμπροσκυνεῖσθαι δεῖν τῷ Θεῷ Λόγῳ καὶ συνδοξάζεσθαι καὶ συγχρηματίζειν
305 Θεόν, ὡς ἕτερον ἐν ἑτέρῳ· τὸ γὰρ Σὺν ἀεὶ προστιθέμενον τοῦτο νοεῖν
ἀναγκάσει· καὶ οὐχὶ δὴ μᾶλλον μιᾷ προσκυνήσει τιμᾷ τὸν Ἐμμανουήλ,
καὶ μίαν αὐτῷ τὴν δοξολογίαν ἀναπέμπει, καθὸ γέγονε σὰρξ ὁ Λόγος,
ἀνάθεμα ἔστω.

θ'. Εἴ τις φησὶ τὸν ἕνα Κύριον Ἰησοῦν Χριστὸν δεδοξάσθαι παρὰ τοῦ
310 Πνεύματος ὡς ἀλλοτρίᾳ δυνάμει τῇ δι' αὐτοῦ χρώμενον, καὶ παρ'
αὐτοῦ λαβόντα τὸ ἐνεργεῖν δύνασθαι κατὰ πνευμάτων ἀκαθάρτων, καὶ
τὸ πληροῦν εἰς ἀνθρώπους τὰς θεοσημίας, καὶ οὐχὶ δὴ μᾶλλον ἴδιον
αὐτοῦ τὸ Πνεῦμα, φησί, δι' οὗ καὶ ἐνήργηκε τὰς θεοσημίας, ἀνάθεμα
ἔστω.

315 Heb. iii. 1.   ι'. Ἀρχιερέα καὶ ἀπόστολον τῆς ὁμολογίας ἡμῶν
γεγενῆσθαι Χριστὸν ἡ θεία λέγει γραφή, προσκεκόμικε δὲ ὑπὲρ ἡμῶν
Eph. v. 2.   ἑαυτὸν εἰς ὀσμὴν εὐωδίας τῷ Θεῷ καὶ Πατρί. εἴ τις
τοίνυν ἀρχιερέα φησὶ καὶ ἀπόστολον ἡμῶν γενέσθαι, οὐκ αὐτὸν τὸν ἐκ
Θεοῦ Λόγον, ὅτε γέγονε σὰρξ καὶ καθ' ἡμᾶς ἄνθρωπος· ἀλλ' ὡς
320 ἕτερον παρ' αὐτὸν ἰδικῶς ἄνθρωπον ἐκ γυναικός· ἢ εἴ τις λέγει καὶ
ὑπὲρ ἑαυτοῦ προσενεγκεῖν αὐτὸν τὴν προσφορὰν καὶ οὐχὶ δὴ μᾶλλον
ὑπὲρ μόνων ἡμῶν· οὐ γὰρ ἂν ἐδεήθη προσφορᾶς ὁ μὴ εἰδὼς ἁμαρτίαν·
2 Cor. v. 21.   ἀνάθεμα ἔστω.

ια'. Εἴ τις οὐχ ὁμολογεῖ τὴν τοῦ Κυρίου σάρκα ζωοποιὸν εἶναι καὶ
325 ἰδίαν αὐτοῦ τοῦ ἐκ Θεοῦ Πατρὸς Λόγου· ἀλλ' ὡς ἑτέρου τινὸς παρ'
αὐτόν, συνημμένου μὲν αὐτῷ κατὰ τὴν ἀξίαν, ἤγουν ὡς μόνην θείαν
ἐνοίκησιν ἐσχηκότος, καὶ οὐχὶ δὴ μᾶλλον ζωοποιόν, ὡς ἔφημεν, ὅτι

γέγονεν ἰδία τοῦ Λόγου τοῦ τὰ πάντα ζωογονεῖν ἰσχύοντος, ἀνάθεμα ἔστω.

ιβ'. Εἴ τις οὐχ ὁμολογεῖ τὸν τοῦ Θεοῦ Λόγον παθόντα σαρκὶ καὶ 330 ἐσταυρωμένον σαρκὶ καὶ θανάτου γευσάμενον σαρκὶ, γεγονότα τε πρωτότοκον ἐκ τῶν νεκρῶν, καθὸ ζωή ἐστι καὶ ζωοποιὸς ὡς Θεός, ἀνάθεμα ἔστω.

Heb. ii. 9.
Col. i. 18.

NOTES ON CYRIL'S THIRD LETTER TO NESTORIUS

16. τῶν σῶν ἐξηγήσεων τὰ βιβλία. The best edition of these sermons with comments on them is Loofs' *Nestoriana*; and see also *Journal of Theological Studies*, viii, pp. 119 ff. (October 1906).

26. ὁμοῦ τῇ ἁγίᾳ συνόδῳ. The synod at Rome under Caelestine, held at the beginning of August 430. Cyril had sent to Rome in April an account of all that had passed, together with copies of his Letter to the Monks and of his two Letters to Nestorius.[1] Caelestine in the synod had quoted the authority of Ambrose (" Veni Redemptor Gentium "), Hilary, and Damasus, with all of whom Cyril was in agreement, and the synod condemned the teaching of Nestorius, committing the execution of the sentence to Cyril. The pope wrote seven letters, all dated August 11, to the bishops of the principal sees in the East and to the clergy of Constantinople. These were sent to Cyril to be forwarded by him. But in no sense was Cyril authorised to preside at the Council of Ephesus (cf. Kidd, *Church History*, vol. iii, pp. 222 ff. and 241–242).

34. κατὰ τὴν ὁρισθεῖσαν προθεσμίαν. Ten days after the receipt of Caelestine's letter was the period assigned in which Nestorius might recant his error.

42. τῆς σῆς εὐλαβείας. I.e. the Archimandrite Basil, who with a deputation of monks went to the episcopal palace to remonstrate, and was imprisoned in its dungeons (Kidd, vol. iii, p. 202).

46. ἐν τῇ ἐπιστολῇ τῇ γραφείσῃ παρὰ σοῦ. This was the letter written about Easter, 429, by Nestorius to Caelestine, in which he advocated the use of *Christotokos* instead of *Theotokos*. It was carried to Rome by Antiochus (cf. Mansi, iv. 1197).

58. ταῖς γραφείσαις ἐπιστολαῖς . . . ἐκκλησίας. The First and Second Letters of Cyril to Nestorius.

82. καθεὶς ἑαυτὸν εἰς κένωσιν. Here, and below, the κένωσις is defined to consist in the condescension involved in the Incarnation. See note on κατελθόντα in Nicene Creed, and cf. Leo's words in the Tome, § 3 (see below, p. 170).

86. μεμενηκὼς ὅπερ ἦν. A watchword again of Cyril and the Athanasian school. But both Antioch and Alexandria repudiated any idea of a *kenosis* in the modern or Lutheran sense of the word

---

[1] They had easily reached Rome, and are referred to in the letter of Caelestine to Cyril.

(see below, p. 121). And cf. the phrase παντελῶς δ' αὐτὸς ἀεὶ μένων (l. 89) ; and for Nestorian and other views see *Bazaar*, p. 70.

90. κατὰ τὰς γραφάς. Cyril evidently had in mind the Scriptural citations in Alexander's encyclical of 324 (apud Socr. i. 6), Πῶς δὲ τρεπτὸς ἢ ἀλλοιωτὸς ὁ λέγων δι' ἑαυτοῦ 'Εγὼ ἐν τῷ Πατρὶ καὶ ὁ Πατὴρ ἐν ἐμοί· καὶ 'Εγὼ καὶ ὁ Πατὴρ ἕν ἐσμεν· διὰ δὲ τοῦ προφήτου Ἴδετέ με ὅτι ἐγὼ εἰμὶ καὶ οὐκ ἠλλοίωμαι (John xiv. 10, x. 30 ; Mal. iii. 6 ; cf. John viii. 35).

91. ὢν ἔτι καὶ ἐν κόλπῳ, κ.τ.λ. This was evidently in opposition to Nestorius's pronouncement that he could not call a baby God, ἐγὼ τὸν γενόμενον διμηναῖον καὶ τριμηναῖον οὐκ ἂν θεόν ὀνομάσαιμι (Socr. vii. 34 ; see vi. 32 for Socrates' fair judgment of Nestorius).

103. τὸ Πνεῦμα διδοὺς αὐτός. Cyril's Text agrees with that of the oldest uncials, א B (John iii. 34). The argument is that Christ cannot be merely an anointed man, because He Himself bestows the Spirit out of His own fulness of possession.

113. ἡ τοῦ ἀνθρώπου ψυχὴ πρὸς τὸ ἴδιον ἑαυτῆς σῶμα. This analogy is not a perfect one, but it is a sufficient illustration of a natural union in which two unconfused " substances " constitute one person. Cyril employs it, Epist. ad Succens., Epist. ad Valer., Schol. 8, 27, and it is also used by Theodoret, Dial. ii, *Inconfusus*, Epist. cxliii ; by the author of the Quicumque ; by Gregory Naz. Epist. 101 (ad Cled. i. 4) ; and by Augustine, Epist. ad Volus. It is discussed by Petavius De Inc. iii. 9 (Ottley, *The Doctrine of Incarnation*, ii, p. 279). Even Theodore of Mopsuestia used this analogy, though with Antiochene emphasis (Swete, vol. ii, p. 318). Cf. Vincent Ler., Common. 37. But subsequently, in the heat of the Eutychian controversy, it was not used freely, because the Eutychians perverted it, pleading for *one* nature in Christ, inasmuch as soul and body make *one* nature in man. Vigilius of Thapsus, in North Africa, *c.* 480, defended it ; contr. Eutych v. 6. Nestorius replied sharply that such a definition of the union implied that Christ's divine nature would thereby be subject to necessity. It was common ground to both sides to use ἄνθρωπος in the sense of the Manhood, see Athanasius, c. Ar. i. 41–45 ; ii. 45 ; iv. 14, and Cyprian, De Dom. Orat. 14, " Dominus infirmitatem hominis quem portabat ostendens . . . " where *homo* = " man's nature," not " a man."

119. κατὰ παράθεσιν, " by juxtaposition," a co-existence of two things or persons one by the side of another.

121. κατὰ μέθεξιν σχετικήν, " by an acquired participation." Cyril's language is tinctured with terms of the Stoic philosophy, in which σχετικός = " non-essential," " accidental," not springing

from the nature of the object. Such qualities were termed σχέσεις. The Stoics, according to Chrysippus (apud Stobaeus, Ecl. i. 17, p. 144, Gaisford ; p. 376, Heeren), distinguished between παράθεσις, μίξις, κρᾶσις, and σύγχυσις. They defined παράθεσις as σωμάτων συναφὴ κατὰ τὰς ἐπιφανείας, ὡς ἐπὶ τῶν σωρῶν ὁρῶμεν, καὶ τῶν ἐπὶ τῶν αἰγιαλῶν ψήφων καὶ ἄμμων. Μίξις is explained as a complete interpenetration, as in the case of red-hot iron. Κρᾶσις applies to a mechanical mixture, as of certain liquids, such as wine and water. Σύγχυσις is a chemical combination resulting in a third substance. The philosophical use of these terms is important in view of the employment of κρᾶσις and σύγχυσις in the Eutychian controversy. Compare, too, Epist. ad Ioan.

123. συνάφεια is rejected as inadequate ; " association," " conjunction," " connexion," stops short of " union." See P. E. Pusey's note on Cyril adv. Nest. i. 3 in *Library of the Fathers*, p. 19.

140. παραιτούμεθα, κ.τ.λ. These were two dicta of Nestorius, Cyr. adv. Nest. ii. 11, 12. Similarly in his Serm. 1 he had said, τὴν θεοδόχον τῷ Θεῷ Λόγῳ συνθεολογῶμεν μορφήν ; and again Serm. 2, τὴν φορουμένην τῷ φοροῦντι συντιμῶμεν φύσιν. In each case the σύν, as Cyril shows in Anath. 8, implies non-identity.

145. ὡς ἕτερος ἑτέρῳ. See note on Anath. 8, p. 132.

151. οἰκειούμενος. " making His own," " appropriating." Cyril uses οἰκειοῦσθαι as Athanasius used ἰδιοποιεῖν, see Orat. c. Ar. iii. 33, τοῦ Λόγου ἰδιοποιουμένου τὰ τῆς σαρκός, ibid. 38 ; De Inc. 6, 8, 31 ; Epist. ad Epict. 6 ; contr. Apoll. i. 12, 13. Cf. ibid. ii. 16 ; Cyril, Apol. adv. Orient. 12 ; Schol. 36. This point is enforced in Anath. 12, and again Epist. ad Ioan.

165. καταγγέλλοντες γὰρ κ.τ.λ. Dr. Swainson gathered from these words that " some Creed was used in Cyril's time in the Eucharistic office " (*Nicene and Apostles' Creeds*, p. 107), but Cyril's meaning surely is that the service itself was a proclamation of the Death, Resurrection, and Ascension of Christ. He evidently had in mind some such words as are found in the Liturgy of St. Mark, τὸν ἐμὸν θάνατον καταγγέλλετε (1 Cor. xi. 26) καὶ τὴν ἐμὴν ἀνάστασιν καὶ ἀνάληψιν ὁμολογεῖτε ἄχρις οὗ ἐὰν ἔλθω (Brightman, p. 133). Cf. Liturgy of Coptic Jacobites (ibid., p. 177) ; Liturgy of St. Basil (ibid., p. 405) ; and Liturgy of St. James (ibid., p. 52). The recital of the Creed in the Liturgy does not seem to have been customary before the latter half of the fifth century. Its first introduction is generally attributed to Peter the Fuller, Patriarch of Antioch, 471–88, whose example was followed at Constantinople by Timothy, 511–17. The custom spread but slowly. From Spain, after the third Council of Toledo, 589, it passed into Gaul and England, and finally was adopted at Rome in the eleventh century, A.D. 1014. Bernon, Abbot of

Reichenau, relates that in his presence the Emperor Henry II induced Pope Benedict VIII (1012–24) to adopt this custom, and so bring the Roman use into line with the rest of the Christian world : Migne, P.L., cxlii, p. 1060, quoted by Duchesne, *Christian Worship*, p. 172. The original Nicene Creed was supplanted by the Constantinopolitan during the sixth century. The recital of a creed at services other than Baptism and the Eucharist cannot be traced earlier than the ninth century. The Apostles' Creed was then said at Prime, and from thence passed into the English daily Mattins.

168. τὴν ἀναίμακτον . . . τελοῦμεν λατρείαν. For the phrase compare the Liturgy of St. James and of Syrian Jacobites, Brightman, pp. 53, 87. This argument from the Eucharist was frequently used in the Christological controversies and has its own importance.[1] Thus Cyril, following Athanasius (Epist. lxi. 2 ; ad Maxim. Phil. 2, οὐκ ἀνθρώπου τε τινες μετέχοντες σώματος ἀλλ' αὐτοῦ τοῦ Λόγου σῶμα λαμβάνοντες θεοποιούμεθα), reasons that we should not eat Christ's flesh in the Sacrament unless we believed it to be the flesh of one who is God and therefore life-giving. Somewhat similarly Irenaeus (iv. 31. 4) had confuted those who denied the resurrection of the flesh from the fact that the flesh was nourished in the Eucharist with the divine life of the Word of God. He concludes " Ἡμῶν δὲ σύμφωνος ἡ γνώμη τῇ εὐχαριστίᾳ καὶ ἡ εὐχαριστία βεβαιοῖ τὴν γνώμην."

Leo again (Epist. lix, Sermon xci) argued against Eutyches that we should not communicate unless we believed Christ's Flesh there received to be most true and real. Christ's perfect manhood is shown from the fact of communion, just as the hypostatic union is shown from the purpose of the sacrament.[2]

Theodoret (Dial. ii *Inconfusus*) argued the coexistence of the two perfect natures in Christ from the fact that the consecrated Elements retain their nature as bread and wine.

Nestorius' argument is somewhat different (*Bazaar*, 37–41). In whatever sense, he writes, the Bread becomes the Body of Christ, in that same sense do we become the Body of Christ by participating in the Sacrament. And since we can only participate in a human body, the Body of Christ must have been human. In other words, he argues, as against the charge that his Christology destroys the universal significance of the Incarnation and Atonement, that his own view alone safeguards their significance ; for the contrary

---

[1] See Gore, *Dissertations*, p. 274 and references. But the parallelism was already a matter of Christian teaching in Justin Martyr's day (Apol. i. 66).

[2] In the first passage there is an allusion to the then universal practice of infant communion (see Cyprian, De Lapsis, ix. 25 ; Augustine, Serm. clxxiv. 7 ; De Pecc. Mer. i. 20. 26 ; 24. 34 ; Apost Const. viii. 13 ; cf. Bingham, xv. 4. 7) ; and in the second to the " Amen " said by the recipient in response to the words of delivery.

doctrine leaves no humanity for us to be incorporated with. But note how both Schools held the sacramental elements to be in a real sense the very Body and Blood of the Saviour ; only they argued in two different ways from that truth. See also Driver and Hodgson, *Bazaar*, p. 333, and cf. Hooker's argument, *Ecclesiastical Polity*, book v, ch. li–lvi, and St. Thomas Aquinas, Summa Theol., Part III, Q. 73, who teaches that the spiritual benefit (Res) received in the Sacrament is the unity of the Mystical Body. Cf. Augustine, Serm. lvii. 7, and for a similar view Leo, Tome, chapter 5, line 235. See G. Dix, *Shape of the Liturgy*, pp. 138 and 139.

On " bloodless " see Gore, *Body of Christ*, p. 159. The word was used by Philo of the meal as distinguished from the animal offerings ; and generally by Christian writers of spiritual as distinct from material sacrifices. Cf. Gregory Nyss., Great Catechism 18, ἀναίμακτον ἱερωσύνην : Gregory Naz., Poem. xi. 1. On the whole subject of the sacramental union see Bright, *Later Treatises*, p. 208.

176. ἀπέφηνεν. An important word in Eucharistic phraseology, *e.g.* the Liturgy of the Apostolic Constitutions, probably based on an ancient Syrian Liturgy, wherein the old idea of the Eucharistic action was regarded as the *manifestation* of what was all the time there rather than the consecration by the Epiclesis of what was not there in the Bread. The Greek word ἀποφαίνειν means " making real or obvious," sc. the memorial of the Passion at the Eucharist. The word " to show " has, however, passed into the Epiclesis of the later Greek liturgies, see Dix, op. cit., pp. 289 and 296, who says that the word may mean either " render " or " show." The word is very common in Cyril of Alexandria in the sense of to " declare " or to " appoint," and so to " make." It is used of the effect of consecration or of communion, cf. ἀποδείκνυναι ἐπὶ τῇ ἀναδείξει τὸν ἄρτον τῆς εὐχαριστίας. See Brightman, *Liturgies Eastern and Western*, pp. 21 and 59 ; and cf. Cyril, Epist. ad Ioan., ll. 14 and 166 ; Gore, *Body of Christ*, p. 79.

182. Τὰς δέ γε ἐν τ. εὐ., κ.τ.λ. On this reference of the Gospel sayings to the two distinct Natures of Christ, see Hilary Poit. De Trin. ix. 5, 6. He further distinguishes three periods in the Word's existence, to each of which certain expressions are properly to be referred : the pre-incarnate (wholly Divine), the incarnate (involving two kinds of expressions applicable to the two Natures) and the post-resurrection period (when the Manhood is perfected in the Godhead). So in Leo's Tome, chapter 4. But it had been a commonplace of Christological expression since the time of St. Irenaeus, whose statement, ἡσυχάζοντος μὲν τοῦ Λόγου ἐν τῷ πειρά-ζεσθαι καὶ ἀτιμάζεσθαι καὶ σταυροῦσθαι καὶ ἀποθνήσκειν, συγγινομένου δὲ τῷ ἀνθρώπῳ ἐν τῷ νικᾶν καὶ ὑπομένειν καὶ χρηστεύεσθαι καὶ ἀνίστασ-θαι καὶ ἀναλαμβάνεσθαι (iii.20.3), was a standard of orthodoxy in the West before Chalcedon ; but not in Alexandria after Apollinarius, who had great influence in that quarter. The revival in the Tome

of Leo of such expressions and their inclusion in the Definition of Chalcedon were reasons which led to the repudiation of the latter by the opposition afterwards known as the Monophysite Schism. (See Duchesne, *Ancient History of the Church*, vol. 3, pp. 318 ff.)

204. κένωσιν. This famous word, taken from Phil. ii. 7 (ἐκένωσεν ἑαυτὸν) will be found in writers of both schools, who agree in referring it to the condescension of the Logos in taking human nature. At the same time, a long tradition, especially in the West, referred the text to the humble condition chosen for the Incarnate life on earth.[1] Cyril often repeated the phrase that the Logos has in the Incarnation undergone a voluntary *kenosis*, suffering as man and energising as God (cf. the fragment Homily 15; Pusey, vol. 5, p. 474). " He went through the laws of human nature " (Adv. Nest. i. 1 ; Pusey, vol. 6, p. 63). See especially Comm. in Io. Ev. vi. 38, 39 (Pusey, vol. 3, p. 487), ἐπιτρέπει γεμὴν ὡς ἐν σαρκὶ γεγονὼς ὑπομένειν τὰ ἴδια τῇ σαρκὶ; Apol. adv. Theod. x. (Pusey, vol. 6, p. 476), ἐφιεὶς τῇ σαρκὶ τὸ πάσχειν ἐσθ' ὅτε τὰ ἴδια ; and in particular Quod Unus Sit Christus (Pusey, vol. 7, i, p. 399), ἐτελεῖτο γὰρ ἀψοφητὶ τὸ μυστήριον. ἠφίει δὴ οὖν οἰκονομικῶς τοῖς τῆς ἀνθρωπότητος μέτροις ἐφ' ἑαυτῷ τὸ κρατεῖν : " The mystery was accomplished noiselessly. Therefore, in accordance with the economy, He permitted the measures of manhood to prevail in Himself " (or " in His own case ".)[2] Cyril did not, however, extend this principle to the intellectual or moral spheres, writing, *e.g.*, of our Lord's apparent ignorance : οὐκοῦν οἶδε μὲν θεικῶς ὡς Σοφία τοῦ πατρὸς, ἐπειδὴ δὲ τὸ τῆς ἀγνοούσης ἀνθρωπότητος ὑπέδυ μέτρον οἰκονομικῶς [οἰκειόντως Loofs], οἰκειοῦται καὶ τοῦτο μετὰ τῶν ἄλλων (Apol. adv. Theod. iv. ; Pusey, vol. 6, p. 432). Note that Cyril here goes on the principle common to all Alexandrian theologians and distinguishes between what belongs to the Logos in His divine nature (θεικῶς) and what is His when He has become incarnate (cf. Adv. Nest. ii. 12 ; Ep. 3 ad Nest., l. 194 ; and see Sellers, op. cit., p. 86).

For Nestorius' view see *Bazaar*, chapter 69, where, using his favourite expression, he states that " God became incarnate in the manhood through His own *prosopon* and made his (the manhood's *prosopon*) His own *prosopon*. There is no condescension comparable with this, that the *prosopon* of the man should become His own, and that He should give His *prosopon* to him ; and therefore He made use of his (the man's) *prosopon* in that He took it for himself ; but He took it in order to make it not honourable but contemptible, that He might show to whoever wished to serve (God) that all greatness grows great by condescension and not in exalting itself, in that He took the likeness of a servant and has been found in

---

[1] See Loofs, *Studien u. Kritiken*, 1927, pp. 1–102, and article " Kenosis " in *Encyclopaedia of Religion and Ethics*.
[2] It is, in the opinion of the present editor, very doubtful whether the usual translation of ἐφ' ἑαυτῷ τὸ κρατεῖν " to prevail *over* Himself," can be extracted from the Greek. See an article in *Laudate*, July 1942, p. 32.

I

fashion (*schema*) as a man. . . . In the same way as He made use of
the likeness of a servant in the *kenosis*, so in the exaltation He
participated in the likeness of God, since He is thus in both, in the
likeness of the servant and in the likeness of God, and possesses the
same *prosopon* of humiliation and exaltation." In these words
Nestorius, while approaching very closely to the orthodoxy of
Cyril, shows himself nearer to that interpretation of the Philippian
text, which refers those words to the incarnate life only and not to
the pre-incarnate Logos. (See further Loofs, *Nestoriana*, pp. 91 ff.,
and Sellers, *Two Ancient Christologies*, pp. 51, 86, and 147.)

206. ὑποστάσει μιᾷ τῇ τοῦ Λόγου σεσαρκωμένῃ. This important
phrase in Cyril's Christology is called by Petavius the "tessera fidei,"
which, with the variations φύσις for ὑπόστασις and then σεσαρκωμένου for σεσαρκωμένη, came to play almost the same part as
the *Theotokos* in Christological controversy. It became, in fact,
a touchstone of orthodoxy. But it was in fact Apollinarian in
origin, and was used in the latter form by one of Apollinarius' disciples,
Eunomius of Beroea. It meant for the Apollinarians that the φύσις
of the Logos—that is, the Logos Himself—was once simple but now is
composite (σύνθετος). The form of the phrase μία φύσις τοῦ λόγου
σεσαρκωμένου became a favourite with Cyril, but the phrase in this
form is first found in the book *Ad Jovianum*, a work probably to be
ascribed to Apollinarius himself, where it is said "And since the
flesh has become compounded into the divine φύσις the Person
Incarnate is one." [1] Considering its origin, it is not surprising that
the phrase in either form was the cause of endless trouble, because
of the ambiguity of its terms, which led to hopeless misunderstanding. In the sense in which Cyril uses it, in the present context,
the meaning is tolerably clear. He is here defending the position
that all the sayings in the Gospels must be attributed to a single
hypostasis, which in the previous words he identifies with the
prosopon. Now if we are able to retain the meaning of *hypostasis*
given above—a single objective reality—Cyril means that the Godhead and manhood came together so closely in Christ that they are
organically one, they constitute a single objective reality, the one
Christ. Whereas Nestorius, following the Antiochene philosophy,
rightly, from his point of view, repudiated the phrase because there
must be two ὑποστάσεις or objective realities in Jesus Christ, however
we may seek to unite them; for ὑποστάσεις like οὐσίαι from the

---

[1] The phrase is also found in a work, De Incarn. Verbi Dei, which Cyril and
others accepted as Athanasius', but which is now regarded as one of the
many [Apollinarian] forgeries circulated under the names of Athanasius,
Gregory Thaumaturgus, Julius, etc. (Robertson, *Athanasius*, p. lxv).
The whole passage is as follows : Ὁμολογοῦμεν καὶ εἶναι τὸν αὐτὸν Υἱὸν Θεοῦ καὶ
Θεὸν κατὰ πνεῦμα, Υἱὸν δὲ ἀνθρώπου κατὰ σάρκα· οὐ δύο φύσεις, τὸν ἕνα Υἱὸν, μίαν προσ-
κυνητὴν καὶ μίαν ἀπροσκύνητον, ἀλλὰ μίαν φύσιν τοῦ Θεοῦ Λόγου σεσαρκωμένην, μετὰ
τῆς σαρκὸς αὐτοῦ μιᾷ προσκυνήσει καὶ προσκυνουμένην (Migne, P.G., 28, p. 25). See
Sellers, op. cit., p. 54.

Antiochene point of view cannot mix. Unfortunately, Cyril used in other places the word *phusis* instead of *hypostasis,* thereby exposing himself to a charge of denying the doctrine common to all Christian orthodoxy, at least since Tertullian, that there are two natures in Christ. But according to Nestorius there can be no such thing as a *prosopon* or a *phusis* without a *hypostasis.* The same sort of difficulty arose later in scholastic theology when St. Thomas Aquinas found it necessary to postulate " accidents " without a " subject " in the doctrine of Transubstantiation. Probably what Cyril meant was that, since the Incarnation, the Logos exists at one and the same time both Godwise and manwise, as we have seen to be true in the Cappadocian Doctrine of Trinity, in which God may be said to exist Fatherwise, Sonwise, and Spiritwise, but is still one God ; so Christ is one God-man. Doubtless Nestorius believed the same thing ; the fault was in his expression of his belief, which never achieved a real unity. We must, however, beware of applying to the doctrine of the Person of Christ in the patristic period modern notions about personality which we have learned to use since the time of Locke. It is rash to use such expressions as that the Logos become the ego, " centre," or " subject " of a human experience in the Incarnation. The ancients could not and did not. They had only the two categories of Manhood and Godhead to deal with.

While, however, it is difficult to acquit Cyril of deliberately playing upon the ambiguities of this formula, it would not be fair to Cyril to say that he taught what later theologians have called an " impersonal " manhood, though he may have approached to a doctrine that Christ was not so much personally as inclusively man (Ottley, *Doctrine of the Incarnation,* vol. ii, p. 160, and cf. Moberly, *Atonement and Personality,* pp. 93, 94).

Whatever may have been the final formulation of Greek Christology, *e.g.* in Leontius of Byzantium and John of Damascus, it is difficult to find evidence in Cyril's writings of doctrines which Dorner and some modern scholars attribute to Apollinarius, that the Logos was the archetype of humanity, and therefore by nature capable of assuming a human nature and experience.[1] Greek Christology was perhaps seeking after a point of view which has been well expressed by a modern theologian (Canon T. A. Lacey). " When the Council of Chalcedon proceeded to attribute to our Lord two natures— Divine and human—it is at least possible that ' human nature ' was taken as including all that is now called ' personality.' In that case the Council implicitly affirmed the human personality." (Quoted by Hodgson, *Essays on the Trinity and the Incarnation,* p. 392.)

[1] Dorner, *Person of Christ,* i. 11, p. 371 ff. This doctrine, according to Dr. Prestige, is wrongly called the Enhypostasia (*God in Patristic Thought,* p. 274).

THE TWELVE ARTICLES

WITH the exception of the seventh, the Twelve Articles deal with points already treated in the Epistle, though the same order of treatment is not observed. They lack the breadth of statement which the Epistle itself displayed, and one may be permitted to regard their composition as an unfortunate mistake, both as a matter of theology and of policy, if, at least, we judge them by their immediate results. It is at the same time quite probable that Cyril and the synod saw no other way of bringing home to Nestorius the fatal error of his teaching. But anathemas are not to be lightly used or lightly put by ; and although Cyril doubtless meant the Letter to explain the Articles, as a matter of fact the Articles were at once separated from the Letter and dealt with alone. In this dislocation they clearly needed amendment, since they emphasised only one side of the truth, and that in the baldest manner, so that they appeared to John of Antioch, to whom Nestorius sent them, and to others, to lean towards Apollinarianism.[1] Indeed, it was with difficulty that they were believed to be the genuine work of Cyril. Andrew of Samosata, representing the " Oriental " bishops, attacked them, and Theodoret criticised them in a series of observations which he sent to John. Nestorius put out Twelve counter-Anathemas (which are here printed from Marius Mercator's Latin translation, Mansi, iv. 1099 ; Hahn, 316).[2] Andrew for the most part criticised Cyril's unguarded wording, which made it too easy for heretical constructions to be put upon them. Theodoret, while approaching closer to Cyril's position, nevertheless continued to maintain the Antiochene tradition, though not to the same extent as Nestorius, whose counter-anathemas if anything re-emphasised his views.

Cyril replied to Andrew (Apol. adv. Orientales) and to Theodoret (Apol. adv. Theodor.), and wrote at length in refutation of Nestorius (Tom. v. contr. Nest.). Later, about August 431, he wrote a further " Explanation " of the Anathemas.

The Anathemas are printed again in full for convenience, and a translation is given on p. 218 f. A translation of Nestorius' counter-Anathemas will be found in *The Seven Ecumenical Creeds* (Library of Nicene and post-Nicene Fathers). The notes on them together with the comments of Theodoret and of Andrew are drawn from Theodoret's *Reprehensio XII Capitum Cyrilli*, from Migne, *P.G.*, vol. 76, pp. 293 ff.

[1] Theodoret, Epist. cxii.
[2] The texts vary in a few places. I have followed Hahn.

ARTICLE I

Cyril.   Εἴ τις οὐχ ὁμολογεῖ Θεὸν εἶναι κατὰ ἀλήθειαν τὸν
Ἐμμανουὴλ, καὶ διὰ τοῦτο θεοτόκον τὴν ἁγίαν παρθένον· γεγέννηκε
γὰρ σαρκικῶς σάρκα γεγονότα τὸν ἐκ Θεοῦ Λόγον· ἀνάθεμα ἔστω.

Nestorius' counter-Anathema.   Si quis eum qui est Emmanuel, Deum Verbum [1] esse dixerit et non potius nobiscum Deum, hoc est, inhabitasse eam quae secundum nos est naturam per id quod unitus est massae nostrae, quam de Maria virgine suscepit, matrem etiam Dei Verbi, et non potius eius qui Emmanuel est sanctam virginem nuncupaverit ipsumque Deum Verbum in carnem versum esse, quam accepit ad ostentationem deitatis suae ut habitu inveniretur ut homo, anathema sit.

Theodoret.   Inasmuch as Divinity is immutable, God the word was not made flesh by nature nor changed into flesh, but He " took " flesh and tabernacled in us. Phil. ii. 5 shows that " the form of God " was not changed, but remaining what it was took the form of a " servant," took, that is, a living and reasonable flesh. He was not " naturally " conceived of the Virgin, thus deriving the beginning of His existence from her ; but He fashioned for Himself a temple in the Virgin's womb, and was with that which was begotten. The Virgin then is called *Anthropotokos* in view of the fashioning and conception, and *Theotokos* not because she bare " naturally " One who was God, but because she bare man united to God, Who had fashioned Him. Otherwise God the Word would be a creature of the Holy Spirit (Matt. i. 23). The child is called Immanuel on account of God Who assumed, and the Virgin is *Theotokos* on account of the union of " the Form of God " with the conceived " form of a servant."

To avoid any idea of change in respect of the divine nature of the Logos, Theodoret on the basis on Phil. ii. 5 insists that He " took " real manhood, which having fashioned it for Himself (ἑαυτῷ), was thus united to God. In consequence of this union, the Virgin can be called both *Theotokos* and *Anthropotokos*, since the Lord Christ is at once God and man, and the Child can be called Immanuel. From the start He wishes to maintain the conception of the immutability of the God-head and the doctrine of the Two Natures.

Orientals.   Σαρκικῶς implies an ordinary natural birth, and that the Word was not thereby changed into flesh. " The Word was made Flesh " (John i. 14) is similar to the expressions " made sin " (2 Cor. v. 21) and " made a curse " (Gal. iii. 13), and must not be understood of a literal change.

Cyril's Reply.   The Incarnation, of course, involved no change in the Divine Nature of the Word. He became Man without ceasing to be God. It was a Union without any confusion, and

[1] *Mansi*, Verum.

the formula *Theotokos* guards the truth of the Union. By σαρκικῶς was meant κατὰ σάρκα, opposed to an Apollinarian θεικῶς, and not implying a denial of the mystery of the Virginal Birth. The phase " made flesh " means " was Incarnate and made Man," born after the Human Nature through the Virgin, and is not on a par with the similar phrases quoted.[1]

ARTICLE II

Cyril.   Εἴ τις οὐχ ὁμολογεῖ σαρκὶ καθ' ὑπόστασιν ἡνῶσθαι τὸν ἐκ Θεοῦ Πατρὸς Λόγον, ἕνα τε εἶναι Χριστὸν μετὰ τῆς ἰδίας σαρκός, τὸν αὐτὸν δηλόνοτι Θεόν τε ὁμοῦ καὶ ἄνθρωπον, ἀνάθεμα ἔστω.

Nestorius.   Si quis in Verbi Dei coniunctione, quae ad carnem facta est, de loco in locum mutationem divinae essentiae dixerit factam, eiusque divinae naturae carnem capacem dixerit ac partiliter unitam carni, aut iterum in infinitum incircumscriptam divinae naturae coextenderit carnem ad capiendum Deum, eandemque ipsam naturam et Deum dicat et hominem, anathema sit.

Nestorius evidently thought that Cyril's teaching on the union of the Word with flesh involved either a local change on the part of the Divine Being or an infinite extension of the flesh to enable it to unite with Deity.

Theodoret.   We confess one Christ, and on account of the union name the same both God and man. But we are wholly ignorant of the phrase " hypostatic union," which is strange and foreign to divine scripture and to the Fathers. Does Cyril mean by it a mixture of flesh and Godhead ? If he does, we shall oppose with all our might the blasphemy of the " confusion," the admission of which destroys the character (ἰδιότητα) of each nature ; for as the Lord Himself testifies, when He says to the Jews " destroy this temple and in three days I will raise it up " (John ii. 19), no thought of mixture (κρᾶσις) is possible, since God remains God who raises the temple, and the temple is recognised as a temple undergoing destruction.

Theodoret upholds the doctrine of the separate reality of the two natures, which in his judgment Cyril wilfully endangers by insisting on his " hypostatic" union. It should be understood that Theodoret uses *hypostasis* here in the sense of *substantia*, whereas Cyril was using it in the sense of *persona*. This anathema was apparently not attacked by Andrew.

Cyril's Reply.   Ἕνωσις καθ' ὑπόστασιν means a union in true personal Being. There is only One Christ, who is both God and man. The denial of this has necessitated some phrase that emphasises the truth.

[1] See this point dealt with again very fully in Quod unus sit Christus, Pusey's translation, *Library of the Fathers*, pp. 241 ff.

ARTICLE III

Cyril. Εἴ τις ἐπὶ τοῦ ἑνὸς Χριστοῦ διαιρεῖ τὰς ὑποστάσεις μετὰ τὴν ἕνωσιν, μόνῃ συνάπτων αὐτὰς συναφείᾳ τῇ κατὰ τὴν ἀξίαν, ἤγουν αὐθεντίαν ἢ δυναστείαν, καὶ οὐχὶ δὴ μᾶλλον συνόδῳ τῇ καθ᾽ ἕνωσιν φυσικήν, ἀνάθεμα ἔστω.

Nestorius. Si quis non secundum coniunctionem unum dixerit Christum, qui est etiam Emmanuel, sed secundum naturam, ex utraque etiam substantia tam Dei Verbi quam etiam assumpti ab eo hominis unam filii connexionem, quam etiam nunc inconfuse servant, minime confiteatur, anathema sit.

Theodoret. Theodoret complained of the subtlety and obscurity of the distinction drawn by Cyril between συνάφεια and σύνοδος. He particularly objected to the phrase καθ᾽ ἕνωσιν φυσικήν, which he understood as implying a union that was involuntary and of necessity, and thus depriving God of His loving kindness. St. Paul teaches, however, that the " self-emptying " was a voluntary act, and shows that He was united to the nature assumed by purpose and will. The term φυσική then is superfluous, and it should be sufficient to speak of " the union "—a union, that is, of things divided. For whatever Cyril may say to the contrary, the hypostases must be divided, and as his use here of the plural ὑποστάσεις shows, he himself knows that each nature is perfect, and that both come together into the Same. So while we confess the one *prosopon*, the one Son and the one Christ, it is not absurd—nay, it is necessary— to hold that the divided natures are two. After all we are but following the blessed Paul, who divides the one man into the in- ward and outward (2 Cor. iv. 14 ; Rom. vii. 22), when we divide the natures and "recognise" (γνωρίζειν) the special properties of each. Theodoret can hardly be accused of Nestorianism when he speaks of a " conjunction " (συνάφεια) and divides the natures. He explicitly states that for him there is one Son in whom the two natures are united. But at the same time he insists that if the reality of the two natures is to be maintained against Eutychian thought, these must be divided (δεῖν τὰς ὑποστάσεις διαιρεῖν), by which he means that they must be recognised, *i.e.* with the reason, each with its properties.[1] Cyril did not stop to think what the Antiochenes meant when they spoke of dividing the natures ; neither did they on their side offer an exact explanation of the sense in which they use the word. Similarly, we should note that Theodoret misunderstands Cyril's " natural union," just as he misunderstands their " hypostatic union." The reason for this is that for him, as for Nestorius, "nature" (φύσις) means *natura*;

---

[1] See Theodoret's direct affirmations on this point. Epists. lxxxiii, xcix, ci, clxxxi, and cf. Sellers, *Two Ancient Christologies*, pp. 195–201, on the meaning given by the Antiochenes to χωρίζειν and on the implications of γνωρίζειν.

whereas Cyril, while at times using the word in this sense also uses it, as here, as the equivalent of *proposon* and *hypostasis*.

Orientals.   In his Epistle to the Monks (15) Cyril had admitted two *Hypostases* with which this present Anathema is inconsistent. φυσική implies an ordinary process of nature, and thus robs the Union of its supernatural character.

Cyril's Reply.   φυσική means a "real" Union καθ' ὑπόστασιν, as opposed to a "moral" or "acquired" one (ἐν σχέσει, σχετική), such as Nestorius held to exist. It involves no notion of necessity. The Godhead and the Manhood are distinct, but the Person is One. The doctrine of the Incarnation is not satisfied by an association of two persons, a Divine and a human.

ARTICLE IV

Cyril.   Εἴ τις προσώποις δυσὶν ἤγουν ὑποστάσεσι τάς τε ἐν τοῖς εὐαγγελικοῖς καὶ ἀποστολικοῖς συγγράμμασι διανέμει φωνάς, ἢ ἐπὶ Χριστῷ παρὰ τῶν ἁγίων λεγομένας, ἢ παρ' αὐτοῦ περὶ ἑαυτοῦ· καὶ τὰς μὲν ὡς ἀνθρώπῳ παρὰ τὸν ἐκ Θεοῦ Λόγον ἰδικῶς νοουμένῳ προσάπτει, τὰς δὲ ὡς θεοπρεπεῖς μόνῳ τῷ ἐκ Θεοῦ Πατρὸς Λόγῳ, ἀνάθεμα ἔστω.

Nestorius.   Si quis eas voces, quae tam evangelicis quam epistulis apostolicis, de Christo, qui est utraque, conscriptae sunt, accipiat tanquam de una natura, ipsique Dei Verbo tribuere passiones tentaverit tam carne quam etiam Deitate, anathema sit.

Here again is a want of definition : *natura* is evidently held to imply its own *persona*, and two natures to demand two persons.

Theodoret.   Cyril seems to think that there has been a "mixture," and in consequence that there is no difference between the sayings in the Gospel and the Apostolic writings, and this while he was against Arius and Eunomius ! These last applied to the Logos what is only appropriate to the "form of the servant," in order that they may make him a creature. Ours is the opposite opinion, who hold that the Son is co-eternal with the Father and no creature. To whom, then, do we apply those passages which speak of His loneliness, hunger and thirst, and all the other human feelings and needs ? Such things cannot belong to the Divine Logos, for how can He who has all that the Father has be ignorant ? Ignorance rather is the part of the "form of the servant," who at that time knew as much as the indwelling God revealed. Thus in regard to the cry in Gethsemane these are the words not of the Logos but of the "form of the servant" afraid of death, because death was not yet destroyed. It was the divine Logos who "allowed" (συνεχώρησεν) the utterance of these words, giving a place for fear in order that the nature of Him who had been born (τοῦ τεχθέντος) might be fully apparent, and that it might not be supposed that the son of Abraham and David was but a phantom.

At first sight, especially in view of Theodoret's constant use of τίς when referring to our Lord's manhood, it might seem that after all he was a Nestorian, for whom the son of Abraham and David is a human person existing alongside of the divine Son. But he expressly denies that he does teach two Sons. His position, it seems clear, is that the "form of the servant" possesses its own human individuality, but that has been united to the Logos. So he can say that the Logos "allows" it to speak and act according to its nature. Thus, Cyril himself implies the same doctrine; "the mystery" (of the Incarnation), he says, "was accomplished noiselessly, the Logos in the economy allowing (ἠφίει) the measures of the manhood to have power in His case" (Quod unus sit Christus, Pusey, vii, Part 1, p. 399). And he uses the very words which Theodoret uses here when he says that the Logos when He became man "allowed Himself" (συνεχώρησεν ἑαυτόν) to hunger and thirst with men and to suffer . . ." (Thesaurus Assert. xxii). Cf. the words of Irenaeus (Adv. Haer. iii. 20, 3 quoted on p. 120).

Orientals. The complete Union is granted, but there is no confusion of the Godhead with the Manhood, otherwise the former is degraded, and that would be Arianism.

Cyril's Reply. Cyril emphatically disclaimed all notion of mixture or confusion. He admitted the distinction of the Scriptural terms, but showed that whether Divinely or Humanly spoken they referred to the One Person of Christ. The texts implying humiliation belonged to the Word in virtue of His Incarnation; He became Man, and therefore spoke and felt as Man.

If the Orientals agreed with him as to the Personal Union they could not object to Theotokos, which asserted it.

Note that in Cyril's anathema πρόσωπον is used synonymously with ὑπόστασις for "Person".

Note also that the last words in the Formulary of Reunion (Epist. ad Joan.) admit the distribution of Gospel sayings to the two different Natures, while ascribing them all to One Person.

ARTICLE V

Cyril. Εἴ τις τολμᾷ λέγειν θεοφόρον ἄνθρωπον τὸν Χριστόν, καὶ οὐχὶ δὴ μᾶλλον Θεὸν εἶναι κατὰ ἀλήθειαν, ὡς Υἱὸν ἕνα καὶ φύσει, καθὸ γέγονε σὰρξ ὁ Λόγος καὶ κεκοινώνηκε παραπλησίως ἡμῖν αἵματος καὶ σαρκός, ἀνάθεμα ἔστω.

Nestorius. Si quis post assumptionem hominis naturaliter Dei Filium unum esse audet dicere, cum sit et Emmanuel, anathema sit.

Theodoret. Certainly God the Word shared with us in blood and flesh and soul; but He was not changed into flesh. The very word "sharing" implies distinction of the two. We worship Him that took and that which was taken as One Son. The term θεοφόρος ἄνθρωπος is not objectionable : it was used by Basil the Great. It does not mean that Christ was a man endowed with some particular divine grace, but with all the Godhead of the Son (Col. ii. 8, 9).

Here we must note that Theodoret first states a truism, and then falls into an error of fact. θεοφόρος ἄνθρωπος (= a God-bearing man ; *i.e.* a human person carrying God) was a distinctly Nestorian phrase, and had not been used by Basil, who wrote ἡ θεοφόρος σάρξ (De Spirit. Sanct. 12) and ἄνθρωπον Θεὸν 'Ιησοῦν Χριστόν. (Hom. in Psal. xlix.) [1]

These terms were orthodox ; just as Athanasius had written 'Ιησοῦς Χριστὸς Θεός ἐστι σάρκα φορῶν, Or. c. Ar. iii. 51. Cf. the decrees of the Illyrian synod in 371 apud Theodoret, HE. iv. 8, ὁμολογοῦμεν . . . Θεὸν ὄντα σαρκοφόρον οὐκ ἄνθρωπον θεοφόρον. The Easterns do not appear to have objected to this and the following Anathema.

Cyril's Reply.   No change of the Word into flesh is implied : but θεοφόρος might be applied to any saint in whom God dwells.

ARTICLE VI

Cyril.   Εἴ τις λέγει Θεὸν ἢ Δεσπότην εἶναι τοῦ Χριστοῦ τὸν ἐκ Θεοῦ Πατρὸς Λόγον, καὶ οὐχὶ δὴ μᾶλλον τὸν αὐτὸν ὁμολογεῖ Θεόν τε ὁμοῦ καὶ ἄνθρωπον, ὡς γεγονότος σαρκὸς τοῦ Λόγου κατὰ τὰς γραφὰς, ἀνάθεμα ἔστω.

Nestorius.   Si quis post incarnationem Deum Verbum alterum quempiam praeter Christum nominaverit, servi sane formam cum Deo Verbo initium non habere et hanc increatam, ut ipse est, esse dicere tentaverit, et non potius ab ipso creatam confiteatur, tamquam a naturali domino et creatore et Deo, quam suscitare propria virtute promisit : Solvite, dicens ad Iudaeos, templum hoc et triduo suscitabo illud, anathema sit.

Theodoret.   Paul calls that which was assumed the " form of the servant," but he was speaking of the act of assuming as such. Once the union is effected, however, the term " servitude " has no longer a place, and we confess even the " form of the servant " still to be God on account of the form of God united to it. For if the Apostle says that the believers are no longer servants but sons (Gal. iv. 7), much more will the first fruits of our nature be released from a title of servant. So also, following the prophet, we call the

---

[1] But Theodoret was aware of the true text and quotes it elsewhere (Dial. i. ad fin.) ; it was not a deliberate misquotation, since he always uses the word ἄνθρωπος as a term explanatory of σάρξ. What he means here is that our Lord's manhood can be called θεοφόρος, since it was united to all the Godhead of the Son. For Him the divine in-dwelling in this manhood differed from that in the saints in that in this unique case the Logos had united to Himself a manhood fashioned by the Holy Spirit, and in consequence dwelt therein in all the fullness of Godhead.

child who was born Immanuel, though the same prophet speaks of Him of the seed of Abraham as servant (Is. vii. 14; xlix. 5, 6). Yet what was fashioned was not God but the form of the servant; for the divine Logos was not changed into flesh, but took flesh with a rational soul.

Theodoret it would seem is here employing the principle of the *communicatio idiomatum*: since in the one person of Jesus Christ man has been united to Godhead and His are at once both divine and human properties, it follows while the properties of each nature are preserved and remain distinct, what is strictly human can be given the divine title and what is strictly divine can be called " man." His reply then stands not only as the acceptance of Cyril's teaching, though with the usual *caveat* in respect of the word ἐγένετο in John i. 14, but also as an enlargement of the fundamental truth that Jesus Christ is one person, at once God and man.

Cyril's Reply. There is no dualism ; Christ is One Person to Whom, as man, the term of servitude belongs. He cannot be God and Lord of Himself.

Note that a distinction is to be drawn between Christ being God and Lord of a human person associated with Himself, which involves a dualism, and His being God and Lord of His Own Manhood.

ARTICLE VII

Cyril. Εἴ τις φησὶν, ὡς ἄνθρωπον ἐνηργῆσθαι παρὰ τοῦ Θεοῦ Λόγου τὸν Ἰησοῦν καὶ τὴν τοῦ μονογενοῦς εὐδοξίαν περιῆφθαι, ὡς ἑτέρῳ παρ᾽ αὐτὸν ὑπάρχοντι, ἀνάθεμα ἔστω.

Nestorius. Si quis hominem, qui de virgine creatus est, hunc esse dixerit Unigenitum, qui ex utero Patris ante luciferum natus est, non magis propter unitionem ad eum qui est Unigenitus naturaliter Patris, Unigeniti cum appellatione confiteatur eumque participem magis factum, Iesum quoque alterum quempiam praeter Emmanuel dicat, anathema sit.

Theodoret. Man's nature is mortal, but the divine Logos, the giver of life, raised up the temple destroyed by the Jews, and so it was made immortal, receiving what it had not, now that it has been glorified by Him who gave.

Theodoret, neither here nor in his replies to Articles 8, 10, and 11, explicitly sides with Cyril in his penetrating view of Nestorianism in the condemnation of the notion that the manhood was " another beside the Logos." Nevertheless, such a condemnation would seem implicit in his teaching on the union of the Logos with a manhood which He takes to Himself. Here as elsewhere he is determined to maintain the position that our Lord is perfect God and perfect man; the human nature, he says, was and remained mortal till it was glorified by the Logos at the Resurrection.

Orientals.   Christ was not "energised" as the saints were, but yet St. Paul speaks of ἡ ἐνέργεια τοῦ κράτους τῆς ἰσχύος αὐτοῦ ἣν ἐνήργησεν ἐν τῷ Χριστῷ ἐγείρας αὐτὸν ἐκ νεκρῶν (Eph. i. 19, 20).

Cyril's Reply.   Christ is not "energised" from without; He is Himself the Word who "energises." His resurrection is claimed as His Own work (John ii. 19), and it was in His Human nature only that He was glorified.   Here we notice for the first time the word ἐνεργεῖσθαι, and its cognates, which became technical in the later Monophysite and Monothelite controversies.

ARTICLE VIII

Cyril.   Εἴ τις τολμᾷ λέγειν τὸν ἀναληφθέντα ἄνθρωπον συμπροσκυνεῖσθαι δεῖν τῷ Θεῷ Λόγῳ καὶ συνδοξάζεσθαι καὶ συγχρηματίζειν Θεόν, ὡς ἕτερον ἐν ἑτέρῳ·[1] τὸ γὰρ Σὺν ἀεὶ προστιθέμενον τοῦτο νοεῖν ἀναγκάσει· καὶ οὐχὶ δὴ μᾶλλον μιᾷ προσκυνήσει τιμᾷ τὸν Ἐμμανουὴλ, καὶ μίαν αὐτῷ τὴν δοξολογίαν ἀναπέμπει, καθὸ γέγονε σὰρξ ὁ Λόγος, ἀνάθεμα ἔστω.

Nestorius.   Si quis servi formam per se ipsam, hoc est, secundum propriae naturae rationem colendam esse dixerit et omnium rerum dominam esse, et non potius per societatem, qua beatae et ex se naturaliter dominicae Unigeniti naturae coniuncta et connexa est, veneratur, anathema sit.

Theodoret.   We offer only one doxology to the Lord Christ, who as it once God and Man; but the properties of the Natures are distinct, for the Word did not change into flesh, nor was the man transmuted into God.   His words are "we worship the Lord of Creation incarnate, the Word of God.   For, if the flesh also is in itself a part of the created world, yet it has become God's body. And we neither divide the body being such from the Word, and worship it by itself, nor when we wish to worship the Word do we set Him apart from the flesh; but knowing, as we said above, that the Word was made flesh, we recognise Him as God also after having come in the flesh . . . nor because the Word was the Maker of all creation did He despise the flesh which he had put on, but He is the Creator of the Universe and worshipped as dwelling in a created temple."

Once again Theodoret does not come to the real point, he does not explicitly deny the Nestorian doctrine of "one in another."   Ever

---

[1] This expression is peculiar.   Nowhere else in this connexion does Cyril write ἐν ἑτέρῳ, and the ἐν seems to be an intrusion, perhaps due to a mistaken reduplication of the last two letters of the preceding word.   We must translate, with Marius Mercator (who cannot have read ἐν), tamquam alterum cum altero, " as if one person *with* another " [so Dr. Bright in a private letter to Dr. Bindley].   Fleury ("comme l'un étant en l'autre") and P. E. Pusey (" as one in another ") miss the point of the emphasis on σύν.

suspicious of the presence of Eutychian thought in Cyril's declarations, he drives home the doctrine, all important to the Antiochenes, that there are two perfect natures in Christ.

Orientals. We do not recognise two Persons or two Sons, but One Son, whom we adore.

Cyril's Reply. Any phrase that involves the notion of a duality of persons is wrong, e.g. ὁ ἀναληφθεὶς ἄνθρωπος, "the man assumed," and Theodoret's antithesis of " the Word " and " the man " ; both of which phrases involve a human personality side by side with the Divine.

Note that this anathema was adopted in an expanded form by the Fifth General Council (see Anath. ix. below, p. 155), and also that Athanasius had already dealt with this question of the one worship of the Incarnate Son, Epist. ad Adelph. 3, Οὐ κτίσμα προσκυνοῦμεν· μὴ γένοιτο· κ.τ.λ.

ARTICLE IX

Cyril. Εἴ τις φησὶ τὸν ἕνα Κύριον Ἰησοῦν Χριστὸν δεδοξάσθαι παρὰ τοῦ Πνεύματος, ὡς ἀλλοτρίᾳ δυνάμει τῇ δι᾽ αὐτοῦ χρώμενον, καὶ παρ᾽ αὐτου λαβόντα τὸ ἐνεργεῖν δύνασθαι κατὰ πνευμάτων ἀκαθάρτων, καὶ τὸ πληροῦν εἰς ἀνθρώπους τὰς θεοσημίας, καὶ οὐχὶ δὴ μᾶλλον ἴδιον αὐτοῦ τὸ Πνεῦμα, φησί, δι᾽ οὗ καὶ ἐνήργηκε τὰς θεοσημίας, ἀνάθεμα ἔστω.

Nestorius. Si quis formae servi consubstantialem esse dixerit Spiritum Sanctum et non potius per illius mediationis, quae est ad Deum Verbum ab ipsa conceptione, habuisse dixerit copulationem seu coniunctionem, per quam in homines communes simul nonnunquam miserandas curationes exercuit, et ex hoc fugandorum spirituum eveniebat esse potestatem, anathema sit.

Theodoret. This exact examiner of the divine Decrees would anathematise prophets, apostles, the Angel Gabriel, and even the Lord Himself, all of whom as the writings show would say that He was "formed" and "anointed" by the Holy Spirit, through whose power also He performed His works (cf. especially Luke iv. 18 ff. ; Matt. xii. 28). At the same time it was not the divine Logos who was thus "formed" and "anointed," but the human nature which He assumed. If, then, Cyril speaks of the Holy Spirit as ὁμοφυής with the Father, and as proceeding from him, we are ready to say with him that the Spirit of the Son is His own. But if he speaks of the Spirit as being from the Son, or as having His origin through the Son (ὡς ἐξ Υἱοῦ ἢ δι᾽ Υἱοῦ τὴν ὕπαρξιν ἔχων), we shall reject such a statement as blasphemous (John xv. 26).

Once more Theodoret cannot refrain from emphasising the difference of the natures. Particularly interesting is his remark concerning the Procession of the Spirit; for here we seem to have traces of a real difference between his view and that of Cyril; Cyril would be ready to accept the Double Procession, while Theodoret refuses to admit the idea of the derivation of the Spirit either from or through the Son, as blasphemous and contrary to Christ's words, though he misquotes John xv. 26 by substituting ἐκ τοῦ Θεοῦ καὶ πατρός for παρὰ τοῦ πατρός.

Orientals. Two points were put forward. First, Cyril had at first, in his Epistle to the Monks, admitted that Christ was influenced and even quickened by the Spirit of God; cf. Matt. xii. 28. Secondly, the emphasis laid on the Spirit being Christ's own tended towards a distinction being made in the " common " action of the Three Persons of the Trinity. They admitted that Christ's miracles were wrought both by His own power (τῇ οἰκείᾳ δυνάμει) and by the Spirit's energy.

Cyril's Reply. He intended the anathema to exclude the notion, which Nestorius seemed to hold, that the action of the Spirit upon Christ was like in kind to His action on ordinary men. The Spirit was His own Spirit, for although He proceeds from the Father He is not alien from the Son (οὐκ ἀλλότριον ἐστὶ τοῦ Υἱοῦ); and since " all that the Father hath " is the Son's too, therefore the Spirit is His. He wrought the miracles, having as His own the Spirit, Who is ἐξ αὐτοῦ καὶ οὐσιωδῶς ἐμπεφυκὸς αὐτῷ (Explic. xii.). Cf. Adv. Nest. iv. 1.

For the bearing of this upon Cyril's views as to the eternal derivation of the Spirit from the Son as well as from the Father, see the note above on *Filioque*, p. 80.

Presumably we have here an indication of the fundamental difference between the two schools of thought in respect of their Trinitarian doctrine; the Alexandrians putting first the thought of the Three *Hypostases*, the doctrine of God of God, while the Antiochenes gave first place to the thought of the divine Unity, the doctrine of God in God. (*Essays on the Trinity and the Incarnation*, pp. 247 ff.)

N.B.—It is worth noting that Theodoret makes use of the word ὁμοφυής where orthodox theology was accustomed to use Nicene *homoousion* for the relation between the Persons of the Trinity. Cf. note on ὁμοούσιος, p. 23.

ARTICLE X

Cyril Ἀρχιερέα καὶ ἀπόστολον τῆς ὁμολογίας ἡμῶν γεγενῆσθαι Χριστὸν ἡ θεία λέγει γραφή, προσκεκόμικε δὲ ὑπὲρ ἡμῶν ἑαυτὸν εἰς ὀσμὴν εὐωδίας τῷ Θεῷ καὶ Πατρί. εἰ τις τοίνυν ἀρχιερέα φησὶ καὶ ἀπόστολον ἡμῶν γενέσθαι, οὐκ αὐτὸν τὸν ἐκ Θεοῦ Λόγον, ὅτε γέγονε σὰρξ καὶ καθ' ἡμᾶς ἄνθρωπος· ἀλλ' ὡς ἕτερον παρ' αὐτὸν ἰδικῶς ἄνθρωπον ἐκ γυναικός· ἢ εἴ τις λέγει καὶ ὑπὲρ ἑαυτοῦ προσενεγκεῖν αὐτὸν τὴν προσφορὰν, καὶ οὐχὶ δὴ μᾶλλον ὑπὲρ μόνων ἡμῶν· οὐ γὰρ ἂν ἐδεήθη προσφορᾶς ὁ μὴ εἰδὼς ἁμαρτίαν· ἀνάθεμα ἔστω.

Nestorius. Si quis illud in principio Verbum pontificem et apostolum confessionis nostrae factum esse seque ipsum obtulisse pro nobis
dicat, et non Emmanuelis esse apostolatum potius dixerit oblatio-
nemque secundum eandem dividat rationem ei, qui univit, et illi,
qui unitus est ad unam societatem Filii, hoc est, Deo, quae Dei
sunt, et homini, quae sunt hominis, non deputans, anathema sit.

Theodoret. It was not God the Word but the human nature assumed
by Him that took the name of the Priesthood of Melchizedek
and experienced the feelings of our mortal nature. The unchangeable nature was not changed into flesh but took " a human
nature " as the Epistle to the Hebrews teaches (Heb. v. 1). Who,
then, is He, who learned obedience by experience ? Who is He
that lived with Godly fear . . . ? It was not the divine Logos,
rather was it the seed of David taken by Him, the nature taken for
us for our salvation. For no one will say that the Logos is a creature,
but that He who is of David's seed, being free from all sin, was made
our High Priest and Victim, and offered himself on our behalf to
God, having in Himself (ἐν ἑαυτῷ) the Logos, God of God, united
to Him and inseparably conjoined.

As in Article IV, Theodoret uses language which can easily be misunderstood. His point is that the manhood which was taken by the
Logos was real manhood possessing a rational soul, and therefore
endowed with freedom of choice. Yet he would deny that for him it
existed alongside of the Logos ; as he says the nature assumed is united
to Him and inseparably conjoined. He may not express approval of
Cyril's condemnation of the Nestorian position of " one beside another,"
but what he does affirm concerning the union is enough to warrant the
conclusion that while the manhood is complete it is inseparably united
to the Logos.

Orientals. The Orientals practically agree with Cyril. Christ
is our High Priest; His Humanity is the sphere of His priesthood.

Cyril's Reply. After citing some words from Nestorius which he
deemed heretical, Cyril proceeded to emphasise the particular
point intended by this Anathema, namely, that our High Priest is
God the Word Incarnate. There was no advancement of a man
towards moral union with the Word. Christ's Human Nature
brought upon Him the function of Priest, but He exercised it as
the Word of God. Cf. Adv. Nest. iii. 3.

ARTICLE XI

Cyril. Εἴ τις οὐχ ὁμολογεῖ τὴν τοῦ Κυρίου σάρκα ζωοποιὸν
εἶναι καὶ ἰδίαν αὐτοῦ τοῦ ἐκ Θεοῦ Πατρὸς Λόγου· ἀλλ' ὡς ἑτέρου
τινὸς παρ' αὐτόν, συνημμένου μὲν αὐτῷ κατὰ τὴν ἀξίαν, ἤγουν ὡς
μόνην θείαν ἐνοίκησιν ἐσχηκότος, καὶ οὐχὶ δὴ μᾶλλον ζωοποιὸν, ὡς

ἔφημεν, ὅτι γέγονεν ἰδία τοῦ Λόγου τοῦ τὰ πάντα ζωογονεῖν ἰσχύοντος, ἀνάθεμα ἔστω.

Nestorius. Si quis unitam carnem Verbo Dei ex naturae propriae possibilitate vivificatricem esse dixerit ipso Domino et Deo pronunciante : Spiritus est qui vivificat, caro nihil prodest, anathema sit. Spiritus est Deus, a Domino pronunciatum est. Si quis ergo Deum Verbum carnaliter secundum substantiam carnem factum esse dicat, hoc autem modo et specialiter custodite, maxime Domino Christo post resurrectionem discipulis suis dicente : Palpate et videte, quoniam spiritus ossa et carnem non habet sicut me videtis habere, anathema sit.

Theodoret. Theodoret detects Apollinarianism in Cyril's anathema. Cyril does not mention an intelligent flesh or confess that the assumed was perfect man. Moreover, he clearly states the flesh to be soulless (ἄψυχον . . . σάρκα φησίν). Since he anathematises anyone who says that it was not the own flesh of the Logos, so does he hold that the Logos takes the place of the soul in the flesh. But we on our side assert that the animate and rational flesh of the Lord is life-giving, because of the life-giving Godhead united to it. The Logos was not changed into flesh but has His own flesh—the assumed nature—which He makes life-giving in the union.

Theodoret altogether misunderstood Cyril, who was certainly no Apollinarian (cf. his explicit statement in Epist. ii ad Succen., *P.G.*, vol. 77, 240c : τὸ δὲ σάρκος ὅταν εἴπωμεν ἄνθρωπον φαμέν). Moreover, as in his explanations of Articles I and II Theodoret often uses the expression σάρξ ψυχὴν ἔχουσα τὴν λογικήν. At the same time this reply well illustrates his position ; at the Incarnation the Logos took complete manhood (for the doctrine of Apollinarius cannot be tolerated), and by uniting it to Himself made it His own.

Orientals. The reiteration of ἰδίαν . . . ἰδία, which lays stress on its being the own flesh of the Word, looks like Apollinarianism, as though His flesh was not of human origin. Again, since Cyril had admitted that the Manhood was glorified by the Spirit, it is out of place to reject the phrase συνημμένος αὐτῷ κατὰ τὴν ἀξίαν.

Cyril's Reply. The emphasis laid upon the flesh being Christ's own is to prevent Nestorius attributing it to a separate human person (cf. contr. Nest. iv. 6). He himself entirely rejected the idea that Christ's flesh was of heavenly origin.

" Flesh " is used, John i. 14, to mean the whole of man, and it is used in the Anathema in the same sense, not as excluding " soul."

ARTICLE XII

Cyril. Εἴ τις οὐχ ὁμολογεῖ τὸν τοῦ Θεοῦ Λόγον παθόντα σαρκὶ καὶ ἐσταυρωμένον σαρκὶ καὶ θανάτου γευσάμενον σαρκὶ, γεγονότα τε πρωτότοκον ἐκ τῶν νεκρῶν, καθὸ ζωή ἐστι καὶ ζωοποιὸς ὡς Θεός, ἀνάθεμα ἔστω.

Nestorius. Si quis confitens passiones carnis has quoque Verbo Dei et carni simul in qua factus est, sine discretione dignitatis naturarum tribuerit, anathema sit.

Theodoret. The passible only can suffer ; the impassible is above passion. The " form of the servant " suffered as the " form of God " dwelling with it allowed (συγχωρούσης) it to suffer for man's salvation, and made the sufferings His own on account of the union. Therefore it was not the divine in Christ who suffered, but the manhood assumed of us by God.

Note here that Nestorius is more orthodox than Theodoret, who carries the separation to an extreme, as Cyril does the union. Note also Theodoret's teaching on the *kenosis*, comparing with this the similar statement in his reply to Cyril's Article IV.

Orientals. How could the Word suffer ? Cyril had himself admitted the impassibility of the Godhead. To say " God suffered in flesh " is inadequate, as it still implies that God was passible, and this is either Patripassianism or Arianism, a degradation of Deity.

Cyril's Reply. To suffer in flesh does not involve suffering in Godhead. The Word could not suffer as God, but only as having become passible Man. It is the Personal Union of One who is God with Human Nature that makes the Atonement efficacious.

Note that the lack of any qualification in this Anathema, such as that in the Epistle itself, which affirms the impassibility of the Word in His own Nature, laid Cyril justly open to the charge of holding that the Deity suffered ; and this was eagerly seized upon by those who were on the look-out for signs of Apollinarianism. Theopaschite language of the strongest kind was common enough in early writers (see Lightfoot's note, Clement ii. 15) in order to emphasise the real Deity of Christ, but it had its own dangers. By Gnostics it might be perverted to imply passibility in the Godhead ; by Apollinarians and Monophysites to denote the obliteration of the Human Nature ; and by Sabellians to destroy the distinction of Persons within the Trinity. Athanasius was more cautious ; cf. *e.g.* Or. c. Ar. iii. 32, ὅθεν τῆς σαρκὸς πασχούσης οὐκ ἦν ἐκτὸς ταύτης ὁ Λόγος· διὰ τοῦτο γὰρ αὐτοῦ λέγεται καὶ τὸ πάθος, κ.τ.λ. Cyril, it is seen, could not maintain his full position without inconsistency ; using the distinction of nature where the Unity of Person seemed to him convenient, *e.g.* where the action of the Holy Spirit was concerned. There were, in fact, two Cyrils, one who spoke in informal, at times in unguarded, language, as in the Anathemas, which never received oecumenical sanction, and another in diplomatic language, as in the Epistle which follows. See Kidd, op. cit., vol. iii, p. 283 and Duchesne, op. cit., vol. iii, p. 405 ; and cf. Article IX, p. 133.

K

THE EPISTLE OF CYRIL TO JOHN OF ANTIOCH

INTRODUCTION

On receipt of the letters from Caelestine and Cyril, Nestorius preached a sermon admitting the use of *Theotokos* alongside of *Anthropotokos*, but preferring *Christotokos*. He then framed the twelve counter-Anathemas to Cyril's, which have been already commented on, and secured the support of John of Antioch, Andrew of Samosata, and Theodoret of Cyrrhos. Andrew and Theodoret, as we have seen, wrote against the Twelve Articles, and Cyril replied, composing also Five Tomes in refutation of Nestorius' sermons.

In June 431 the prelates were assembling at Ephesus for the great Council. Some of them, John of Antioch and his party, were late. Cyril disastrously insisted on opening the Synod on June 22 ; and in consequence Nestorius refused to appear. Cyril almost certainly feared the influence of John, and that it would be exerted to annul his Twelfth Anathema. Without doubt he intended to get Nestorius condemned out of hand. For this he risked the appearance of having snatched the verdict ; and his procedure brought its own punishment in the confusion that ensued. Cyril presided either on the ground of the importance of his see or because he regarded himself as representing Pope Caelestine in virtue of the commission of the previous year (see above, p. 116).

Cyril's Second Letter was read and approved, and Nestorius' reply condemned. The Letter of Caelestine to Nestorius, and Cyril's Third Letter with the Anathemas, were then read and inserted in the Acts. They were accepted as orthodox, although no special acclamations of approval are recorded.[1] The deposition of Nestorius followed. A Synodal Letter to Theodosius informed him of all that had been done, and that the Council had found that the Epistles (ἐπιστόλας) of Cyril agreed with the Nicene Creed. Nestorius also wrote inveighing against the Council's actions.

On June 27 John and the Easterns arrived, held a separate council, deposed Cyril and Memnon of Ephesus, and excommunicated the rest pending their condemnation of Cyril's Anathemas. A record of their proceedings was also sent to the Emperor.

Two days later the true Council was severely reprimanded in a letter from the Emperor, and its acts annulled.

After the arrival of the Roman legates early in July several further

---

[1] Mansi, iv. 1139. The Easterns certainly believed that the Council had approved of Cyril's Articles (see their second petition to the Emperor, Mansi, v. 403), and such was the belief of the Commissioners at Chalcedon, Sess. i., Mansi, vi. 937. Both were probably in error.

sessions were held, and John of Antioch was excommunicated. The Emperor and the Pope were informed of these actions, but Theodosius sent a commissioner, Count John, with full powers and a letter which betrayed an entire misunderstanding of the position of affairs. It assented to the deposition of Cyril, Memnon, and Nestorius, who were thereupon placed under arrest. A demonstration of monks at Constantinople awakened Theodosius to his mistake, and in September a deputation from each party met him at Chalcedon. He ordered a new patriarch to be consecrated for Constantinople, and the rest of the prelates to return to their homes. John of Antioch continued to condemn Cyril and his supporters, and the Emperor endeavoured in vain to effect a reconciliation by means of a conference. An Antiochene council framed six Articles [1] in opposition to Cyril's, who replied that he insisted only on Nestorius' condemnation, and explained that his own Articles meant nothing but a rejection of Nestorian tenets. He anathematised Apollinarius and all other heretics. John was now satisfied, but the " Easterns " wavered. Eventually Paul of Emesa was sent to confer with Cyril. Confessions of faith were interchanged, and the terms of reunion embodied in a letter addressed to Cyril. This was sent to Antioch for John to subscribe ; it included the condemnation of Nestorius' writings and the recognition of his successor at Constantinople. After a little time, under pressure from the Court, John agreed, and Cyril announced the restoration of communion on April 23, 433. He then wrote the following Letter (*Laetentur caeli*) to John, inserting in it the Formulary of Reunion.

Dr. Kidd, summing up the controversy, remarks that Cyril has been very badly used by modern writers because they could not understand his zeal for a doctrine. Cyril made mistakes in the conduct of the controversy, but we must never lose sight of the fact that the issues were vital. His title to our veneration is that the contest has been decided long since in Cyril's way ; and Cyril's judgment has been ratified by all subsequent Christendom. The letter *Laetentur caeli* was recognised as oecumenical by the Council of Chalcedon. The authority of the Council of Ephesus, however unworthy its proceedings, depends upon the subsequent acceptance of its decisions by the Church. (Kidd, op. cit., vol. 3, pp. 253-6.)

[1] " We adhere to the Nicene Creed and the exposition of it by the blessed Athanasius in his letter to Epictetus. But the new dogmas, advanced in certain letters or articles, we reject as calculated to create disturbance." So ran the first article, the only one now extant (Fleury, Oxford translation, iii, p. 155).

ANALYSIS OF CYRIL'S EPISTLE TO JOHN OF ANTIOCH

A. *Introduction.*

The happiness of peace.
The visit of Paul of Emesa.

B. *Doctrinal.*

It is now clear that dissension was unnecessary.
The Formulary of Reunion.
    The Nicene Creed is sufficient, yet, as expressive of our convictions,
We confess
    Jesus Christ, Perfect God and Perfect Man,
    Co-essential with the Father as to Godhead,
    And with us as to Manhood : in Union of Two Natures One Christ.
    The Virgin is Theotokos, because from the moment of conception Her Offspring was God the Word. There is a Unity of Person with distinction of Natures, as the Gospel sayings imply.

I am accused of saying that the Flesh of Christ came down from heaven ; but this is excluded by my insistence upon Theotokos, and by the words of Isaiah vii. 14, and of Gabriel, Luke i. 30 and Matt. i. 23.
    We say that Christ came down from heaven, following St. Paul (1 Cor. xv. 47), because He is One with His own flesh which was born of the Virgin. The Word in His own Nature is unchangeable and unalterable.
    There was no mixture, or confusion, or blending. He, impassible, suffered for us in the flesh by an " economic " appropriation. We follow the Fathers, especially Athanasius, and the unalterable Nicene Symbol.

C. *Conclusion.*

You will know how to treat our calumniators.
    We send you a correct copy of Athanasius' Epistle to Epictetus, since many of the current copies are corrupt.

ΕΠΙΣΤΟΛΗ ΤΟΥ ΑΓΙΟΥ

ΚΥΡΙΛΛΟΥ

ΠΡΟΣ ΙΩΑΝΝΗΝ ΕΠΙΣΚΟΠΟΝ ΑΝΤΙΟΧΕΙΑΣ

Κυρίῳ μου ἀγαπητῷ ἀδελφῷ καὶ συλλειτουργῷ Ἰωάννῃ Κύριλλος ἐν κυρίῳ χαίρειν

ΕΥΦΡΑΙΝΕΣΘΩΣΑΝ οἱ οὐρανοὶ καὶ ἀγαλλιάσθω ἡ Psalm xcv. 11. 5
γῆ· λέλυται γὰρ τὸ μεσότοιχον τοῦ φραγμοῦ καὶ πέπαυται Eph. ii. 14.
τὸ λυποῦν καὶ διχονοίας ἁπάσης ἀνήρηται τρόπος, τοῦ πάντων ἡμῶν
Σωτῆρος Χριστοῦ ταῖς ἑαυτοῦ ἐκκλησίαις τὴν εἰρήνην βραβεύοντος·
κεκληκότων δὲ πρὸς τοῦτο ἡμᾶς καὶ τῶν εὐσεβεστάτων καὶ θεοφιλεσ-
τάτων βασιλέων· οἳ προγονικῆς εὐσεβείας ἄριστοι ζηλωταὶ γεγονότες, 10
ἀσφαλῆ μὲν καὶ ἀκατάσειστον ἐν ἰδίαις ψυχαῖς τὴν ὀρθὴν φυλάττουσι
πίστιν· ἐξαίρετον δὲ ποιοῦνται φροντίδα τὴν ὑπὲρ τῶν ἁγίων ἐκκλησιῶν,
ἵνα καὶ διαβόητον ἔχωσιν εἰς αἰῶνα τὴν δόξαν, καὶ εὐκλεεστάτην
ἀποφήνωσι τὴν ἑαυτῶν βασιλείαν· οἷς καὶ αὐτὸς ὁ τῶν δυνάμεων
Κύριος πλουσίᾳ χειρὶ διανέμει τὰ ἀγαθά· καὶ δίδωσι μὲν κατακρατεῖν 15
τῶν ἀνθεστηκότων, χαρίζεται δὲ τὸ νικᾶν. οὐ γὰρ ἂν διαψεύσαιτο
λέγων Ζῶ ἐγώ, λέγει Κύριος· ὅτι τοὺς δοξάζοντάς με 1 Sam. ii. 30.
δοξάσω.
Ἀφικομένου τοίνυν εἰς τὴν Ἀλεξάνδρειαν τοῦ κυρίου μου τοῦ
θεοφιλεστάτου ἀδελφοῦ καὶ συλλειτουργοῦ Παύλου, θυμηδίας ἐμπεπλή- 20
σμεθα καὶ σφόδρα εἰκότως, ὡς ἀνδρὸς τοιούτου μεσιτεύοντος, καὶ τοῖς
ὑπὲρ δύναμιν πόνοις ἑλομένου προσομιλεῖν, ἵνα τὸν τοῦ διαβόλου
νικήσῃ φθόνον, καὶ συνάψῃ τὰ διηρημένα, καὶ τὰ μεταξὺ διερριμμένα
σκάνδαλα περιελών, ὁμονοίᾳ καὶ εἰρήνῃ στεφανώσῃ τάς τε παρ' ἡμῖν
καὶ τὰς παρ' ὑμῖν ἐκκλησίας. τίνα μὲν γὰρ διήρηνται τρόπον, περιττὸν 25
εἰπεῖν· χρῆναι δὲ μᾶλλον ὑπολαμβάνω τὰ τῷ τῆς εἰρήνης πρέποντα
καιρῷ καὶ φρονεῖν καὶ λαλεῖν. ἤσθημεν τοίνυν ἐπὶ τῇ συντυχίᾳ τοῦ
μνημονευθέντος θεοσεβεστάτου ἀνδρός· ὃς τάχα που καὶ ἀγῶνας ἕξειν
οὐ μικροὺς ὑπενόησεν, ἀναπείθων ἡμᾶς ὅτι χρὴ συνάψαι πρὸς εἰρήνην
τὰς ἐκκλησίας, καὶ τὸν τῶν ἑτεροδόξων ἀφανίσαι γέλωτα, ἀπαμβλῦναί 30
τε πρὸς τούτῳ τῆς τοῦ διαβόλου δυστροπίας τὸ κέντρον. ἑτοίμως δὲ
οὕτως ἔχοντας εἰς τοῦτο κατέλαβεν, ὡς μηδένα πόνον ὑποστῆναι
παντελῶς· μεμνήμεθα γὰρ τοῦ Σωτῆρος λέγοντος Εἰρήνην John xiv. 27.
τὴν ἐμὴν δίδωμι ὑμῖν, εἰρήνην τὴν ἐμὴν ἀφίημι ὑμῖν. δεδιδάγμεθα δὲ
καὶ λέγειν ἐν προσευχαῖς Κύριε ὁ Θεὸς ἡμῶν εἰρήνην δὸς Isaiah xxvi. 12. 35
ἡμῖν, πάντα γὰρ ἀπέδωκας ἡμῖν. ὥστε εἴ τις ἐν μεθέξει γένοιτο τῆς
παρὰ Θεοῦ χορηγουμένης εἰρήνης, ἀνενδεὴς ἔσται παντὸς ἀγαθοῦ.
Ὅτι δὲ περιττὴ παντελῶς καὶ οὐκ εὐάφορμος τῶν ἐκκλησιῶν ἡ
διχοστασία γέγονε, νυνὶ μάλιστα πεπληροφορήμεθα, τοῦ κυρίου μου
τοῦ θεοφιλεστάτου Παύλου τοῦ ἐπισκόπου χάρτην προκομίσαντος, 40
ἀδιάβλητον ἔχοντα τῆς πίστεως τὴν ὁμολογίαν, καὶ ταύτην συντετάχθαι

141

διαβεβαιουμένου παρά τε τῆς σῆς ὁσιότητος καὶ τῶν αὐτόθι θεοσεβεστά-
των ἐπισκόπων. ἔχει δὲ οὕτως ἡ συγγραφὴ, καὶ αὐταῖς λέξεσιν ἐν-
τέθειται τῇδε ἡμῶν τῇ ἐπιστολῇ.

45 Περὶ δὲ τῆς θεοτόκου παρθένου ὅπως καὶ φρονοῦμεν καὶ λέγομεν, τοῦ τε τρόπου τῆς
ἐνανθρωπήσεως τοῦ Μονογενοῦς Υἱοῦ τοῦ Θεοῦ, ἀναγκαίως, οὐκ ἐν προσθήκης μέρει, ἀλλ᾽ ἐν
πληροφορίας εἴδει, ὡς ἄνωθεν ἔκ τε τῶν θείων γραφῶν, ἔκ τε τῆς παραδόσεως τῶν ἁγίων
πατέρων παρειληφότες ἐσχήκαμεν, διὰ βραχέων ἐροῦμεν, οὐδὲν τὸ συνόλου προστιθέντες τῇ
τῶν ἁγίων πατέρων τῶν ἐν Νικαίᾳ ἐκτεθείσῃ πίστει. ὡς γὰρ ἔφθημεν εἰρηκότες, πρὸς
50 πᾶσαν ἐξαρκεῖ καὶ εὐσεβείας γνῶσιν, καὶ πάσης αἱρετικῆς κακοδοξίας ἀποκήρυξιν. ἐροῦμεν
δὲ οὐ κατατολμῶντες τῶν ἀνεφίκτων, ἀλλὰ τῇ ὁμολογίᾳ τῆς οἰκείας ἀσθενείας, ἀποκλείοντες
τοῖς ἐπιφύεσθαι βουλομένοις, ἐν οἷς τὰ ὑπὲρ ἄνθρωπον διασκεπτόμεθα.

Ὁμολογοῦμεν τοιγαροῦν τὸν Κύριον ἡμῶν Ἰησοῦν τὸν Χριστόν, τὸν Υἱὸν τοῦ Θεοῦ τὸν
Μονογενῆ, Θεὸν τέλειον καὶ ἄνθρωπον τέλειον ἐκ ψυχῆς λογικῆς καὶ σώματος· πρὸ αἰώνων
55 μὲν ἐκ τοῦ Πατρὸς γεννηθέντα κατὰ τὴν θεότητα, ἐπ᾽ ἐσχάτου δὲ τῶν ἡμερῶν τὸν αὐτὸν δι᾽
ἡμᾶς καὶ διὰ τὴν ἡμετέραν σωτηρίαν, ἐκ Μαρίας τῆς παρθένου κατὰ τὴν ἀνθρωπότητα·
ὁμοούσιον τῷ Πατρὶ τὸν αὐτὸν κατὰ τὴν θεότητα, καὶ ὁμοούσιον ἡμῖν κατὰ τὴν ἀνθρωπότητα·
δύο γὰρ φύσεων ἕνωσις γέγονε· διὸ ἕνα Χριστόν, ἕνα Υἱόν, ἕνα Κύριον ὁμολογοῦμεν. κατὰ
ταύτην τὴν τῆς ἀσυγχύτου ἑνώσεως ἔννοιαν ὁμολογοῦμεν τὴν ἁγίαν παρθένον θεοτόκον, διὰ
60 τὸ τὸν Θεὸν Λόγον σαρκωθῆναι καὶ ἐνανθρωπῆσαι, καὶ ἐξ αὐτῆς τῆς συλλήψεως ἑνῶσαι
ἑαυτῷ τὸν ἐξ αὐτῆς ληφθέντα ναόν. τὰς δὲ εὐαγγελικὰς καὶ ἀποστολικὰς περὶ τοῦ Κυρίου
φωνὰς, ἴσμεν τοὺς θεολόγους ἄνδρας, τὰς μὲν κοινοποιοῦντας, ὡς ἐφ᾽ ἑνὸς προσώπου, τὰς δὲ
διαιροῦντας, ὡς ἐπὶ δύο φύσεων· καὶ τὰς μὲν θεοπρεπεῖς κατὰ τὴν θεότητα τοῦ Χριστοῦ, τὰς
δὲ ταπεινὰς κατὰ τὴν ἀνθρωπότητα παραδιδόντας.

65 Ταύταις ὑμῶν ἐντυχόντες ταῖς ἱεραῖς φωναῖς, οὕτω τε καὶ ἑαυτοὺς
Eph. iv. 5. φρονοῦντας εὑρίσκοντες· εἷς γὰρ Κύριος, μία πίστις,
ἓν βάπτισμα· ἐδοξάσαμεν τὸν τῶν ὅλων Σωτῆρα Θεόν· ἀλλήλοις
συγχαίροντες, ὅτι ταῖς θεοπνεύστοις γραφαῖς καὶ τῇ παραδόσει τῶν
ἁγίων ἡμῶν πατέρων, συμβαίνουσαν ἔχουσι πίστιν αἵ τε παρ᾽ ἡμῖν καὶ
70 αἱ παρ᾽ ὑμῖν ἐκκλησίαι· ἐπειδὴ δὲ ἐπυθόμην τῶν φιλοψογεῖν εἰωθότων
τινὰς, σφηκῶν ἀγρίων δίκην περιβομβεῖν, καὶ μοχθηροὺς ἐρεύγεσθαι
κατ᾽ ἐμοῦ λόγους, ὡς ἐξ οὐρανοῦ κατακομισθὲν, καὶ οὐκ ἐκ τῆς ἁγίας
παρθένου λέγοντος τὸ ἅγιον σῶμα Χριστοῦ δεῖν ᾠήθην ὀλίγα περὶ
τούτου πρὸς αὐτοὺς εἰπεῖν Ὦ ἀνόητοι καὶ μόνον εἰδότες τὸ συκοφαντεῖν·
75 πῶς εἰς τοῦτο παρηνέχθητε γνώμης καὶ τοσαύτην νενοσήκατε τὴν
μωρίαν; ἔδει γὰρ ἔδει σαφῶς ἐννοεῖν, ὅτι σχεδὸν ἅπας ἡμῖν ὁ ὑπὲρ τῆς
πίστεως ἀγὼν συγκεκρότηται, διαβεβαιουμένοις, ὅτι θεοτόκος ἐστὶν ἡ
ἁγία παρθένος. ἀλλ᾽ εἴπερ ἐξ οὐρανοῦ, καὶ οὐκ ἐξ αὐτῆς τὸ ἅγιον
σῶμα γεγενῆσθαί φαμεν τοῦ πάντων ἡμῶν σωτῆρος Χριστοῦ, πῶς ἂν
80 ἔτι νοοῖτο θεοτόκος; τίνα γὰρ ὅλως τέτοκεν, εἰ μή ἐστιν ἀληθὲς, ὅτι
γεγέννηκε κατὰ σάρκα τὸν Ἐμμανουήλ; γελάσθωσαν τοίνυν οἱ ταῦτα
περὶ ἐμοῦ πεφλυαρηκότες· οὐ γὰρ ψεύδεται λέγων ὁ μακάριος προφήτης
Isaiah vii. 14. Ἡσαΐας Ἰδοὺ ἡ παρθένος ἐν γαστρὶ ἕξει, καὶ τέξεται
Matt. i. 23. Υἱόν, καὶ καλέσουσι τὸ ὄνομα αὐτοῦ Ἐμμανουήλ· ὅ ἐστι
85 μεθερμηνευόμενον Μεθ᾽ ἡμῶν ὁ Θεός, ἀληθεύει δὲ πάντως καὶ ὁ ἅγιος
Luke i. 30, 31. Γαβριὴλ πρὸς τὴν μακαρίαν παρθένον εἰπὼν Μὴ φοβοῦ
Μαριάμ· εὗρες γὰρ χάριν παρὰ τῷ Θεῷ· καὶ ἰδοὺ συλλήψῃ ἐν γαστρὶ,
Matt. i. 21. καὶ τέξῃ υἱόν, καὶ καλέσεις τὸ ὄνομα αὐτοῦ Ἰησοῦν. Αὐτὸς
γὰρ σώσει τὸν λαὸν αὐτοῦ ἀπὸ τῶν ἁμαρτιῶν αὐτῶν.
90 Ὅταν δὲ λέγομεν ἐξ οὐρανοῦ καὶ ἄνωθεν τὸν Κύριον ἡμῶν Ἰησοῦν
τὸν Χριστόν, οὐχ ὡς ἄνωθεν καὶ ἐξ οὐρανοῦ κατενεχθείσης τῆς ἁγίας
αὐτοῦ σαρκὸς, τὰ τοιαῦτά φαμεν, ἑπόμενοι δὲ μᾶλλον τῷ θεσπεσίῳ

Παύλῳ διακεκραγότι σαφῶς Ὁ πρῶτος ἄνθρωπος ἐκ γῆς, 1 Cor. xv. 47.
χοϊκός, ὁ δεύτερος ἄνθρωπος [ὁ Κύριος] ἐξ οὐρανοῦ. μεμνήμεθα δὲ
καὶ αὐτοῦ τοῦ Σωτῆρος λέγοντος Οὐδεὶς ἀναβέβηκεν εἰς τὸν οὐρανόν, 95
εἰ μὴ ὁ ἐκ τοῦ οὐρανοῦ καταβάς, ὁ υἱὸς τοῦ ἀνθρώπου· John iii. 13.
καίτοι γεγέννηται κατὰ σάρκα, καθάπερ ἔφην ἀρτίως, ἐκ τῆς ἁγίας
παρθένου. ἐπειδὴ δὲ ὁ ἄνωθεν καὶ ἐξ οὐρανοῦ καταφοιτήσας Θεὸς
Λόγος κεκένωκεν ἑαυτόν, μορφὴν δούλου λαβών, καὶ Phil. ii. 7.
κεχρημάτικεν υἱὸς ἀνθρώπου, μετὰ τοῦ μεῖναι ὃ ἦν, τουτέστι Θεός. 100
ἄτρεπτος γὰρ καὶ ἀναλλοίωτος κατὰ φύσιν ἐστίν· ὡς εἰς ἤδη νοούμενος
μετὰ τῆς ἰδίας σαρκός, ἐξ οὐρανοῦ λέγεται κατελθεῖν, ὠνόμασται
δὲ καὶ ἄνθρωπος ἐξ οὐρανοῦ, τέλειος ὢν ἐν θεότητι, καὶ 1 Cor. xv. 47.
τέλειος ἐν ἀνθρωπότητι ὁ αὐτός, καὶ ὡς ἐν ἑνὶ προσώπῳ νοούμενος·
εἷς γὰρ Κύριος Ἰησοῦς Χριστός, κἂν ἡ τῶν φύσεων μὴ 1 Cor. viii. 6. 105
ἀγνοῆται διαφορά, ἐξ ὧν τὴν ἀπόρρητον ἔνωσιν πεπρᾶχθαι φαμέν.
Τοὺς δὲ λέγοντας ὅτι κρᾶσις ἢ σύγχυσις ἢ φυρμὸς ἐγένετο τοῦ Θεοῦ
Λόγου πρὸς τὴν σάρκα, καταξιωσάτω ἡ σὴ ὁσιότης ἐπιστομίζειν.
εἰκὸς γάρ τινας καὶ ταῦτα περὶ ἐμοῦ θρυλεῖν, ὡς ἢ πεφρονηκότος ἢ
εἰρηκότος. ἐγὼ δὲ τοσοῦτον ἀφέστηκα τοῦ φρονῆσαί τι τοιοῦτον, 110
ὥστε καὶ μαίνεσθαι νομίζω τοὺς οἰηθέντας ὅλως, ὅτι James i. 17.
τροπῆς ἀποσκίασμα περὶ τὴν θείαν τοῦ Λόγου φύσιν συμβῆναι δύναται·
μένει γὰρ ὅ ἐστιν ἀεί, καὶ οὐκ ἠλλοίωται· ἀλλ᾿ οὐδ᾿ ἂν Mal. iii. 6.
ἀλλοιωθείη πώποτε καὶ μεταβολῆς ἔσται δεκτική. ἀπαθῆ δὲ πρὸς
τούτῳ τὸν τοῦ Θεοῦ Λόγον ὑπάρχειν ὁμολογοῦμεν ἅπαντες, κἂν εἰ 115
πανσόφως αὐτὸς οἰκονομῶν τὸ μυστήριον, ἑαυτῷ προσνέμων ὁρῶτο τὰ
τῇ ἰδίᾳ σαρκὶ συμβεβηκότα πάθη. ταύτῃ τοι καὶ ὁ πάνσοφος Πέτρος
Χριστοῦ οὖν, φησί, παθόντος ὑπὲρ ἡμῶν σαρκί, καὶ οὐχὶ 1 Peter iv. 1.
τῇ φύσει τῆς ἀρρήτου θεότητος. ἵνα γὰρ αὐτὸς ὁ τῶν ὅλων Σωτὴρ
εἶναι πιστεύηται, κατ᾿ οἰκείωσιν οἰκονομικὴν εἰς ἑαυτόν, ὡς ἔφην, τὰ 120
τῆς ἰδίας σαρκὸς ἀναφέρει πάθη· ὁποῖόν ἐστι τὸ διὰ τῆς τοῦ προφήτου
φωνῆς προαναφωνούμενον, ὡς ἐξ αὐτοῦ Τὸν νῶτόν μου Isaiah i. 6.
δέδωκα εἰς μάστιγας, τὰς δὲ σιαγόνας μου εἰς ῥαπίσματα, τὸ δὲ
πρόσωπόν μου οὐκ ἀπέστρεψα ἀπὸ αἰσχύνης ἐμπτυσμάτων.
Ὅτι δὲ ταῖς τῶν ἁγίων πατέρων δόξαις ἑπόμεθα πανταχοῦ, μάλιστα 125
δὲ ταῖς τοῦ μακαρίου καὶ πανευφήμου πατρὸς ἡμῶν Ἀθανασίου, τὸ
κατά τι γοῦν ὅλως ἔξω φέρεσθαι παραιτούμενοι, πεπείσθω μὲν ἡ σὴ
ὁσιότης, ἐνδοιαζέτω δὲ τῶν ἄλλων μηδείς. παρέθηκα δ᾿ ἂν καὶ
χρήσεις αὐτῶν πολλάς, τοὺς ἐμαυτοῦ λόγους ἐξ αὐτῶν πιστούμενος, εἰ
μὴ τὸ μῆκος ἐδεδίειν τοῦ γράμματος, μὴ ἄρα πως γένηται διὰ τοῦτο 130
προσκορές. κατ᾿ οὐδένα δὲ τρόπον σαλεύεσθαι παρά τινων ἀνεχόμεθα
τὴν ὁρισθεῖσαν πίστιν, ἤτοι τὸ τῆς πίστεως σύμβολον, παρὰ τῶν
ἁγίων ἡμῶν πατέρων, τῶν ἐν Νικαίᾳ συνελθόντων κατὰ καιρούς· οὔτε
μὴν ἐπιτρέπομεν ἑαυτοῖς ἢ ἑτέροις, ἢ λέξιν ἀμεῖψαι τῶν ἐγκειμένων
ἐκεῖσε, ἢ μίαν γοῦν παραβῆναι συλλαβήν, μεμνημένοι τοῦ λέγοντος 135
Μὴ μέταιρε ὅρια αἰώνια ἃ ἔθεντο οἱ πατέρες σου· οὐ γὰρ Prov. xxii. 28.
ἦσαν αὐτοὶ οἱ λαλοῦντες, ἀλλὰ τὸ Πνεῦμα τοῦ Θεοῦ καὶ Matt. x. 20.
Πατρός· ὃ ἐκπορεύεται μὲν ἐξ αὐτοῦ, ἔστι δὲ οὐκ ἀλλότριον
τοῦ Υἱοῦ κατά γε τὸν τῆς οὐσίας λόγον. καὶ πρός γε τοῦτο ἡμᾶς οἱ
τῶν ἁγίων μυσταγωγῶν πιστοῦνται λόγοι. ἐν μὲν γὰρ ταῖς πράξεσι 140

John xv. 26. τῶν ἀποστόλων γέγραπται Ἐλθόντες δὲ κατὰ τὴν Μυσίαν
Acts xvi. 7. ἐπείραζον εἰς τὴν Βιθυνίαν πορευθῆναι, καὶ οὐκ εἴασεν
αὐτοὺς τὸ πνεῦμα Ἰησοῦ· ἐπιστέλλει δὲ καὶ ὁ θεσπέσιος Παῦλος Οἱ
Rom. viii. 8, 9. δὲ ἐν σαρκὶ ὄντες Θεῷ ἀρέσαι οὐ δύνανται, ὑμεῖς δὲ οὐκ
145 ἐστὲ ἐν σαρκὶ ἀλλ᾽ ἐν πνεύματι, εἴπερ Πνεῦμα Θεοῦ οἰκεῖ ἐν ὑμῖν. εἰ
δέ τις πνεῦμα Χριστοῦ οὐκ ἔχει, οὗτος οὐκ ἔστιν αὐτοῦ.

Ὅταν δέ τινες τῶν τὰ ὀρθὰ διαστρέφειν εἰωθότων τὰς ἐμὰς παρατ-
ρέπωσι φωνὰς εἰς τὸ αὐτοῖς δοκοῦν, μὴ θαυμαζέτω τοῦτο ἡ σὴ ὁσιότης,
εἰδυῖα ὅτι καὶ οἱ ἀπὸ πάσης αἱρέσεως ἐκ τῆς θεοπνεύστου γραφῆς τὰς
150 τῆς ἑαυτῶν πλάνης συλλέγουσιν ἀφορμάς, τὰ διὰ τοῦ Ἁγίου Πνεύματος
ὀρθῶς εἰρημένα ταῖς ἑαυτῶν κακονοίαις παραφθείροντες, καὶ ταῖς
ἰδίαις κεφαλαῖς τὴν ἄσβεστον ἐπαντλοῦντες φλόγα.

Ἐπεὶ δὲ μεμαθήκαμεν ὅτι καὶ τὴν πρὸς τὸν μακάριον Ἐπίκτητον
ἐπιστολὴν τοῦ πανευφήμου πατρὸς ἡμῶν Ἀθανασίου, ὀρθοδόξως
155 ἔχουσαν, παραφθείραντές τινες ἐκδεδώκασιν, ὡς ἐντεῦθεν ἀδικεῖσθαι
πολλούς, διὰ τοῦτο χρήσιμόν τι καὶ ἀναγκαῖον ἐπινοοῦντες τοῖς
ἀδελφοῖς, ἐξ ἀντιγράφων ἀρχαίων τῶν παρ᾽ ἡμῖν καὶ ἀπλανῶς ἐχόντων,
ἀπεστείλαμεν τὰ ἴσα τῇ σῇ ὁσιότητι.

Ἐρρωμένον σε καὶ ὑπερευχόμενον ἡμῶν ὁ Κύριος διαφυλάξει
160 τιμιώτατε ἀδελφέ.

NOTES ON CYRIL'S LETTER TO JOHN OF ANTIOCH

9. τῶν . . . βασιλέων. Theodosius II and Valentinian III.

27. συντυχίᾳ, "intercourse," "conference." The word often bears this sense of "interview" in ecclesiastical Greek, being almost synonymous with ὁμιλία.

40. Paul, when he visited Cyril, brought with him : (1) the six propositions of the recent Synod of Antioch ; (2) the doctrinal formulary drawn up by Theodoret and presented to the Emperor by Count John on behalf of the Orientals, but without the anti-Cyrilline preface and peroration ; and containing an introduction and a creed, afterwards called the Formulary of Union, or the Reunion Creed of the Antiochenes, which is the document here referred to (συγγραφή). What was its origin ? Presumably it was drawn up by Theodoret as a basis of the reconciliation in August 431. Count John had tried without success to bring the parties together again (see Kidd, op. cit., vol. 3, p. 259 and cf. Sellers, op. cit., p. 235).

43. συγγραφή. Note with regard to the Formulary of Union :
(1) The emphasis laid upon the two Natures. In his subsequent letter to his anti-Nestorian supporters who complained that Cyril, in accepting the phrases about the ascription of the words of Christ to the two Natures separately and even pressing them, was giving in to those who opposed him at Ephesus, Cyril remarks that Nestorius was right in insisting on two Natures, demonstrating thereby the difference between the flesh and the divine Logos (Ep. ad Eulog., P.G., vol. 77, p. 255a). This was a remarkably frank statement, which if made earlier with charity would have avoided the controversy. Moreover, he remarks that it is possible to speak of two Natures in respect of Christ Incarnate, though only in θεωρία ("contemplation") ; which way of thinking belongs to the brethren in Antioch, who, accepting simply as though in imagination or contemplation only the diversity of Natures, in no wise divide the things that have been united (Ep. ad Acac., P.G., vol. 77, p. 193D). This phrase (θεωρίᾳ μόνῃ), afterwards brought into prominence by Severus of Antioch, was not welcomed by the anti-Nestorians as giving their opponents a loop-hole of escape into orthodoxy, and they urged that it should be dropped (see Sellers, op. cit., p. 101).
(2) δυό φυσέων ἕνωσις γέγονε. This phrase seems to regard Christ as the result of the union of the two Natures rather than its ground. It is Immanuel who is one, as Nestorius was never

tired of saying. In this respect Cyril was in substantial agreement and supported it in the phrase ἐξ ὧν (φυσέων) τὴν ἀπόρρητον ἕνωσιν πεπράχθαι φαμέν ; but as usual he was not consistent and often spoke in the Alexandrian fashion as if the only element that mattered was the *Hypostasis* of the Logos as the ground of the Union.

(3) The Antiochenes on their side have dropped, as a concession to Cyril, Nestorius' phrases Χριστοτόκος and ἀνθρωποτόκος.

(4) The position of this formulary in subsequent history is interesting. It was in no sense acceptable to Dioscorus, Cyril's successor in the See of Alexandria. To his mind the Formulary was now regarded as a form of orthodoxy, but should never have been so accepted. With its mention of a union of two natures it was simply a shield behind which the Nestorianisers could hide and proclaim themselves sound in the faith. Ultimately Dioscorus found in Eutyches a valuable ally ; and it was he who insisted on securing the trial and deposition of Bishop Ibas of Edessa, the translator of the works of Diodore and Theodore into Syrian, in spite of Ibas' declaration of belief in the Formulary and anathematisation of Nestorius.

46. οὐκ ἐν προσθήκης μέρει, ἀλλ' ἐν πληροφορίας εἴδει, " not by way of a supplement (to the Nicene Symbol)." προσθεῖναι is thus used here by the bishops at Antioch in 341 at the end of their first creed, Socr. ii. 10, Athan. De Synod. 22 (see their words cited, p. 62).

57. ὁμοούσιον τῷ Πατρί, κ.τ.λ. This phrase finds a place again in the Chalcedonian Definition. The latter half, " co-essential with us as to manhood," had occurred in Nestorius' Sermon 3, and had no doubt come into partial use before this as a " counter-statement to the doctrine of Apollinarius that Christ's Body was consubstantial with the Godhead." It was not, as yet, a well-known and accepted Catholic phrase ; and this may explain Eutyches' subsequent hesitation respecting it (see below, pp. 191, 207, 239). Cf. Vincent Lerin., Common. 13 (written in 434), " In uno eodemque Christo duae substantiae sunt, sed una Divina altera humana . . . una consubstantialis Patri, altera consubstantialis matri ; unus tamen idemque Christus in utraque substantia."

72. ὡς ἐξ οὐρανοῦ . . . τὸ ἅγιον σῶμα Χριστοῦ. The doctrine of the Synousiasts (Athanasius, Epist. ad Epictetum ; see Sellers, op. cit., p. 53).

88. Αὐτὸς γὰρ σώσει, κ.τ.λ. This is added from the Angel's words to Joseph, Matt. i. 21.

94. [ὁ Κύριος] ἐξ οὐρανοῦ. The text is doubtful. The reference to it just below implies the omission of ὁ Κύριος. Cyril " apparently knew and used both readings " (Hort) of this verse. But in John iii. 13 next quoted he certainly omitted ὁ ὢν ἐν τῷ οὐρανῷ.

101. ἄτρεπτος γὰρ καὶ ἀναλλοίωτος. This phrase, which Cyril had already used in his Third Letter to Nestorius, occurred both in the Creed of Alexandria and in that of Antioch, and was therefore naturally employed by the bishop of the one city writing to the bishop of the other. See above, pp. 62, 110.

105. εἶς . . . Κύριος Ἰησοῦς Χριστός. Here again Cyril cites the Creed, or perhaps directly from 1 Cor. viii. 6, as in Epist. ad Nest. 3.

107. κρᾶσις ἢ σύγχυσις. The terms used here were, indeed, used by Apollinarius and his followers (Fragment 10, line 113, Raven, p. 204). But they were also used by Origen and his followers (e.g. c. Celsum iii. 43 and 66); by Irenaeus (Adv. Haer. iv. 34, 4), and by Epiphanius (Ancoratus 8) and even Cyril himself (Epist. xl ad Acacium). κρᾶσις received its final use in Eutychianism. Cf. also Leo, Sermon lviii, in which he speaks of one nature being blended (" miscetur," see above, p. 118). The phrase also occurs in the Cappadocian Fathers, e.g. Gregory Naz., Orat. de Epiphan., 38. 13.

120. οἰκονομικὴν, " economic," i.e. " inherent in the Incarnation. οἰκονομία is constantly used by ecclesiastical writers for the " Dispensation " whereby the Son of God manifested Himself in flesh, while θεολογία expressed the Divinity of His Person. Eusebius, HE. i. 1 ; Basil, Epist. viii. 3 ; Athanasius, Or. c. Ar. ii. 9 ; c. Apollin. i. 2, 18 ; Theodoret, Dial. ii., τὴν ἐνανθρώπησιν τοῦ Θεοῦ Λόγου καλοῦμεν οἰκονομίαν : cf. ibid., iii. juxta fin. ; Def. Chalc. 3. See Lightfoot's note on Eph. i. 10 and on Ignat. Eph. 18 (ii. 75). Tertullian had used θεολογία in a different sense, of the relations of the Divine Persons in the Trinity (Adv. Prax. 2, 3, 8).

125. ταῖς τῶν ἁγ. π. δόξαις, κ.τ.λ. Cyril no doubt had in mind the Fathers from whose writings extracts had been made in the Sixth Session of the Council of Ephesus, and appended to the Nicene Creed as a kind of Definition of Faith. They comprised passages from Peter of Alexandria, Athanasius' Orations and Epistle to Epictetus, Julius' Epistle to Docimus, Felix' Epistle to Maximus, the Paschal Letters of Theophilus of Alexandria, Cyprian, Ambrose, Gregory Nazianzen, Basil, Gregory of Nyssa, Atticus of Constantinople, and Amphilochius of Iconium. See Vincent Ler., Common. 79, who omits the last two.

135. ἢ μίαν γοῦν παραβῆναι συλλαβήν. So Basil (Epist. ccxlviii) had written to Epiphanius in 377 " that ' not the smallest addition ' could be made to the Nicene Creed except on the Divinity of the Holy Spirit " (Bright, Canons, p. 39).

153. τὴν πρὸς τ. μ. Ἐπίκτητον ἐπιστολήν. On the Letter of Athanasius to Epictetus Bishop of Corinth (c. 371) see Raven, Apollinarianism, pp. 102 f. For another view see Tixeront, History of Dogmas,

vol. ii, pp. 109 f.   Together with the letters to Adelphius, an Egyptian Bishop, and to Maximus, a philosopher friend of Gregory Nazianzen, it is one of the most important documents in early Church history and was regarded by antiquity as a standard work on Christology.   It was regularly used by Cyril of Alexandria, Epiphanius, and the unknown author of the two books against Apollinarius.   Its importance lies in the fact that it occasioned the false estimate of Apollinarius, as being the author of the cruder forms of the heresy which goes by his name, afterwards revived by Eutyches, *e.g.* that the flesh of the Logos was consubstantial with the Godhead, was not from Mary, and was the seat of suffering, all of which propositions are expressly condemned in the various fragments of Apollinarius which have survived.   Alone of ancient authors Epiphanius definitely connected the Letter with Apollinarius, but many modern writers have wrongly attributed to Apollinarius the troubles at Corinth with which Athanasius was concerned in this Letter.   It may be added that the conciliar letter addressed by the Athanasian Council of Alexandria in 362 to the same Corinthian Church is referred to with approval by Apollinarius in a personal letter to Basil (Raven, op. cit., pp. 134–6). The innocence of Apollinarius is further demonstrated by the fact that the Letter *Ad Epictetum* appears actually to have been sent to him by Athanasius for his approval and comments.   (See Lietzman, *Fragments*, pp. 159–61, including a letter to Serapion of Thmuis, the trusty supporter of the exiled Athanasius, in which Apollinarius acknowledged the receipt of the letter.)

APPENDIX
TO THE EPISTLES OF CYRIL

ANATHEMATISMS OF THE FIFTH GENERAL COUNCIL AT CONSTANTINOPLE

A.D. 553

APPENDIX TO THE EPISTLES OF CYRIL

This Appendix, as also that printed after the Definition of Chalcedon, is added to complete the story of the Oecumenical Councils of the early and undivided Church. The Definition of the Council of Chalcedon, as is now generally recognised, was the first general acknowledgment of that side of the truth about Christ which had always been recognised by Antioch. It was, however, unfortunate that in its terminology the Council was so unrepresentative of the East and especially of the Alexandrian school of thought: with the result that it was the occasion of a worse schism than any of the preceding ones, such as Apollinarianism. This was the Monophysite schism which dominated the Christian East for centuries and still survives in the Coptic, Syrian Jacobite, and, in a qualified sense, the Armenian Churches to-day. Those on the Alexandrian side could not, on reflection, see that any satisfactory expression was given at Chalcedon of the unity of Christ's Person. Indeed, it came to be thought that, on Leo's showing, a distinction of the Natures after the Union was inconsistent with any real preservation of the Unity; and in consequence there came into being a school of scientific Monophysitism, which, as in the case of Apollinarianism, was often little more than a verbal or philosophical argument against the imperfect logic of the Catholics.

The publication of the decrees of Chalcedon was therefore only the signal for a final outburst of Eutychianism throughout the East. To the great body of monks in particular it came with all the force of a compulsory establishment of Nestorianism. Everywhere the most determined opposition instantly developed; not only in Alexandria but also in Jerusalem, Constantinople, and even Antioch. The Emperor Marcian's Decrees enforcing uniformity followed one another in rapid succession. In A.D. 457, however, he was succeeded by Leo the First, who tried to test the feeling of the Church by a sort of plebiscite of the hierarchy: the result of which was an overwhelming vote in favour of the Decrees from 1,600 bishops. But the opposition continued in the great centres of the East. In 470 Peter the Fuller ousted the orthodox Patriarch at Antioch, and became very active and successful in propagating Monophysitism by means of interpolations in the Liturgy, just as Arius had popularised his views by means of popular songs. Phrases such as " the Mother of God," " God was Crucified," began to assume a meaning which referred the whole incarnate activity of Christ to His Godhead to the ignoring of all human activity in Him. The Emperor Leo was succeeded in 474 by Zeno, who was the leader in a futile scheme of reconciliation, the only effect of which was to divide the parties even more hopelessly than before; and, under the influence of the Monophysite Peter Mongus of Alexandria, the Emperor with the aid of Acacius, Patriarch of Alexandria, drew up a Confession of Faith called the *Henotikon*, based upon the first three General Councils, but ignoring Chalcedon, and accordingly all controversial terms.   Such an attempt on the part of the secular powers to define the Faith and enforce conformity to it was resisted by Rome under Pope Felix the Third, who excommunicated Acacius. This was, of course, resented, and the first great schism between East and West lasted for forty years.   In 518 Justinian, whose long and illustrious reign followed Zeno's, succeeded in restoring all the centres of the East except Alexandria to the Chalcedonian fold; and communion was resumed with Rome.   But under the patronage of the Empress Theodora, a violent Monophysite, the schism revived and reorganised itself everywhere, especially in Constantinople itself.   Justinian himself began as a convinced Chalcedonian, but subsequently weakened; and it was a sign which way the wind was blowing when Justinian, as an act of conciliation, sanctioned in 533 the liturgical formula "One of the Trinity was born and crucified." Twenty years later the Fifth General Council anathematised all who should reject it.   After attempting to suppress and again to reconcile Monophysitism, Justinian in 544 issued his edict of *The Three Chapters*, in which were anathematised the person and works of Theodore, and the works but not the persons of Theodoret and Ibas; thereby acting contrary to the decisions of Chalcedon which had acquitted them of all charges of heresy, condemning only their own charge of Apollinarianism against Cyril. This Edict was opposed by Pope Vigilius, who had at first inclined towards Monophysitism and the Empress Theodora, to whose influence he owed his See.   After much vacillation, for which he was strongly rebuked by a storm of opposition from the West, he prevailed upon the Emperor to summon a Council, to which Justinian agreed, subject to the condition that he should not withdraw his assent to the condemnation of the three Doctors.   In 553 accordingly the Fifth General Council was held, the second of Constantinople, and the fourteen anathematisms of this Council are printed below. It was, however, only after prolonged debate that the opposition of Vigilius was broken down, and the Decrees of the Council and its authority accepted afterwards in the West.   The motto of this Council might be said to be μία θεανδρικὴ ἐνέργεια; the latter word being its peculiarly new form of expression.   This sketch is mainly taken from the *Oecumenical Councils*, by the late W. P. Du Bose (Edinburgh, T. and T. Clark, 2nd Edn., 1897), to which the reader is referred for more detailed information.   Translations of this and the later Appendix will be found in Wace and Schaff, *Library of Nicene and post-Nicene Fathers*, vol. xiv, *The Seven Oecumenical Councils*, pp. 312 ff.

ANATHEMATISMS OF THE FIFTH GENERAL COUNCIL AT CONSTANTINOPLE

A.D. 553

Mansi, ix. 367 ; Hahn, p. 168.

I. Εἴ τις οὐχ ὁμολογεῖ Πατρὸς καὶ Υἱοῦ καὶ Ἁγίου Πνεύματος μίαν φύσιν ἤτοι οὐσίαν μίαν τε δύναμιν καὶ ἐξουσίαν, τριάδα ὁμοούσιον, μίαν θεότητα ἐν τρισὶν ὑποστάσεσιν ἤγουν προσώποις προσκυνουμένην· ὁ τοιοῦτος ἀνάθεμα ἔστω. Εἷς γὰρ Θεὸς καὶ Πατήρ, ἐξ οὗ τὰ πάντα, καὶ εἷς Κύριος Ἰησοῦς Χριστός, δι' οὗ τὰ πάντα, καὶ ἓν Πνεῦμα Ἅγιον, ἐν ᾧ τὰ πάντα.

II. Εἴ τις οὐχ ὁμολογεῖ, τοῦ Θεοῦ Λόγου εἶναι τὰς δύο γεννήσεις, τήν τε πρὸ αἰώνων ἐκ τοῦ Πατρός, ἀχρόνως καὶ ἀσωμάτως, τήν τε ἐπ' ἐσχάτων τῶν ἡμερῶν τοῦ αὐτοῦ κατελθόντος ἐκ τῶν οὐρανῶν καὶ σαρκωθέντος ἐκ τῆς ἁγίας ἐνδόξου θεοτόκου καὶ ἀειπαρθένου Μαρίας καὶ γεννηθέντος ἐξ αὐτῆς· ὁ τοιοῦτος ἀνάθεμα ἔστω.

III. Εἴ τις λέγει, ἄλλον εἶναι τοῦ Θεοῦ Λόγον τὸν θαυματουργή-σαντα καὶ ἄλλον τὸν Χριστὸν τὸν παθόντα, ἢ τὸν Θεὸν Λόγον συνεῖναι λέγει τῷ Χριστῷ γενομένῳ ἐκ γυναικός, ἢ ἐν αὐτῷ εἶναι ὡς ἄλλον ἐν ἄλλῳ, ἀλλ' οὐχ ἕνα καὶ τὸν αὐτὸν Κύριον ἡμῶν Ἰησοῦν Χριστόν, τὸν τοῦ Θεοῦ Λόγον σαρκωθέντα καὶ ἐνανθρωπήσαντα, καὶ τοῦ αὐτοῦ τά τε θαύματα καὶ τὰ πάθη, ἅπερ ἑκουσίως ὑπέμεινε σαρκί· ὁ τοιοῦτος ἀνάθεμα ἔστω.

IV. Εἴ τις λέγει, κατὰ χάριν ἢ κατὰ ἐνέργειαν ἢ κατὰ ἰσοτιμίαν ἢ κατὰ αὐθεντίαν ἢ ἀναφορὰν ἢ σχέσιν ἢ δύναμιν τὴν ἕνωσιν τοῦ Θεοῦ Λόγου πρὸς ἄνθρωπον γεγενῆσθαι ἢ κατὰ εὐδοκίαν, ὡς ἀρεσθέντος τοῦ Θεοῦ Λόγου τοῦ ἀνθρώπου, ἀπὸ τοῦ εὖ καὶ καλῶς δόξαι αὐτῷ περὶ αὐτοῦ, καθὼς Θεόδωρος μαινόμενος λέγει, ἢ κατὰ ὁμωνυμίαν, καθ' ἣν οἱ Νεστοριανοὶ τὸν Θεὸν Λόγον Ἰησοῦν καὶ Χριστὸν καλοῦντες, καὶ τὸν ἄνθρωπον κεχωρισμένως Χριστὸν καὶ υἱὸν ὀνομάζοντες, καὶ δύο πρόσωπα προφανῶς λέγοντες κατὰ μόνην τὴν προσηγορίαν καὶ τιμὴν καὶ ἀξίαν καὶ προσκύνησιν, καὶ ἓν πρόσωπον καὶ ἕνα Χριστὸν ὑποκρί-νονται λέγειν· ἀλλ' οὐχ ὁμολογεῖ τὴν ἕνωσιν τοῦ Θεοῦ Λόγου πρὸς σάρκα ἐμψυχωμένην ψυχῇ λογικῇ καὶ νοερᾷ κατὰ σύνθεσιν ἤγουν καθ' ὑπόστασιν γεγενῆσθαι, καθὼς οἱ ἅγιοι πατέρες ἐδίδαξαν· καὶ διὰ τοῦτο μίαν αὐτοῦ τὴν ὑπόστασιν, ὅ ἐστιν ὁ Κύριος Ἰησοῦς Χριστός, εἷς τῆς ἁγίας τριάδος· ὁ τοιοῦτος ἀνάθεμα ἔστω. Πολυτρόπως γὰρ νοουμένης τῆς ἑνώσεως οἱ μὲν τῇ ἀσεβείᾳ Ἀπολιναρίου καὶ Εὐτυχοῦς ἀκολου-θοῦντος τῷ ἀφανισμῷ τῶν συνελθόντων προκείμενοι, τὴν κατὰ σύγχυσιν τὴν ἕνωσιν πρεσβεύουσιν· οἱ δὲ τὰ Θεοδώρου καὶ Νεστορίου φρονοῦντες τῇ διαιρέσει χαίροντες σχετικὴν τὴν ἕνωσιν ἐπεισάγουσιν. Ἡ μέντοι ἁγία τοῦ Θεοῦ ἐκκλησία, ἑκατέρας αἱρέσεως τὴν ἀσέβειαν ἀποβαλλομένη, τὴν ἕνωσιν τοῦ Θεοῦ Λόγου πρὸς τὴν σάρκα κατὰ

L

σύνθεσιν ὁμολογεῖ, ὅπερ ἐστὶ καθ᾽ ὑπόστασιν. Ἡ γὰρ κατὰ σύνθεσιν
ἕνωσις ἐπὶ τοῦ κατὰ Χριστὸν μυστηρίου οὐ μόνον ἀσύγχυτα τὰ
συνελθόντα διαφυλάττει, ἀλλ᾽ οὐδὲ διαίρεσιν ἐπιδέχεται.

V. Εἴ τις τὴν μίαν ὑπόστασιν τοῦ Κυρίου ἡμῶν Ἰησοῦ Χριστοῦ
οὕτως ἐκλαμβάνει, ὡς ἐπιδεχομένην πολλῶν ὑποστάσεων σημασίαν, καὶ
διὰ τούτου εἰσάγειν ἐπιχειρεῖ ἐπὶ τοῦ κατὰ Χριστὸν μυστηρίου δύο
ὑποστάσεις ἤτοι δύο πρόσωπα, καὶ τῶν παρ᾽ αὐτοῦ εἰσαγομένων δύο
προσώπων ἐν πρόσωπον λέγει κατὰ ἀξίαν καὶ τιμὴν καὶ προσκύνησιν,
καθάπερ Θεόδωρος καὶ Νεστόριος μαινόμενοι συνεγράψαντο· καὶ
συκοφαντεῖ τὴν ἁγίαν ἐν Χαλκηδόνι σύνοδον ὡς κατὰ ταύτην τὴν
ἀσεβῆ ἔννοιαν χρησαμένην τῷ τῆς μιᾶς ὑποστάσεως ῥήματι, ἀλλὰ μὴ
ὁμολογεῖ τὸν τοῦ Θεοῦ Λόγον σαρκὶ καθ᾽ ὑπόστασιν ἑνωθῆναι καὶ διὰ
τοῦτο μίαν αὐτοῦ τὴν ὑπόστασιν ἤτοι ἐν πρόσωπον, οὕτως τε καὶ τὴν
ἁγίαν ἐν Χαλκηδόνι σύνοδον μίαν ὑπόστασιν τοῦ Κυρίου ἡμῶν Ἰησοῦ
Χριστοῦ ὁμολογῆσαι· ὁ τοιοῦτος ἀνάθεμα ἔστω. Οὔτε γὰρ προσθήκην
προσώπου ἤγουν ὑποστάσεως ἐπεδέξατο ἡ ἁγία τριὰς καὶ σαρκωθέντος
τοῦ ἑνὸς τῆς ἁγίας τριάδος, Θεοῦ Λόγου.

VI. Εἴ τις καταχρηστικῶς, ἀλλ᾽ οὐκ ἀληθῶς, θεοτόκον λέγει τὴν
ἁγίαν ἔνδοξον ἀειπαρθένον Μαρίαν ἢ κατὰ ἀναφοράν, ὡς ἀνθρώπου
ψιλοῦ γεννηθέντος, ἀλλ᾽ οὐχὶ τοῦ Θεοῦ Λόγου σαρκωθέντος [καὶ τῆς]
ἐξ αὐτῆς, ἀναφερομένης δὲ κατ᾽ ἐκείνου τῆς τοῦ ἀνθρώπου γεννήσεως
ἐπὶ τὸν Θεὸν Λόγον, ὡς συνόντα τῷ ἀνθρώπῳ γενομένῳ· καὶ συκοφαντεῖ
τὴν ἁγίαν ἐν Χαλκηδόνι σύνοδον, ὡς κατὰ ταύτην τὴν ἀσεβῆ ἐπινοηθεῖ-
σαν παρὰ Θεοδώρου ἔννοιαν θεοτόκον τὴν παρθένον εἰποῦσαν· ἢ εἴ τις
ἀνθρωποτόκον αὐτὴν καλεῖ ἢ χριστοτόκον, ὡς τοῦ Χριστοῦ μὴ ὄντος
Θεοῦ, ἀλλὰ μὴ κυρίως καὶ κατὰ ἀλήθειαν θεοτόκον αὐτὴν ὁμολογεῖ,
διὰ τὸ τὸν πρὸ τῶν αἰώνων ἐκ τοῦ Πατρὸς γεννηθέντα Θεὸν Λόγον ἐπ᾽
ἐσχάτων τῶν ἡμερῶν ἐξ αὐτῆς σαρκωθῆναι, οὕτω τε εὐσεβῶς καὶ τὴν
ἁγίαν ἐν Χαλκηδόνι σύνοδον θεοτόκον αὐτὴν ὁμολογῆσαι· ὁ τοιοῦτος
ἀνάθεμα ἔστω.

VII. Εἴ τις ἐν δύο φύσεσι λέγων μὴ ὡς ἐν θεότητι καὶ ἀνθρωπότητι
τὸν ἕνα Κύριον ἡμῶν Ἰησοῦν Χριστὸν γνωρίζεσθαι ὁμολογεῖ, ἵνα διὰ
τούτου σημάνῃ τὴν διαφορὰν τῶν φύσεων, ἐξ ὧν ἀσυγχύτως ἡ ἄφραστος
ἕνωσις γέγονεν, οὔτε τοῦ Λόγου εἰς τὴν τῆς σαρκὸς μεταποιηθέντος
φύσιν οὔτε τῆς σαρκὸς πρὸς τὴν τοῦ Λόγου φύσιν μεταχωρησάσης,—
μένει γὰρ ἑκάτερον ὅπερ ἐστὶ τῇ φύσει, καὶ γενομένης τῆς ἑνώσεως
καθ᾽ ὑπόστασιν,— ἀλλ᾽ ἐπὶ διαιρέσει τῇ ἀνὰ μέρος τὴν τοιαύτην λαμβάνει φωνὴν ἐπὶ τοῦ κατὰ Χριστὸν μυστηρίου ἢ τὸν ἀριθμὸν τῶν
φύσεων ὁμολογῶν ἐπὶ τοῦ αὐτοῦ ἑνὸς Κυρίου ἡμῶν Ἰησοῦ τοῦ Θεοῦ
λόγου σαρκωθέντος, μὴ τῇ θεωρίᾳ μόνῃ τὴν διαφορὰν τούτων λαμβάνει,
ἐξ ὧν καὶ συνετέθη, οὐκ ἀναιρουμένην διὰ τὴν ἕνωσιν,—εἷς γὰρ ἐξ
ἀμφοῖν καὶ δι᾽ ἑνὸς ἀμφότερα—ἀλλ᾽ ἐπὶ τούτῳ κέχρηται τῷ ἀριθμῷ
ὡς κεχωρισμένας καὶ ἰδιοϋποστάτους ἔχει τὰς φύσεις· ὁ τοιοῦτος
ἀνάθεμα ἔστω.

VIII. Εἴ τις ἐκ δύο φύσεων, θεότητος καὶ ἀνθρωπότητος ὁμολογῶν
τὴν ἕνωσιν γεγενῆσθαι, ἢ μίαν φύσιν τοῦ Θεοῦ Λόγου σεσαρκωμένην
λέγων, μὴ οὕτως αὐτὰ λαμβάνῃ, καθάπερ καὶ οἱ ἅγιοι πατέρες ἐδίδαξαν,
ὅτι ἐκ τῆς θείας φύσεως καὶ τῆς ἀνθρωπίνης, τῆς ἑνώσεως καθ᾽

ὑπόστασιν γενομένης, εἰς Χριστὸς ἀπετελέσθη, ἀλλ' ἐκ τῶν τοιούτων φωνῶν μίαν φύσιν ἤτοι οὐσίαν θεότητος καὶ σαρκὸς τοῦ Χριστοῦ εἰσάγειν ἐπιχειρεῖ· ὁ τοιοῦτος ἀνάθεμα ἔστω. Καθ' ὑπόστασιν γὰρ λέγοντες τὸν μονογενῆ Λόγον ἡνῶσθαι οὐκ ἀνάχυσίν τινα τὴν εἰς ἀλλήλους τῶν φύσεων πεπρᾶχθαί φαμεν, μενούσης δὲ μᾶλλον ἑκατέρας ὅπερ ἐστὶν ἡνῶσθαι σαρκὶ νοοῦμεν τὸν Λόγον. Διὸ καὶ εἷς ἐστιν ὁ Χριστός, Θεὸς καὶ ἄνθρωπος, ὁ αὐτὸς ὁμοούσιος τῷ Πατρὶ κατὰ τὴν θεότητα, καὶ ὁμοούσιος ἡμῖν ὁ αὐτὸς κατὰ τὴν ἀνθρωπότητα. Ἐπίσης γὰρ καὶ τοὺς ἀνὰ μέρος διαιροῦντας ἤτοι τέμνοντας καὶ τοὺς συγχέοντας τὸ τῆς θείας οἰκονομίας μυστήριον τοῦ Χριστοῦ ἀποστρέφεται καὶ ἀναθεματίζει ἡ τοῦ Θεοῦ ἐκκλησία.

IX. Εἴ τις προσκυνεῖσθαι ἐν δυσὶ φύσεσι λέγει τὸν Χριστόν, ἐξ οὗ δύο προσκυνήσεις εἰσάγονται, ἰδίᾳ τῷ Θεῷ Λόγῳ καὶ ἰδίᾳ τῷ ἀνθρώπῳ· ἢ εἴ τις ἐπὶ ἀναιρέσει τῇ σαρκὸς ἢ ἐπὶ συγχύσει τῆς θεότητος καὶ τῆς ἀνθρωπότητος, ἢ μίαν φύσιν ἤγουν οὐσίαν τῶν συνελθόντων τερατευόμενος, οὕτω προσκυνεῖ τὸν Χριστόν, ἀλλ' οὐχὶ μιᾷ προσκυνήσει τὸν Θεὸν Λόγον σαρκωθέντα μετὰ τῆς ἰδίας αὐτοῦ σαρκὸς προσκυνεῖ, καθάπερ ἡ τοῦ Θεοῦ ἐκκλησία παρέλαβεν ἐξ ἀρχῆς· ὁ τοιοῦτος ἀνάθεμα ἔστω.

X. Εἴ τις οὐχ ὁμολογεῖ, τὸν ἐσταυρωμένον σαρκὶ Κύριον ἡμῶν Ἰησοῦν Χριστὸν εἶναι Θεὸν ἀληθινὸν καὶ Κύριον τῆς δόξης καὶ ἕνα τῆς ἁγίας τριάδος· ὁ τοιοῦτος ἀνάθεμα ἔστω.

XI. Εἴ τις μὴ ἀναθεματίζει Ἄρειον, Εὐνόμιον, Μακεδόνιον, Ἀπολινάριον, Νεστόριον, Εὐτυχέα καὶ Ὠριγένην μετὰ τῶν ἀσεβῶν αὐτῶν συγγραμμάτων, καὶ τοὺς ἄλλους πάντας αἱρετικοὺς τοὺς κατακριθέντας καὶ ἀναθεματισθέντας ὑπὸ τῆς ἁγίας καθολικῆς καὶ ἀποστολικῆς ἐκκλησίας καὶ τῶν προειρημένων ἁγίων τεσσάρων συνόδων, καὶ τοὺς τὰ ὅμοια τῶν προειρημένων αἱρετικῶν φρονήσαντας ἢ φρονοῦντας καὶ μέχρι τέλους τῇ οἰκείᾳ ἀσεβείᾳ ἐμμείναντας· ὁ τοιοῦτος ἀνάθεμα ἔστω.

XII. Εἴ τις ἀντιποιεῖται Θεοδώρου τοῦ ἀσεβοῦς, τοῦ Μοψουεστίας, τοῦ εἰπόντος, ἄλλον εἶναι τὸν Θεὸν Λόγον καὶ ἄλλον τὸν Χριστὸν ὑπὸ παθῶν ψυχῆς καὶ τῶν τῆς σαρκὸς ἐπιθυμιῶν ἐνοχλούμενον καὶ τῶν χειρόνων κατὰ μικρὸν χωριζόμενον, καὶ οὕτως ἐκ προκοπῆς ἔργων βελτιωθέντα καὶ ἐκ πολιτείας ἄμωμον καταστάντα, ὡς ψιλὸν ἄνθρωπον βαπτισθῆναι εἰς ὄνομα Πατρὸς καὶ Υἱοῦ καὶ Ἁγίου Πνεύματος, καὶ διὰ τοῦ βαπτίσματος τὴν χάριν τοῦ Ἁγίου Πνεύματος λαβεῖν, καὶ υἱοθεσίας ἀξιωθῆναι, καὶ κατ' ἰσότητα βασιλικῆς εἰκόνος εἰς πρόσωπον τοῦ Θεοῦ Λόγου προσκυνεῖσθαι, καὶ μετὰ τὴν ἀνάστασιν ἄτρεπτον ταῖς ἐννοίαις καὶ ἀναμάρτητον παντελῶς γενέσθαι· καὶ πάλιν εἰρηκότος τοῦ αὐτοῦ ἀσεβοῦς Θεοδώρου, τὴν ἕνωσιν τοῦ Θεοῦ Λόγου πρὸς τὸν Χριστὸν τοιαύτην γεγενῆσθαι, οἵαν ὁ ἀπόστολος ἐπὶ ἀνδρὸς καὶ γυναικός· ἔσονται οἱ δύο εἰς σάρκα μίαν· καὶ πρὸς ταῖς ἄλλαις ἀναριθμήτοις αὐτοῦ βλασφημίαις τολμήσαντος εἰπεῖν, ὅτι μετὰ τὴν ἀνάστασιν ἐμφυσήσας ὁ Κύριος τοῖς μαθηταῖς καὶ εἰπών· Λάβετε Πνεῦμα Ἅγιον, οὐ δέδωκεν αὐτοῖς Πνεῦμα Ἅγιον, ἀλλὰ σχήματι μόνον ἐνεφύσησεν· οὗτος δὲ καὶ τὴν ὁμολογίαν Θωμᾶ τὴν ἐπὶ τῇ ψηλαφήσει τῶν χειρῶν καὶ τῆς πλευρᾶς τοῦ Κυρίου μετὰ τὴν ἀνάστασιν, τό· Ὁ Κύριός μου καὶ ὁ Θεός μου, εἶπε, μὴ εἰρῆσθαι περὶ τοῦ Χριστοῦ παρὰ τοῦ Θωμᾶ, ἀλλ' ἐπὶ τῷ

παραδόξῳ τῆς ἀναστάσεως ἐκπλαγέντα τὸν Θωμᾶν ὑμνῆσαι τὸν Θεόν,
τὸν ἐγείραντα τὸν Χριστόν· τὸ δὲ χεῖρον, καὶ ἐν τῇ τῶν πράξεων τῶν
ἀποστόλων γενομένῃ παρ' αὐτοῦ δῆθεν ἑρμηνείᾳ συγκρίνων ὁ αὐτὸς
Θεόδωρος τὸν Χριστὸν Πλάτωνι καὶ Μανιχαίῳ καὶ Ἐπικούρῳ καὶ
Μαρκίωνι λέγει, ὅτι, ὥσπερ ἐκείνων ἕκαστος εὑράμενος οἰκεῖον δόγμα
τοὺς αὐτῷ μαθητεύσαντας πεποίηκε καλεῖσθαι Πλατωνικοὺς καὶ
Μανιχαίους καὶ Ἐπικουρείους καὶ Μαρκιωνιστάς, τὸν ὅμοιον τρόπον
καὶ τοῦ Χριστοῦ εὑραμένου δόγμα ἐξ αὐτοῦ Χριστιανοὺς καλεῖσθαι· εἴ
τις τοίνυν ἀντιποιεῖται τοῦ εἰρημένου ἀσεβεστάτου Θεοδώρου καὶ τῶν
ἀσεβῶν αὐτοῦ συγγραμμάτων, ἐν οἷς τάς τε εἰρημένας καὶ ἄλλας
ἀναριθμήτους βλασφημίας ἐξέχεε κατὰ τοῦ μεγάλου Θεοῦ καὶ Σωτῆρος
ἡμῶν Ἰησοῦ Χριστοῦ· ἀλλὰ μὴ ἀναθεματίζει αὐτὸν καὶ τὰ ἀσεβῆ
αὐτοῦ συγγράμματα καὶ πάντας τοὺς δεχομένους ἢ καὶ ἐκδικοῦντας
αὐτὸν ἢ λέγοντας, ὀρθοδόξως αὐτὸν ἐκθέσθαι, καὶ τοὺς γράψαντας
ὑπὲρ αὐτοῦ καὶ τῶν ἀσεβῶν αὐτοῦ συγγραμμάτων, καὶ τοὺς τὰ ὅμοια
φρονοῦντας ἢ φρονήσαντας πώποτε καὶ μέχρι τέλους ἐμμείναντας τῇ
τοιαύτῃ αἱρέσει· ἀνάθεμα ἔστω.

XIII. Εἴ τις ἀντιποιεῖται τῶν ἀσεβῶν συγγραμμάτων Θεοδωρίτου,
τῶν κατὰ τῆς ἀληθοῦς πίστεως καὶ τῆς ἐν Ἐφέσῳ πρώτης καὶ ἁγίας
συνόδου καὶ τοῦ ἐν ἁγίοις Κυρίλλου καὶ τῶν δώδεκα αὐτοῦ κεφαλαίων,
καὶ πάντων ὧν συνεγράψατο ὑπὲρ Θεοδώρου καὶ Νεστορίου, τῶν
δυσσεβῶν, καὶ ὑπὲρ ἄλλων τῶν τὰ αὐτὰ τοῖς προειρημένοις Θεοδώρῳ
καὶ Νεστορίῳ φρονούντων καὶ δεχομένων αὐτοὺς καὶ τὴν αὐτῶν
ἀσέβειαν, καὶ δι' αὐτῶν ἀσεβεῖς καλεῖ τοὺς τῆς ἐκκλησίας διδασκάλους,
τοὺς καθ' ὑπόστασιν τὴν ἕνωσιν τοῦ Θεοῦ λόγου φρονοῦντας· καὶ εἴπερ
οὐκ ἀναθεματίζει τὰ εἰρημένα ἀσεβῆ συγγράμματα καὶ τοὺς τὰ ὅμοια
τούτοις φρονήσαντας ἢ φρονοῦντας, καὶ πάντας δὲ τοὺς γράψαντας κατὰ
τῆς ὀρθῆς πίστεως ἢ τοῦ ἐν ἁγίοις Κυρίλλου καὶ τῶν δώδεκα αὐτοῦ κεφαλαίων, καὶ ἐν τοιαύτῃ ἀσεβείᾳ τελευτήσαντας· ὁ τοιοῦτος ἀνάθεμα ἔστω.

XIV. Εἴ τις ἀντιποιεῖται τῆς ἐπιστολῆς τῆς λεγομένης παρὰ Ἴβα
γεγράφθαι πρὸς Μάρην τὸν Πέρσην, τῆς ἀρνουμένης μὲν τὸν Θεὸν
Λόγον ἐκ τῆς ἁγίας θεοτόκου καὶ ἀειπαρθένου Μαρίας σαρκωθέντα
ἄνθρωπον γεγενῆσθαι, λεγούσης δὲ ψιλὸν ἄνθρωπον ἐξ αὐτῆς γεννηθῆναι, ὃν ναὸν ἀποκαλεῖ, ὡς ἄλλον εἶναι τὸν Θεὸν Λόγον καὶ ἄλλον
τὸν ἄνθρωπον· καὶ τὸν ἐν ἁγίοις Κύριλλον τὴν ὀρθὴν τῶν χριστιανῶν
πίστιν κηρύξαντα διαβαλλούσης ὡς αἱρετικὸν καὶ ὁμοίως Ἀπολιναρίῳ
τῷ δυσσεβεῖ γράψαντα· καὶ μεμφομένης τὴν ἐν Ἐφέσῳ πρώτην ἁγίαν
σύνοδον, ὡς χωρὶς κρίσεως καὶ ζητήσεως Νεστόριον καθελοῦσαν· καὶ
τὰ δώδεκα κεφάλαια τοῦ ἐν ἁγίοις Κυρίλλου ἀσεβῆ καὶ ἐναντία τῇ
ὀρθῇ πίστει ἀποκαλεῖ ἡ αὐτὴ ἀσεβὴς ἐπιστολή, καὶ ἐκδικεῖ Θεόδωρον
καὶ Νεστόριον καὶ τὰ ἀσεβῆ αὐτῶν δόγματα καὶ συγγράμματα· εἴ τις
τοίνυν τῆς εἰρημένης ἐπιστολῆς ἀντιποιεῖται, καὶ μὴ ἀναθεματίζει
αὐτὴν καὶ τοὺς ἀντιποιουμένους αὐτῆς, καὶ λέγοντας αὐτὴν ὀρθὴν
εἶναι ἢ μέρος αὐτῆς, καὶ γράψαντας καὶ γράφοντας ὑπὲρ αὐτῆς ἢ τῶν
περιεχομένων αὐτῇ ἀσεβειῶν, καὶ τολμῶντας ταύτην ἐκδικεῖν ἢ τὰς
περιεχομένας αὐτῇ ἀσεβείας ὀνόματι τῶν ἁγίων πατέρων ἢ τῆς ἁγίας
ἐν Χαλκηδόνι συνόδου, καὶ τούτοις μέχρι τέλους ἐμμείναντας· ὁ τοιοῦτος
ἀνάθεμα ἔστω.

THE TOME OF LEO

THE TOME OF LEO

INTRODUCTION

I. HISTORICAL

THE circumstances under which the Tome was written were these. Eutyches was the archimandrite of some three hundred monks in a large monastery near Constantinople. In 431 he had joined the long train of anti-Nestorian abbots and monks, whose representations to the Emperor Theodosius had led to the release of Cyril and to the imperial acceptance of Nestorius' deposition. He was now an old man of seventy, and his life had been passed in the seclusion of his monastery. An unfortunate obstinacy of mind, united with an incapacity for holding the balance of theological truth,[1] led him in his zealous opposition to Nestorianism to emphasise the Divinity at the expense of the reality of the Human Nature in Christ. On this ground a charge was brought against him by a former intimate friend, Eusebius of Dorylaeum, in a synod which happened to be sitting at Constantinople on November 8, 448, under the presidency of the Archbishop Flavian.[2] So high was the estimation in which Eutyches was held that it was only with the greatest reluctance that Flavian consented to hear the formal charge of heresy, and to summon the archimandrite to make his defence. The synod adjourned, but it was not until the seventh session, on November 22, that Eutyches appeared, accompanied by soldiers and monks and an imperial commissioner. Confronted with the teaching of Cyril in his Letter to John, on the distinction of the Two Natures in Christ,

[1] So Leo speaks of him as " multum imprudens et nimis imperitus " ; and again (Epist. xxix) as erring " imperite atque imprudenter " ; and still more strongly (Epist. xxxiii ad Synod. Ephes.) as " ostendens se nullum unquam studium cognoscendae veritatis habuisse, et superfluo honorabile visum, qui nulla maturitate cordis ornavit canitiem senectutis " (cf. also Epist. xxxviii ad Flav.).

[2] There was always a large number of Bishops staying in Constantinople on business connected with their own churches. These " could easily be collected by a message from the Archbishop," and this σύνοδος ἐνδημοῦσα " became a recognised part of the ecclesiastical machinery, and as time ran on gained a prescriptive authority " (note in Oxford translation of Fleury, iii. 406). It was not a permanent assembly, but an irregular convocation, which was found very useful for the despatch of the business of the Patriarchate. Its practical usefulness is illustrated by the words of Anatolius in the Fourth Session of the Council of Chalcedon (Mansi, vii. 92), " A custom has long prevailed that Bishops who are staying (ἐνδημοῦντας) in Constantinople should assemble when occasion requires for such ecclesiastical affairs as accidentally occur." Its existence undoubtedly had aided largely in establishing the Patriarchal jurisdiction of Constantinople, which was confirmed, in spite of the Roman protest, by Chalc. canon 28.

Eutyches admitted a "Union out of Two Natures" (ἕνωσις ἐκ δύο φύσεων), but declined to acknowledge the existence of Two Natures after the Incarnation, and wished to put in a written statement of his own. This, however, he appeared unwilling to read out,[1] but said that he confessed Christ as Perfect Man from the flesh of the Virgin.[2] In deference to the synod he further admitted, though reluctantly, that Christ was co-essential with us as to His Manhood,[3] and repeatedly said that he did not wish to speculate upon the Nature (φυσιολογεῖν) of One who was his God. Much reasoning and argument were expended, and when the discussion finally narrowed down to the question, "Do you confess Two Natures after the Union?" Eutyches' reply in the negative, from which nothing could move him, left no room for doubt as to his heresy.[4] Only one course was open, and immediately Flavian, in the name of the synod, pronounced sentence of excommunication and deposition on the archimandrite and any who should adhere to him. Eutyches intimated to the commissioner, Florentius, his intention of appealing to Rome, Alexandria, and Jerusalem, and wrote to Pope Leo complaining of ill-treatment, and anathematising Apollinarius, Valentinus, Manes, Nestorius, and all heresies. Flavian also wrote to inform Leo of the facts of the case, but his letter met with some delay in transit, for on February 18, 449, Leo, who had surmised from Eutyches' letter and from another which he had received from the Emperor that Flavian had acted with some want of charity, wrote to Flavian expressing his surprise that he had not been informed of the case (Epist. xxiii). Flavian's original letter, with the acts of the synod, arrived later, and was acknowledged on May 21. His second letter, in response to Leo's of February 18, did not reach Rome until near the end of June, after Leo had written the Tome (Epist. xxvi, xxxvi). Meanwhile Theodosius, in response to the desire of Dioscorus of Alexandria, who had become a zealous partisan of Eutyches, had written on March 30 summoning a General Council to meet at Ephesus on August 1.

Eutyches possessed a good deal of court influence, and by the Emperor's orders a preliminary synod sat at Constantinople on

---

[1] He appended it to his letter to Leo (apud Leon. Epist. xxi), but it has not been preserved.

[2] "I adore the Father with the Son, and the Son with the Father, and the Holy Spirit with the Father and the Son. I confess that His Incarnate Presence came from the flesh of the holy Virgin, and that he was made Perfect Man for our salvation."

[3] See note above on Formulary of Union, p. 145 ; and below on the Tome, p. 175, and again on Chalc. Def., p. 196. The admission was evidently so reluctant that it failed to convey the impression of sincerity, for Flavian twice asserted that Eutyches did not admit the Human co-essentiality (Epist. xxii and xxvi in the Leonine collection).

[4] From evidence subsequently given by Basil of Seleucia it appeared that Eutyches had said that he would agree to abide by the ruling of the Bishops of Rome and of Alexandria on the point, implying that he did not believe that they would admit the Two Natures.

April 8 to revise the acts of the " Home Synod," which Eutyches asserted were inaccurate, but which were confirmed in all essential particulars. Another petition was presented by Eutyches to the Emperor, who ordered Flavian to produce a written statement of his faith. This he did in spite of the strangeness of the procedure that a prince should make himself the judge of his own archbishop's faith. In this confession he adhered to Nicaea, Constantinople, and Ephesus, acknowledged in Christ *after the Incarnation* Two Natures ἐν μιᾷ ὑποστάσει καὶ ἐν ἑνὶ προσώπῳ, and would admit (in Cyrilline language) One Nature of the Divine Word Incarnate and Made Man.[1]

The Emperor nominated Dioscorus as President of the coming Council, and invited the Western Bishops and Pope Leo. The latter saw no necessity for a Council, and would have preferred it to have been held, if at all, in Italy. He nominated three legates to represent him at Ephesus : Julius, Bishop of Puteoli ; Renatus, a priest ; and Hilarus, a deacon.

On June 13, 449, amongst other letters, he wrote, as a fuller answer to Flavian's first letter, the celebrated Tome, which as a doctrinal formulary was subsequently accepted at Chalcedon, and declared authoritative on the subject of the mystery of the Incarnation.

II. THEOLOGICAL

The Tome of Leo has rightly been called the final defender of the truth of our Lord's Person against both of its assailants. To compare it, however, with special treatises on the Incarnation such as Cyril's

[1] It is, however, probable that the text in this place has been tampered with to bring it into conformity with the Definition of Chalcedon, and that what he acknowledged was " Two Natures " (Mansi, vi. 541a, and Kidd, vol. 3, p. 302). The text of Flavian's confession is here printed from Hahn :

Οὐδὲν οὕτω πρέπει ἱερεῖ Θεοῦ καὶ τῷ τὰ θεῖα παιδευθέντι δόγματα ὡς ἕτοιμον εἶναι πρὸς ἀπολογίαν παντὶ τῷ αἰτοῦντι αὐτὸν λόγον περὶ τῆς ἐν ἡμῖν ἐλπίδος καὶ χάριτος. Οὐ γὰρ ἐπαισχύνομαι τὸ εὐαγγέλιον τοῦ Χριστοῦ. Δύναμις γὰρ Θεοῦ ἐστιν εἰς σωτηρίαν παντὶ τῷ πιστεύοντι. Ἐπεὶ οὖν καὶ ἡμεῖς ἐλέει τοῦ παμβασιλέως ἡμῶν Χριστοῦ τοῦ Θεοῦ ἱερουργοὶ τοῦ εὐαγγελίου ἐκληρώθημεν, φρονοῦμεν ὀρθῶς καὶ ἀνεπιλήπτως, πάντοτε ταῖς θείαις γραφαῖς ἑπόμενοι καὶ ταῖς ἐκθέσεσι τῶν ἁγίων πατέρων, τῶν ἐν Νικαίᾳ καὶ ἐν Κωνσταντινουπόλει συνελθόντων καὶ τῶν ἐν Ἐφέσῳ ἐπὶ τοῦ τῆς ὁσίας μνήμης Κυρίλλου, τοῦ γενομένου ἐπισκόπου τῆς Ἀλεξανδρέων· καὶ κηρύττομεν τὸν ἕνα κύριον ἡμῶν Ἰησοῦν Χριστὸν πρὸ αἰώνων μὲν ἐκ Θεοῦ πατρὸς ἀνάρχως γεννηθέντα κατὰ τὴν θεότητα, ἐπ' ἐσχάτων δὲ τῶν ἡμερῶν τὸν αὐτὸν δι' ἡμᾶς καὶ διὰ τὴν ἡμετέραν σωτηρίαν ἐκ Μαρίας τῆς παρθένου κατὰ τὴν ἀνθρωπότητα, Θεὸν τέλειον καὶ ἄνθρωπον τέλειον τὸν αὐτὸν ἐν ψυχῇ λογικῇ καὶ σώματος, ὁμοούσιον τῷ πατρὶ κατὰ τὴν Θεότητα καὶ ὁμοούσιον τῇ μητρὶ τὸν αὐτὸν κατὰ τὴν ἀνθρωπότητα. Καὶ γὰρ ἐν δύο φύσεσιν ὁμολογοῦντες τὸν Χριστὸν μετὰ τὴν σάρκωσιν τὴν ἐκ τῆς ἁγίας παρθένου καὶ ἐνανθρώπησιν ἐν μιᾷ ὑποστάσει καὶ ἐν ἑνὶ προσώπῳ, ἕνα Χριστόν, ἕνα υἱόν, ἕνα κύριον ὁμολογοῦμεν καὶ μίαν μὲν τοῦ Θεοῦ λόγου φύσιν, σεσαρκωμένην μέντοι καὶ ἐνανθρωπήσασαν, λέγειν οὐκ ἀρνούμεθα διὰ τὸ ἐξ ἀμφοῖν ἕνα καὶ τὸν αὐτὸν εἶναι τὸν κύριον ἡμῶν Ἰησοῦν τὸν Χριστόν. Τοὺς δὲ δύο υἱοὺς ἢ δύο ὑποστάσεις ἢ δύο πρόσωπα καταγγέλλοντας, ἀλλ' οὐχὶ ἕνα καὶ τὸν αὐτὸν κύριον Ἰησοῦν Χριστόν, τὸν υἱὸν τοῦ Θεοῦ τοῦ Ζῶντος, κηρύττοντας ἀναθεματίζομεν καὶ ἀλλοτρίους εἶναι τῆς ἐκκλησίας κρίνομεν. καὶ πρῶτον πάντων Νεστόριον τὸν δυσσεβῆ ἀναθεματίζομεν καὶ τοὺς τὰ αὐτοῦ φρονοῦντας ἢ λέγοντας καὶ ἐκπέσωσιν οἱ τοιοῦτοι τῆς υἱοθεσίας τῆς ἀπηγγελμένης τοῖς ὀρθῶς πιστεύουσιν.

Quod Unus Sit Christus, or that of Hilary of Poitiers in the *De Trinitate* or with those of Apollinarius or Theodore of Mopsuestia, as "inferior in theological inspiration," is to misunderstand its origin and purpose, which was not to speculate on the mystery but to declare once more the Rule of Faith as it had been handed down from the beginning in its Western form. Hence the Tome is not an original work: it does little more than reproduce the teaching and even the phraseology of Irenaeus, Tertullian, and Cyprian, as developed by Athanasius, Hilary, and St. Augustine, or again such teachers as Gaudentius of Brescia (*c.* 410) and other Fathers of the West. Eastern and Western traditions met in Athanasius during his exiles, and in Hilary through his association with the Cappadocian Fathers. But Leo manifests the close association existing, at least since the time of Irenaeus and Tertullian, between Antioch and the Western tradition. And just as there is a well-known theological kinship between Pelagius and Theodore [1] of Mopsuestia and Nestorius, so the same might be said to be the case with their contemporaries Leo and Theodoret. It should, however, be noted in Leo that the word "tradition" is still used in the sense of teaching and custom transmitted by word of mouth; and that Leo, together with Cyril and Nestorius, marks a new stage in the history of doctrine, in that all three recognise side by side with the Creed a twofold authority for doctrine in the Church, the Scriptures along with the Fathers as the organ of the Church in teaching and interpretation. [2] Hence it is that Leo's method is to quote, in some cases verbally, statements of recognised Fathers which afterward became the accepted theological practice among theologians in East and West alike. In the same way, as we have seen, Cyril appeals to the teaching of Athanasius even when the reference is a mistaken one. In the Tome there are passages of almost verbal quotation from Tertullian and Augustine, *e.g.* Adv. Praxean (27) "et adeo salva est utriusque proprietas substantiae", etc., where, however, we note the change from *substantia* in Tertullian to *natura* in Leo. Again verbal dependence upon St. Augustine appears in the opening words of Chapter 4, about the *communicatio idiomatum*, *e.g.* where St. Augustine, expounding Rom. v. 19, goes on to say "nec quia dixit hominis separavit Deum, qui hominem assumpsit; quia, sicut dixi et valde commendandum est, una persona est; . . . ac per hoc propter istam unitatem personae in utraque natura intelligendam, et Filius hominis dicitur descendisse de caelis, . . . et Filius Dei dicitur crucifixus et sepultus, quamvis haec non in divinitate ipsa qua est Unigenitus Patri coaeternus, sed in naturae humanae sit infirmitate perpessus . . . Unigenitum vero Filium Dei crucifixum et sepultum, omnes etiam in Symbolo confitemur."

[1] Cf. Bishop Gore, "The Nestorian Christ is the natural Saviour of the Pelagian Man" (*Church Quarterly Review*, xvi, p. 298).
[2] See Tixeront, *History of Dogma*, vol. 3, pp. 326 ff. Cf. Cyril, Epist. to John (p. 142).

(See c. Serm. Arianorum 8.) And with the opening words of this chapter we may compare Sermon 184, "in homine ad nos venisse et a Patre non recessisse." In the same chapter, though he does not quote, Leo was evidently depending upon St. Athanasius, of whom he remarks, quoting the Epistle to Epictetus, that "he set forth the Incarnation so luminously and carefully that even in the presence of heretics of that age he has defeated Nestorius and Eutyches." "Whence it was, when the flesh suffered, the Word was not external to it, and therefore is the Passion said to be His : and when He did divinely His Father's works, the flesh was not external to Him, but in the body itself did the Lord do them. . . . In the case of Lazarus He gave forth a human voice, as man, but divinely, as God, did he raise Lazarus from the dead." (c. Ar. iii. 32.) Above all, the Tome is permeated with the thought and spirit if not the actual sayings of Irenaeus who could sum up the Christology of the Rule of Faith in a whole series of passages, such as those in Adv. Haer. 3.16–22, in which, he says, that "Christ is the Word or Son of the Father who became the Son of Man . . . the humanity carrying and holding and embracing the Son of God," and that "His only begotten Word, who became flesh, is Himself Jesus Christ our Lord, who suffered for us and rose again . . . and in all respects is man." We may note Leo's emphasis on the Son as the "visible of the invisible Father," taken directly from Irenaeus. But the doctrine of the two natures in one Lord Jesus Christ may be said to go back to St. Ignatius himself (Eph. vii. 2, xviii. 2), "Our Lord Jesus Christ was conceived in the womb of Mary, and is God in Man, Son of Man, Son of God " ; and from Ignatius to St. Paul, who himself declares of Christ that He is Son of God κατὰ πνεῦμα born of the seed of David κατὰ σάρκα (Rom. i. 3). Clearly Leo's Christology may be said to sum up the whole of the Western and much of the classical Eastern tradition, and to define the area of agreement between them. It is this that limits its value. The Tome is the Rule of Faith, as far as it had got in the oecumenical agreements of the Church ; and for this reason it was rightly said by the Bishops at Chalcedon that "Leo and Cyril think alike." Nevertheless, it is no less true that, in point of language and terminology, Leo does come down somewhat too heavily on the side of the Antiochenes, when he expounds the doctrine of the two " Natures " so characteristic of that school. That such was thought to be the case is shown by the objections taken by the Monophysite Bishops at Chalcedon. The passages objected to were three :

(1) c. 3 : " In order to pay the debt of our condition, the invisible Nature was united to a passible, so that, as was necessary for our healing, one and the same Mediator between God and man, the Man Jesus Christ, should be able from one to die and from the other should not be able to die."

(2) " Each Nature performs what is proper to itself in common

with the other; the Word, that is, performing what is proper to the Word, and the flesh carrying out what is proper to the flesh. The one shines out in miracles, the other succumbs to injuries " (c. 4).

(3) " Although there is in the Person of the Lord Jesus one Person of God and man, yet that wherein the suffering is common to both is one thing, and that wherein the glory is common is another, for from us He has the humanity inferior to the Father, and from the Father He has the divinity equal to the Father " (c. 4).

Does Leo in these passages of the Tome propound a theory of alternative action and parallelism so distasteful to Alexandrian thought, as if nothing had happened to discredit it? It must be admitted that in language he comes near to the Antiochene position of ἄλλος καὶ ἄλλος in Christ, but it is equally obvious that he has in mind only the time-honoured Christology of Athanasius, Tertullian, Irenaeus, and Justin. The full answers to these objections, which, as will be seen, were not sustained at Chalcedon, are found in the other Sermons of Leo on the Incarnation (See Bright, *St. Leo's Sermons on the Incarnation*); and in his Letters, especially in that to the Palestinian monks (Library of the Nicene and the Post-Nicene Fathers, *St. Leo*, p. 91) in which he shows himself well aware of the objections raised and of the recent developments of Christology, but also confirms the verdict of the Chalcedonian Fathers that Leo and Cyril think alike.

That the objections were not well founded appears, however, from the Tome itself. The following points may be noticed:

(1) The unambiguous insistence on the unity of the Subject in all statements in which the actions and words of Christ are assigned to the two Natures respectively, " in unam coeunte personam," where *coeunte* agrees with *proprietate*, the respective quality of either nature. In this mode of expression Leo's *coire* or *convenire* is the exact equivalent of Cyril's συνδρομή and σύνοδος. Again, compare " unus atque idem mediator Dei et hominis "; and while the language in Chapter 4, " Verbo . . . operante quod Verbi est et carne exsequente quod carnis est," was singularly unfortunate, Aetius was able at the Council to refer to Cyril's own admission (in spite of his Fourth Anathema) in the Formulary of Union (p. 142). " Some theologians have treated some of the expressions concerning Our Lord as common, as referring to one Person, and have distinguished others as referring to two Natures, and have taught us to refer to Christ's Godhead those which were appropriate to divinity and to the Manhood those which imply humiliation." He, nevertheless, goes on to explain that the Easterns had no thought of distributing the expressions between two Persons. Here again Cyril and Leo think the same thing, and both agree with Theodoret (Eranistes, Dial. iii), who, while insisting that the properties of both natures must be severally recognised, fully owns that " to be wearied and not wearied belong to the same *hypostasis*." So again though there might seem to be a certain inaccuracy in Leo's use of " verbo

operante," etc. (2) which Cyril might legitimately have rejected as a case of ἄλλος καὶ ἄλλος Christology, whereby some expressions could be predicated of the Logos and others assigned to the human nature, such objections could easily be met, and were met by Eulogius, by reference to the words at the end of Chapter 4 " unus . . . idemque est . . . vere Dei Filius et vere hominis Filius "; and again " in Domino Iesu Christo Dei et hominis una Persona sit " ; and still more by the elaborate expression of the *communicatio idiomatum* which follows in Chapter 5 and corresponds with the use of Cyril, Athanasius and the whole Alexandrian school ; especially the words " ut . . . in eo proprietas divinae humanaeque naturae individua permanere et ita . . . verbum non hoc esse quod carnem, ut unum Dei Filium et Verbum confiteremur et carnem." The denial of the permanent human nature, he says, is really the *solvere Iesum* (c. 5), not the recognition of the two natures.

Such was the defence of Leo against the Monophysite objections at Chalcedon ; and in spite of Dorner's view that there was a serious difference between Leo and Cyril (*Person of Christ*, Div. ii, vol. i, pp. 70 ff.), it would seem that both thought alike in this matter. Nevertheless, the question may be asked : did the *una persona* of Leo mean quite the same thing as Cyril's μία φύσις or ὑπόστασις ? If the meaning to be attached to this kind of phrase was in reality that we cannot rightly equate the Divine and Human as if they were on the same level and comparable—that the nature of the Logos is only the Logos himself, and one cannot truly speak of the Logos as a nature at all—then there can be only one *hypostasis*, the uncreated, if there is to be a true incarnation. In this case Leo says exactly the same thing as Cyril was trying to say. There is only one Christ, and He is the Logos or Son, and the human nature, utterly real as it was, is something added; in modern language an experience or event or fact " conditioning " (by a vast condescension) that Divinity. If, on the other hand, by μία φύσις was meant that the human nature was in some way swallowed up, overwhelmed, or rendered docetic by the mystery of the Deity, then Leo is against Cyril. But, as we have seen, Cyril, like Athanasius, seems to speak with two voices on this point, though not in the documents recognised as oecumenical, that is to say, apart from the Anathemas. Both alike emphasise the mysterious character of the union.

More probably, however, the explanation alike of their agreement and difference, as in so many other cases which we have noted, is to be found in the difference of approach. The Westerns had, like the Antiochenes, started from the *una substantia* of God in Three Persons, which, as in Antioch, naturally tended towards a "dyoprosopic" Christology; whereas the Alexandrians and Origenists, starting from a pluralistic conception of the Trinity, found no difficulty in the idea of the Godhead in the Person of the Son becoming the subject of a human experience, and so tending towards a " henprosopic " Christology. Leo therefore can speak of the

" Filius Dei," the Christ, as identical with the Logos, and Cyril of the Logos incarnate who is identical with Jesus Christ. There can, however, be little doubt that Leo's version of the Rule of Faith is nearer to the more primitive Christology than Cyril's, which has passed through the Origenist climate of thought, while adopting, as we have seen, a mediating position. And it must not be forgotten that it is the Cyrilline form, if not actually the Monophysite, which, largely under the influence of the system of Dionysius the Areopagite, followed only too closely by that of St. Thomas Aquinas, has, until the liberal reaction, almost universally prevailed in the Church.

How the union between the two natures or substances could happen, Leo was no more able to say than Cyril had been; both fell back on its mysterious character. But it is noteworthy that in one of his Sermons (ii) Leo uses the word *misceretur*, " because both substances did not in any such sense retain their properties that there could be in them a difference of persons ; nor was the creation in such wise taken into fellowship with the Creator that He should be the inhabitant and it the habitation ; but in this way that the one nature should be united to the other (*misceretur*)." Here Leo was again echoing the language of Irenaeus and of Tertullian " homo Deo mixtus" (Apol. 21), followed by Cyprian " Deus cum homine miscetur " (De Idol. Van. XI), and Hilary " hujus admixtionis " (De Trin. ii. 24) and finally Augustine " in illa ergo persona mixtura est animi et corporis, in hac Persona mixtura est Dei et hominis " (Epist. cxxxvii). Cyril, who had himself at one time employed such language, remarks (Adv. Nest. i. 3), however, that some of the Fathers had used the word κρᾶσις, not with any idea of ἀνάχυσις as when liquids are blended, but to set forth the perfect ἕνωσις.[1] But such language did not survive after Eutychianism had rendered it dangerous. Cf. Cyril, Ad Succensum 1, Adv. Nest. 2, Epist. to John of Antioch, the Defence against Theodoret (1), Explanation of Anathema I, and Epist. to Acacius (1) ; all of which only go to show more clearly the agreement between East and West reflected by the great protagonists in the controversy ; or rather that of both with the Rule of Faith.

The care with which the expressions are guarded by Cyril confirms the verdict of Bethune-Baker (*Nestorius*, pp. 171 ff.) that Cyril's use of the expression ἕνωσις φυσική gives strong support to the view that he used the parallel expression καθ' ὑπόστασιν in the sense of substantial rather than personal unity. Lastly, Cyril and Leo agreed in the strong soteriological interest which, though far from absent, yet is not so prominent in the Antiochene theologians, who were perhaps more preoccupied, as was Theodore, with the nature of man and the question of his freewill, which engaged the attentions of theologians in the West at this period. But see Sellers, *Two Ancient Christologies*, pp. 184 ff.

[1] Gregory Nazianzen, perhaps under Apollinarian influence, had used the same language ; see Sellers, op. cit., pp. 75–6.

ANALYSIS OF LEO'S TOME

A. *Introductory.*

§ 1. Eutyches has fallen into error through ignorance and theological incompetence.

B. *Doctrinal.*

§ 2. He should have studied the Creed, St. Matthew and St. Paul, and Old Testament prophecies, which teach the reality of the Incarnation.

§ 3. Two Natures without confusion met in One Person.

§ 4. The Son of God is born after a new order—in time, and by a new mode of birth—from a Virgin; yet with Flesh like ours, only faultless. The Selfsame is Very God and Very Man, each Nature working in its own sphere.

§ 5. The *communicatio idiomatum.* The properties of each Nature, while remaining distinct, are yet referable to the One Person of the Son of God. Eutyches has rejected this truth, and " dissolved " Jesus by denying His Human Nature, and by holding Docetic views of His Body and His Passion.

§ 6. Eutyches' confession—" of two natures before the union "— is as impious as his denial of the Two Natures after the Incarnation.

C. *Hortatory.*

Endeavour to reclaim him, and if he repents and condemns these errors in writing, restore him.

D. *Conclusion.*

For the due execution of the matter we are sending three legates to the Council.

THE TOME OF LEO

DILECTISSIMO FRATRI FLAVIANO LEO

I. Lectis dilectionis tuae litteris, quas miramur fuisse tam seras, et gestorum episcopalium ordine recensito, tandem quid apud vos scandali contra integritatem fidei exortum fuisset, agnovimus ; et 5 quae prius videbantur occulta, nunc nobis reserata patuerunt. Quibus Eutyches, qui presbyterii nomine honorabilis videbatur, multum imprudens et nimis imperitus ostenditur, ut etiam de ipso Ps. xxxv. 4. dictum sit a propheta : *Noluit intelligere, ut bene ageret, iniquitatem meditatus est in cubili suo.* Quid autem iniquius, quam 10 impia sapere, et sapientioribus doctioribusque non cedere ? Sed in hanc insipientiam cadunt, qui cum ad cognoscendam veritatem aliquo impediuntur obscuro, non ad propheticas voces, non ad apostolicas litteras nec ad evangelicas auctoritates, sed ad semetipsos recurrunt ; et ideo magistri erroris exsistunt, quia veritatis discipuli 15 non fuere. Quam enim eruditionem de sacris novi et veteris testamenti paginis acquisivit, qui ne ipsius quidem Symboli initia comprehendit ? Et quod per totum mundum omnium regenerandorum voce depromitur, istius adhuc senis corde non capitur.

II. Nesciens igitur, quid deberet de Verbi Dei incarnatione sentire, 20 nec volens ad promerendum intelligentiae lumen in sanctarum scripturarum latitudine laborare illam saltem communem et indiscretam confessionem sollicito recepisset auditu, qua fidelium universitas pro-
Rom. Symb. fitetur : *Credere se in Deum Patrem omnipotentem et in Iesum Christum Filium eius unicum, Dominum nostrum, qui natus est* 25 *de Spiritu sancto et Maria virgine.* Quibus tribus sententiis omnium fere haereticorum machinae destruuntur. Cum enim Deus et omnipotens et Pater creditur, consempiternus eidem Filius demon-
Nic. Symb. stratur, in nullo a Patre differens, quia *de Deo Deus*, de omnipotente omnipotens, de aeterno natus est coaeternus, non 30 posterior tempore, non inferior potestate, non dissimilis gloria, non divisus essentia ; idem vero sempiterni genitoris unigenitus sempiternus natus est de Spiritu sancto et Maria virgine. Quae nativitas temporalis illi nativitati divinae et sempiternae nihil minuit, nihil contulit, sed totam se reparando homini, qui erat deceptus, impendit, 35 ut et mortem vinceret et diabolum, qui mortis habebat imperium, sua virtute destrueret. Non enim superare possemus peccati et mortis auctorem, nisi naturam nostram ille susciperet et suam faceret, quem nec peccatum contaminare nec mors potuit detinere. Conceptus quippe est de Spiritu sancto intra uterum matris virginis, 40 quae illum ita salva virginitate edidit, quemadmodum salva virginitate concepit.

168

Sed si de hoc christianae fidei fonte purissimo sincerum intellectum haurire non poterat, quia splendorem perspicuae veritatis obcaecatione sibi propria tenebrarat; doctrinae se evangelicae subdidisset. Et dicente Matthaeo : *Liber generationis Iesu Christi* *filii David, filii Abraham*, apostolicae quoque praedicationis expetisset instructum. Et legens in epistola ad Romanos : *Paulus, servus Iesu Christi, vocatus apostolus, segregatus in evangelium Dei, quod ante promiserat per prophetas suos in scripturis sanctis de Filio suo, qui factus est Ei ex semine David secundum carnem,* ad propheticas paginas piam sollicitudinem contullisset. Et inveniens promissionem Dei ad Abraham dicentis : *In semine tuo benedicentur omnes gentes*, ne de huius seminis proprietate dubitaret, secutus fuisset apostolum dicentem : *Abrahae dictae sunt promissiones et semini eius. Non dicit : et seminibus, quasi in multis, sed quasi in uno : et semini tuo, quod est Christus.* Isaiae quoque praedicationem interiore apprehendisset auditu dicentis : *Ecce virgo in utero accipiet et pariet filium, et vocabunt nomen eius Immanuel, quod est interpretatum : nobiscum Deum.* Eiusdem prophetae fideliter verba legisset : *Puer natus est nobis, filius datus est nobis, cuius potestas super humerum eius, et vocabunt nomen eius : Magni Consilii Angelus, Admirabilis Consiliarius, Deus fortis, Princeps pacis, Pater futuri saeculi.* Nec frustratorie loquens ita Verbum diceret carnem factum, ut editus utero virginis Christus haberet formam hominis et non haberet materni corporis veritatem. An forte ideo putavit Dominum nostrum Iesum Christum non nostrae esse naturae, quia missus ad beatam Mariam semper virginem angelus ait : *Spiritus sanctus superveniet in te, et virtus Altissimi obumbrabit tibi ; ideoque et quod nascetur ex te sanctum vocabitur Filius Dei ?* ut quia conceptus virginis divini fuit operis, non de natura concipientis fuerit caro concepti. Sed non ita intelligenda est illa generatio singulariter mirabilis et mirabiliter singularis, ut per novitatem creationis proprietas remota sit generis. Fecunditatem enim virgini Spiritus sanctus dedit, veritas autem corporis sumpta de corpore est ; et *aedificante sibi sapientia domum : Verbum caro factum est, et habitavit in nobis*, hoc est in ea carne, quam assumpsit ex homine et quam spiritu vitae rationalis animavit.

III. Salva igitur proprietate utriusque naturae et substantiae, et in unam coëunte personam, suscepta est a maiestate humilitas, a virtute infirmitas, ab aeternitate mortalitas ; et ad resolvendum conditionis nostrae debitum natura inviolabilis naturae est unita passibili, ut, quod nostris remediis congruebat, unus atque idem mediator Dei et hominum, homo Iesus Christus, et mori posset ex uno et mori non posset ex altero. In integra ergo veri hominis perfectaque natura versus natus est Deus, totus in suis, totus in nostris. " Nostra " autem dicimus, quae in nobis ab initio Creator condidit et quae reparanda suscepit. Nam illa, quae deceptor intulit et homo

M

Marginal references:
45 Matt. i. 1.
Rom. i. 1 ff.
50
Gen. xii. 3, xxii. 18.
Gal. iii. 16. 55
Isa. vii. 14. Matt. i. 23.
60 Isa. ix. 6.
Luc. i. 35.
70
75 Prov. ix. 1. Ioan. i. 14.
80
85

90 deceptus admisit, nullum habuerunt in Salvatore vestigium. Nec quia communionem humanarum subiit infirmitatum, ideo nostrorum fuit particeps delictorum. Assumpsit formam servi sine sorde peccati, humana augens, divina non minuens; quia *exinanitio illa*, qua se invisibilis visibilem praebuit, et creator ac Dominus
95 omnium rerum unus voluit esse mortalium, inclinatio fuit miserationis, non defectio potestatis. Proinde qui manens in forma Dei fecit hominem, idem in forma servi factus est homo. Tenet enim sine defectu proprietatem suam utraque natura; et sicut formam servi Dei forma non adimit, ita formam Dei servi forma non minuit.
100 Nam quia gloriabatur diabolus, hominem sua fraude deceptum divinis caruisse muneribus, et immortalitatis dote nudatum duram mortis subiisse sententiam, seque in malis suis quoddam de praevaricatoris consortio invenisse solatium; Deum quoque, iustitiae exigente ratione, erga hominem, quem in tanto honore condiderat,
105 propriam mutasse sententiam; opus fuit secreti dispensatione consilii, ut incommutabilis Deus, cuius voluntas non potest sua benignitate privari, primam erga nos pietatis suae dispositionem sacramento occultiore compleret, et homo diabolicae iniquitatis versutia actus in culpam contra Dei propositum non periret.
110 IV. Ingreditur ergo haec mundi infima Filius Dei, de caelesti sede descendens et a paterna gloria non recedens, novo ordine, nova nativitate generatus. Novo ordine, quia invisibilis in suis visibilis factus est in nostris, incomprehensibilis voluit comprehendi; ante tempora manens esse coepit ex tempore; universitatis
115 Dominus servilem formam obumbrata maiestatis suae immensitate suscepit; impassibilis Deus non dedignatus est homo esse passibilis, et immortalis mortis legibus subiacere. Nova autem nativitate generatus, quia inviolata virginitas concupiscentiam nescivit, carnis materiam ministravit. Assumpta est de matre Domini natura,
120 non culpa; nec in Domino Iesu Christo ex utero virginis genito, quia nativitas est mirabilis, ideo nostri est natura dissimilis. Qui enim verus est Deus, idem verus est homo; et nullum est in hac unitate mendacium, dum invicem sunt et humilitas et altitudo deitatis. Sicut enim Deus non mutatur miseratione, ita homo non
125 consumitur dignitate. Agit enim utraque forma cum alterius communione quod proprium est; Verbo scilicet operante quod Verbi est, et carne exsequente quod carnis est. Unum horum coruscat miraculis, aliud succumbit iniuriis. Et sicut Verbum ab aequalitate paternae gloriae non recedit, ita caro naturam nostri
130 generis non relinquit. Unus enim idemque est, quod saepe dicendum est, vere Dei Filius et vere hominis Filius. Deus per id quod *in principio erat Verbum, et Verbum erat apud Deum, et*

Ioan. i. 1.   *Deus erat Verbum ;* homo per id quod *Verbum caro factum*
ibid. 14.
ibid. 3.   *est, et habitavit in nobis.* Deus per id quod *omnia per*
135 Gal. iv. 4.   *ipsum facta sunt, et sine ipso factum est nihil ;* homo per id
quod *factus est ex muliere, factus sub lege.* Nativitas carnis
manifestatio est humanae naturae; partus virginis divinae est

virtutis indicium. Infantia parvuli ostenditur humilitate cunarum ; magnitudo Altissimi declaratur vocibus angelorum. Similis est *rudimentis* hominum, quem Herodes impie molitur occidere ; sed 140 Dominus est omnium, quem Magi gaudent suppliciter adorare. Iam cum ad praecursoris sui Ioannis baptismum venit, ne lateret, quod carnis velamine divinitas tegeretur, vox Patris de caelo intonans dixit : *Hic est Filius meus dilectus, in quo mihi bene* Matt. iii. 17. *complacui.* Quem itaque sicut hominem diabolica tentat astutia, 145 eidem sicut Deo angelica famulantur officia. Esurire, sitire, lassescere atque dormire evidenter humanum est. Sed quinque panibus millia hominum satiare et largiri Samaritanae aquam vivam, cuius haustus bibenti praestet, ne ultra iam sitiat ; supra dorsum maris plantis non desidentibus ambulare, et *elationes fluctuum* 150 increpata tempestate consternere, sine ambiguitate Cf. Ps. xcii. 3 f. divinum est. Sicut ergo, ut multa praeteream, non eiusdem naturae est flere miserationis affectu amicum mortuum, et eundem remoto quatriduanae aggere sepulturae ad vocis imperium excitare redivivum ; aut in ligno pendere, et in noctem luce conversa omnia 155 elementa tremefacere ; aut clavis transfixum esse, et paradisi portas fidei latronis aperire ; ita non eiusdem naturae est dicere : *Ego et Pater unum sumus*, et dicere : *Pater maior Me est.* Ioan. x. 30; Quamvis enim in Domino Iesu Christo Dei et hominis xiv. 28. una persona sit, aliud tamen est unde in utroque communis est 160 contumelia, aliud unde communis est gloria. De nostro enim illi est minor Patre humanitas ; de Patre illi est aequalis cum Patre divinitas.

V. Propter hanc ergo unitatem personae in utraque natura intelligendam et Filius hominis legitur descendisse de caelo, cum Filius 165 Dei carnem de ea virgine, de qua est natus, assumpserit, et rursus Filius Dei crucifixus dicitur ac sepultus, cum haec non in divinitate ipsa, qua Unigenitus consempiternus et consubstantialis est Patri, sed in naturae humanae sit infirmitate perpessus. Unde unigenitum Filium Dei crucifixum et sepultum omnes etiam in Symbolo confite- 170 mur secundum illud apostoli : *Si enim cognovissent, numquam Dominum maiestatis crucifixissent.* Cum autem ipse 1 Cor. ii. 8. Dominus noster atque Salvator fidem discipulorum suis interrogationibus erudiret, *Quem me*, inquit, *dicunt homines esse* Matt. xvi. 13 ff. *Filium hominis ?* Cumque illi diversas aliorum opiniones retexuis- 175 sent, *Vos autem*, ait, *quem me esse dicitis ?* Me utique, qui sum Filius hominis, et quem in forma servi atque in veritate carnis aspicitis, quem me esse dicitis ? Ubi beatus Petrus divinitus inspiratus et confessione sua omnibus gentibus profuturus *Tu es*, inquit, *Christus Filius Dei vivi.* Nec immerito beatus est pro- 180 nuntiatus a Domino et a principali petra soliditatem et virtutis traxit et nominis, qui per revelationem Patris eundem et Dei Filium est confessus et Christum, quia unum horum sine alio receptum non proderat ad salutem ; et aequalis erat periculi Dominum Iesum Christum aut Deum tantummodo sine homine aut sine Deo solum 185

hominem credidisse. Post resurrectionem vero Domini (quae utique veri corporis fuit, quia non alter est resuscitatus, quam qui fuerat crucifixus et mortuus) quid aliud quadraginta dierum mora gestum est, quam ut fidei nostrae integritas ab omni caligine mun-
190 daretur ? Colloquens enim cum discipulis suis et cohabitans atque convescens et pertractari se diligenti curiosoque contactu ab eis, quos dubietas perstringebat, admittens, ideo et clausis ad discipulos januis introibat, et flatu suo dabat Spiritum sanctum, et donato intelligentiae lumine sanctarum Scripturarum occulta pandebat;
195 et rursus idem vulnus lateris, fixuras clavorum et omnia recentissimae passionis signa monstrabat dicens : *Videte manus meas et*
Luc. xxiv. 39.   *pedes quia ego sum. Palpate et videte, quia spiritus carnem et ossa non habet, sicut me videtis habere ;* ut agnosceretur in eo proprietas divinae humanaeque naturae individua permanere;
200 et ita sciremus, Verbum non hoc esse quod carnem, ut unum Dei Filium et Verbum confiteremur et carnem. Quo fidei sacramento Eutyches iste nimium aestimandus est vacuus, qui naturam nostram in Unigenito Dei nec per humilitatem mortalitatis nec per gloriam resurrectionis agnovit. Nec sententiam beati apostoli et evange-
205 I Ioan. iv. 2 f.   listae Ioannis expavit dicentis : *Omnis spiritus, qui confitetur Iesum Christum in carne venisse, ex Deo est ; et omnis spiritus, qui solvit Iesum, ex Deo non est ; et hic est Antichristus.* Quid autem est solvere Iesum, nisi humanam ab eo separare naturam, et sacramentum, per quod unum salvati sumus, impudentissimis
210 evacuare figmentis ? Caligans vero circa naturam corporis Christi necesse est, ut etiam in passione eius eadem obcaecatione desipiat. Nam si crucem Domini non putat falsam, et susceptum pro mundi salute supplicium verum fuisse non dubitat ; cuius credit mortem, agnoscat et carnem ; nec diffiteatur nostri corporis hominem, quem
215 cognoscit fuisse passibilem, quoniam negatio verae carnis negatio est etiam corporeae passionis. Si ergo christianam suscipit fidem et a praedicatione evangelii suum non avertit auditum, videat, quae natura transfixa clavis pependerit in crucis ligno, et aperto per militis lanceam latere crucifixi intelligat, unde *sanguis et aqua* fluxerit,
220 Ioan. xix. 34.   ut ecclesia Dei et lavacro rigaretur et poculo. Audiat et beatum Petrum apostolum praedicantem, quod sanctificatio Spiritus per aspersionem fiat sanguinis Christi. Nec transitorie
I Pet. i. 18.   legat eiusdem apostoli verba dicentis : *Scientes, quod non corruptibilibus argento et auro redempti estis de vana vestra conver-*
225 *satione paternae traditionis, sed pretioso sanguine quasi agni incontaminati et immaculati Iesu Christi.* Beati quoque Ioannis apostoli
I Ioan. i. 7.   testimonio non resistat dicentis : *Et sanguis Iesu Filii Dei*
I Ioan. v. 4.   *emundat nos ab omni peccato.* Et iterum : *Haec est victoria, quae vincit mundum, fides nostra.* Et : *Quis est, qui vincit*
230 ibid. 5 ff.   *mundum, nisi qui credit, quoniam Iesus est Filius Dei ? Hic est, qui venit per aquam et sanguinem, Iesus Christus ; non in aqua solum, sed in aqua et sanguine. Et Spiritus est, qui testificatur, quoniam Spiritus est veritas. Quia tres sunt, qui testimonium dant,*

Spiritus, aqua et sanguis, et tres unum sunt. Spiritus utique sancti-
ficationis et sanguis redemptionis et aqua baptismatis; quae tria 235
unum sunt et individua manent nihilque eorum a sui connexione
seiungitur: quia catholica ecclesia hac fide vivit, hac proficit, ut
in Christo Iesu nec sine vera divinitate humanitas nec sine vera
humanitate divinitas.

VI. Cum autem ad interlocutionem examinis vestri Eutyches re- 240
sponderit dicens: *Confiteor ex duabis naturis fuisse Dominum nostrum
ante adunationem ; post adunationem vero unam naturam confiteor ;*
miror tam absurdam tamque perversam eius professionem, nulla
iudicantium increpatione reprehensam, et sermonem nimis insi-
pientem nimisque blasphemum ita omissum, quasi nihil quod 245
offenderet esset auditum; cum tam impie duarum naturarum ante
incarnationem unigenitus Dei Filius fuisse dicatur, quam nefarie,
postquam *Verbum caro factum est,* natura in eo singularis   Ioan. i. 14.
asseritur. Quod ne Eutyches ideo vel recte vel tolerabiliter aestimet
dictum, quia nulla vestra est sententia confutatum, sollicitudinis 250
tuae diligentiam commonemus, frater carissime, ut si per inspira-
tionem misericordiae Dei ad satisfactionem caussa perducitur,
imprudentia hominis imperiti etiam ab hac sensus sui peste purgetur.
Qui quidem, sicut gestorum ordo patefecit, bene coeperat a sua
persuasione discedere, cum vestra sententia coarctatus profiteretur 255
se dicere, quod ante non dixerat, et ei fidei acquiescere, cuius prius
fuisset alienus. Sed cum anathematizando impio dogmati noluisset
praebere consensum, intellexit eum fraternitas vestra in sua manere
perfidia, dignumque esse, qui iudicium condemnationis exciperet.
De quo si fideliter atque utiliter dolet, et quam recte mota sit episco- 260
palis auctoritas vel sero cognoscit, vel si ad satisfactionis plenitudinem
omnia, quae ab eo male sunt sensa, viva voce et praesenti subscrip-
tione damnaverit: non erit reprehensibilis erga correctum quanta-
cumque miseratio, quia Dominus noster verus et bonus pastor,
qui *animam suam posuit pro ovibus suis,* et qui *venit*   Ioan. x. 15. 265
animas hominum salvare, non perdere, imitatores, nos   Luc. ix. 56.
suae vult esse pietatis; ut peccantes quidem iustitia coërceat,
conversos autem misericordia non repellat. Tunc enim demum
fructuosissime fides vera defenditur, quando etiam a sectatoribus
suis opinio falsa damnatur. Ad omnem vero caussam pie ac fideliter 270
exsequendam fratres nostros Iulium episcopum et Renatum presbyterum sed et filium meum Hilarum diaconum vice nostra direximus.
Quibus Dulcitium notarium nostrum, cuius fides nobis est probata,
sociavimus; confidentes adfuturum divinitatis auxilium, ut is, qui
erraverat, damnata sensus sui pravitate salvetur.   275
Deus te incolumem custodiat, frater carissime.
Data Idibus Iunii, Asturio et Protogene viris clarissimis consulibus.

NOTES ON THE TOME

2. *litteris.* Flavian's first letter.

3. *gestorum episcopalium ordine.* The acts of the Home Synod of November 448.

ordine. The " record " or " minutes " : so *ordo* is used again § 6, line 254, and Epist. xxix.

10. *impia sapere.* Sapere is used to translate φρονεῖν in the Vulg. of Matt. xvi. 23, Mark viii. 33 ; and that is its sense here : " to be impiously (or undutifully) minded." Cf. " recta sapere," "to be rightly minded " in the Collect for Pentecost in the Gregorian Sacramentary.

16. *Symboli initia.* On the meaning of *Symbolum* see H. J. Carpenter, *Journal of Theological Studies,* xliii, who thinks that the associations of the word in its Latin form were legal = partnership.

17. *regenerandorum voce depromitur.* Leo refers to the " Redditio symboli " or recitation of the Creed by the candidates or their sponsors immediately before the administration of Baptism ; a practice certainly established in the fourth and fifth centuries.

21. *indiscretam.* Either " uniform," " confessed by all in common," or else " indivisible," with reference to the articles of the Christian Faith ; by articles is meant little joints, each of which is dependent on the rest.

23. *Credere se in Deum,* etc. Leo here quotes the Roman Creed with the reading " de Spiritu Sancto et Maria Virgine." See note above (pp. 39, 67).

25. *Quibus tribus sententiis,* etc. Cf. Epist. xxxi ad Pulcher. " Ipsa Catholica symboli brevis et perfecta confessio . . . tam instructa sit munitione caelesti ut omnes haereticorum opiniones solo ipsius possint gladio detruncari."

28. *de Deo Deus.* This is a reminiscence of the Nicene Θεὸν ἐκ Θεοῦ, which was sometimes rendered " Deum ex Deo," as by Hilary, De Synod. 84 ; and sometimes " Deum de Deo," as by Dionysius Exiguus, Mansi, iii. 567.

40. *salva virginitate.* Cf. Tertullian, De Carne Chr. 23, and see below on *semper virginem.*

45. *Liber generationis.* This argument from the genealogy in the Gospel for the reality of Christ's Humanity had been used by

Tertullian, De Carne Chr. 20—a treatise which formed a storehouse of material for subsequent writers.

50. *Ei.* The Vulg. reading in Rom. 1. 3.

62. *Magni Consilii Angelus.* So the old Latin versions following the LXX, which condenses the whole of the titles of the Messiah into Μεγάλης βουλῆς ἄγγελος. Leo supplements this with the Vulg. reading " Admirabilis," etc.

64. *frustratorie.* " Evasively," " deceptively," *i.e.* emptying the statement " The Word was made Flesh " of its real and proper meaning.

66. *materni corporis veritatem.* Eutyches himself was scarcely committed to this view, since he had under pressure admitted that Christ was co-essential with His mother and with us as to His Manhood (see above, p. 159 f.). But Leo was right in noting that the trend of the Eutychian position was to deny the reality of the Manhood, and therefore of Christ's Human Body. Some of the extreme Eutychians did actually reproduce the tenet of some Apollinarians (and of the Valentinians) that Christ's Body was not derived from the substance of the Virgin. Tertullian had argued the point very fully in De Carne Chr. 15, 20, 21. Cf. Leo, Epist. xxxv, ad Iulian., " Qui enim negat verum hominem Iesum Christum necesse est in multis impietatibus impleatur, eumque aut Apollinaris sibi vindicat, aut Valentinus usurpet, aut Manichaeus obtineat: quorum nullus in Christo humanae carnis credidit veritatem."

The same views were revived at the time of the Reformation by some of the anabaptist sects : see the recantation of Michael Tombe in 1549 (Strype, *Memorials*, vol. i, p. 357) ; and how widely and persistently they were disseminated may be gathered from their reiterated condemnation (see the Reform. Leg. Eccles. 5 ; 32 Henry VIII. cap. 49, § 11, cited by Hardwick, *Articles*, p. 87), and from the emphasis laid upon the true doctrine in the Interpretation of the Creed, Art. III, in the Institution of a Christian Man, 1537 ; and again in the Necessary Doctrine and Erudition, 1543 ; the XLII Articles of 1552, Art. II ; and the Proper Preface for Christmas, 1549.

68. *Mariam semper virginem.* Athanasius is apparently the first writer to give this title (ἀειπαρθένος) to the Virgin, Orat. c. Ar. ii. 70. Augustine held the same view (Tract. x. in Joan. ii. 12–21, " Unde fratres Domino ? Num enim Maria iterum peperit ? Absit. Inde coepit dignitas virginum." Serm. li ; De Fid. et Symb. 11, " in illo utero nec ante nec postea quidquam mortale conceptum est " ; De Cat. Rud. 40, " virgo concipiens, virgo pariens, virgo moriens ") ; and such has been the general belief of the majority of Church writers upon the subject. For these see Pearson on the Creed, Article " Born of the Virgin Mary " ; Jeremy

Taylor, *Life of Christ*, chapter 3 ; Bishop Bull, Sermon 4, (1. 96) ; Hooker, *Ecclesiastical Polity*, Book ii, 7. 5 ; Bishop Andrewes' *Devotions*, p. 93. The question has been very fully treated by Lightfoot (Essay in his *Galatians*), who upholds the perpetual virginity, and still later by Professor J. B. Mayor (*Epistle of St. James*, chapter 1), who rejects it. It must, however, be noticed that the term " brethren " used by the Evangelists and by St. Paul (cf. Luke ii. 33, 48) cannot in view of the miraculous conception be taken in its simple natural meaning, and therefore demands some explanation. The early tradition deduced from some remarks of Hegesippus (Eusebius, HE. iii. 11 ; iv. 22), that the " brethren " of the Lord were the children of Mary, wife of Clopas, St. Joseph's brother, seems deserving of credence. Tertullian's language (Adv. Marc. iv. 19 ; De Carne Chr. 7) merely cites the N.T. phrases, and cannot be appealed to on either side, though see a passage, De Monogam. 8. See further an able paper in *The Guardian* (June 7, 1899) and Dom Chapman, *Journal of Theological Studies*, vol. vii, p. 412 (April 1906).

72. *non . . . ut per novitatem creationis proprietas remota sit generis*, *i.e.* the novel mode of the cause of the Birth did not remove it from the category of real births.

76. *aedificante sibi sapientia domum.* Cf. Pseudo-Athanasius, Or. c. Arian. iv. 34.

78. *ex homine.* " From a Human Being." Latin examples of the use of the word meaning Human Nature will be found in Tertullian, Apol. 21 ; Augustine, Encheir. 36, De Civ. Dei xi. 2 ; Leo Serm. xxviii. 6 ; and cf. the Te Deum, " Tu suscepisti hominem."

80. *salva igitur*, etc. See note above on Cyril, Epist. 2 ad Nest. (p. 101). Leo is here verbally echoing the famous statement of Tertullian (Adv. Prax. 27).

82. *ab aeternitate mortalitas.* The orthodoxy of this phrase was scrutinised at Chalcedon (Mansi, vi. 972), and defended as agreeable with Cyril's teaching.

88. " *Nostra* " *autem dicimus*, etc. Sin is no part of human nature, but its corruption. The idea is Athanasian, De Incarn. 5.

93. *divina non minuens.* This passage is paraphrased by Pearson on Art. iv. (Oxford Edn. 1877, p. 336) ; cf. Hooker, *Ecclesiastical Polity*, v. 54. 4 ; Athanasius De Inc. 17.

102. *praevaricatoris.* In ecclesiastical Latin this word (with its cognates) loses its technical forensic sense, and is simply equivalent to " peccator." See Rom. ii. 25 ; Gal. ii. 18 (Vulg.) ; Tertullian, adv. Marc. iv. 43.

107. *pietatis.* Of God's affection and loving kindness towards us, as in the Gregorian Collects, which stand in our Prayer Book (mistranslated) for v Epiphany and xxii Trinity.

108. *sacramento occultiore.* "A more hidden mystery." *Sacramentum* frequently represents the N.T. μυστήριον. So again below, § 5.

110. *mundi infima.* There is probably an allusion to Eph. iv. 9. The Greek translator had this reading before him (εἰς τὸ ταπεινὸν τοῦτο τοῦ κόσμου), but some Latin MSS. read *infirma.*

113. *incomprehensibilis.* Literally, of physical, not intellectual, apprehension, " that which cannot be held in the grasp or enclosed in space."

123. *mendacium.* " Unreality." The Godhead and the Manhood were both equally real. Eutyches' real difficulty was that he shrank from the condescension involved in the Incarnation and from the voluntary limitations which real Manhood implies.

125. *Agit enim utraque forma . . . iniuriis.* This was the second passage questioned at Chalcedon as tending to divide the Two Natures. It was defended by Aetius from Cyril's second letter to Successus, in which he showed that the Gospel expressions, whether θεοπρεπεῖς or ἀνθρωποπρεπεῖς, belonged to the same *Hypostasis*, not to two Personalities. See Sellers, op. cit., p. 249, and for the expression *invicem sunt* in line 123 meaning " alternate in activity," literally " are by turns," see Bethune-Baker, *Introduction to the Early History of Christian Doctrine*, p. 290 n.

136. *Nativitas Carnis,* etc. For this phraseology Leo was apparently indebted to Gaudentius of Brescia (*c.* A.D. 394). See C. R. Norcock, *Journal of Theological Studies*, July 1914, p. 593. Eutyches had long fought under the banner of Cyril, but did not confine himself to the doctrine of the anathemas. He challenged the view that the humanity of Christ was consubstantial with that of other men. He revived the unguarded language of Apollinarius in which the terms κρᾶσις and σύγχυσις had occurred, which Apollinarius contrasted with the Antiochene position and language ; without, however, using the qualifying reservations which Apollinarius had added to those expressions. Cf. Contr. Diod., fr. 127 ; Raven, *Apollinarianism*, p. 205.

146. *Esurire,* etc. Cf. Athanasius, Or. c. Ar. iii. 32, 34 ; Cyril Jer., Catech. iv. 9.

157. *non eiusdem naturae est dicere,* etc. Leo is here following the later and, for the most part, Western explanation of John xiv. 28. Cf. Epist. lix, " Nec dicimus eius humanitatem, qua maior est Pater, minuere aliquid eius naturae, quae aequalis est Patri. Hoc aut utrumque unus est Christus qui verissime dixit et secundum

Deum ' Ego et Pater unum sumus,' et secundum hominem ' Pater maior Me est.' ''

Earlier writers, Origen, Tertullian, Alexander, Athanasius, Hilary, understood the " principatus Patris " as inherent in His Person as the Πηγὴ θεότητος. He alone is "of none," while the Son is " begotten of the Father." Thus the Son was regarded as equal in essence but inferior in Person. This was termed the " subordination " of the Persons in the Trinity, springing from Their eternal and absolute relations to each other, whereby we speak of Them in the " order" of Father, Son, and Spirit. After the Arian controversy the Son's inferiority was more generally referred to His Incarnation. Chrysostom, Cyril of Alexandria, and Augustine admit both interpretations; Amphilochius, Ambrose, and the author of the " Quicunque " adopt the latter. See West-cott's additional note on John xiv. 28.

For the Western view cf. Augustine, Tract 78 in Ioan xiv. 27 ff. ; for the Eastern view De Fide et Symbolo 18, where he remarks that in saying these words our Lord was speaking from His experience as a man. For English writers see Bull, *Nicene Creed*, and Pearson, *On the Creed*, Art. I.

159. *Quamvis enim*, etc. This passage was also objected to at Chalcedon and defended by Theodoret from Cyril's Scholia on the Incarnation, 27.

164. *Propter hanc ergo unitatem*, etc. Leo here clearly illustrates the Hypostatic Union and Communicatio Idiomatum. See note on Cyril, Epist. 2 ad Nest., p. 103 f.

181. *a principali petra. i.e.* Christ. Peter as the rock derived his character and name from the Divine archetypal Rock, Christ. So Augustine (Serm. lxxvi in Matt. xiv.), whose words Leo apparently had in mind, " Christus est Petra . . . Petra enim principale nomen est." There is an important passage on this text which discloses Leo's views, in his Serm. iv (De Nat. ips. 4). " Tu es Petrus : id est, cum Ego sim inviolabilis petra Ego lapis angularis qui facio utraque unum, Ego fundamentum praeter quod nemo potest aliud ponere; tamen tu quoque petra es quia Mea virtute solidaris, ut quae Mihi potestate sunt propria, sint tibi Mecum participatione communia." [He had said a little before, speaking of Christian pastors, " Omnes proprie regat Petrus quos principaliter regit et Christus."] But he goes on to explain " super hanc petram " of Peter's confession, " Super hanc fortitudinem aeternum exstruam templum, et ecclesiae Meae caelo inferenda sublimitas in huius fidei firmitate consurget. Hanc confessionem portae inferi non tenebunt." The point of view, as often in the Fathers, keeps changing. Sometimes Christ is the Rock, sometimes Peter, sometimes Peter's confession. The more general rule of the Fathers is that of St. Ambrose that Peter's primacy was one of honour

rather than of office (De Incarn. iv. 32). The peculiar view of St. Cyprian worked out in the " De Unitate Ecclesiae," that the primacy was the symbol rather than the centre of unity is summed up in the sentence " for power that was afterwards given to all the apostles was first for the sake of emphasis on unity bestowed upon one." See Kidd, *Documents Illustrative of Church History*, No. 147 ; Gore, *Church and Ministry*, 2nd Edn., 1919, pp. 151 ff. ; Bigg, *Origins*, p. 363, note 4. Cf. Bindley's note on Tertullian, De Praescr. Haer. 22. Lightfoot, *Clement of Rome II*, pp. 482 ff. ; and the interesting monograph of G. Goetz, *Petrus als Gründer und Oberhaupt der Kirche*; and cf. Jalland, *Bampton Lectures*, pp. 161–5.

184. *aequalis erat periculi*, etc. Leo expresses the double truth which avoids Docetism on the one side and Psilanthropism on the other. The Saviour of mankind must be God to recreate, redeem, and atone ; and Man to discharge the law of obedience and death.

200. *ita sciremus. i.e.* holding the indivisible union of the Two Natures unconfused. Cf. the ἀδιαιρέτως, ἀσυγχύτως of the Chalcedonian Definition.

207. *qui solvit Iesum.* This is the Vulgate reading in 1 John iv. 3, and represents a Greek text such as is given in Socr. vii. 32, ὃ λύει τὸν Ἰησοῦν. It was probably an early gloss upon ὃ μὴ ὁμολογεῖ τὸν Ἰησοῦν, which recorded another Johannine phrase, λύειν Ἰησοῦν Χριστόν, and which from the Greek crept into the African Latin version, and thence into the Vulgate. Tertullian used it quite naturally (De Ieiun. 1 ; adv. Marc. v. 16), and so also the Latin translator of Irenaeus (iii. 17. 8 ; Harvey, ii. 90) and the Latin Fathers, who were familiar with the Vulgate. Socrates cited it against the Nestorian separation of the Godhead from the Virgin-born. Leo uses it here against the Eutychian annihilation of the Human Nature in Christ.

218. *aperto.* Use of this word is no doubt due to the Vulgate of John xix. 34, which represents a false reading, ἤνοιξεν for ἔνυξεν. So also Augustine Commentary, ad loc.

219. *sanguis et aqua.* John xix. 34. That the issue of the blood showed the reality of Christ's flesh, and that of the water its spotless purity as being the Body of God was urged by Ps.-Athanasius, c. Apollin. i. 18. That the double stream symbolised the Atonement and the Cleansing, and was therein connected with the two sacraments, was a general patristic belief. Cf. Leo again, Epist. xiv. " Tunc regenerationis potentiam sanxit quando de latere Ipsius profluxerunt sanguis redemptionis et aqua baptismatis." Cf. the prayer for the sanctification of the Water in the English Baptismal Service. St. Cyril of Jerusalem (Cat. Lect. iii. 10) interprets the double stream of Baptism with water in times of peace and with the martyrs' own blood in times of persecution. See also ibid., xiii. 21, where other interpretations are given : Augustine, De Civ. Dei xxii. 17 ; Tract.

ix in Ioan. 10 " mortuo Christo lancea percutitur latus ut profluant sacramenta quibus formetur ecclesia."

223. *Scientes*, etc.   1 Pet. i. 18 and 19.   This and the following citations are not in verbal agreement with the Vulgate.   See Westcott and Hort on 1 John v. 8 and " the Three Heavenly Witnesses " admitted in late MSS. of the Vulgate.

231. *non in aqua solum.*   St. John had in mind the Cerinthian separation of the Divine Christ of the Baptism from the human Jesus of the Passion.   Leo's application of the text involves the interpretation of " The Spirit " as the Divinity of Christ (a meaning of the " Spirit," which had a long and widespread tradition in Western Christology (see above, p. 45), and the " Water " and the " Blood " as His humanity.   By " The Spirit " was probably meant in this context the Christian community and its experience of the Resurrection of Christ and His living power in the Church and its sacraments.

241. *Confiteor*, etc.   See above, p. 160 ;   and cf. Theodoret, Dial. ii (Later Treatises of Athanasius, *Library of the Fathers*, p. 197).

250. *quia nulla vestra est sententia confutatum.*   Eutyches' con-demnation in the Home Synod had turned rather on his denial of Two Natures after the Union than on his affirmation of Two Natures before it.   Probably he did not mean actually to assert that Christ's Manhood existed before the Incarnation, and so the phrase was passed over.   But Leo, in his letter to Julian of Cos (Epist. xxxv) of the same date as the Tome, dwells upon it further, and under-stands Eutyches to have expressed his belief that the Saviour's soul had had a previous existence *in caelis* before its birth of the Virgin, and that Eutyches consequently held a belief which had already been condemned in the case of Origen.

254. *a sua persuasione discedere.   i.e.* Eutyches had consented, in deference to the synod, to say what he had never said before, that Christ was co-essential with us as to His Manhood.

271. *Iulium.*   Of the three legates, Julius shrinks into the back-ground at Ephesus before the resolute and tenacious Hilarus ;   nor do we hear of him again after the close of that disastrous meeting from which Hilarus made his escape without compromising himself or the See of Rome.   Renatus died at Delos on his way to Ephesus.

Renatum presbyterum.   A marginal gloss which has crept into some MSS. tells us that Renatus was in charge of the " titular " Church of St. Clement (*tituli sancti Clementis*).   On *titulus* see Bingham, *Ant.* viii. 1. 10, and cf. Batiffol, *Histoire du Bréviaire Romain*, on the four kinds of churches in Rome : patriarchal, titular (= parochial), diaconal, and martyral (p. 37 ; edn. 1894).

272. *Hilarum.*   Hilarus was Archdeacon of Rome.

THE CHALCEDONIAN DEFINITION
OF THE FAITH

ΑΥΤΗ Η ΠΙΣΤΙΣ ΤΩΝ ΠΑΤΕΡΩΝ
ΑΥΤΗ Η ΠΙΣΤΙΣ ΤΩΝ ΑΠΟΣΤΟΛΩΝ
ΤΑΥΤΗ ΠΑΝΤΕΣ ΣΤΟΙΧΟΥΜΕΝ
ΠΑΝΤΕΣ ΟΥΤΩ ΦΡΟΝΟΥΜΕΝ

THE CHALCEDONIAN DEFINITION
OF THE FAITH

INTRODUCTION

I. HISTORICAL

THE Council summoned for August 1, 449, met in the church of St. Mary at Ephesus on August 8, under the presidency of Dioscorus of Alexandria. About one hundred and thirty bishops were present. After the Emperor's letter convening the Council had been read, Hilarus, the Papal legate, requested that Leo's Letters to the Council should be received.[1] Dioscorus agreed, but some other letters from the Emperor were put in, and in accordance with the wish therein expressed the Council proceeded at once to the question of the Faith. Eutyches was introduced. He produced a written confession of faith, to which, when it was read, he added some indignant words concerning the manner of his condemnation by Flavian. Flavian then asked that Eusebius, Eutyches' accuser, should be admitted. This was most inequitably refused, and the Acts of the Home Synod were proceeded with, notwithstanding another attempt on the part of Julius and Hilarus to get Leo's Letters read first.

It was soon obvious that the majority of the members of the Council was dominated by Dioscorus, and when, during the reading of the minutes which recorded Eusebius' demand that Eutyches should confess " Two Natures after the Union," Dioscorus asked if such language was to be endured, his followers anathematised the Eusebian teaching, and acclaimed that of Eutyches as orthodox. Eutyches was then by vote of the Council restored to his position, and the ban of excommunication taken off his community.

The Council proceeded to read and approve the decrees of the Council of Ephesus in 431, and to condemn those who should add to the Nicene Faith. Once again Hilarus tried, but unsuccessfully, to bring forward Leo's Letters as agreeable to the truth. Dioscorus now proposed that, in accordance with the Ephesine decrees which laid penalties upon those persons who disturbed them, Flavian and Eusebius should be deposed; and this was actually done, notwithstanding the protest of Flavian and the *contradicitur* of the Roman legates.[2] At the actual pronouncement of the sentence,

[1] These were Epist. xxviii (The Tome) to Flavian, and Epist. xxxiii, of the same date, to the Synod.
[2] Both Flavian and Eusebius addressed Pope Leo in written appeals. These documents, long looked upon as lost, were discovered by Amelli in

however, some of the bishops, ashamed and alarmed, entreated
Dioscorus to desist. He instantly called in the army, and amid a
scene of incredible uproar and violence the majority of the bishops
were compelled to sign a blank paper, and agree to Flavian's deposition. Those who refused were banished, while Flavian and Eusebius
were imprisoned. Such was the tragedy of the " Latrocinium." [1]
With the greatest difficulty Hilarus escaped unhurt, and by taking
unusual roads eventually got to Rome. [2] Three days after the
Council closed, Flavian, at Hypepe in Lydia, whither he had been
banished, died of the brutal injuries he had sustained in the Synod,
and Anatolius, Dioscorus' apocrisiarius at Constantinople, was
consecrated to succeed him.

Dioscorus' next step was to excommunicate Leo, [3] who hitherto
had received no news of the Council. Hilarus arrived at Rome at
the end of September, and the annual autumn synod promptly
condemned the Acts of Epheus, and requested Theodosius to summon a General Council in Italy (Epist. xliii and xliv ad Theodos.).
But Theodosius had meanwhile given his authoritative approval
to the proceedings at Ephesus, and was not to be moved from this
position (Leo, Epist. lxii, lxiii, lxiv). His reply to Leo required
him to approve of Anatolius' consecration, which Leo refused to do
unless Anatolius would heartily assent to Cyril's Second Letter to
Nestorius, the Ephesine Acts of 431, and his own Tome (Epist. lxix).

Matters were thus at a deadlock when the death of Theodosius
on July 29, 450, and the retirement of Eudocia left Pulcheria sole
Empress of the East. On August 25 she married Marcian, a distinguished Thracian soldier, who was elected Emperor, and both
she and her husband were devoted to the Catholic cause. Leo
had sent four legates to Constantinople to enquire into Anatolius'
faith, who were received by the archbishop on their arrival, and Leo's
Tome was accepted in a synod and subscribed (Mansi, vii. 92).
When Leo was informed of the restoration of union he wished the
proposed General Council to be deferred on account of the difficulties
which the Western bishops would experience in leaving their sees,
owing to the ravages of the Huns. But Marcian thought it best

---

1874 and published in 1882. They have been edited with a historical
Introduction, and translated by T. A. Lacey, Church Historical Society's
Publications LXX, " Appellatio Flaviani " (1903).

[1] Leo's description of the iniquitous assembly. " Nec opus est epistulari
pagina comprehendi quidquid in illo Ephesino non iudicio sed latrocinio
potuit perpetrari " (Epist. xcv ad Pulch.). Cf. Epist. lxxxv, " Illa synodus
quae nomen synodi nec habere poterit nec meretur." Latrocinium was a
Ciceronian phrase (pro Roscio Amerino, 61), " quod putares hoc latrocinium non iudicium futurum."

[2] Leo wrote of him (Epist. xliv), " Qui vix, ne subscribere per vim
coneretur, effugit." Epist. xlv ad Pulch., and Hilarus' own letter to the
Empress (Epist. xlvi), which describes the Council.

[3] So Fleury, xxvii. 41, and Neale ; Bright would place it later—in the
spring of 450, when at Nicaea (Roman See, etc., p. 276).

to proceed, and accordingly on May 17, 451, issued the summons convening a General Council at Nicaea for September 1. Leo appointed five legates to represent him, Paschasinus, Lucentius, Boniface, and Basil, who were to act with Julian, Bishop of Cos, who was Leo's resident agent at Constantinople.

The Council met at Nicaea, but was transferred to Chalcedon, as more convenient for the Emperor, and opened in the Martyry of Euphemia on October 8. Five hundred and twenty bishops were present, the Roman legates presiding, and nineteen imperial commissioners attended from the Emperor. Dioscorus and Eusebius occupied places in the middle as parties concerned.

In the first session the records of the Latrocinium were read, and Dioscorus with some others was condemned. In the second session (October 10) the question of the faith was debated. The Nicene Creed, the " Creed of the Second General Council," Cyril's Second Letter to Nestorius, and Letter to John of Antioch, and Leo's Tome (in a Greek translation) were read and approved. Some difficulty was at first felt by the Palestinian and Illyrian bishops about three passages in the Tome which insisted upon the distinction of the Two Natures, but they were shown by Aetius of Constantinople and Theodoret to agree with Cyrilline teaching. The Council was adjourned, and five days granted for the examination of patristic teaching on the question of the faith.

The third session (October 13) was wholly occupied with the trial of Dioscorus. He disregarded three citations to attend, and was finally deposed on the ground of his uncanonical actions ; viz., communion with the condemned Eutyches, tyranny at the Latrocinium, excommunication of Leo, and disobedience to synodical citation.

In the fourth session (October 17) the doctrinal question was resumed. The Tome of Leo was subscribed as agreeable to Nicaea, Constantinople, and Cyril's exposition at Ephesus. Some other matters were disposed of, and the Council adjourned to the following day.

In the fifth session (October 22) a Definition of the Faith was presented, to which the Roman legates and some Easterns took exception on the ground that it did not speak of Christ as existing *in* Two Natures, as Leo's Tome had implied, but only as *from* Two Natures, which had been accepted in a Eutychian sense. Dioscorus, for instance, had assented to the phrase " from two," but rejected " two." [1] Others, imagining the opposition to be due to Nestorian sympathies, urged the insertion of *Theotokos*. Eventually a committee, consisting of Anatolius, four Roman legates, and eighteen bishops, was appointed to revise it, and it was finally accepted in its present form after immense pressure had been put on them by the

---

[1] Mansi, vi. 692. Cf. Eranistes in Theodoret, Dial. ii, " I say that Christ was ἐκ δύο φύσεων, but δύο φύσεις I do not say."

N

Imperial Commissioners. See Kidd, op. cit., vol. iii, pp. 324-36, for a vivid description of the closing scene of the Council.

Three days later the Emperor and Empress visited the Council to confirm the faith, and the *Definitio* was ratified anew.

II. THEOLOGICAL

The Definition put forth by the Fathers at Chalcedon has been described on the one hand as " a great utterance of faith aware of the many turnings which theory may take so easily " (Mackintosh) : on the other as the " bankruptcy of Greek theology " (Harnack). In view of its close affinity with the Tome, the latter opinion is scarcely tenable, but it was meant to call attention to the fact that it provided no solution to the mystery of the Person of Christ. The Definition has been compared to buoys anchored along a difficult estuary on the right and left to guide the ship of truth. Perhaps this apt comparison could with advantage be carried a step farther, for the estuaries are only so much evidence of the vastness of the continents which they water ; and thus the Definition, which Dorner regards as short-sighted, is evidence itself of the background of Divine Revelation lying behind it, which stretches out to the infinite and manifests what those writers of the New Testament thought but could not express of what they had heard and seen and their hands had handled of the Word of Life, the object of Christian Faith and Worship. In any case it cannot be called the " bare skeleton of a dogma " (Mackintosh). Against the unfortunate results of its too ready acceptance of St. Leo's words regarding the *two natures*, must be set its refusal thereby to exclude all that was specially valuable in the theology of Antioch, a course justified by the revival of that aspect of Christology in recent times.[1] Nor can it be said to have excluded progress in Christology in view of the later developments along the lines of the Cyrilline doctrine of *kenosis*. It enshrines the truth contained in the judgment of Professor Bethune-Baker that there is in the theology of Paul of Samosata that to which the Church must return in its attempt to formulate a better definition of the mystery of the Incarnation (quoted by Dr. Raven, *Apollinarianism*, preface), as also the verdict of Dr. Quick that some theory of *kenosis* is inevitable in any restatement of the Doctrine of the Person of Christ (*Doctrines of the Creed*, p. 138). Above all, it must be read in the light of the subsequent Definitions of the Fourth and Fifth Oecumenical Councils which are included in this volume. It is, in fact, in its recognition of the Creed, both the Nicene and that of Constantinople now made for the first time Oecumenical, a republication and a reassertion of the ancient Rule of Faith, explained in view of the Eutychian heresy. Beyond that it does not pretend to go.

We may note its chief and characteristic pronouncements agreeing

---

[1] Kidd, op. cit., iii, 324 ff.

with and incorporating for the first time new and important developments in theology. First of all famous four adverbs ἀσυγχύτως, ἀτρέπτως, ἀδιαιρέτως, ἀχωρίστως, qualifying and defining the ἐν δύο φύσεσιν. At the same time the unity of the Person is positively defined, as may have been done already in the Athanasian Creed, which is perhaps a little earlier, "unus Christus non confusione substantiae sed unitate personae." Above all there is a clearly felt soteriological interest behind the careful phrasing which enables us to interpret the whole as a combination of the vital elements which Faith has always insisted on combining in its view of Christ the Saviour. Thus the reality and integrity of each nature, of Godhead and Manhood, is upheld; and the Incarnation has not issued in a Being that is somehow neither Divine nor human nor either exclusively. On the other hand, the theanthropic life is a personal unity, not severed into two independent subjects, but *hypostatically* and substantially one. The question which Loofs asks (*Leitfaden*[3], p. 172) namely whether, when the Definition had to be interpreted, it would be read in the light of Cyril's teaching, or Theodoret's, or Leo's, is perhaps theologically, as well as historically, the justification of its claim to have defined the Doctrine of the Person of Christ in such terms, that it has been the starting-point for a large and fruitful range of Christological thought through the centuries, which is by no means yet exhausted, because the Subject itself is inexhaustible.

ANALYSIS OF THE CHALCEDONIAN DEFINITION OF THE FAITH

§ 1. Introductory.

§ 2. For the preservation of peace, and the removal of error by the grace of Christ we assemble. Holding the Creeds of Nicaea and of Constantinople, and preserving the traditions of Ephesus, we solemnly ratify the

Creed of Nicaea, and the
Creed of Constantinople.

§ 3. Although the Nicene Creed is really sufficient on the doctrines of the Holy Trinity and the Incarnation, yet since heresies have arisen—

    1. Corrupting the mystery of the Incarnation, and denying to the Virgin Mary the title " Theotokos " (Nestorians);

    2. Introducing a mixture or fusion of the Two Natures, making the Divine Nature of the Son passible (Eutychians);

therefore we confirm—

    1. The Nicene Creed;

    2. The Constantinopolitan Creed;

    3. The Two Synodical Epistles of Cyril;

    4. The Tome of Leo.

§ 4. The Holy Synod condemns—

    1. A Dyad of Sons;

    2. A passible Divinity in the Son;

    3. A mixture or fusion of the Two Natures;

    4. A non-human origin of Christ's Body;

    5. Two Natures before, but only one after, the Union;

and confesses One and the Self-same Son our Lord Jesus Christ—

    { Perfect in Godhead;
    { Perfect in Manhood:

    { Truly God;
    { Truly Man:

    { Co-essential with the Father as to Godhead;
    { Co-essential with us as to Manhood:

    { Begotten of the Father eternally as to Divinity;
    { Born of the Virgin, Theotokos, temporally as to Humanity:

One Christ IN TWO NATURES, unconfusedly, unchangeably, indivisibly, inseparably, according to Holy Scripture, the teaching of Christ, and tradition.

§ 5. No other Creed than the Symbol of the Fathers to be composed or imposed upon intending converts.

DEFINITIO FIDEI APUD
CONCILIUM CHALCEDONENSE

DEFINITIO FIDEI APUD
CONCILIUM CHALCEDONENSE

Η ΑΓΙΑ καὶ μεγάλη καὶ οἰκουμενικὴ σύνοδος, ἡ κατὰ Θεοῦ χάριν
καὶ θέσπισμα τῶν εὐσεβεστάτων καὶ φιλοχρίστων ἡμῶν βασιλέων
Μαρκιανοῦ καὶ Οὐαλεντιανοῦ Αὐγούστων, συναχθεῖσα ἐν τῇ Καλχηδο- 5
νέων, μητροπόλει τῆς Βιθυνῶν ἐπαρχίας, ἐν τῷ μαρτυρίῳ τῆς ἁγίας
καὶ καλλινίκου μάρτυρος Εὐφημίας, ὥρισε τὰ ὑποτεταγμένα.
Ὁ Κύριος ἡμῶν καὶ Σωτὴρ Ἰησοῦς Χριστὸς τῆς πίστεως τὴν
γνῶσιν τοῖς μαθηταῖς βεβαιῶν, ἔφη· Εἰρήνην τὴν ἐμὴν ἀφίημι ὑμῖν,
εἰρήνην τὴν ἐμὴν δίδωμι ὑμῖν· ὥστε μηδένα πρὸς τὸν John xiv. 27. 10
πλησίον διαφωνεῖν ἐν τοῖς δόγμασι τῆς εὐσεβείας, ἀλλ' ἐπίσης ἅπασι τὸ
τῆς ἀληθείας ἐπιδείκνυσθαι κήρυγμα. ἐπειδὴ δὲ οὐ παύεται διὰ τῶν
ἑαυτοῦ ζιζανίων ὁ πονηρὸς τοῖς τῆς εὐσεβείας ἐπιφυόμενος σπέρμασι,
καί τι καινὸν κατὰ τῆς ἀληθείας ἐφευρίσκων ἀεί, διὰ τοῦτο συνήθως ὁ
Δεσπότης προνοούμενος τοῦ ἀνθρωπίνου γένους, τὸν εὐσεβῆ τοῦτον καὶ 15
πιστότατον πρὸς ζῆλον ἀνέστησε βασιλέα, καὶ τοὺς ἀπανταχῇ τῆς
ἱερωσύνης πρὸς ἑαυτὸν ἀρχηγοὺς συνεκάλεσεν· ὥστε, τῆς χάριτος τοῦ
πάντων ἡμῶν Δεσπότου Χριστοῦ ἐνεργούσης, πᾶσαν μὲν τοῦ ψεύδους
τῶν τοῦ Χριστοῦ προβάτων ἀποσείσασθαι λύμην, τοῖς δὲ τῆς ἀληθείας
αὐτὴν καταπιαίνειν βλαστήμασιν. ὃ δὴ καὶ πεποιήκαμεν, κοινῇ ψήφῳ 20
τὰ τῆς πλάνης ἀπελάσαντες δόγματα, τὴν δὲ ἀπλανῆ τῶν πατέρων
ἀνανεωσάμενοι πίστιν, τὸ τῶν τριακοσίων δεκαοκτὼ σύμβολον τοῖς
πᾶσι κηρύξαντες, καὶ ὡς οἰκείους τοὺς τοῦτο τὸ σύνθεμα τῆς εὐσεβείας
δεξαμένους πατέρας ἐπιγραψάμενοι· οἵπερ εἰσὶν οἱ μετὰ ταῦτα ἐν τῇ
μεγάλῃ Κωνσταντινουπόλει συνελθόντες ἑκατὸν πεντήκοντα, καὶ αὐτοὶ 25
τὴν αὐτὴν ἐπισφραγισάμενοι πίστιν. ὁρίζομεν τοίνυν, τὴν τάξιν καὶ
τοὺς περὶ τῆς πίστεως ἅπαντας τύπους φυλάττοντες καὶ ἡμεῖς τῆς κατ'
Ἔφεσον πάλαι γεγενημένης ἁγίας συνόδου, ἧς ἡγεμόνες οἱ ἁγιώτατοι
τὴν μνήμην Κελεστῖνος ὁ τῆς Ῥωμαίων, καὶ Κύριλλος ὁ τῆς Ἀλεξανδρέων, ἐτύγχανον, προλάμπειν μὲν τῆς ὀρθῆς καὶ ἀμωμήτου πίστεως 30
τὴν ἔκθεσιν τῶν τριακοσίων δεκαοκτὼ ἁγίων καὶ μακαρίων πατέρων
τῶν ἐν Νικαίᾳ ἐπὶ τοῦ εὐσεβοῦς μνήμης Κωνσταντίνου τοῦ γενομένου
βασιλέως συναχθέντων· κρατεῖν δὲ καὶ τὰ παρὰ τῶν ἑκατὸν πεντήκοντα
ἁγίων πατέρων ἐν Κωνσταντινουπόλει ὁρισθέντα, πρὸς ἀναίρεσιν μὲν
τῶν τότε φυεισῶν αἱρέσεων, βεβαίωσιν δὲ τῆς αὐτῆς καθολικῆς καὶ 35
ἀποστολικῆς ἡμῶν πίστεως.

Τὸ τῶν τριακοσίων δεκαοκτὼ ἐν Νικαίᾳ σύμβολον.

Πιστεύομεν εἰς ἕνα Θεόν, Πατέρα παντοκράτορα, πάντων ὁρατῶν τε καὶ ἀοράτων
ποιητήν. Καὶ εἰς ἕνα Κύριον Ἰησοῦν Χριστόν, τὸν Υἱὸν τοῦ Θεοῦ, γεννηθέντα ἐκ τοῦ
Πατρός, μονογενῆ, τουτέστιν ἐκ τῆς οὐσίας τοῦ Πατρός· Θεὸν ἐκ Θεοῦ, Φῶς ἐκ Φωτός, 40
Θεὸν ἀληθινὸν ἐκ Θεοῦ ἀληθινοῦ, γεννηθέντα οὐ ποιηθέντα, ὁμοούσιον τῷ Πατρί· δι' οὗ τὰ
πάντα ἐγένετο· τὸν δι' ἡμᾶς τοὺς ἀνθρώπους, καὶ διὰ τὴν ἡμετέραν σωτηρίαν κατελθόντα ἐκ
τῶν οὐρανῶν, καὶ σαρκωθέντα ἐκ Πνεύματος Ἁγίου καὶ Μαρίας τῆς παρθένου, καὶ ἐνανθρωπή-

σαντα· σταυρωθέντα τε ὑπὲρ ἡμῶν ἐπὶ Ποντίου Πιλάτου, καὶ παθόντα, καὶ ταφέντα· καὶ
45 ἀναστάντα τῇ τρίτῃ ἡμέρᾳ κατὰ τὰς γραφάς· καὶ ἀνελθόντα εἰς τοὺς οὐράνους, καὶ καθεζόμενον
ἐν δεξιᾷ τοῦ Πατρός· καὶ πάλιν ἐρχόμενον μετὰ δόξης κρῖναι ζῶντας καὶ νεκρούς· οὗ τῆς
βασιλείας οὐκ ἔσται τέλος. Καὶ εἰς τὸ Πνεῦμα τὸ ἅγιον τὸ κύριον τὸ ζωοποιόν. Τοὺς δὲ
λέγοντας· Ἦν ποτε ὅτε οὐκ ἦν, καὶ Πρὶν γεννηθῆναι οὐκ ἦν, καὶ ὅτι ἐξ οὐκ ὄντων ἐγένετο, ἢ
ἐξ ἑτέρας ὑποστάσεως ἢ οὐσίας φάσκοντας εἶναι, ἢ τρεπτόν, ἢ ἀλλοιωτὸν τὸν Υἱὸν τοῦ Θεοῦ,
50 τούτους ἀναθεματίζει ἡ καθολικὴ καὶ ἀποστολικὴ ἐκκλησία.

Τὸ τῶν ἑκατὸν πεντήκοντα ἐν Κωνσταντινουπόλει σύμβολον.

Πιστεύομεν εἰς ἕνα Θεόν, Πατέρα παντοκράτορα, ποιητὴν οὐρανοῦ καὶ γῆς, ὁρατῶν τε
πάντων καὶ ἀοράτων. Καὶ εἰς ἕνα Κύριον Ἰησοῦν Χριστόν, τὸν Υἱὸν τοῦ Θεοῦ τὸν μονογενῆ,
τὸν ἐκ τοῦ Πατρὸς γεννηθέντα πρὸ πάντων τῶν αἰώνων· Φῶς ἐκ Φωτός, Θεὸν ἀληθινὸν ἐκ
55 Θεοῦ ἀληθινοῦ· γεννηθέντα, οὐ ποιηθέντα, ὁμοούσιον τῷ Πατρί, δι' οὗ τὰ πάντα ἐγένετο· τὸν
δι' ἡμᾶς τοὺς ἀνθρώπους, καὶ διὰ τὴν ἡμετέραν σωτηρίαν, κατελθόντα ἐκ τῶν οὐρανῶν, καὶ
σαρκωθέντα ἐκ Πνεύματος ἁγίου καὶ Μαρίας τῆς παρθένου, καὶ ἐνανθρωπήσαντα· σταυρωθέντα
τε ὑπὲρ ἡμῶν ἐπὶ Ποντίου Πιλάτου, καὶ παθόντα, καὶ ταφέντα, καὶ ἀναστάντα τῇ τρίτῃ
ἡμέρᾳ κατὰ τὰς γραφάς· καὶ ἀνελθόντα εἰς τοὺς οὐρανούς, καὶ καθεζόμενον ἐκ δεξιῶν τοῦ
60 Πατρός· καὶ πάλιν ἐρχόμενον μετὰ δόξης κρῖναι ζῶντας καὶ νεκρούς· οὗ τῆς βασιλείας οὐκ
ἔσται τέλος. Καὶ εἰς τὸ Πνεῦμα τὸ ἅγιον, τὸ κύριον, καὶ τὸ ζωοποιόν, τὸ ἐκ τοῦ Πατρὸς
ἐκπορευόμενον, τὸ σὺν Πατρὶ καὶ Υἱῷ συμπροσκυνούμενον καὶ συνδοξαζόμενον, τὸ λαλῆσαν
διὰ τῶν προφητῶν· εἰς μίαν ἁγίαν καθολικὴν καὶ ἀποστολικὴν ἐκκλησίαν· ὁμολογοῦμεν ἓν
βάπτισμα εἰς ἄφεσιν ἁμαρτιῶν· προσδοκῶμεν ἀνάστασιν νεκρῶν, καὶ ζωὴν τοῦ μέλλοντος
65 αἰῶνος. Ἀμήν.

Ἥρκει μὲν οὖν εἰς ἐντελῆ τῆς εὐσεβείας ἐπίγνωσίν τε καὶ βεβαίωσιν
τὸ σοφὸν καὶ σωτήριον τοῦτο τῆς θείας χάριτος σύμβολον· περί τε γὰρ
τοῦ Πατρὸς καὶ τοῦ Υἱοῦ καὶ τοῦ Ἁγίου Πνεύματος ἐκδιδάσκει τὸ
τέλειον, καὶ τοῦ Κυρίου τὴν ἐνανθρώπησιν τοῖς πιστῶς δεχομένοις
70 παρίστησιν. ἀλλ' ἐπειδήπερ οἱ τῆς ἀληθείας ἀθετεῖν ἐπιχειροῦντες τὸ
κήρυγμα, διὰ τῶν οἰκείων αἱρέσεων τὰς κενοφωνίας ἀπέτεκον, οἱ μὲν
τὸ τῆς δι' ἡμᾶς τοῦ Κυρίου οἰκονομίας μυστήριον παραφθείρειν
τολμῶντες, καὶ τὴν θεοτόκον ἐπὶ τῆς παρθένου φωνὴν ἀπαρνούμενοι·
οἱ δὲ σύγχυσιν καὶ κρᾶσιν εἰσάγοντες, καὶ μίαν εἶναι φύσιν τῆς σαρκὸς
75 καὶ τῆς θεότητος ἀνοήτως ἀναπλάττοντες, καὶ παθητὴν τοῦ μονογενοῦς
τὴν θείαν φύσιν τῇ συγχύσει τερατευόμενοι· διὰ τοῦτο πᾶσαν αὐτοῖς
ἀποκλεῖσαι κατὰ τῆς ἀληθείας μηχανὴν βουλομένη ἡ παροῦσα νῦν αὕτη
ἁγία μεγάλη καὶ οἰκουμενικὴ σύνοδος, τὸ τοῦ κηρύγματος ἄνωθεν
ἀσάλευτον ἐκδιδάσκουσα, ὥρισε προηγουμένως, τῶν τριακοσίων δε-
80 καοκτὼ ἁγίων πατέρων τὴν πίστιν μένειν ἀπαρεγχείρητον. καὶ διὰ
μὲν τοὺς τῷ Πνεύματι τῷ Ἁγίῳ μαχομένους, τὴν χρόνοις ὕστερον
παρὰ τῶν ἐπὶ τῆς βασιλευούσης πόλεως συνελθόντων ἑκατὸν πεντήκοντα
ἁγίων πατέρων περὶ τῆς τοῦ Πνεύματος οὐσίας παραδοθεῖσαν διδασκαλίαν κυροῖ· ἣν ἐκεῖνοι τοῖς πᾶσιν ἐγνώρισαν, οὐκ ὥς τι λεῖπον τοῖς
85 προλαβοῦσιν ἐπάγοντες, ἀλλὰ τὴν περὶ τοῦ Ἁγίου Πνεύματος αὐτῶν
ἔννοιαν κατὰ τῶν τὴν αὐτοῦ δεσποτείαν ἀθετεῖν πειρωμένων γραφικαῖς
μαρτυρίαις τρανώσαντες. διὰ δὲ τοὺς τὸ τῆς οἰκονομίας παραφθείρειν
ἐπιχειροῦντας μυστήριον, καὶ ψιλὸν ἄνθρωπον εἶναι τὸν ἐκ τῆς ἁγίας
τεχθέντα Μαρίας ἀναιδῶς ληρωδοῦντας, τὰς τοῦ μακαρίου Κυρίλλου,
90 τοῦ τῆς Ἀλεξανδρέων ἐκκλησίας γενομένου ποιμένος, συνοδικὰς
ἐπιστολὰς πρὸς Νεστόριον καὶ πρὸς τοὺς τῆς ἀνατολῆς, ἁρμοδίους
οὔσας ἐδέξατο, εἰς ἔλεγχον μὲν τῆς Νεστορίου φρενοβλαβείας, ἑρμηνείαν
δὲ τῶν ἐν εὐσεβεῖ ζήλῳ τοῦ σωτηρίου συμβόλου ποθούντων τὴν ἔννοιαν·

αἷς καὶ τὴν ἐπιστολὴν τοῦ τῆς μεγίστης καὶ πρεσβυτέρας Ῥώμης
προέδρου τοῦ μακαριωτάτου καὶ ἁγιωτάτου ἀρχιεπισκόπου Λέοντος, 95
τὴν γραφεῖσαν πρὸς τὸν ἐν ἁγίοις ἀρχιεπίσκοπον Φλαυιανὸν ἐπ᾿
ἀναιρέσει τῆς Εὐτυχοῦς κακονοίας, ἅτε δὴ τῇ τοῦ μεγάλου Πέτρου
ὁμολογίᾳ συμβαίνουσαν, καὶ κοινήν τινα στήλην ὑπάρχουσαν κατὰ τῶν
κακοδοξούντων, εἰκότως συνήρμοσε πρὸς τὴν τῶν ὀρθοδόξων δογμάτων
βεβαίωσιν.   100
   Τοῖς τε γὰρ εἰς υἱῶν δυάδα τὸ τῆς οἰκονομίας διασπᾶν ἐπιχειροῦσι
μυστήριον, παρατάττεται· καὶ τοὺς παθητὴν τοῦ μονογενοῦς λέγειν
τολμῶντας τὴν θεότητα, τοῦ τῶν ἱερῶν ἀπωθεῖται συλλόγου· καὶ τοῖς
ἐπὶ τῶν δύο φύσεων τοῦ Χριστοῦ κρᾶσιν, ἢ σύγχυσιν ἐπινοοῦσιν
ἀνθίσταται· καὶ τοὺς οὐρανίου, ἢ ἑτέρας τινὸς ὑπάρχειν οὐσίας τὴν ἐξ 105
ἡμῶν ληφθεῖσαν αὐτῷ τοῦ δούλου μορφὴν παραπαίοντας ἐξελαύνει·
καὶ τοὺς δύο μὲν πρὸ τῆς ἑνώσεως φύσεις τοῦ Κυρίου μυθεύοντας, μίαν
δὲ μετὰ τὴν ἕνωσιν ἀναπλάττοντας ἀναθεματίζει. Ἑπόμενοι τοίνυν
τοῖς ἁγίοις πατράσιν, ἕνα καὶ τὸν αὐτὸν ὁμολογοῦμεν Υἱὸν τὸν Κύριον
ἡμῶν Ἰησοῦν Χριστόν, καὶ συμφώνως ἅπαντες ἐκδιδάσκομεν, τέλειον 110
τὸν αὐτὸν ἐν θεότητι, τέλειον τὸν αὐτὸν ἐν ἀνθρωπότητι, Θεὸν ἀληθῶς,
καὶ ἄνθρωπον ἀληθῶς, τὸν αὐτὸν ἐκ ψυχῆς λογικῆς καὶ σώματος,
ὁμοούσιον τῷ Πατρὶ κατὰ τὴν θεότητα, καὶ ὁμοούσιον τὸν αὐτὸν ἡμῖν
κατὰ τὴν ἀνθρωπότητα, κατὰ πάντα ὅμοιον ἡμῖν χωρὶς   Heb. iv. 15.
ἁμαρτίας· πρὸ αἰώνων μὲν ἐκ τοῦ Πατρὸς γεννηθέντα κατὰ τὴν θεότητα, 115
ἐπ᾿ ἐσχάτων δὲ τῶν ἡμερῶν τὸν αὐτὸν δι᾿ ἡμᾶς καὶ διὰ τὴν ἡμετέραν
σωτηρίαν ἐκ Μαρίας τῆς παρθένου τῆς θεοτόκου κατὰ τὴν ἀνθρωπότητα,
ἕνα καὶ τὸν αὐτὸν Χριστόν, Υἱόν, Κύριον, μονογενῆ, ἐν δύο φύσεσιν
ἀσυγχύτως, ἀτρέπτως, ἀδιαιρέτως, ἀχωρίστως γνωριζόμενον· οὐδαμοῦ
τῆς τῶν φύσεων διαφορᾶς ἀνῃρημένης διὰ τὴν ἕνωσιν, σωζομένης δὲ 120
μᾶλλον τῆς ἰδιότητος ἑκατέρας φύσεως, καὶ εἰς ἓν πρόσωπον καὶ μίαν
ὑπόστασιν συντρεχούσης, οὐκ εἰς δύο πρόσωπα μεριζόμενον ἢ διαιρού-
μενον, ἀλλ᾿ ἕνα καὶ τὸν αὐτὸν Υἱὸν καὶ μονογενῆ Θεόν, Λόγον, Κύριον
Ἰησοῦν Χριστόν· καθάπερ ἄνωθεν οἱ προφῆται περὶ αὐτοῦ, καὶ αὐτὸς
ἡμᾶς ὁ Κύριος Ἰησοῦς Χριστὸς ἐξεπαίδευσε, καὶ τὸ τῶν πατέρων ἡμῖν 125
παραδέδωκε σύμβολον. Τούτων τοίνυν μετὰ πάσης πανταχόθεν ἀκριβείας τε καὶ ἐμμελείας παρ᾿ ἡμῶν διατυπωθέντων, ὥρισεν ἡ ἁγία καὶ
οἰκουμενικὴ σύνοδος, ἑτέραν πίστιν μηδενὶ ἐξεῖναι προφέρειν, ἤγουν
συγγράφειν, ἢ συντιθέναι, ἢ φρονεῖν, ἢ διδάσκειν ἑτέρους. τοὺς δὲ
τολμῶντας ἢ συντιθέναι πίστιν ἑτέραν, ἤγουν προκομίζειν, ἢ διδάσκειν, 130
ἢ παραδιδόναι ἕτερον σύμβολον τοῖς ἐθέλουσιν ἐπιστρέφειν εἰς ἐπίγνωσιν
ἀληθείας ἐξ Ἑλληνισμοῦ, ἢ ἐξ Ἰουδαϊσμοῦ, ἤγουν ἐξ αἱρέσεως οἱασδη-
ποτοῦν, τούτους, εἰ μὲν εἶεν ἐπίσκοποι ἢ κληρικοί, ἀλλοτρίους εἶναι
τοὺς ἐπισκόπους τῆς ἐπισκοπῆς, καὶ τοὺς κληρικοὺς τοῦ κλήρου· εἰ δὲ
μονάζοντες ἢ λαϊκοὶ εἶεν, ἀναθεματίζεσθαι αὐτούς.   135

NOTES ON THE CHALCEDONIAN
DEFINITION OF THE FAITH

6. μαρτυρίῳ. A martyry was a memorial church erected over a martyr's tomb, or which contained a martyr's relics. Euphemia was a virgin martyred under Galerius in the Great Persecution in 307. She was regarded with great veneration, and was the patroness of the city of Chalcedon. Arcadius and Gainas had met here in 400 to take a solemn oath of peace (Socr. vi. 6). The church was a stately and magnificent edifice ; its beautiful situation is described in picturesque terms by Evagrius, ii. 3.

16. καὶ τοὺς ἁπανταχῇ. Routh, following two Latin versions which read " qui undique," suggested ὃς καὶ, but unnecessarily.

20. αὐτήν. Either a mistake for αὐτά, or = ποίμνην, implied in the mention of προβάτα.

22. τὸ τῶν τριακοσίων δεκαοκτὼ σύμβολον. This was the generally reckoned number of the Nicene Fathers : so Athanasius, ad Afr. 2, ad Jovian. ap. Theodoret, HE. iii. 3, Socr. i. 8, Profess. of Eustathius to Liberius ap. Socr. iv. 12, Evagr. iii. 31, Syn. Epist. of Rom. Counc. in 371 ap. Theodoret ii. 17, Canon 1 of Constantinople.

The number was suggestive of the 318 servants of Abram who rescued Lot, Gen. xiv. 4 (Liberius ap. Socr. loc. cit.), and, as T I H, had been already allegorised as prospective of the Cross and Jesus by the writer of the Epistle of Barnabas, ch. 9 ; by Clement of Alexandria, Strom. vi. 11 ; and by Ambrose, de Fide, *prol.*

38. Πιστεύομεν, κ.τ.λ. In the second session the Nicene Creed had been read nearly in its original form (see note above, p. 66) ; but it appears here in a peculiar recension, expanded by the addition of several phrases taken from the Constantinopolitan Creed. The additions to the original are these :

1. ἐκ τῶν οὐρανῶν.
2. ἐκ Πνεύματος Ἁγίου καὶ Μαρίας τῆς παρθένου.
3. σταυρωθέντα τε ὑπὲρ ἡμῶν ἐπὶ Ποντίου Πιλάτου.
4. καὶ ταφέντα.
5. κατὰ τὰς γραφάς.
6. καὶ καθεζόμενον ἐν δεξιᾷ τοῦ Πατρός.
7. καὶ πάλιν . . . μετὰ δόξης.
8. οὗ τῆς βασιλείας οὐκ ἔσται τέλος.

Besides these additions τὸ Ἅγιον Πνεῦμα of Nicaea becomes τὸ Πνεῦμα τὸ ἅγιον τὸ κύριον τὸ ζωοποιόν, while τά τε ἐν τῷ οὐρανῷ καὶ τὰ ἐν τῇ γῇ is omitted after δι' οὗ τὰ πάντα ἐγένετο, and κτιστόν disappears from the anathemas.

Nestorius was evidently familiar with this form of the Creed, for he quoted (1) and (2), apud Cyril, Adv. Nest. i. 7, 8, as Nicene, and was corrected by Cyril ; while Diogenes of Cyzicus actually accused Eutyches (in session i) of Apollinarianism because he omitted (3), and was himself set right by the Egyptian bishops (Mansi, vi. 632).

For dogmatic notes on the additional clauses in the " creed of the 150," see above, pp. 69 f.

72. οἰκονομίας. See note on οἰκονομικήν, p. 147.

80. διὰ μὲν τοὺς τῷ Π. τ. Ἁ. μαχομένους. The Macedonians, who were known as the " Pneumatomachi." See Constant., Canon 1 and Socr. ii. 45, Ὁ Μακεδόνιος τὸ Ἅγιον τὸ Πνεῦμα συναναλαβεῖν εἰς τὴν θεολογίαν τῆς Τριάδος ἐξέκλινε . . . διὰ ταύτην δὲ τὴν αἰτίαν καὶ Πνευματομάχους ἀποκαλοῦσιν αὐτοὺς οἱ τὸ ὁμοούσιον φρονοῦντες.

86. γραφικαῖς μαρτυρίαις. The context seems to show that by this term the Chalcedonian Fathers meant " Scriptural," not merely " written," testimonies : γραφικαῖς will thus refer to the Scriptural epithets added to τὸ Πνεῦμα. See the notes above, pp. 69 ff.

90. συνοδικὰς ἐπιστολάς. The Second Letter to Nestorius, and the Letter to John of Antioch. The Third Letter to Nestorius with the schedule of anathemas had been read at Ephesus, but, doubtless in consequence of the anathemas, had not been so thoroughly accepted as the Second Letter (see above, p. 138). It was passed over at Chalcedon, but accepted as authoritative along with the Second Letter at the Fifth General Council in 553, apparently on the mistaken ground that it had been similarly received at Chalcedon (Mansi, ix. 341).

105. ἢ ἑτέρας τινὸς . . . οὐσίας. i.e. " any other non-human substance" ; cf. Cyril ad Ioan., above, pp. 142, 143.

108. Ἑπόμενοι τοίνυν, κ.τ.λ. Here the language of the Definitio is an amplification of a portion of Flavian's " Confession of Faith " which he sent to Theodosius in 449. It may be interesting to give Flavian's words (Mansi, vi. 539 ; Hahn, p. 320), so that they may be compared with those of the Council. After a brief preamble he proceeds : Πάντοτε ταῖς θείαις γραφαῖς ἑπόμενοι καὶ ταῖς ἐκθέσεσι τῶν ἁγίων πατέρων, τῶν ἐν Νικαίᾳ καὶ ἐν Κωνσταντινουπόλει συνελθόντων καὶ τῶν ἐν Ἐφέσῳ ἐπὶ τοῦ τῆς ὁσίας μνήμης Κυρίλλου τοῦ γενομένου ἐπισκόπου τῆς Ἀλεξανδρέων· καὶ κηρύττομεν τὸν ἕνα Κύριον ἡμῶν Ἰησοῦν Χριστὸν πρὸ αἰώνων μὲν ἐκ Θεοῦ Πατρὸς ἀνάρχως γεννηθέντα κατὰ τὴν θεότητα, ἐπ' ἐσχάτων δὲ τῶν ἡμερῶν τὸν αὐτὸν δι' ἡμᾶς καὶ διὰ τὴν ἡμετέραν σωτηρίαν ἐκ Μαρίας τῆς παρθένου κατὰ τὴν ἀνθρωπότητα, Θεὸν τέλειον καὶ ἄνθρωπον τέλειον τὸν αὐτὸν ἐν

προσλήψει ψυχῆς λογικῆς καὶ σώματος, ὁμοούσιον τῷ Πατρὶ κατὰ τὴν θεότητα καὶ ὁμοούσιον τῇ μητρὶ τὸν αὐτὸν κατὰ τὴν ἀνθρωπότητα. Καὶ γὰρ ἐκ ¹ δύο φύσεων ὁμολογοῦντες τὸν Χριστὸν μετὰ τὴν σάρκωσιν τὴν ἐκ τῆς ἁγίας παρθένου καὶ ἐνανθρώπησιν ἐν μιᾷ ὑποστάσει καὶ ἐν ἑνὶ προσώπῳ, ἕνα Χριστόν, ἕνα Υἱόν, ἕνα Κύριον ὁμολογοῦμεν· καὶ μίαν μὲν τοῦ Θεοῦ Λόγου φύσιν, σεσαρκωμένην μέντοι καὶ ἐνανθρω-πήσασαν, λέγειν οὐκ ἀρνούμεθα διὰ τὸ ἐξ ἀμφοῖν ἕνα καὶ τὸν αὐτὸν εἶναι τὸν Κύριον ἡμῶν Ἰησοῦν τὸν Χριστόν. Τοὺς δὲ δύο υἱοὺς ἢ δύο ὑποστάσεις ἢ δύο πρόσωπα καταγγέλλοντας, ἀλλ᾽ οὐχὶ ἕνα καὶ τὸν αὐτὸν Κύριον Ἰησοῦν Χριστόν, τὸν Υἱὸν τοῦ Θεοῦ τοῦ ζῶντος, κηρύτ-τοντας ἀναθεματίζομεν καὶ ἀλλοτρίους εἶναι τῆς ἐκκλησίας κρίνομεν.

113. ὁμοούσιον . . . ἡμῖν. We have already noticed Eutyches hesita-tion on this point (see pp. 159 f.). It was probably due to a misunder-standing of two passages in Athanasius, (a) ad Serap. ii. 3, where, in reference to the Nature of the Son, he asserts his co-essentiality with the Father but not with creatures; (b) De Sent. Dion. 10, where he distinguishes the Divine nature co-essential with the Father, and the Human nature diverse in essence from the Father.

The more usual phrase was " co-essential with Mary " or " with His Mother " ; so Flavian, as cited in the last note, and Leo, Epist. xxxi ad Pulch. Eutyches in the Home Synod confessed Christ to be " from the flesh of the Virgin, and that He was Perfect Man " ; and again, " I confess that the holy Virgin is co-essential with us, and that our God was incarnate of her " ; upon which Basil of Seleucia remarked, " If the mother is co-essential with us, He is also, for He was called the Son of Man " (Mansi, vii. 747).

ὁμοούσιον ἡμῖν was no doubt at first an anti-Apollinarian watch-word adopted by some Catholics as a useful guard against the notion of any conversion of the Godhead into flesh, or non-human origin of Christ's Body. It was not brought into general use until its employment by the Chalcedonian Council in this passage (see Newman's note, Athan. Orations, *Library of the Fathers*, p. 168).

114. κατὰ πάντα ὅμοιον ἡμῖν χωρὶς ἁμαρτίας. This phrase is equivalent to Rom. viii. 3, ἐν ὁμοιώματι σαρκὸς ἁμαρτίας. Our Lord took *perfect* Manhood, not *fallen* manhood. His was not " flesh of sin," but like it in every respect, except its sinfulness. Cf. the similar language of the longer Epiphanian Creed : ἐναν-θρωπήσαντα, τουτέστι τέλειον ἄνθρωπον λαβόντα, ψυχὴν καὶ σῶμα καὶ νοῦν καὶ πάντα, εἴ τι ἐστὶν ἄνθρωπος χωρὶς ἁμαρτίας. Cf. Heb. iv. 15 with Westcott's notes.

¹ This is the form in which the words were afterwards cited (see Bright, *St. Leo*, p. 241), and is probably what Flavian wrote. If so, it would account for ἐκ δύο φύσεων appearing in the first draft of the *Definitio*. The ordinary Greek Text, both here (ἐν) and in the revised *Definitio* (ἐκ), is thus the result of two mistaken attempts at emendation, the true text of both passages having been interchanged.

118. ἐν δύο φύσεσιν. So Evagr. ii. 4, Euthymius ap. Mansi, vii. 776, and the Latin versions (*in duabus naturis*); and it is undoubtedly the right reading, although the Greek text of the Acts gives ἐκ δύο φύσεων. The very point of the Roman legates' objection to the first draft of the *Definitio* was that its ἐκ δύο φύσεων was ambiguous and must be altered (Mansi, vii. 105). Routh conjectured that both phrases were admitted into the text ἐκ δύο φύσεων καὶ ἐν δύο φύσεσιν (Opusc. ii. 119), but this is not probable. Vincent of Lerins also has *ex duabus substantiis*, Common. 12.

The phrase "In Two Natures" was misunderstood by the Armenians as favouring Nestorianism, for the translator unfortunately used an Armenian word, in rendering "the one" and "the other" Nature of Christ, which could in that language be applied only to *persons*, not to *things*. Political disturbances had prevented the Armenian bishops from being present at the Council, just as for the same reasons they had been absent from Ephesus in 431, though they loyally accepted the Ephesine decrees. Consequently, the Armenian Church never received the Council of Chalcedon as an orthodox synod, and even took the extreme step in 491 of anathematising its decrees. To this day the Armenian Church remains separated from the Orthodox Churches of the East, although the difference between them is one rather of expression than of doctrine. The Armenians hold that the Divine and Human Natures are united in Christ; and this doctrine is formulated in the phrase "One United Nature," and is publicly professed by every Armenian cleric at his ordination. The doctrine is that of an *Unconfused* Union, not the *confused* union of Monophysitism. They profess the Perfection of the Two Natures, and do not admit either a Eutychian absorption or a Monophysite mixture or fusion. Cf. a valuable note in Bright's *Waymarks in Church History*, p. 399.

One may conveniently at this point add that while Eutychianism proper asserted the entire absorption of the Human Nature by the Divine, it was modified after Chalcedon so as to assert one compound nature, neither wholly Divine nor wholly human. This was Monophysitism. Still later, in the seventh century, the controversy assumed another guise, the Monophysites proceeding to the logical consequence of their belief, and denying Two Wills in Christ corresponding to His Two Natures. To exclude this Monothelite heresy the Sixth General Council at Constantinople in 681 found it necessary to insert in its *Definitio Fidei* the affirmation of δύο φυσικὰ θελήματα and δύο φυσικαὶ ἐνέργειαι in Christ. See below in Appendix, p. 205. Cf. Hooker, E.P. v. 48. 9. On the history of this subject and its later developments see Ottley, *The Doctrine of the Incarnation*, ii, pp. 113 ff.

On the oft-quoted phrase of the human mind in Christ being indeed present but swallowed up in the Divine "like a drop of vinegar in the ocean" which occurs first in Gregory of Nyssa (ad Theoph. 3), see Raven, *Apollinarianism*, p. 182.

119. ἀσυγχύτως. This teaching was practically that of Tertullian adv. Prax. 27. See also Athan. c. Apoll. i. 10, where he urges a real but unconfused union between the Word and the flesh that He made His own.

ἀσυγχύτως and ἀτρέπτως are directed against the Apollinarian and Eutychian heresies, and exclude the notion of any intermingling of the Natures or alteration of their distinct properties : ἀδιαιρέτως and ἀχωρίστως against the Nestorian, and exclude any division of person or separation of the once-for-all united Natures. Compare the words put into the mouth of the celebrant, as he holds the Sacred Elements in his hands, in the Liturgy of the Coptic Jacobites (Brightman, p. 185), " I believe that this is the quickening flesh which Thine Only begotten Son our Lord and our God and our Saviour Jesus Christ took of the Lady of us all, the holy Theotokos Saint Mary : He made it one with His Godhead without confusion and without mixture and without alteration . . . I verily believe that His Godhead was not severed from His Manhood for one moment, nor for the twinkling of an eye." And the emphatic statement of our Second Article (taken from Art. III of the Augsburg Confession), " ita ut duae naturae divina et humana integre atque perfecte in unitate personae fuerint inseparabiliter coniunctae." And the well-known passage in Hooker (v. 54. 10), who sums up the Christological work of the first four Councils in the words ἀληθῶς (" truly God "), τελέως (" perfectly Man "), ἀδιαιρέτως (" indivisibly of Both One "), ἀσυγχύτως (" distinctly in that One Both ").

119. οὐδαμοῦ τῆς τ. φύσ. διαφορᾶς, κ.τ.λ. See the note on Epist. 2 ad Nest., p. 101.

126. Τούτων τοίνυν κ.τ.λ. This section merely re-enacts the decision of the Council of Ephesus in 431 canon 7 ; ἑτέρα πίστις meaning here, as there, any other Creed than the Nicene. No doubt the decisions of Ephesus and Chalcedon on this point were regarded as disciplinary rather than doctrinal. It is individual action in composing a different creed that is forbidden. On this question see an interesting article in The Church Quarterly Review, vol. iii, p. 422. On the other hand, Dr. Badcock wrote to the present editor, " I have little doubt that the Alexandrian Council of Ephesus intended to condemn the Constantinopolitan additions to the Creed of Nicaea; but the Constantinopolitan Council of Chalcedon accepted the two Creeds as being one." Certain it is that in the Western Church the Nicene symbol has never displaced the baptismal formularies which more or less approximated to the form known as the Apostles' Creed (Swainson, pp. 22 f.). Further, the original text of the Nicene Creed, when used in Western liturgies, has been supplanted by the longer Creed " of the 150," and even that has been supplemented by the unauthorised " Filioque." Before reading

the Appendix to the Definition of Chalcedon printed in the next Section it is interesting to insert the judgment on the Council of a recent Catholic historian. He remarks that the Definition corresponded only imperfectly with the convictions of the majority. The Monophysite party may be said to have inaugurated at Chalcedon the attitude they were henceforward to adopt concerning Eutyches' protest against the doctrine of two natures as expressed in the Tome (Duchesne, *Ancient History of the Church*, vol. iii, pp. 316 ff. Cf. Bright, *Canons*, p. 243 and Dorner, op. cit., i. 11, p. 195).

APPENDIX

TO

THE CHALCEDONIAN DEFINITION

APPENDIX TO
THE CHALCEDONIAN DEFINITION

The progress of events from the Fifth General Council to the Sixth may be briefly sketched. Soon after the victory of Alexandrine theology at Constantinople, which has been described above, of which the key word was no longer *phusis* or *hypostasis* but *energeia*, one step nearer perhaps to our modern conception ego or personality, an event happened which changed the entire situation—namely, the Mohammedan invasion in the time of the Emperor Heraclius. As so often happens, external events stimulated the efforts towards reunion, and in this case especially in Egypt, the centre of Monophysitism. The Patriarch Cyrus of Alexandria was approached for this purpose, but encountered opposition from a monk named Sophronius, who became soon afterwards Patriarch of Jerusalem. This opposition led to a reference to the Patriarch Sergius of Constantinople of the question of one *energeia* of the Incarnate (μία θεανδρική ἐνέργεια). Sergius, however, expressed himself as in substantial agreement with Cyrus, but advised against the use both of one *energeia* and of two *energeiai*; the first because it was a novelty, and the second as necessarily involving two wills, and therefore amounting to a reversal of Chalcedon in a Nestorian direction. Fearing, however, the continued opposition of Sophronius, now Patriarch of Jerusalem, he submitted the whole matter to Pope Honorius, who decided in favour of a formula, of which the keynote was *una operatio* rather than *unius operatio*. In other words, our Lord being One Person possessed one will which was exercised in two modes of operation, just as we have already seen in the previous controversies it was maintained that the one hypostasis of the Incarnate Christ acted both humanly and divinely. Honorius' statement was, in fact, a reassertion of the position of Cyril of Alexandria. At this stage of the controversy the theologian Marius greatly cleared the air by reasserting the *totus in suis, totus in nostris* of Leo's Tome. Unfortunately the Emperor, who took the Monothelite side, resorted to persecution, and Pope Martin the First and Marius himself died like Nestorius in cruel exile. In 678 the Emperor Constantine Pogonatus, " the bearded," ended the controversy by entering into negotiation with the new Pope Domnus with a view to securing a general council, which assembled in Constantinople in the year 680. Like the Council of Chalcedon, it was preceded by an Encyclical Letter from the next Pope Agatho, who had in the meantime succeeded Domnus. In this he affirmed two wills and two *energeiai*, as well as two natures in the Incarnate.

This council condemned Cyril, Sergius, and Honorius, and in the definition which it issued : (1) agreed with the five General Councils preceding, (2) re-affirmed acceptance of both the Nicene and Constantinopolitan Creeds, (3) issued its own definition of the Faith about Jesus Christ, which is printed below.

Thus ends the conciliar or oecumenical period of Church history, which passes thereafter in its Greek form into the body contained in the system of St. John of Damascus, " Concerning the Orthodox Faith "; and in the West under the growing influence of the great work of Dionysius the Areopagite, into scholasticism ; not, however, without an intervening period of revived interest in the *humanity* of our Lord. This was known as " adoptionism," a controversy in which the English theologian Alcuin took a leading part, but without any lasting influence upon Christology until modern times. For the last see Ottley, *Doctrine of the Incarnation*, vol. ii, pp. 151 ff. ; and on the whole question see Du Bose, *Oecumenical Councils*, whose views upon the position of Pope Honorius must, however, be read with caution.

THE DEFINITIO FIDEI OF THE SIXTH
GENERAL COUNCIL AT CONSTANTINOPLE
A.D. 681

Mansi, xi. 636 ; Hahn, p. 172.

ἙΠΟΜΕΝΗ (ἁγία καὶ οἰκουμενικὴ σύνοδος) ταῖς τε ἁγίαις καὶ
οἰκουμενικαῖς πέντε συνόδοις καὶ τοῖς ἁγίοις καὶ ἐκκρίτοις πατράσι καὶ
συμφώνως ὁρίζουσα ὁμολογεῖν τὸν Κύριον ἡμῶν Ἰησοῦν Χριστόν, τὸν
ἀληθινὸν Θεὸν ἡμῶν, τὸν ἕνα τῆς ἁγίας ὁμοουσίου καὶ ζωαρχικῆς
τριάδος, τέλειον ἐν θεότητι καὶ τέλειον τὸν αὐτὸν ἐν ἀνθρωπότητι,
Θεὸν ἀληθῶς καὶ ἄνθρωπον ἀληθῶς αὐτόν, ἐκ ψυχῆς λογικῆς καὶ
σώματος, ὁμοούσιον τῷ Πατρὶ κατὰ τὴν θεότητα καὶ ὁμοούσιον ἡμῖν
τὸν αὐτὸν κατὰ τὴν ἀνθρωπότητα, κατὰ πάντα ὅμοιον ἡμῖν χωρὶς
ἁμαρτίας· τὸν πρὸ αἰώνων μὲν ἐκ τοῦ Πατρὸς γεννηθέντα κατὰ τὴν
θεότητα, ἐπ' ἐσχάτων δὲ τῶν ἡμερῶν τὸν αὐτὸν δι' ἡμᾶς καὶ διὰ τὴν
ἡμετέραν σωτηρίαν ἐκ Πνεύματος Ἁγίου καὶ Μαρίας τῆς παρθένου,
τῆς κυρίως καὶ κατὰ ἀλήθειαν θεοτόκου, κατὰ τὴν ἀνθρωπότητα, ἕνα
καὶ τὸν αὐτὸν Χριστόν, Υἱόν, Κύριον, μονογενῆ, ἐν δύο φύσεσιν
ἀσυγχύτως, ἀτρέπτως, ἀχωρίστως, ἀδιαιρέτως γνωριζόμενον· οὐδαμοῦ
τῆς τῶν φύσεων διαφορᾶς ἀνῃρημένης διὰ τὴν ἕνωσιν, σωζομένης δὲ
μᾶλλον τῆς ἰδιότητος ἑκατέρας φύσεως καὶ εἰς ἓν πρόσωπον καὶ μίαν
ὑπόστασιν συντρεχούσης, οὐκ εἰς δύο πρόσωπα μεριζόμενον ἢ διαιρού-
μενον, ἀλλ' ἕνα καὶ τὸν αὐτὸν Υἱὸν μονογενῆ, Θεοῦ Λόγον, Κύριον
Ἰησοῦν Χριστόν, καθάπερ ἄνωθεν οἱ προφῆται περὶ αὐτοῦ καὶ αὐτὸς
ἡμᾶς Ἰησοῦς ὁ Χριστὸς ἐξεπαίδευσε καὶ τὸ τῶν ἁγίων πατέρων ἡμῖν
παραδέδωκε σύμβολον. Καὶ δύο φυσικὰς θελήσεις ἤτοι θελήματα ἐν
αὐτῷ καὶ δύο φυσικὰς ἐνεργείας ἀδιαιρέτως, ἀτρέπτως, ἀμερίστως,
ἀσυγχύτως κατὰ τὴν τῶν ἁγίων πατέρων διδασκαλίαν ὡσαύτως κηρύτ-
τομεν· καὶ δύο μὲν φυσικὰ θελήματα οὐχ ὑπεναντία, μὴ γένοιτο, καθὼς
οἱ ἀσεβεῖς ἔφησαν αἱρετικοί, ἀλλ' ἑπόμενον τὸ ἀνθρώπινον αὐτοῦ
θέλημα, καὶ μὴ ἀντιπίπτον ἢ ἀντιπαλαῖον, μᾶλλον μὲν οὖν καὶ ὑποτασ-
σόμενον τῷ θείῳ αὐτοῦ καὶ πανσθενεῖ θελήματι· ἔδει γὰρ τὸ τῆς
σαρκὸς θέλημα κινηθῆναι, ὑποταγῆναι δὲ τῷ θελήματι τῷ θεϊκῷ κατὰ
τὸν πάνσοφον Ἀθανάσιον. Ὥσπερ γὰρ ἡ αὐτοῦ σὰρξ σὰρξ τοῦ Θεοῦ
Λόγου λέγεται καὶ ἔστιν, οὕτω καὶ τὸ φυσικὸν τῆς σαρκὸς αὐτοῦ
θέλημα ἴδιον τοῦ Θεοῦ Λόγου λέγεται καὶ ἔστι, καθά φησιν αὐτός.
ὅτι καταβέβηκα ἐκ τοῦ οὐρανοῦ, οὐχ ἵνα ποιῶ τὸ θέλημα τὸ ἐμόν, ἀλλὰ
τὸ θέλημα τοῦ πέμψαντός με Πατρός, ἴδιον λέγων θέλημα αὐτοῦ· τὸ
τῆς σαρκός, ἐπεὶ καὶ ἡ σὰρξ ἰδία αὐτοῦ γέγονεν· ὃν γὰρ τρόπον ἡ
παναγία καὶ ἄμωμος ἐψυχωμένη αὐτοῦ σὰρξ θεωθεῖσα οὐκ ἀνῃρέθη,
ἀλλ' ἐν τῷ ἰδίῳ αὐτῆς ὅρῳ τε καὶ λόγῳ διέμεινεν, οὕτω καὶ τὸ ἀνθρώπινον αὐτοῦ θέλημα θεωθὲν οὐκ ἀνῃρέθη, σέσωσται δὲ μᾶλλον κατὰ τὸν
θεολόγον Γρηγόριον λέγοντα· τὸ γὰρ ἐκείνου θέλειν, τὸ κατὰ τὸν
σωτῆρα νοούμενον, οὐδὲ ὑπεναντίον θεῷ θεωθὲν ὅλον. δύο δὲ φυσικὰς

ἐνεργείας ἀδιαιρέτως, ἀτρέπτως, ἀμερίστως, ἀσυγχύτως ἐν αὐτῷ τῷ
Κυρίῳ ἡμῶν Ἰησοῦ Χριστῷ, τῷ ἀληθινῷ Θεῷ ἡμῶν δοξάζομεν,
τουτέστι θείαν ἐνέργειαν καὶ ἀνθρωπίνην ἐνέργειαν, κατὰ τὸν θεηγόρον
Λέοντα τρανέστατα φάσκοντα· ἐνεργεῖ γὰρ ἑκατέρα μορφὴ μετὰ τῆς
θατέρου κοινωνίας ὅπερ ἴδιον ἔσχηκε, τοῦ μὲν Λόγου κατεργαζομένου
τοῦτο, ὅπερ ἐστὶ τοῦ Λόγου, τοῦ δὲ σώματος ἐκτελοῦντος ἅπερ ἐστὶ
τοῦ σώματος. οὐ γὰρ δήπου μίαν δώσομεν φυσικὴν τὴν ἐνέργειαν
Θεοῦ καὶ ποιήματος, ἵνα μήτε τὸ ποιηθὲν εἰς τὴν θείαν ἀναγάγωμεν
οὐσίαν μήτε μὴν τῆς θείας φύσεως τὸ ἐξαίρετον εἰς τὸν τοῖς γεννητοῖς
πρέποντα καταγάγωμεν τόπον· ἑνὸς γὰρ καὶ τοῦ αὐτοῦ τά τε θαύματα
καὶ τὰ πάθη γινώσκομεν κατ᾽ ἄλλο καὶ ἄλλο τῶν, ἐξ ὧν ἐστι, φύσεων,
καὶ ἐν αἷς τὸ εἶναι ἔχει, ὡς ὁ θεσπέσιος ἔφησε Κύριλλος. Πάντοθεν
γοῦν τὸ ἀσύγχυτον καὶ ἀδιαίρετον φυλάττοντες συντόμῳ φωνῇ τὸ πᾶν
ἐξαγγέλλομεν· ἕνα τῆς ἁγίας τριάδος καὶ μετὰ σάρκωσιν τὸν Κύριον
ἡμῶν Ἰησοῦν Χριστόν, τὸν ἀληθινὸν Θεὸν ἡμῶν, εἶναι πιστεύοντές
φαμεν δύο αὐτοῦ τὰς φύσεις ἐν τῇ μιᾷ αὐτοῦ διαλαμπούσας ὑποστάσει,
ἐν ᾗ τά τε θαύματα καὶ τὰ παθήματα δι᾽ ὅλης αὐτοῦ τῆς οἰκονομικῆς
ἀναστροφῆς οὐ κατὰ φαντασίαν, ἀλλὰ ἀληθῶς ἐπεδείξατο, τῆς φυσικῆς
ἐν αὐτῇ τῇ μιᾷ ὑποστάσει διαφορᾶς γνωριζομένης τῷ μετὰ τῆς
θατέρου κοινωνίας ἑκατέραν φύσιν θέλειν τε καὶ ἐνεργεῖν τὰ ἴδια· καθ᾽
ὃν δὴ λόγον καὶ δύο φυσικὰ θελήματά τε καὶ ἐνεργείας δοξάζομεν πρὸς
σωτηρίαν τοῦ ἀνθρωπίνου γένους καταλλήλως συντρέχοντα. Τούτων
τοίνυν μετὰ πάσης πανταχόθεν ἀκριβείας τε καὶ ἐμμελείας παρ᾽ ἡμῶν
διατυπωθέντων ὁρίζομεν ἑτέραν πίστιν μηδενὶ ἐξεῖναι προφέρειν, ἤγουν
συγγράφειν ἢ συντιθέναι ἢ φρονεῖν ἢ διδάσκειν ἑτέρως. Τοὺς δὲ
τολμῶντας ἢ συντιθέναι πίστιν ἑτέραν ἢ προκομίζειν ἢ διδάσκειν, ἢ
παραδιδόναι ἕτερον σύμβολον τοῖς ἐθέλουσιν ἐπιστρέφειν εἰς ἐπίγνωσιν
τῆς ἀληθείας ἐξ Ἑλληνισμοῦ ἢ ἐξ Ἰουδαϊσμοῦ ἢ γοῦν ἐξ αἱρέσεως οἵας
οὖν, ἢ καινοφωνίαν ἤτοι λέξεως ἐφεύρεσιν πρὸς ἀνατροπὴν εἰσάγειν
τῶν νυνὶ παρ᾽ ἡμῶν διορισθέντων, τούτους, εἰ μὲν ἐπίσκοποι εἶεν ἢ
κληρικοί, ἀλλοτρίους εἶναι τοὺς ἐπισκόπους τῆς ἐπισκοπῆς καὶ τοὺς
κληρικοὺς τοῦ κλήρου, εἰ δὲ μονάζοντες εἶεν ἢ λαϊκοί, ἀναθεματίζεσθαι
αὐτούς.

TRANSLATIONS

THE EPISTLES OF CYRIL
THE TOME OF LEO
THE CHALCEDONIAN DEFINITION OF THE FAITH

THE SECOND EPISTLE OF CYRIL TO NESTORIUS

Cyril to the Most Reverend and God-beloved Fellow-Minister Nestorius, greeting in the Lord.

Certain persons, as I am informed, are, to the detriment of my character, gossiping to thy Piety, and this incessantly, making a special point of attending the gatherings of officials ; and, thinking perhaps to bring not altogether unwelcome news to thy ears, they make groundless statements, for they have by no means suffered any injustice, but were quite rightly convicted—one, for having treated the blind and the poor with injustice ; another, for having drawn sword against his mother ; and the third, for having been associated along with a maidservant in a theft of money, besides bearing generally a permanent character of a kind that one would not like to attach even to one's bitterest enemy. But what such people say is not a matter of much moment to me, who may not exaggerate my littleness above my Master and Teacher, nor yet above the Fathers. For it is not possible to escape the mischievous attacks of the wicked however one may order one's life. But those men, " whose mouth is full of cursing and bitterness," will render their account to the Judge of all. I will turn on the other hand to what more especially becomes my position, and will put thee in mind even now, as a brother in Christ, to make thy method of teaching and thy mental attitude towards the faith free from all danger to the people, and to bear in mind that " to offend " even only " one of the little ones that believe " in Christ is a ground for the intolerable displeasure (of God). But when the number of those aggrieved is very great we surely stand in need of all possible skill, both prudently to remove the offence and to extend the wholesome doctrine of the faith to those who seek the truth ; and this we shall do most properly by being zealous to hold in high esteem the words of the holy Fathers when we light upon them, and, " proving ourselves (as it is written) to see whether we are in the faith," by fashioning right well our own conceptions according to their safe and impregnable opinions.

Now the holy and great Synod (of Nicaea) said that the Only-begotten Son Himself, by nature begotten from God even the Father, Very God from Very God, Light from Light, through whom the Father made all things, came down, was incarnate, lived as Man, suffered, rose the third day, and ascended into heaven. These words and doctrines it behoves us to follow, recognising what is meant by the Word who is from God being incarnate, and living as

Man. For we do not say that the Nature of the Word was changed and became flesh, nor that He was transformed into a complete human being, I mean one of soul and body; but this rather, that the Word, having united to Himself in His Own Hypostasis, in an ineffable and inconceivable manner, flesh animated with a rational soul, became Man, and was called Son of Man; not being united merely as a result of will or good pleasure, nor yet by His assumption of a single (human) person; and that while the Natures which were brought together into this genuine unity were different, yet of them both is the One Christ and Son, not as though the difference of the Natures was abolished by the union, but rather the Godhead and the Manhood, by their ineffable and unspeakable consilience into unity, perfected for us the One Lord and Christ and Son. And thus, although He had His existence and was begotten from the Father before the ages, He is spoken of as begotten also after the flesh from a woman; not as though His Divine Nature received its beginning of existence in the holy Virgin, nor yet as though a second generation were necessarily wanting for its own sake after that from the Father, for it is altogether ridiculous and stupid to say that He, who existed before every aeon and is co-eternal with the Father, had need of a second beginning of existence. But when for our sakes and for our salvation the Word, having united humanity to Himself hypostatically, came forth from a woman, He is for this reason said to have been born after the flesh. For it was not an ordinary man, who was first born of the holy Virgin, and upon whom afterwards the Word descended, but Himself, united to humanity from the womb itself, is said to have undergone fleshly birth, as making His own the birth of His own flesh. Thus we say that He both suffered and rose again; not meaning that the Word of God, in His own proper (Divine) Nature, suffered either stripes or the piercing of the nails or any other wounds at all; for the Divinity is impassible because it is also incorporeal. But when that which was made His own body suffered, He Himself is said to suffer these things for us: for the Impassible was in the suffering body.

After the same manner, too, we conceive of His dying. For the Word of God is by nature immortal and incorruptible and life and life-giving; but when His own body " by the grace of God tasted death for every man " (as Paul saith), He Himself is said to have suffered death for us; not meaning that He experienced death at all in so far as touches His (Divine) Nature—for it were sheer madness to say or think that—but that His flesh tasted death, as I have just said.

Thus again, too, when His flesh was raised, the resurrection is spoken of as His; not meaning that He fell into corruption, certainly not, but that it was His body that was again raised.

Thus we acknowledge One Christ and Lord; not worshipping a man along with the Word, lest a semblance of division might secretly creep in through the use of the words " along with," but worshipping One and the Same (Lord), because the Word's body wherein He shares the Father's throne is not alien to Himself; in this case again not meaning that there are two Sons in co-session, but One (Son), by reason of His union with His flesh. But if we reject this Hypostatic Union as impossible or as unseemly, we fall into saying " two Sons," and then there will be every necessity for drawing a distinction, and for speaking of the one as properly a man honoured with the title of " Son," and again of the other as properly the Word of God, having naturally the name and possession of Sonship.

Accordingly we must not divide into two Sons the One Lord Jesus Christ; for it will in no way assist the right expression of the faith so to do, even though some promise to admit a Unity of Prosopa. For the Scripture hath not declared that the Word united to Himself a man's person, but that He hath become Flesh. Now the Word becoming Flesh is nothing else but that " He partook of blood and flesh like us," and made His own a body which was taken (from us), and came forth a man from a woman; not laying aside His being God and His generation from God the Father, but even in His assumption of flesh remaining what He was.

This (teaching) the statement of the correct faith everywhere sets forth. Thus we shall find the holy Fathers have been minded. Accordingly, they confidently called the holy Virgin Theotokos; not meaning that the Nature of the Word or His Godhead received its beginning from the holy Virgin, but that, inasmuch as His rationally animated body to which the Word was hypostatically united was born of her, He is said to have been born after the flesh.

I have thus written to thee out of the love which I have in Christ, and I beseech thee as a brother and " charge thee before Christ and the elect angels " thus to think and teach with us, that the peace of the Churches may be preserved, and the bond of unanimity and love between the priests of God may remain unbroken.

THE THIRD (SYNODICAL) EPISTLE OF
CYRIL TO NESTORIUS

Cyril and the Synod assembled in Alexandria from the Egyptian diocese, to the Most Reverend and Pious Fellow-Minister Nestorius, greeting in the Lord.

Whereas our Saviour plainly said, " He that loveth father or mother more than Me is not worthy of Me, and he that loveth son or daughter more than Me is not worthy of Me," what must we feel who are expected by thy Reverence to love thee more than Christ our common Saviour ? Who will be able to aid us in the day of judgment ? Or what defence shall we invent for thus preserving silence for so long in the face of the blasphemies uttered against Him by thee ? And if thou wast injuring thyself only by holding and teaching such things the matter would be of less consequence, but when the whole Church is scandalised and thou hast cast the leaven of thy unwonted and strange heresy amongst the laity—and not only amongst the laity in thy own city, but also in all other places, for the books containing thy expositions are widely circulated —what reason can any longer be given for our silence, or for our forgetfulness of Christ's words, " Think not that I came to send peace upon the earth : I came not to send peace, but a sword. For I came to set a man against his father, and a daughter against her mother " ? For when the faith is wronged, away with filial reverence as inexpedient and precarious ; the law of parental and fraternal affection must be abjured ; nay, death must be counted as better than life to the godly, " that they may obtain a better resurrection," as it is written.

Now therefore, in harmony with the holy Synod which was assembled in great Rome under the presidency of our most holy and pious brother and fellow-minister Bishop Caelestine, we earnestly conjure thee in this our Third Letter, and counsel thee to desist from those doctrines so mischievous and perverse which thou both holdest and teachest, and to choose instead the right faith which was delivered to the Churches from the beginning through the holy apostles and evangelists who were " eye-witnesses and ministers of the Word " ; else, if thy Reverence will not do this within the time appointed in the letters of the said most holy and pious bishop, our fellow-minister of the Church of the Romans, Caelestine, know that thou thyself hast no lot with us, nor place or rank amongst the priests and bishops of God. For it is not possible for us to overlook Churches thus disturbed and laity scandalised and the right faith set at naught and the flock scattered by thee who ought to preserve it, even though thou wert like ourselves a lover of right doctrine following the pious steps of the holy Fathers. Moreover, we are all in communion with every one of those who have been excommunicated by thy Reverence on account of the faith, or deposed, both laics and clerics. For it is not just that those who have known how to think aright should be treated unjustly by thy decrees, because they have done well and have spoken in opposition to thee. For this very point hast thou notified in the letter written by thee to Caelestine our most holy fellow-bishop of great Rome.

Now it will not be sufficient for thy Reverence simply to agree to the symbol of the faith which was put forth in its time by the Holy Spirit by the hand of the great and holy Synod duly assembled in the city of the Nicaeans ; for thou hast not rightly understood and interpreted it, but perversely rather, although thou confessest its words with thy mouth. It is more fitting that thou confess in writing and on oath that thou anathematisest thy foul and profane doctrines, and that thou wilt hold and teach what we all do, bishops and teachers and leaders of the laity throughout the West and East. Moreover, both the holy Synod at Rome and all of us have assented, as being orthodox and irreproachable, to the letters written to thy Reverence by the Church of the Alexandrians. And we have appended to this our Letter the things which it is necessary to hold and teach and what it is beseeming to reject.

For this is the Faith of the Catholic and Apostolic Church, in the approval of which all the orthodox bishops throughout the West and East unite :

> We believe in One God the Father All Sovereign, Maker of all things visible and invisible ;
> And in One Lord Jesus Christ, the Son of God, begotten from the Father, Only-begotten, that is From the Essence of the Father, God from God, Light from Light, Very God from Very God, Begotten not made, co-essential with the Father ; through whom all things were made both in heaven and in earth ; who for us men and for our salvation came down and was incarnate and lived as Man ; suffered, and rose the third day ; ascended into heaven ; cometh to judge quick and dead : And in the Holy Spirit.
> But those who say " Once He was not," and " Before He was begotten He was not," and that " He was made out of nothing," or who affirm that " the Son of God is of a different Hypostasis or Substance," or " mutable," or " changeable "— these the Catholic and Apostolic Church anathematises.

Following in every respect the confessions of the holy Fathers which they made by the Holy Spirit speaking in them, and pursuing their line of thought and taking as it were the royal highway, we say that the Only-begotten Word of God Himself, who is begotten from the Father's very Substance, who is Very God from Very God, Light from Light, through whom all things were made both in heaven and in earth, came down for the sake of our salvation and abased Himself unto emptying and was incarnate and lived as Man; that is, He took flesh of the holy Virgin and made it His own from the womb, and underwent a birth like ourselves and came forth Man from a woman, not indeed casting off what He was, but even though He became Man by the assumption of flesh and blood He still remained God in Nature and in truth. And we do not say either that the flesh was changed into the Nature of Godhead, or indeed that the ineffable Nature of God the Word was perverted into that of flesh, for He is immutable and unalterable, ever abiding the Same, according to the Scriptures; but while visible as a babe in swaddling clothes, and yet in the bosom of the Virgin who bare Him, He was filling all creation as God, and was enthroned with Him who begat Him. For the Divinity is immeasurable and without magnitude, nor does it admit of circumscription.

Confessing then that the Word was united hypostatically to flesh, we worship One Son and Lord Jesus Christ, neither putting apart and dividing Man and God as though they were joined to one another in a union of dignity or authority, for this would be empty words and nothing else; nor again calling the Word from God " Christ " separately, and in like manner the one (born) from a woman another " christ " separately; but knowing One only Christ, the Word from God the Father, with His own flesh; for then (when He became flesh) He was anointed as Man with us, while yet it is He Himself that giveth the Spirit to those who are worthy to receive it, and that " not by measure," as saith the blessed evangelist John. Nor again do we say that the Word from God dwelt in one who was born of the holy Virgin as in an ordinary man, lest Christ should be thought of as a man carrying God (within him). For though " the Word did tabernacle amongst us," and it is also said that in Christ there dwelt " all the fulness of the Godhead bodily," yet we understand that when He became Flesh the indwelling is not to be defined as existing in Him after the same mode that there is said to be an indwelling in the saints, but being united as to Nature and not turned into flesh He effected such an indwelling as the soul of man may be said to have in its own body.

There is therefore One Christ and Son and Lord, not as though a man were joined with God in a unity of dignity or authority, for equality of honour does not unite natures, as for instance in the case of Peter and John, who are equal in honour with one another, inasmuch as they are apostles and holy disciples, yet the two are not one; nor again do we understand the mode of the conjunction to be that of juxtaposition, for this is inadequate to express a union of natures; nor again of acquired participation, such as that whereby we, " being joined to the Lord," are (as it is written) " one spirit " with Him. Indeed, we reject the term " conjunction " as not sufficiently expressive of the " union." Nor again do we call the Word from God the Father the God or Lord of Christ, lest we should again manifestly sever into two the One Christ and Son and Lord, and fall under the charge of blasphemy by making Him God and Lord of Himself. For the Word of God, hypostatically united to flesh, as we have already said, is God of the universe and Lord of all. He is neither His own servant nor His own Lord; for it were folly or rather positive impiety so to think or say. He did, indeed, say that God was His own Father, while yet being God by Nature and from the substance of the Father, but we are not ignorant that along with His being God He also became Man and was under God, according at least to the law which is becoming to the nature of humanity. But how could He become the God or Lord of Himself? Therefore, as Man and as far as pertains to what befits the measures of His emptying, He says that He is under God along with us. So He became also " under law," while yet as God He Himself spake the Law and is originally the Law-giver.

We refuse to say of Christ, " I reverence him that was borne on account of the Bearer : for the sake of Him who is invisible I worship him who is seen." It is, moreover, horrible to say, " He that is assumed is styled God along with Him who assumed him." For he who thus speaks makes again two separate Christs, and sets a man on one side apart by himself, and God similarly. For such a one confessedly denies the union, according to which He is not worshipped as one person with another, nor does He share the style of God, but One Christ Jesus is conceived of, the Only-begotten Son, honoured with one worship along with His own flesh.

Now we confess that He Himself, the Son begotten from God the Father, and God Only-begotten, while yet in His own Nature impassible, suffered in the flesh for us according to the Scriptures, and was in His crucified body impassibly making His own the sufferings of His own flesh ; for " by the grace of God He tasted death for every man," yielding His own body to it, while yet by Nature He was " Life " and Himself " the Resurrection." For having trampled upon death in His ineffable might, it was in order that He might in His own flesh become " the first-begotten from the dead " and " the firstfruits of them that slept," and open a way for the nature of man to return to incorruption, that " by the grace of God He tasted death for every man," as we just said, and returned to life again on the third day, having spoiled Hades. So that even if it be said, " By man came the resurrection of the dead," yet we understand that " man " to be the Word begotten from God, and that through Him has the might of death been destroyed. And He will come in due season as One Son and Lord in the glory of the Father " to judge the world in righteousness," as it is written.

And we must add this also. Proclaiming the death in the flesh of the Only-begotten Son of God, that is, of Jesus Christ, and confessing His return to life from the dead and His ascension into heaven, we celebrate the bloodless service in the Churches, and we thus approach the sacramental gifts and are sanctified, being partakers both of the holy flesh and of the precious blood of Christ the Saviour of us all ; not receiving it as common flesh—surely not !—nor as the flesh of a man sanctified and associated with the Word in a unity of dignity, or at least as having a Divine indwelling, but as truly life-giving, and as the Word's very own. For being naturally Life as God, when He became One with His own flesh He rendered [1] it life-giving. So that although He says to us, " Verily, verily, I say unto you, Except ye eat the flesh of the Son of Man and drink His blood " ; yet we shall not reckon it to be the flesh of a man like one of ourselves—for how could the flesh of a man be life-giving in its own nature ?—but as having become truly the own flesh of Him who for our sakes both became and was called Son of Man.

Again, we do not assign the sayings of our Saviour in the Gospels to two several hypostases or two several persons. For the One and Only Christ is not twofold, although He is understood as constituted out of two different elements into an inseparable unity ; just as man also is understood to consist of soul and body, and yet is not twofold, but one out of both. But if we think aright we shall hold that both the human sayings and the Divine were spoken by One Person. For when He says, appropriately to His Divine Nature, " He that hath seen Me hath seen the Father," and " I and the Father are One," we recognise His Divine and ineffable Nature, according to which He is One with His own Father because of the identity of Substance, being His " Image " and " Expression " and " the Effulgence of His Glory." But when, not despising the limita- tion involved in His Humanity, He says to the Jews, " Now ye seek Me, a man who hath spoken to you the truth," again we no less fully know Him, even from the limitations of His Humanity, as God the Word in equality and likeness of His Father. For if it is necessary to believe that, being God by Nature, He became Flesh, that is, Man endowed with a rational soul, what reason could one have for feeling ashamed of certain sayings of His being such as befit His Humanity ? For if He were to decline to use the words which befit Him as Man, who compelled Him to become Man like ourselves ? Why should He, who for our sakes humbled Himself unto a voluntary Self-emptying, decline to use words befitting that Self-emptying ? To One Person then undoubtedly must be attributed all the say- ings in the Gospel, namely, to the One Hypostasis Incarnate of the Word. For " there is One Lord Jesus Christ," according to the Scriptures.

And if He is called also " the Apostle and High-priest of our confession," as being the priestly minister to God the Father of the confession of faith which is offered on our part to Him, and through Him to God the Father, and moreover also to the Holy Spirit, again we say that He is by Nature the Only-begotten Son of God, and we do not attribute to a man other than He either the

[1] For this sense of ἀποφαίνειν see Epist. ad Ioan. *ad init.* ; Lit. of Apost. Const., ὅπως ἀποφήνῃ τὸν ἄρτον τοῦτον σῶμα τοῦ Χριστοῦ (Brightman, p. 21).

name or the actuality of the priesthood. For He has become a
" Mediator between God and men " and a Reconciler for peace,
having offered Himself " for an odour of a sweet savour " to God
even the Father. Wherefore also He affirmed, " Sacrifice and offering Thou wouldest not : in whole burnt offerings and sin offerings
Thou hast no pleasure, but a body didst Thou prepare for Me. Then
said I, Lo, I am come (in the roll of the book it is written concerning
Me) to do, O God, Thy will." For He hath offered His own body
" as an odour of a sweet savour " for us, and not surely for Himself.
For what offering or sacrifice did He need for Himself, who as God
was superior to all sin ? For if " all sinned and came short of the
glory of God," inasmuch as we have become inclined to turn aside,
and the nature of man is diseased with sin—though He is not so—
and we have therefore failed of His glory, how can there be any
doubt left that the True Lamb has been slain for us men and on
our behalf ? And to say that He offered Himself both for Himself
and for us will by no means escape the charge of blasphemy. For
He hath not offended in any way nor committed sin. What offering
then was needed, when there was no sin for which it could be made
with any show of reason ?

And when He says concerning the Spirit " He shall glorify Me,"
we shall not say, if we understand it aright, that the One Christ
and Son received glory from the Holy Spirit as though He needed
a glory which was from Another ; for His Spirit is not superior to
Him and above Him. But since for the manifestation of His Godhead He used His own Spirit for majestic works, He says that He
was glorified by Him ; just as if one of us were to say concerning
his strength, for instance, or his skill in anything. " They shall
glorify me." For although the Spirit exists in His own proper
Hypostasis and inasmuch as He is Spirit and not Son, yet He is
not therefore alien from Him ; for He is named " Spirit of Truth,"
and Christ is " the Truth " ; and He is poured forth from Him
just as He is also, of course, from God the Father. Accordingly
the Spirit, even by working wonders through the hand of the holy
Apostles after the Ascension of our Lord Jesus Christ into heaven,
glorified Him. For it was believed that He must be God by Nature
when He Himself was working through His own Spirit. Wherefore
also He affirmed " He shall receive of Mine and shall announce it
to you." And we are not at all intending to say by this that the
Spirit is wise and powerful by participation ; for He is all-Perfect,
and not lacking in all (possible) good. And since He is Spirit of
the Father's Power and Wisdom, that is, of the Son, He is Wisdom
and Power in very deed.

But since the holy Virgin brought forth after the flesh God
personally united to flesh, for this reason we say that she is Theotokos ;
not as though the nature of the Word had its beginning of existence
from flesh ;—for He " was in the beginning," and " the Word was
God," and " the Word was with God," and He is Himself the Maker

P

of the ages, co-eternal with the Father, and the Creator of the whole ; but, as we have already said, since He personally united to Himself Manhood, He also underwent a fleshly birth from her womb—not that He needed either necessarily or on account of His own Nature the birth in time and in the last ages of the world ; but that He might bless the very beginning of our existence ; and that the curse on all the race which sends to death our bodies, which are from the earth, might be made to cease thenceforth by a woman bearing Him united to flesh ; and that when the sentence " In sorrow shalt thou bring forth children " was annulled by Him, the prophet's words should be shown to be true, " Death in its might swallowed [us] up, and on the other hand God wiped away every tear from every face." For, for this cause we say that He Himself in virtue of His Incarnation blessed marriage, and went when He was invited in Cana of Galilee with His holy apostles.

These doctrines we have been taught to hold by the holy apostles and evangelists and all the God-breathed Scriptures, and from the true confession of the blessed Fathers. And all these it behoves thy Reverence to agree to and maintain without any guile.

Now the points which it is necessary for thy Reverence to anathematise are appended to this our Letter.

I. If anyone confesseth not Immanuel to be God in truth and the holy Virgin on this ground to be Theotokos, since she brought forth after the flesh the Word of God who became flesh, be he anathema.

II. If anyone confesseth not that the Word who is from God the Father hath been hypostatically united to flesh, and is One Christ with His own flesh—the Same, that is to say, God and Man alike— be he anathema.

III. If anyone divideth the hypostases after the union in respect of the One Christ, connecting them by a mere association in dignity or authority or rule, and not rather by a conjunction of real union, be he anathema.

IV. If anyone assigns to two persons or hypostases the words of the evangelic or apostolic writings, which are spoken either of Christ by the saints or of Himself by Himself, and applies some to a man considered apart from the Word who is from God, and others, as God-befitting, solely to the Word from God the Father, be he anathema.

V. If anyone dares to call Christ a God-bearing man, and not rather truly God, as being One Son, and that by Nature, inasmuch as the Word has become Flesh and partaken of blood and flesh like unto us, be he anathema.

VI. If anyone says that the Word who is from God the Father is God or Lord of Christ, and does not rather confess the Self-same to be alike God and Man, the Word having become Flesh, according to the Scriptures, be he anathema.

VII. If anyone says that Jesus, as a man, was energised by God the Word and clothed with the glory of the Only-begotten, as being different from Him, be he anathema.

VIII. If anyone dares to assert that the man assumed ought to be co-worshipped with God the Word and co-glorified (with Him) and with Him styled God as if one person with another—for the continual addition of the word " with " compels one to understand this—and does not rather honour Immanuel with one worship and render to Him one doxology, inasmuch as the Word has become Flesh, be he anathema.

IX. If anyone says that the One Lord Jesus Christ was glorified by the Spirit, using the power which came through Him as if it were foreign to Himself, and that He received from Him the power of working against unclean spirits and of fulfilling divine signs and tokens, and does not rather say that the Spirit was His own, through whom also He wrought the divine signs, be he anathema.

X. The divine Scripture asserts that Christ was made " the High Priest and Apostle of our confession " ; moreover, He offered Himself for us " as an odour of sweet savour " to God even the Father. If anyone therefore says that it was not the Word Himself who is from God who was made High Priest and our Apostle when He was made flesh and man like us, but as it were another one born of a woman, considered separately from Him : or if anyone says that He offered the sacrifice for Himself also and not rather solely for our sakes—for He " who knew no sin " would have no need of a sacrifice—be he anathema.

XI. If anyone does not confess the flesh of our Lord to be life-giving and the own flesh of the Word Himself who is from God, but (regards it) as the flesh of some other than Himself conjoined to Him in dignity, or having a mere divine indwelling, and not rather life-giving, as we affirm, because it became the own flesh of the Word who hath strength to quicken all things, be he anathema.

XII. If anyone does not confess that the Word of God suffered in flesh and was crucified in flesh and " tasted of death " in flesh and became " Firstborn from the dead," inasmuch as He is Life and Life-giving, as God, be he anathema.

THE EPISTLE OF CYRIL TO JOHN OF ANTIOCH

To my lord, beloved brother, and fellow-minister John, Cyril, greeting in the Lord.

" Let the heavens rejoice and let the earth be glad," for "the middle-wall of the hedge " has been broken down and the distress has been made to cease and the cause of all dissension has been removed, Christ our common Saviour rewarding His Churches with peace, the most orthodox and God-beloved emperors, more-over, inviting us thereto, who, having become most excellent imitators of ancestral orthodoxy, preserve the right faith sure and unshaken in their own souls : moreover, they make a special care of His holy Churches, that they themselves may have renowned glory for ever and render their empire most illustrious : to whom also the Lord of Hosts assigns blessings with a rich hand, and permits them to prevail over their antagonists and graces them with victory. For He might not speak falsely who said, " As I live, saith the Lord, them that honour Me I will honour."

When, then, my lord Paul, the brother and fellow-minister most dear to God, arrived at Alexandria, we were filled with joy—and very reasonably, seeing that such a man was acting as mediator, and had elected to encounter excessive toils in order to vanquish the envy of the devil and to heal divisions and, by the removal of the stumbling-blocks cast between us, to crown both our Churches and yours with unanimity and peace. It is needless to recount the ground of their division : better is it, I take it, to think and speak rather of matters which befit a time of peace.

Delighted were we at our intercourse [1] with that most pious man, who probably thought that he would have no little difficulty in persuading us that it was a duty to unite the Churches in peace and to stop the laughter of the heterodox and to blunt the sting of the devil's contumacy. But he found us so readily disposed for this that he had absolutely no trouble at all ; for we remembered the words of the Saviour, " My peace I give to you, My peace I leave with you " ; moreover, we have been taught to pray, " O Lord our God, give us peace, for Thou gavest us all things." So that if one becomes a participator in the peace which is abundantly supplied by God, he will not lack any good thing.

But that the dissension which arose between the Churches was quite needless and inexcusable we have now been fully convinced,

---

[1] συντυχία often bears the sense of " conference," " interview," in ecclesiastic Greek, being almost synonymous with ὁμιλία. E. A. Sophocles' Lexicon gives several examples.

since my lord the most God-beloved bishop Paul has proffered a paper which contained an unimpeachable confession of the faith, which he affirmed had been drawn up by thy Holiness and the most pious bishops in that place. The document is as follows, and it is inserted in this our letter word for word :

Now in the matter of how we think and speak concerning the Virgin Theotokos and the manner of the Incarnation of the Only-begotten Son of God, we must briefly state, not by way of supplement (to the Nicene Creed), but in the nature of full belief, as we have held from the first, having received it both from the divine Scriptures and from the tradition of the holy fathers, making no addition at all to the Creed of the holy fathers put forth at Nicaea. For, as we have just said, it suffices both for all knowledge of orthodoxy and for the exclusion of all heretical blasphemy. And we will state it, not daring impossibilities, but in the acknowledgment of our own infirmity, to exclude those who attack us on the ground that we are looking into things beyond the power of man.

We confess, then, our Lord Jesus Christ, the Only-begotten Son of God, Perfect God and Perfect Man of a rational soul and body ; before the ages begotten from the Father as to His Godhead, and in the last days the Self-same for us and for our salvation, (born) of Mary the Virgin as to His Manhood ; the Same co-essential with the Father as to Godhead and co-essential with us as to Manhood, for there was a Union of Two Natures, whereby we confess One Christ, One Son, One Lord. And according to this idea of the unconfused Union we confess the holy Virgin to be Theotokos, because that God the Word was incarnate, and lived as Man, and from the very conception united to Himself the temple which He took of her.

And with regard to the evangelic and apostolic sayings concerning the Lord, we know that theologians make some common, as relating to One Person, and distinguish others, as relating to Two Natures, interpreting the God-befitting ones of the Godhead of Christ, and the lowly ones of His Humanity.

On reading these your holy words and finding that we ourselves also thus think—for " there is One Lord, One Faith, One Baptism " —we gave glory to God the Saviour of the world, and congratulated each other that both our Churches and yours hold a faith agreeing with the God-breathed Scriptures and with the tradition of the holy Fathers. But when I learnt that certain of those who are wont to be censorious were buzzing around like fierce wasps, and were spitting out villainous words against me as though I said that the holy body of Christ was brought down from heaven and was not (taken) from the holy Virgin, I thought it necessary to add a few words on this topic in answer to them. O foolish ones, knowing only how to accuse falsely! How were ye thus mentally perverted so as to have fallen sick of such monstrous folly? For it is your absolute duty clearly to understand that well-nigh the whole of our contest for the faith has been waged round our affirmation that the holy Virgin is Theotokos. But if we say that the holy body of Christ our common Saviour is from heaven and was not made from her, how could she be any longer understood to be Theotokos? For whom has she at all brought forth, if it is not true that she begat after the flesh Immanuel? Let those, then, who have prated these things about me be ridiculed; for the blessed prophet Isaiah did not lie when he said, " Behold, the Virgin shall be with Child and shall bear a Son, and they shall call His Name Immanuel "; and altogether truly did the holy Gabriel speak to the blessed Virgin, " Fear not, Mary; for thou didst find favour with God; and behold, thou shalt conceive and bear a Son, and thou shalt call His Name Jesus." " For He shall save His people from their sins." But when we speak of our Lord Jesus Christ being " from heaven " and from above, we do not use these expressions as meaning that His holy flesh was brought from above and from heaven, but we follow rather the divinely speaking Paul, who plainly cried, " The first man is from earth, of mould : the Second Man is [the Lord] from heaven." Moreover, we remember, too, the Saviour saying, " No one hath ascended into heaven but He that came down from heaven, the Son of Man "; although He was born according to the flesh, as I have just said, of the holy Virgin. But since God the Word who came down from above and from heaven " emptied Himself, taking servant's form," and was called " Son of Man," still remaining what He was, that is, God—for He is immutable and unalterable by Nature—He is therefore now conceived of as One with His own flesh, and is said to have come down from heaven, and is, moreover, named " Man from heaven," being perfect in Godhead and perfect in Manhood, and conceived of as in One Person; for " there is One Lord Jesus Christ," although the difference of the Natures is not ignored, from both of which we say that the ineffable Union hath been wrought.

As for those who say there was a mixture or confusion or blending of God the Word with the flesh, let thy Holiness deem it well to stop their mouths; for it is likely that some are commonly reporting this also about me, as though I had either thought or said so. But I am so far from thinking such a thing that I deem those to be actually out of their mind who can for a moment suppose it possible for a shadow of turning " to take place in respect of the Divine Nature of the Word; for He ever abides what He is and has not been changed, neither, indeed, could He ever be changed or be capable of variation. Besides, we all confess the Word of God to be naturally impassible, although in His all-wise administration of the mystery (of the Incarnation) He is seen to attribute to Himself the suffering which befell His own flesh. Thus likewise, saith the all-wise Peter, " Christ then suffered for us in flesh," and not in the nature of the ineffable Godhead. For in order that He Himself may be believed to be the Saviour of the world He takes upon Himself, as I said, the sufferings of His own flesh in accordance with the appropriation inherent in the Incarnation ; much as He was foreannounced by the prophet's voice as of Him, " I gave My back to the scourges, My cheeks to blows, and My face I turned not away from the shame of spitting."

Now that we follow in all respects the opinions of the holy fathers, but especially those of our blessed and all-renowned father Athanasius, refusing to be carried in the very least beyond them, let thy Holiness be persuaded and let no one else feel any doubt. I would also have set down many passages of theirs, guaranteeing my own words from theirs, had not I feared the length of the letter lest it should thereby become tedious.

And we do not suffer the faith to be in any way shaken by anyone, which was defined—I mean the Symbol of the faith—by our holy fathers who assembled in their time at Nicaea ; nor do we permit either ourselves or others either to alter a word of what is there laid up, or to transgress a single syllable ; remembering Him who said, " Remove not the eternal bounds which thy fathers set." For they themselves were not the speakers, but the Spirit of God even the Father, who proceedeth indeed from Him, yet is not alien from the Son, at least in respect of substance. Indeed, the words of the holy teachers guarantee this to us. For in the Acts of the Apostles it is written, " When they came opposite Mysia they attempted to go into Bithynia, and the Spirit of Jesus suffered them not." The divinely uttering Paul also writes, " They that are in the flesh cannot please God, but ye are not in the flesh, but in the Spirit, if so be that the Spirit of God dwell in you. Now if anyone have not the Spirit of Christ he is not His." But when any of those who are wont to pervert the right turn aside my words to what they please, let not thy Holiness marvel, being aware that those also of every heresy find the starting-points for their own error out of the God-breathed Scriptures, corrupting by their own evil notions what has been rightly written by the Holy Spirit, and pouring over their own heads the unquenchable flame.

But since we have learnt that certain persons have corrupted the epistle of our all-renowned father Athanasius to the blessed Epictetus, which is orthodox, and have published it so that thereby many are injured, we have therefore, in our thought of something useful and necessary for the brethren, sent duplicates to thy Holiness made from ancient copies which are here with us, and which are free from error.

The Lord shall keep thee in good health and praying for us, most honoured brother.

THE TOME OF LEO

Leo, bishop, to his dearest brother Flavian, Bishop of Constantinople.

On reading the letter of your Affectionateness, at the late arrival of which we wonder, and on reviewing the minutes of the acts of the bishops, we at length discovered the scandal which had arisen in your midst in opposition to the integrity of the faith, and what formerly appeared obscure, now that it has been explained to us, has become perfectly clear. In this matter Eutyches, who might reasonably have been thought worthy of esteem as a presbyter, shows himself to have been very short-sighted and far too inexperienced, so that the prophet's words are true, too, of him : " He was unwilling to learn that he might do good ; he meditated wickedness upon his bed." For what is more wicked than to be undutifully minded, and to refuse to yield to those who are wiser and more learned than ourselves ? But into this folly do those persons fall who, when they are hindered from arriving at the truth by some obscurity, have recourse not to the voices of the prophets or the letters of the apostles or the gospel authorities, but to themselves, and on this account they become teachers of error because they were not disciples of the truth. For what learning has such a one acquired from the sacred pages of the New and the Old Testament, seeing that he does not understand even the opening words of the creed ? And that which is proclaimed throughout the whole world by the voices of all candidates for baptismal regeneration has not yet been understood by the heart of your aged presbyter.

2. And so, being ignorant of what he ought to think about the Incarnation of the Word of God, and unwilling, with a view to acquiring the light of intelligence, to make research in the wide extent of the Holy Scriptures, he yet might at least have received with careful attention the general and common confession with which all the faithful profess that they

" believe in God the Father Omnipotent,
and in Jesus Christ His Only Son our Lord,
who was born of the Holy Spirit and the Virgin Mary,"

by which three sentences the machinations of almost all heretics are destroyed. For when God is believed to be both Omnipotent and Father, and the Son is shown to be co-eternal with Him, in nothing differing from the Father because He is " God of God," Omnipotent of Omnipotent, begotten Co-eternal of the Eternal ; not later in time, not unlike in glory, not divided in essence ; but the Self-same,

who was the Only-begotten and Everlasting One of the Everlasting
Parent, was born of the Holy Spirit and the Virgin Mary. And
this birth in time takes away nothing from that divine and eternal
birth, nor does it add anything to it, but it is entirely concerned
with the reparation of man who had been deceived, so that it might
both conquer death and by its own power destroy the devil, who held
the sovereignty of death. For we should not have been able to
overcome the author of sin and death had He not taken our nature
and made it His own, whom neither could sin pollute nor death
detain. For He was conceived of the Holy Spirit within the womb
of the Virgin Mary, who brought Him forth just as she had conceived
Him, preserving her virginity. But if he was not able to imbibe
a right knowledge from this purest fount of Christian faith, because
he had obscured the brightness of the clear truth by a darkness
peculiar to himself, Eutyches might have submitted to the Gospel
teaching, and on reading Matthew's words: " The book of the
generation of Jesus Christ, the Son of David, the Son of Abraham,"
he should have sought further instruction from the apostle's preaching; and when he read in the Epistle to the Romans: " Paul, a
servant of Jesus Christ, a called apostle, separated for the Gospel of
God which He had promised before by His prophets in the Holy
Scriptures about His Son who became to Him of the seed of David
according to the flesh," he should have studied the pages of the
prophets with dutiful attention. And when he found the promise
of God to Abraham, which says, " In thy seed shall all nations be
blessed," to prevent all doubt as to the peculiar privilege of this
seed, he should have given heed to the apostle when he says, " To
Abraham were the promises made, and to his seed. He saith not
' and to seeds,' as if it applied to many, but as to one—' and to thy
seed,' which is Christ." Isaiah's prophecy also he should have
listened to with the inward ear when he says, " Behold a virgin shall
be with child, and shall bring forth a Son, and they shall call His
name ' Immanuel,' which is, being interpreted, ' God is with us.' "
And he should have read with faith the words of the same prophet,
" Unto us a Child is born, unto us a Son is given, whose power is
on His shoulder, and they shall call His name the Angel of Great
Counsel, Wonderful, Counsellor, the Mighty God, the Prince of
Peace, the Father of the Coming Age." And he should not, using
deceptive words, say that the Word was made Flesh in such wise as
to imply that Christ, having been conceived in the Virgin's womb,
possessed the form of a man without a real body taken from His
mother. Perhaps he thought that our Lord Jesus Christ was not
of our nature because the angel sent to the blessed Mary ever-virgin
said, " The Holy Spirit shall come upon thee and the power of the
Highest shall overshadow thee, therefore also that Holy Thing that
shall be born of thee shall be called the Son of God "—as if, because
the conception by the Virgin was of Divine operation, the flesh of
Him conceived was not of the nature of her who conceived it. But

that birth, uniquely wonderful and wonderfully unique, is not to be understood as losing its true character because of the novelty of its origin. For the Holy Spirit made the Virgin bring forth, but it was a real body taken from her body ; and " when Wisdom was building for Herself a house " " the Word was made Flesh and dwelt amongst us "—that is, in that flesh which He took from a human being, and which He animated with the spirit of a rational life.

3. Since then the properties of both natures and substances were preserved and co-existed in One Person, humility was embraced by majesty, weakness by strength, mortality by eternity ; and to pay the debt of our condition the inviolable nature was united to a passible nature ; so that, as was necessary for our healing, there was one and the same " Mediator between God and men, the man Jesus Christ," who was capable of death in one nature and incapable of it in the other. In the complete and perfect nature, therefore, of very man, very God was born—complete in what belonged to Him, complete in what belonged to us. And by " what belonged to us " we mean what the Creator put in us from the beginning, and what He undertook to repair. For that which the Deceiver brought upon us and that which deceived man admitted found no trace in the Saviour. And it does not follow that because He shared in human weakness He therefore shared in our sins. He assumed the " form of a servant " without the stain of sin, enhancing what was human, not detracting from what was Divine ; because that " Self-emptying," by which He who is invisible rendered Himself visible and He who alone is the Creator and " Lord of all " willed to be mortal, was a condescension of pity, not a loss of power. Hence, He who, remaining in the " form of God," made man was the Same who was made man in the " form of a servant." For each nature retains without loss its own properties ; and as the " form of God " does not take away the " form of a servant," so the " form of a servant " does not detract from the " form of God." For because the devil was boasting that man, deceived by his fraud, had lost the Divine gifts, and, being stript of the dowry of im- mortality, was undergoing the hard sentence of death, and that he himself derived a certain solace in his woes from his having a partner in guilt, and that God, too, had changed His intention towards man (as justice demanded), whom He had fashioned and endowed with so much honour ; there was need of the dispensation of a secret counsel so that the unchangeable God, whose will cannot be deprived of its own benignity, might perfect His first dispensation of kindness towards us by a more hidden mystery, and that man, who had been lured into guilt by the craftiness of diabolical wickedness, might not perish contrary to the purpose of God.

4. So, then, the Son of God enters upon this lower world, descend- ing from His heavenly seat without retiring from the Father's glory, generated in a new order by a novel kind of birth. In a new order, because He who is invisible in what belongs to Himself was made

visible in what belongs to us, the Incomprehensible willed to be comprehended, He who continued to exist before time began to exist in time, the Lord of the universe took upon Him a servant's form shrouding the immensity of His majesty, the impassible God did not disdain to be passible man, nor the Immortal to be subject to the laws of death ; and by a novel kind of birth, because inviolate virginity, without knowing desire, furnished the material of the flesh.   Nature it was that was taken by the Lord from His mother, not defect, and it does not follow in the case of our Lord Jesus Christ, born from the Virgin's womb, that because His nativity was wonderful His nature is therefore unlike ours.   For the Self-same who is very God is also very Man ; and there is nothing false in this union, whilst the lowliness of the Manhood and the loftiness of the Divinity have their separate spheres.   For as the Godhead is not changed by the compassion, so the Manhood is not absorbed by the dignity.   For each nature performs what is proper to itself in communion with the other ; the Word, that is, performing what is proper to the Word, and the flesh carrying out what is proper to the flesh.   The one of these is brilliant with miracles, the other succumbs to injuries.   And just as the Word does not retire from the Father's glory, so neither does the flesh abandon the nature of our race.   For He is One and the Same—a fact which we must often insist upon—truly the Son of God, and truly the Son of Man. God, inasmuch as " In the beginning was the Word, and the Word was with God, and the Word was God " : Man, inasmuch as " The Word was made Flesh and dwelt amongst us " ; God, inasmuch as " All things were made by Him, and without Him was nothing made " ; Man, inasmuch as " He was made of a woman, made under law."   The birth of the flesh is a manifestation of the human nature, the Virgin's bringing-forth is a proof of the Divine Power. The infancy of the little Child is shown by His lowly cradle, the greatness of the Most High is declared by the voices of Angels. He whom Herod impiously tries to slay is like a human infant, but He whom the Magi are glad humbly to adore is the Lord of all. And even as early as the time when He came to the baptism of his forerunner John, lest He should escape notice because the Divinity was hidden by the veil of the flesh, the Father's voice spake in thunder from heaven, " This is My Beloved Son, in whom I am well pleased." And so He who as Man is tempted by the devil's craft is the Same that is ministered unto by angels as God.   To feel hunger, thirst, and weariness, and to sleep, is evidently human ; but to satisfy thousands of men with five loaves, and to bestow living water on the Samaritan woman, the drinking of which would cause her who drank it to thirst no more ; to walk on the surface of the sea with feet which did not sink, and to allay the " rising billows " by rebuking the tempest, is without doubt Divine.   As then, to omit many other examples, it does not belong to the same nature to weep in an emotion of pity for a dead friend, and to raise that same friend from the dead with a word of power, after the stone over the tomb where he had been for four days buried had been removed ; or, to hang on the wood and, changing the light into darkness to make all the elements tremble ; or, to be pierced with nails and to open the gates of Paradise to the faith of the robber ; so it does not belong to the same nature to say, " I and the Father are One," and " the Father is greater than I." For although in the Lord Jesus Christ there is One Person of God and man, yet that whence the suffering is common to both is one thing, and that whence the glory is common to both is another ; for from us He has the Humanity inferior to the Father, and from the Father He has the Divinity equal to the Father.

5. It is on account of this Unity of Person which is to be understood as existing in both the Natures that, on the one hand, the Son of Man is read of as descending from heaven when the Son of God took flesh from the Virgin from whom He was born, and on the other hand, that the Son of God is said to have been crucified and buried, although he suffered these things not in His Godhead itself, in virtue of which the Only-begotten is both Co-eternal and Co-essential with the Father, but in the weakness of the Human Nature. And this is the reason why we all confess, too, in the Creed that " the Only-begotten Son of God was crucified and buried " in accordance with that saying of the Apostle, " For had they known they would not have crucified the Lord of Majesty." Now when our Lord and Saviour Himself was bringing out the faith of His disciples by His questions, He asked, " Who do men say that I the Son of Man am ? " And when they had declared the different opinions of others, He said, " But ye, who say ye that I am ?—I, that is, who am Son of Man, and whom in the form of a servant and in true flesh ye behold—who do ye say that I am ? " Whereupon blessed Peter, being divinely inspired, and about to benefit all nations by his confession, said, " Thou art the Christ, the Son of the Living God." And it was not without good reason that he was pronounced blessed by the Lord, and derived the firmness of his power and of his name from the original Rock, who confessed through the revelation of the Father that the Self-same Person was both the Son of God and the Christ. For one of these truths without the other would not profit unto salvation ; and there was equal danger in believing the Lord Jesus Christ to be only God and not Man, or only Man and not God. But after the Lord's Resurrection (which surely was a resurrection of a true body, because there was no other body raised than that which had been crucified and died), for what other purpose did He stay on earth for forty days than to clear the integrity of our faith from all obscurity ? For conversing with His disciples, and dwelling and eating with them, and allowing Himself to be handled with a loving and heedful touch by those whom doubt oppressed, it was on this account also that He entered into His disciples when the doors were shut, and by His breath gave them the

Holy Spirit, and, when He had given them the light of understanding, opened the hidden mysteries of the Holy Scriptures, and again, showed them the wound in His side, the marks of the nails, and the most recent signs of the passion, saying, " Behold My hands and My feet, that it is I Myself. Handle Me and see, for a spirit hath not flesh and bones as ye see Me have " ; it was on this account, I say, that the properties of the Divine and the Human Nature might be recognised as remaining in Him undivided, and that we might so know the Word to be not the same as the flesh as to confess the One Son of God to be both Word and Flesh. Which mystery of the faith this Eutyches must be deemed to have utterly failed to grasp, for he hath not recognised our nature in the Only-begotten of God, either in the humility of the mortality or in the glory of the resurrection. Nor hath he feared the sentence of the blessed apostle and evangelist John : " Every spirit which confesseth Jesus Christ come in flesh is of God, and every spirit that dissolveth Jesus is not of God, and this is Antichrist." Now what is it to dissolve Jesus but to separate the human nature from Him, and to make void by the most shameless fictions the mystery whereby alone we have all been saved ? Moreover, being in darkness as to the Body of Christ, he must necessarily show the same blindness and folly in relation to His Passion also. For if he does not think the cross of the Lord an unreality, and does not doubt that He underwent true punishment for the salvation of the world, let him acknowledge also the flesh of Him whose death he believes ; and let him not deny that He whom he admits to have been passible was a man with a body like ours : for to deny the reality of His flesh is to deny also His sufferings in a body. If, then, he embraces the Christian faith and does not refuse to listen to the preaching of the Gospel, let him consider which nature it was that was pierced by the nails and hung upon the wood of the cross, and let him understand from which nature it was, when the side of the Crucified had been opened by the soldier's spear, that the blood and the water flowed out, to invigorate the Church of God with the laver and with the cup. Let him also listen to the blessed apostle Peter declaring that " the sanctification of the Spirit " is wrought out through " the sprinkling of the blood of Christ " ; and let him read attentively the words of the same apostle, " Knowing that ye were redeemed from your vain manner of life which ye inherited from your fathers, not with corruptible things as silver and gold, but with the precious blood of Jesus Christ, as of a Lamb without blemish and without spot." Let him also not resist the testimony of the blessed apostle John, " And the blood of Jesus the Son of God cleanseth us from all sin." And again, " This is the victory which overcometh the world, even our faith." And, " Who is he that overcometh the world but he that believeth that Jesus is the Son of God ? This is He that came by water and blood, even Jesus Christ ; not in water only, but in water and blood. And it is the Spirit that beareth witness, because the Spirit is truth

For there are three that bear witness, the Spirit, the water, and the blood ; and the three are one." The Spirit of sanctification, namely ; and the blood of redemption ; and the water of baptism : which three are one and remain undivided, and not one of them is separated from its union with the others : because the Catholic Church lives and makes progress by this faith, that in Christ Jesus neither Humanity without true Divinity, nor Divinity without true Humanity, may be believed to exist.

6. When, however, Eutyches, in response to your cross-examination, said, " I confess that our Lord was from two Natures before the Union, but after the Union I admit but One Nature," I am amazed that so absurd and perverse a profession as this of his was not severely censured by the judges, and that an exceedingly foolish and blasphemous phrase was passed over, just as though nothing which could be matter of offence had been heard : since it is just as impious to say that the Only-begotten Son of God was from two Natures before the Incarnation, as to assert that after the Word was made Flesh but a single Nature remained in Him. But lest Eutyches should think that his words were correct or tolerable because they were not silenced by any expression of opinion on your part, we exhort you to be carefully solicitous, dearly beloved brother, that if by God's merciful inspiration the case is brought to a satisfactory conclusion, this short-sighted and inexperienced man may be purged also from this pestilent notion of his. For he, as the minutes of the Acts have made plain, had well begun to retreat from his opinion when, pressed by your judgment, he agreed to say what he had not said before, and to acquiesce in that faith to which he had formerly been a stranger. But when he refused to anathematise the impious doctrine, your Fraternity understood that he adhered to his false doctrine, and deserved to be condemned. For which if he is genuinely and efficaciously sorry, and recognises, though late, how rightly the episcopal authority has been set in motion against him ; or if for the fulfilment of expiation he shall condemn all his errors viva voce and by actual subscription, you cannot be blamed for showing him pity to any extent when he has been convinced of his error ; for our Lord, the true and good Shepherd, who laid down His life for His sheep, and who came to save men's souls, not to destroy them, wishes us to imitate His loving affection ; so that justice should indeed restrain sinners, but compassion should not repel those who have renounced their errors. For then, indeed, is the true faith defended most profitably when a false opinion is condemned by its actual former adherents.

But with a view to concluding the whole case religiously and faithfully, we have directed our brothers Julius the bishop and Renatus the presbyter and also my son Hilarus the deacon to act for us : and with them we have sent as companion Dulcitius our notary, of whose fidelity we are assured ; being confident that the help of God will be with you, so that he who has erred may be saved by condemning his depraved opinion.

May God keep you safe, dearest brother.

Given on the Ides of June, in the distinguished consulship of Asturius and Protogenes.

THE CHALCEDONIAN DEFINITION OF THE FAITH

§ 1. THE Holy, Great, and Oecumenical Synod, by the grace of God and the command of our most orthodox and Christ-loving Emperors, Marcian and Valentinian Augusti, assembled in the metropolis of Chalcedon, in the Bithynian province, in the martyry of the holy and nobly triumphant martyr Euphemia, hath decreed as follows :

§ 2. Our Lord and Saviour Jesus Christ, confirming the knowledge of the Faith to His disciples, said, " My peace I leave with you, My peace I give to you," to the end that no one should differ from his neighbour in the doctrines of orthodoxy, but that the proclamation of the truth should be shown forth equally by all.

But since the evil one ceaseth not, by means of his own tares, to supplant the seeds of orthodoxy, and ever inventeth something new against the truth, therefore the Lord, in His wonted care for the human race, excited to zeal this orthodox and most faithful Emperor, and called together to Himself the chiefs of the priesthood from all parts, in order that, by the action of the grace of Christ the Lord of us all, we might remove every noxious element from the sheep of Christ, and enrich them with the fresh herbage of the truth.

And this, in fact, we have accomplished, having by a unanimous vote driven away the dogmas of error, and having renewed the undeviating Creed of the Fathers, proclaiming to all the Symbol of the Three Hundred and Eighteen ; and, in addition, accepting as our own fathers those who received that statement of orthodoxy— we mean the One Hundred and Fifty who subsequently met together in Great Constantinople, and themselves set their seal to the same Creed.

Therefore (preserving the order and all the decrees concerning the Faith passed by the Holy Synod held formerly at Ephesus, the leaders of which were Caelestine of Rome and Cyril of Alexandria of most holy memory) we decree that the exposition of the right and blameless Faith of the Three Hundred and Eighteen holy and blessed Fathers, assembled in Nicaea, in the time of the Emperor Constantine of orthodox memory, be pre-eminent ; and moreover, that the definitions made by the One Hundred and Fifty holy Fathers in Constantinople, for the removal of the heresies then rife, and for the confirmation of the same Catholic and Apostolic Faith, remain valid.

The Symbol of the Three Hundred and Eighteen : [1]

---

[1] On the peculiarities of this recension see the notes on p. 194. The additions are here printed in italics.

" We believe in One God the Father All-sovereign, Maker of all things visible and invisible :

" And in One Lord Jesus Christ, the Son of God, Begotten from the Father, Only-begotten, that is, from the substance of the Father ; God from God, Light from Light, Very God from Very God ; Begotten, not made ; Consubstantial with the Father ; through whom all things were made [both in heaven and in earth] ; who for us men and for our salvation came down *from the heavens,* and was incarnate *of the Holy Spirit and the Virgin Mary,* and lived as Man ; *was crucified also for us under Pontius Pilate, and* suffered, *and was buried,* and rose the third day *according to the Scriptures, and* ascended into the heavens ; *and sitteth on the right hand of the Father, and again* cometh *with glory* to judge the quick and the dead, *of whose kingdom there shall be no end :*

" And in the Spirit, Holy, *Lord, and Life-giving.*

" But those who say, ' Once He was not,' and ' Before He was begotten He was not,' and that ' He was made out of nothing,' or who say that ' the Son of God is of a different Hypostasis or Essence,' or ' mutable ' or ' changeable ' ; these the Catholic and Apostolic Church anathematises."

The Symbol of the One Hundred and Fifty :

" We believe in One God the Father All-sovereign, Maker of heaven and earth, and of all things visible and invisible :

" And in One Lord Jesus Christ, the Only-begotten Son of God, Begotten of the Father before all worlds ; Light from Light, Very God from Very God ; Begotten, not made ; Consubstantial with the Father ; through whom all things were made ; who for us men and for our salvation came down from the heavens, and was incarnate of the Holy Spirit and the Virgin Mary, and lived as Man ; was crucified also for us under Pontius Pilate, and suffered, and was buried and rose the third day according to the Scriptures ; and ascended into the heavens, and sitteth on the right hand of the Father ; and cometh again with glory to judge both the quick and the dead, of whose kingdom there shall be no end :

" And in the Spirit, Holy, Lord, and Life-giving, who proceedeth from the Father ; who with the Father and the Son is together worshipped and glorified ; who spake by the prophets :

" In One Holy Catholic and Apostolic Church :

" We acknowledge One Baptism for the remission of sins :

" We look for a Resurrection of the dead, and a Life of the world to come. Amen."

§ 3. Although this wise and saving Symbol of the Divine Grace would have been sufficient for complete knowledge and confirmation

Q

of orthodoxy, for it both teaches the perfect doctrine concerning the Father and the Son and the Holy Spirit, and sets forth the Incarnation of the Lord to those who receive it faithfully ; yet, forasmuch as those who attempt to set aside the preaching of the truth have produced foolish utterances through their own heresies—some daring to corrupt the mystery of the Lord's Incarnation for us, and denying the title " Theotokos " to the Virgin ; others introducing a confusion and mixture, shamelessly imagining, too, the Nature of the flesh and of the Godhead to be one, and absurdly maintaining that the Divine Nature of the Only-begotten is by this confusion passible ; therefore the present Holy, Great, and Oecumenical Synod, being minded to exclude all their machinations against the truth, and affirming the doctrine as unchangeable from the first, hath decreed primarily that the Creed of the Three Hundred and Eighteen holy Fathers should remain inviolate ; and, on account of those who contend against the Holy Spirit, it ratifies the teaching subsequently set forth by the One Hundred and Fifty holy Fathers assembled in the imperial city concerning the substance of the Spirit, which they made known to all, not as adducing anything left lacking by their predecessors, but making distinct by scriptural testimonies their conception concerning the Holy Spirit against those who were trying to set aside His Sovereignty ; and, on account of those who attempt to corrupt the mystery of the Incarnation, and who shamelessly pretend that He who was born of the holy Mary was a mere man, it hath received the Synodical Epistles of the blessed Cyril, Pastor of the Church of Alexandria, to Nestorius and to the Easterns, as being agreeable thereto, for the refutation of the wild notions of Nestorius and for the instruction of those who in pious zeal desire to understand the saving Symbol. To these also it hath suitably united, for the confirmation of the right doctrines, the Epistle of the Prelate of the great and older Rome, the most blessed and most holy Archbishop Leo, which was written to the saintly Archbishop Flavian for the exclusion of the wrong opinion of Eutyches, inasmuch as it agrees with the confession of the great Peter, and is a common pillar against the heterodox.

§ 4. For the Synod opposes those who presume to rend the mystery of the Incarnation into a Duality of Sons ; and it expels from the company of the priests those who dare to say that the Godhead of the Only-begotten is passible, and it withstands those who imagine a mixture or confusion of the Two Natures of Christ, and it drives away those who fancy that the form of a servant, taken by Him of us, is of a heavenly or different nature ; and it anathematises those who imagine Two Natures of the Lord before the Union, but fashion anew One Nature after the Union. Following, then, the holy Fathers, we all unanimously teach that our Lord Jesus Christ is to us One and the same Son, the Self-same Perfect in Godhead, the Self-same Perfect in Manhood ; truly God and truly Man ; the Self-same of a rational soul and body ; consubstantial with the Father according to the Godhead, the Self-same consubstantial with us according to the Manhood ; like us in all things, sin apart ; before the ages begotten of the Father as to the Godhead, but in the last days, the Self-same, for us and for our salvation (born) of Mary the Virgin Theotokos as to the Manhood ; One and the Same Christ, Son, Lord, Only-begotten ; acknowledged in Two Natures unconfusedly, unchangeably, indivisibly, inseparably ; the difference of the Natures being in no way removed because of the Union, but rather the property of each Nature being preserved, and (both) concurring into One Prosopon and One Hypostasis ; not as though He were parted or divided into Two Prosopa, but One and the Self-same Son and Only-begotten God, Word, Lord, Jesus Christ ; even as from the beginning the prophets have taught concerning Him, and as the Lord Jesus Christ Himself hath taught us, and as the Symbol of the Fathers hath handed down to us.

§ 5. These things having been defined by us with all possible accuracy and care, the Holy and Oecumenical Synod hath decreed that it is unlawful for any one to present, write, compose, devise, or teach to others any other Creed ; but that those who dare either to compose another Creed, or to bring forward or teach or deliver another Symbol to those wishing to turn to the full knowledge of the truth from Paganism or from Judaism, or from heresy of any kind whatsoever—that such persons, if bishops or clerics, shall be deposed, the bishops from the episcopate and clerics from the clerical office, and, if monks or laics, they shall be anathematised.

GENERAL INDEX

INDEX OF TEXTS QUOTED OR REFERRED TO

INDEX OF PATRISTIC REFERENCES